SOUTHERN
GARDENER'S HANDBOOK

First published in 2014 by Cool Springs Press, an imprint of Quarto Publishing Group USA Inc.,
400 First Avenue North, Suite 400, Minneapolis, MN 55401

The information in this book is true and complete to the best of our knowledge. All
recommendations are made without any guarantee on the part of the author or Publisher,
who also disclaims any liability incurred in connection with the use of this data or
specific details.

Cool Springs Press titles are also available at discounts in bulk quantity for industrial or sales-
promotional use. For details write to Special Sales Manager at Quarto Publishing Group USA Inc.,
400 First Avenue North, Suite 400, Minneapolis, MN 55401 USA. To find out more about our books,
visit us online at www.coolspringspress.com.

Library of Congress Cataloging-in-Publication Data

Marden, Troy B.
    Southern gardener's handbook : your complete guide : select, plan, plant, maintain, problem-solve / Troy Marden.
        pages cm
    Includes bibliographical references and index.
    ISBN 978-1-59186-592-6 (sc)
    1. Gardening—Southern States. I. Title.

SB453.2.S66M37 2014
635—dc23
                                2014017680

Acquisitions Editor: Billie Brownell
Art Director: Cindy Samargia Laun
Layout: S. E. Anglin

Printed in China
10 9 8 7 6 5 4 3 2 1

SOUTHERN
GARDENER'S HANDBOOK

ALABAMA, ARKANSAS, GEORGIA, KENTUCKY,
LOUISIANA, MISSISSIPPI, TENNESSEE

YOUR COMPLETE GUIDE:
SELECT · PLAN · PLANT · MAINTAIN · PROBLEM-SOLVE

TROY B. MARDEN

**COOL
SPRINGS
PRESS**

Home and Garden Experts™
MINNEAPOLIS, MINNESOTA

DEDICATION

This book is dedicated to Cheekwood Botanical Garden and Museum of Art. If not for them, I would not have ended up in Nashville more than twenty years ago to begin learning about gardening in the South. And to the many clients I have been privileged to work with during the past two decades: each of your gardens taught me something about how to garden successfully in a sometimes challenging climate and, hopefully, those lessons appear on these pages.

ACKNOWLEDGMENTS

To Billie Brownell, Tracy Stanley, and the team at Cool Springs Press and the Quarto Group—you have my gratitude for helping to produce another beautiful book!

CONTENTS

FEATURED PLANTS

PERENNIALS

SHRUBS

TREES

TROPICALS

VINES

WHAT IS A HARDINESS ZONE?

When you pick up a gardening book like this one and begin reading about plants, you may see frequent references to a plant's hardiness or what zone a plant is hardy to. What are these hardiness zones that are referenced in almost every gardening book? Hardiness zones are fairly broad bands that run more or less horizontally (at least east of the Rocky Mountains) from north to south across the United States and define the average minimum winter temperatures experienced within those territories based on data collected over twenty-year periods of time. It is important to keep in mind that these are *average* minimums and that extremes can happen in any climate, in any given year. They are guidelines, but not written in stone.

In most of the South, we land somewhere between Zone 6 in the colder regions and Zone 8 in the warmer regions, with a few areas along the Gulf Coast, south Georgia, and coastal South Carolina reaching Zone 9. This means that most of us, in a normal year, experience relatively mild winters that afford us the opportunity to grow a very diverse selection of plants ranging from cold-hardy perennials like purple coneflower and daylilies to exotic-looking subtropical plants like some of the hardier palms and bananas. It also means that, when well planned, our gardens can be in bloom nearly year-round, an obvious advantage over gardeners who live farther north.

While milder winters work to our advantage in most cases by extending the seasons and allowing us to enjoy blooming plants almost year-round, they can work against us in some cases. Lilacs and peonies are classic examples of plants that Southern gardeners long to grow well, but the fact is that our winters are often too warm for them to thrive here. The mild temperatures that let us enjoy the blooms of hellebores and witch hazel in January and February mean that the cold requirements of the peonies and lilacs may not be met, leading to them not growing and blooming properly in most years.

IT'S NOT JUST ABOUT WINTER

There is more to plants thriving in the South than just their cold hardiness. Surviving the winter is one thing, but for some plants, surviving our hot, humid summers, which, in some years, seem to go on forever, can be an even greater challenge. There has been some preliminary work done on creating "heat zone" designations for plants, but the jury is still out on exactly how helpful that information is.

When talking about plants' heat tolerance, it's not just about the heat of the day, but also the average lows at night. For many plants, nighttime temperatures in the 60s are ideal and nighttime temperatures in the 70s are tolerable. When night temperatures rise and stay above 80 degrees, the plants' internal systems can't slow down and rest, and important internal processes can't occur. If this continues over several weeks, plants can suffer and possibly die. Watering during the nighttime hours with overhead irrigation or sprinklers can help plants survive extended periods of heat, not just by keeping the soil moist, but by physically cooling the plants. Watering at night is not something that I do on a regular basis or that I encourage most gardeners to do because it can encourage foliar disease-like powdery mildew, blackspot (in roses) and other leaf spot diseases. However, most foliar diseases, while unsightly, are not deadly. In the end it may be better to tolerate a little powdery mildew than to lose a plant or plants entirely. This is the point where we all, as gardeners, have to make a call as to what's best for the long-term success of the garden and the plants growing there and, in some cases, go against what might be a more common approach or logic.

USDA COLD-HARDINESS ZONES

ALABAMA

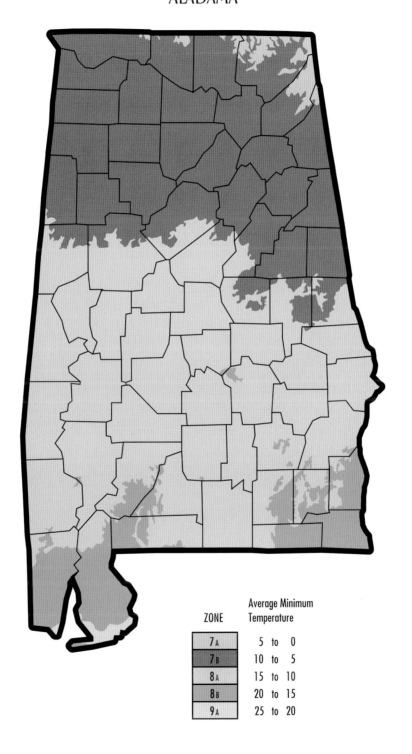

ZONE	Average Minimum Temperature
7A	5 to 0
7B	10 to 5
8A	15 to 10
8B	20 to 15
9A	25 to 20

USDA Plant Hardiness Zone Map, 2012. Agricultural Research Service, U.S. Department of Agriculture. Accessed from http://planthardiness.ars.usda.gov.

ARKANSAS

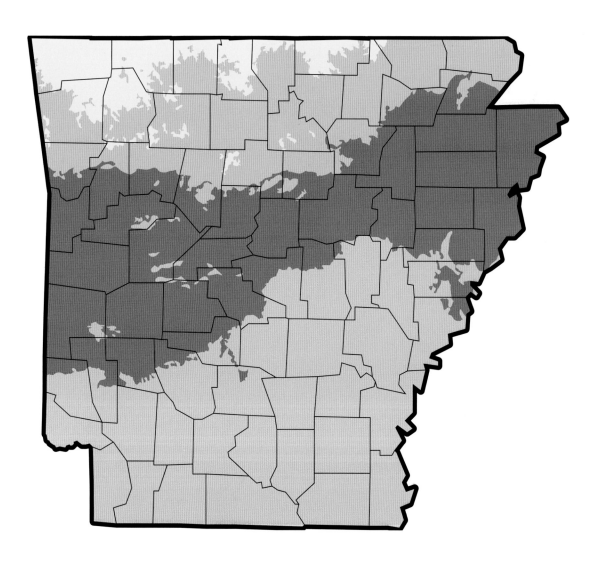

ZONE	Average Minimum Temperature
6B	0 to 5
7A	5 to 0
7B	10 to 5
8a	15 to 10

USDA Plant Hardiness Zone Map, 2012. Agricultural Research Service, U.S. Department of Agriculture. Accessed from http://planthardiness.ars.usda.gov.

GEORGIA

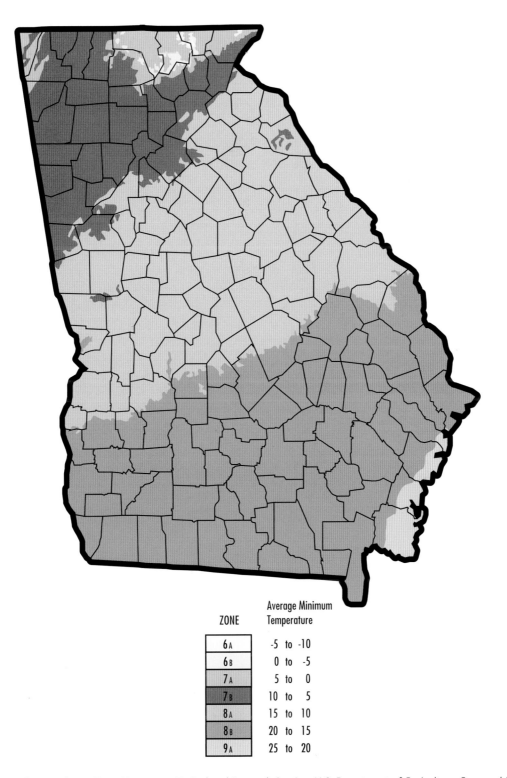

ZONE	Average Minimum Temperature
6 A	-5 to -10
6 B	0 to -5
7 A	5 to 0
7 B	10 to 5
8 A	15 to 10
8 B	20 to 15
9 A	25 to 20

USDA Plant Hardiness Zone Map, 2012. Agricultural Research Service, U.S. Department of Agriculture. Accessed from http://planthardiness.ars.usda.gov.

KENTUCKY

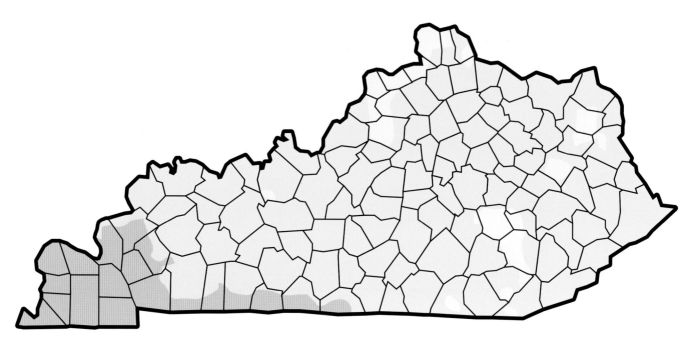

ZONE	Average Minimum Temperature
6 A	-5 to -10
6 B	0 to -5
7 A	5 to 0

USDA Plant Hardiness Zone Map, 2012. Agricultural Research Service, U.S. Department of Agriculture. Accessed from http://planthardiness.ars.usda.gov.

LOUISIANA

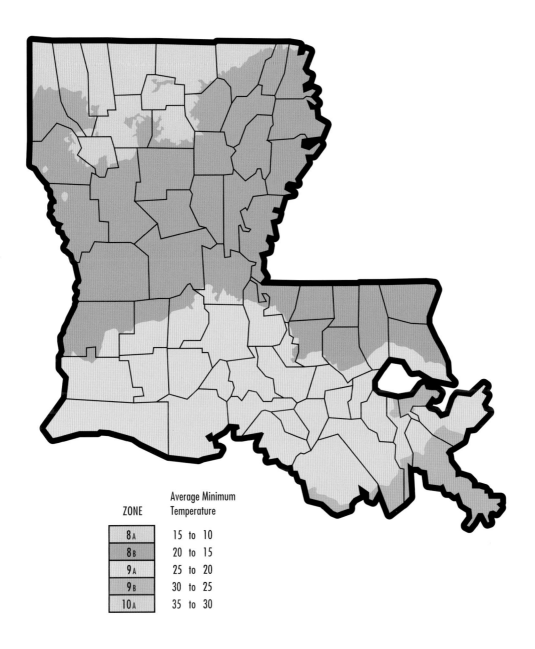

ZONE	Average Minimum Temperature
8A	15 to 10
8B	20 to 15
9A	25 to 20
9B	30 to 25
10A	35 to 30

USDA Plant Hardiness Zone Map, 2012. Agricultural Research Service, U.S. Department of Agriculture. Accessed from http://planthardiness.ars.usda.gov.

MISSISSIPPI

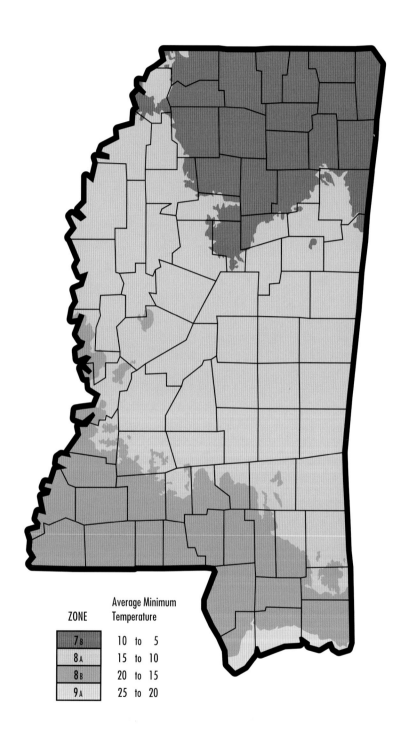

ZONE	Average Minimum Temperature
7 B	10 to 5
8 A	15 to 10
8 B	20 to 15
9 A	25 to 20

USDA Plant Hardiness Zone Map, 2012. Agricultural Research Service, U.S. Department of Agriculture. Accessed from http://planthardiness.ars.usda.gov.

TENNESSEE

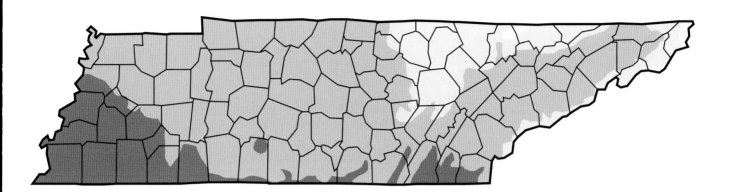

ZONE	Average Minimum Temperature
6 A	-5 to -10
6 B	0 to -5
7 A	5 to 0
7 B	10 to 5

USDA Plant Hardiness Zone Map, 2012. Agricultural Research Service, U.S. Department of Agriculture. Accessed from http://planthardiness.ars.usda.gov.

WELCOME TO GARDENING
in the South

For those of us lucky enough to garden in the South, it can be a most rewarding experience. We have a long list of advantages. Mild temperatures at the beginning and end of the growing season allow us to stretch the flowering time of perennial beds and cutting gardens from early spring to late autumn. In some locations we can harvest vegetables nearly year-round, based on the planting of cool-season and warm-season crops at the appropriate time. Gentler winters encourage the use of plants like Lenten roses, witch hazels, camellias, pansies, and many others whose blooms continue right on through the drabbest days of winter, in spite of any cold weather we may experience. Broadleaf evergreens, such as hollies, azaleas, boxwoods, and our grand Southern magnolia, lend color, form, and texture to our landscapes and gardens throughout the year.

Gardening in the South can also be a challenge. Extreme heat places undue stress on plants in summer, while high humidity encourages a variety of diseases. The mild winters that afford us the opportunity to have plants in bloom are only occasionally cold enough to help control the insect population. Clay, a primary ingredient in much of our Southern soil, is also problematic. It restricts root growth, retains water, and warms slowly in spring while frequent summertime droughts, even when brief, bake the soil to an almost brick-like consistency.

For those of us who love to garden, we face these challenges knowing they are outweighed by the advantages and that with a little planning, a generous dose of ingenuity, and the willingness to work hard, we can have a garden that will delight and provide for us in every season.

While I had been gardening for most of my life and had been educated in the art and science of horticulture through my schooling when I moved to the South more than twenty years ago, there is no substitute for experience. My indoctrination to the weather extremes that can occur in the South came during the ice storm of 1994, which paralyzed Nashville and many other southern cities for days,

if not weeks. Over the years, there have been record-setting freezes, destructive tornadoes, and a Nashville flood of epic proportions. Then, there was the soil. Let's just say it was not the deep, rich, black topsoil of the Kansas prairie that I had grown up planting and growing flowers and vegetables in. In fact, it wasn't even close!

These kinds of extremes and inconsistencies in the weather and soil do not make gardening easy for Southern gardeners. Those of us who love it, though, pay little heed to the challenges and restrictions that Mother Nature places on us. We garden in spite of them. I hope the following pages bring some of my many years of experience to life for you and that your successes in your garden, while they may not outnumber your failures (mine certainly don't!), will surely outshine them.

ASSESSING YOUR SITE AND ITS MICROCLIMATES

When I moved to my current home, a gardener had occupied the house before me, so many of the garden's bones were already in place, and much of the garden, at least in its beginning stages, had already been sited around the property. The first thing I did was take a basic inventory, not just of plants that were already in place, but also of the garden's basic features. Beds, I noted, were laid out and edged in brick, a garden shed stood near the rear of the yard, paths were laid from the house to the shed, and certain decorative elements within the garden already existed. Two magnificent white oaks flanked the front entrance of the house with a white picket fence forming the front boundary near the road, and a black four-board horse fence framed the remainder of the property. While these were all advantages and did much to put me ahead of the game, the weed problem that existed in the larger part of the garden was mind-boggling, and the quality of the soil around most of the property left much to be desired.

Many gardeners would consider this a bleak prospect, but in my initial assessment I saw potential in spite of the challenges.

The initial assessment of my new garden continued with the most easily defined areas—sun and shade. By defining these two basic exposures, I could begin formulating a plan for incorporating the large number of plants I had moved from my previous garden. The front of the house, I discovered, faces almost due west, but two giant oaks provide considerable shade, making the microclimate of the front garden much different than it would be were it not for those trees. I also found the soil to be better in this part of the garden than anywhere else on the property, which was an enormous advantage in getting the shade garden established quickly and to good effect.

As easy as it was to get the shade garden looking good and the plants performing well, the sunny parts of the garden presented considerably more challenges. For one, the sunny areas were fully exposed to the elements. The wind blows across a nearby ridge almost continually, drying out the soil and drawing water from the plants' leaves faster than their roots are able to absorb more. Freezing and thawing are also a problem. During

the coldest winter weather, the top layer of soil may freeze solid at night, but warms enough in the sun during the day to thaw and become a muddy mess. Continual freezing and thawing around the roots and crowns of the plants—especially around perennial garden flowers—may actually break roots and heave the plants out of the ground, causing next year's dormant buds to be exposed to freezing weather. Heavy rains pound the ground and wash rivulets through the mulched beds and paths, exposing roots and storage organs (bulbs, rhizomes, corms, and so forth) to the elements where they can quickly shrivel, freeze, or be eaten. Each of these challenges and more come into play when I am considering a site for a new garden or garden bed, as they will wherever *you* garden.

MICROCLIMATES

Within every garden there exist small **microclimates** where the average conditions of the larger garden are modified. Protected areas—where the shelter of a wall, building, or even a larger plant form a shield from the elements, tempering exposure to sun, wind, cold, or moisture—allow you to grow varieties that might otherwise be less successful. Warm microclimates around the garden permit those of us who call ourselves "zone pushers" to grow plants like palm trees, bananas, or other more tropical species outside of regions where they would customarily be hardy. Taking advantage of these warmer locations can gain us as much as a full zone of hardiness, allowing a gardener in Zone 6 to grow plants typically only hardy to Zone 7 or a Zone 7 gardener to grow plants meant for Zone 8.

Drier microclimates allow for growing cacti, agave, and other hardy succulents where winter moisture combined with cold temperatures would, by and large, cause them to rot. These drier microclimates might occur naturally on steep slopes and in rocky areas, or they may be created by the gardener by building berms, amending soil with coarse gravel or turkey grit to increase drainage and reduce the chances of plants succumbing to root and crown rot in cold, wet soil, especially in winter.

Perhaps a low area in the garden holds moisture and provides an opportunity to grow water-loving plants or even to create a bog. Water-loving irises, sedges, sweet flag, Virginia sweetspire, and many other plants will thrive in these damp areas where other plants may suffer from having wet feet. In especially wet areas or where the water table is high, it may even be possible to excavate and create shallow watering holes or ponds for wildlife. It all depends on the extent and the expense you want to go to.

Exposed corners and open sites where cold winter winds prevail offer a chance for success with shrubs like lilacs that, on average, need longer periods of cold weather than our Southern winters provide. The same is true of perennials like hostas, peonies, and lily-of-the-valley, as well as bulbs such as tulips, daffodils and hyacinths. Take advantage of the coldest microclimates you have to give these plants the winter chilling they need to grow to fulfill their greatest potential.

SUN VS. SHADE

When it comes to assessing how much sun a given area receives, I ask myself one question: How many hours of **direct sun** is the area I'm planting exposed to on a sunny day in midsummer? I use "midsummer" specifically, because of the intensity of the summer sun in the South. The varying degrees of sun and shade warrant a detailed explanation. Understanding them will help you make wise choices when it comes to selecting plants for your landscape or garden.

Full sun is any area of your garden that receives a minimum of eight hours of uninterrupted sun each day. It is important to note the word "uninterrupted" since, on occasion, parts of a garden may receive a total of eight hours of direct sun at various times during the day, but will be shaded in between. Some plants that require full sun will not thrive in these locations where the periods of sun are interrupted. Often, their growth will be weaker, stems may flop, and they will flower less. Annuals such as zinnias (*Zinnia elegans*)

Many sedges thrive in low, wet areas of the garden.

The same garden space that is pictured on page 18, but three years later. Growth was lush and flowers, abundant. Change was coming!

and perennials like hollyhock (*Alcea rosea*) and baptisia (*Baptisia* spp. and hybrids) are plants that thrive in full sun.

Part sun areas receive more sun than shade, but less than eight hours of direct sun. Perhaps you have places in the garden that receive five or six hours of direct morning sun, but are shaded by the overhead tree canopy by lunch time. Foundation plantings or garden beds along the east side of your home, with good morning sun but shade from the house in the afternoon, may also be considered part sun. Some sun-loving perennials such as daylilies (*Hemerocallis* hybrids) and garden phlox (*Phlox paniculata*) may still grow here, though their growth may be slowed and their flowering somewhat reduced.

Part shade can be found where some sunlight still reaches the ground throughout the day, but the overall effect is that of cooler and more pleasant shade. In my garden, part shade exists at the front of my house where two large oaks have been limbed up high. The sun streams through their branches from midmorning until late afternoon, but its intensity is diminished by the overhead limbs and leaves of the trees. No part of the garden is in direct sun for more than a few hours at a time, and most of it receives only the dappled sunlight that shines through the tree canopy. Here, most spring wildflowers will thrive, as will a variety of ferns, Lenten rose (*Helleborus*), the majority of hostas (*Hosta*), Solomon's seal (*Polygonatum*), and an enormous range of other shade-loving plants.

Shade exists where very little direct sunlight reaches the ground, but bright, ambient light still exists and allows certain shade-loving plants to flourish. Full shade conditions are frequently found in wooded areas where the tree canopy is fairly dense but high, and light still reaches the forest floor. Full shade may also exist under a vine-covered arbor or pergola where overhead light is at a minimum but ambient light reaches the ground from the sides of the structure. In full shade, the beautiful blue-leaved forms of hosta will thrive, joined by wild ginger (*Asarum*), the more shade-tolerant ferns like Christmas fern (*Polystichum acrostichoides*), and annuals such as caladiums (*Caladium*).

Deep shade is present where no direct sunlight ever reaches the ground and where very little to no ambient light is able to filter through. Deep shade may exist on the north side of a tall building or solid structure or in the dense, deep shade under the canopy of a Southern magnolia, which are some of the most difficult places to get plants to grow. Your plant palette will be limited only to the most shade-tolerant plants and even those may require some experimentation to see which ones will thrive. Cast-iron plant (*Aspidistra*), while eschewed by some gardeners as common and utilitarian, is one of the toughest and most shade-tolerant plants you can grow. Sometimes, we have to accept the challenges before us and plant what works.

Full Sun   Part Sun   Part Shade   Shade

UNDERSTANDING YOUR SOIL

Soil is the first and most basic component of almost every garden. Rare exceptions might occur in modern gardens where hydroponics or other growing methods are used, but for most of us who garden in the traditional sense, it all begins with our soil. Unfortunately, soil isn't always a very sexy or exciting topic, and often, the soil itself is neglected or—especially on new home sites—destroyed. Instead of being seen as a living, dynamic organism, too many people, gardeners included, simply see their soil as an inanimate or even "dead" object, a support mechanism in which we bury the roots that hold our plants upright and not as the vibrant biological system it truly is.

Because every great garden starts with the soil, whatever gardening success you enjoy will have a direct correlation to how much effort you put into preparing that soil at the outset and how well you continue caring for your soil throughout the life of the garden. To understand how to treat your soil and get the most from it, it's important to know what it is actually made of. For the purpose of gardening, soil is made up of four basic but very different particles.

A healthy garden can be coaxed out of even the heaviest clay soil if you're willing to spend the time it takes to amend it properly and maintain it regularly.

SOIL PARTICLES

Gravel is the largest and coarsest of all of the particles, with very little in the way of water or nutrient-holding capacity. Both pass directly through, so gravelly soils are generally very dry and have few nutrients, even if they are irrigated and fertilized.

Sand is still a large particle, but is smaller than gravel and does have some water-holding capacity. Most nutrients pass through without being captured, though, so gardens with sandy soils often require a different approach to fertilizing (usually in greater quantity and more frequently) than soils that are silt- or clay-based.

Silt is the next smallest particle down from sand and is what most of us would prefer to have as the basis for our garden soil. Its medium-sized particles have a texture similar to coarsely ground flour or cornmeal and are often the result of the complete decomposition of plant (and sometimes animal) matter—sticks, twigs, leaves, manure, bones, and more. Silt easily retains moisture and nutrients and has plenty of spaces between the particles for the exchange of air, water, and nutrients within the soil—all crucial to the soil's health and well-being, as well as the health and wellness of the plants residing there.

Clay is the tiniest of the soil particles and if you were to ask most gardeners, the bane of their existence. If you were to look at a clay sample under a microscope you would see that these particles have notched and jagged edges. They are also highly ionized, meaning they have a positive (+) or negative (-) charge like a magnet. When clay soils become damp, these positive and negative ions bind tightly and seal the notched and jagged edges of the particles together like tiny puzzle pieces. They drive out nearly all remaining air and become so tightly bound to one another they can actually repel water. Nutrients (fertilizer) may bind so tightly to clay soil that plants are unable to use them to grow. By now, you can see where this is going and why plants growing in clay soil often look drought-stressed and deprived of food.

While we're on the topic of clay, let's take a moment to dispel a gardening myth that has been perpetuated for far too long. **Sand does not "fix" clay soil. Sand + clay + water = concrete!** I am unsure as to where the idea came from that adding sand to clay would improve it, but nothing could be further from the truth. Sand is only effective on clay soil when combined with equal (or more) parts of organic matter like garden compost, composted manure, or rotted leaves.

Now that you know about soil particles, let's talk about that one last and very elusive soil type—loam. **Loam** is not a soil particle in and of itself. Instead, loam is a blend of soil particles (usually without the gravel) and can come in a wide array of mixtures from very sandy loams at one end of the spectrum to very clayey loams at the other, depending on how much of each particle is present. Unfortunately, most of us are not gardening with perfect loam under our feet. What we do have is a living, dynamic biological system that will respond to our care and nurturing in much the same way other living organisms do, be they pets, plants, or people.

ORGANIC MATTER

How, then, do you go about affecting positive changes in your soil, its physical composition, and its biological activity and health? **Organic matter.** These two words will become more important in your soil vocabulary than any other. Organic matter comes in many forms, from commercial "soil conditioner" (usually finely ground pine bark), to garden compost, to well-rotted leaves or manure. The key to enhancing almost any problem soil—from tight, waterlogged clay with poor drainage, to dry, barren sand—is the addition of organic matter that occurs in many forms. In clay soil, the addition of organic matter (*not* sand) will help to break tightly bound clay particles apart, improving drainage and aeration, two of the most serious problems with heavy clay soils. In sandy soil, organic matter will help to fill the spaces between the sand particles, improving water- and nutrient-holding capacity and keeping both available in the root zone where plants need them.

If you are fortunate enough to have good garden soil already, maintenance of that soil is paramount. By regularly adding organic matter, you continue to enhance the soil's structure and feed the beneficial microbes it contains. Intensive gardening will deplete even the best soil, so regular maintenance through the addition of organic matter is simply a must.

FERTILIZING

In Southern gardens, fertilizing is important. Our growing seasons are long, and plants can easily use up the naturally occurring elements in the soil that help keep our plants happy and healthy, so it is up to us to supplement with fertilizer. Also, many of us are gardening in clay-based soils, which, as you've already learned in this chapter, can bind up nutrients and make them unavailable to the plants. When this happens, we have to supplement so that our plants have some chance of receiving the nutrients they need in order to thrive and grow.

The three basic nutrients that plants need are nitrogen (N), phosphorus (P), and potassium (K). These are the primary or macronutrients plants need and are indicated as a series of three numbers on every bag or bottle of fertilizer you buy. Those with a higher nitrogen concentration are best for leafy green foliage plants, lawns, and other plants whose leaves are their prominent feature and whose robust growth you want to encourage. Fertilizers with a high middle number are frequently referred to as "bloom boosters" because they encourage flowering, and those that are higher in potassium are often used as root stimulators. There are a number of lesser nutrients, called micronutrients, that plants also need, but they are needed in such small quantities that they are rarely deficient in garden soil. Nitrogen, phosphorous, and potassium, however, can be depleted over time. With occasional application of a complete fertilizer containing all three elements (and nearly all basic fertilizers contain them all, plus more), you ensure the continued growth and good health of your plants.

WATERING

Proper watering will be addressed in greater detail in the following pages, as will the advantages and disadvantages of automatic irrigation systems, water conservation, collecting your own rainwater, and more. The one basic rule of watering that you should remember is that it is almost always better to water deeply and less frequently, thoroughly saturating the root zone each time you water, than it is to sprinkle the soil lightly every day, soaking only the top few inches of soil. Roots follow water, and the whole idea is to get them to grow deep into the soil where they will anchor plants firmly and be able to draw water and nutrients from deep within the soil during periods of drier weather. There is more on this topic as we talk about "Greener Ways to Garden."

To some more experienced gardeners, these discussions of site and microclimate assessment, basic soil science, fertilizing and watering, may seem simple, but I am always amazed at the number of gardeners—even seasoned gardeners—who don't have a firm grasp of the basic elements of successful gardening. Soil is not just an inanimate object that holds a plant upright. A microclimate can be a friend or foe. Proper fertilizing and watering can mean the difference between tremendous success and dismal failure in your gardening endeavors. You don't have to become a soil scientist or a climate expert. There is no need to be a chemist or to understand every molecular chain in a fertilizer granule. A basic understanding, though, of all of these things and how they work together to create a dynamic garden system will help to ensure the best possible success as you work in and learn from your garden.

Rudbeckia 'LITTLE HENRY'

GREENER WAYS
TO GARDEN

Gardeners are a conscientious group of people who, by the very nature of our love of gardening, enjoy nurturing things. We want to coddle and encourage things to grow, creating beautiful surroundings for our own enjoyment, while at the same time protecting and contributing to the natural environment around us. Sometimes this is a challenge when we are faced with the inevitable trials and tribulations that come along with gardening. We wake up one morning to Japanese beetles *devouring* the roses or to deer having come in overnight and eaten the daylilies to the ground. We notice a hosta or two looking poorly and suddenly a whole swath through the garden collapses, infected with Southern blight and gone so quickly all we can hope for is to slow its spread through the rest of the garden. On these occasions, our knee-jerk reaction is to eradicate—at any cost—the offender. How dare something eat or infect our precious plants!

I think most of us struggle with walking that fine line between wanting to truly be a 100 percent earth-friendly and organic gardener, doing everything the "green" and "right" way, but also wanting our gardens to look great and be as weed and pest free as possible without completely monopolizing our free time. I know I certainly do, and no doubt you do, too. We do our very best to use the most effective, earth-friendly practices in our gardens by using organic fertilizers, composting, and recycling as many of the plastics as the recycling center will take. In my own garden I use pesticides and fungicides that are approved for organic gardening and even then, only when they are absolutely necessary to control a problem. I do my very best to leave the chemicals on the garden shed shelf and use them only as a last resort, when all other methods have failed and the life of a valuable plant or plants is at stake, and would encourage you to do the same. But still, it is a fine line to walk.

At the end of the day, I find it easiest to commit myself to being the best possible gardener I can be. To use the most earth-friendly practices I can without letting the garden be in control of me, monopolizing my time by demanding constant care. My friend Joe Lamp'l literally "wrote the book" on earth-friendly gardening in *The Green Gardener's Guide*. There would be no point in me trying to rewrite it here, but I did feel it important to include a chapter in this book on some of the "Greener Ways to Garden" and the importance of taking an environmentally responsible approach to gardening. Most of these ideas are not new or original, but they are what work for me in maintaining what could be a fairly labor-intensive garden in the greenest way I can in the limited amount of time I have to dedicate to it.

MODERN-DAY MIRACLES AND AUTOMATIC IRRIGATION

As a professional in the field of horticulture and landscape design, I understand the need for convenience and ease of care and maintenance when it comes to landscaping. We are all dedicated gardeners, but that doesn't mean we want our gardens to monopolize our time. When it comes to the modern-day miracle of automatic irrigation systems, though, whose timers and clocks require an advanced math degree to operate, I fall more into the category of calling them a "necessary evil" in today's modern world than truly "necessary" for the long-term survival of the landscape. We've become dependent on irrigation systems, and like so many things we've become dependent on, we now believe (and are told by landscape companies that make a lot of money installing them) that our plants and gardens won't survive without them.

Before I make a lot of enemies out of my professional colleagues, let me go ahead and state now that at least some of the time, the misuse and overuse of irrigation (I keep wanting to type "irritation"—I wonder why!) systems is not entirely their fault. Some of it is, but much of it lies squarely on the shoulders of the gardener. Yes, *you*. But instead of playing the blame game, let's talk about how to fix the problem and end the abuse of automatic irrigation systems and the water they waste. Properly programmed and used correctly, they can be of enormous benefit both to garden and gardener.

SWAMP HIBISCUS (*Hibiscus coccineus*)

So what is this common abuse of irrigation systems I keep referring to? It's quite simple. The single greatest abuse of automatic irrigation is running it too often, for too short a period of time. There is absolutely no need—none—for an irrigation system to run daily or, in the vast majority of landscapes (unless you are a golf course superintendent trying to keep bent grass putting greens alive), more than twice weekly, and really even less, for most landscape plants to thrive. The daily irrigation of landscape beds, gardens, and lawns is not only wasteful of water, but is actually detrimental to the plants. Why? That's another easy answer.

When irrigation systems run on a daily basis, or even three or four days per week and for only a few minutes per station, all of the water either runs off, evaporates, or what does soak in remains in the top few inches of the soil. As we all know, where the water goes, so go the roots. So if you are irrigating frequently and in short bursts, wetting only the top few inches of soil, all of the roots of all of your plants are going to remain at the soil's surface where water is readily available to them. Then, when hot weather, drought, or both arrive and the top few inches of soil dry out almost daily, you are forced to turn the irrigation up even more, running it more frequently, using more water, and pushing your water bill up, up, up. And that's just one problem you're creating for yourself. By watering more often, you are only exacerbating the original problem *and* you are now wetting the leaves and stems of the plant on a daily basis, encouraging all kinds of fungal and bacterial diseases to grow and spread. Do you see where this is going? What, then, is the solution?

The solution is simple. Treat your irrigation system the same way you would treat your garden if you were running hoses and setting up sprinklers by hand. You wouldn't go out and move the sprinkler every five to ten minutes, just wetting the leaves of the plants and letting barely any water reach the ground. You would allow the sprinkler to run long enough to give the ground a thorough soaking. The same should be done with your automatic irrigation system, with some adjustments for the greater volume of water that it puts out versus a single sprinkler on the end of a hose.

If you have an irrigation system that currently runs three days per week in the spring, but by summer you feel the need to water every day to "keep things alive," try this instead. Instead of adding to the number of days you water in summer, add to the amount of time you water on the days when the system is already running. So if your lawn zones are running three days per week and fifteen minutes per zone, instead of adding another day of the week to your watering schedule, keep the three-day schedule, but increase the watering time to twenty or even twenty-five minutes per zone, soaking the soil more deeply with each watering and encouraging roots to grow deep into the soil in search of moisture. Do the same for garden beds. Instead of adding days to the schedule, add time to the days when the irrigation is already running. If an increase from ten minutes per zone to fifteen minutes per zone doesn't seem to be enough to keep annuals and perennials happy in July and August, add another five minutes to the time and water even deeper. Encourage roots to reach far down into the soil for their moisture and nutrients and both you and your landscape will be better off.

FIVE TIPS FOR CONSERVING WATER

1. Use less water by not watering too often. I spent many years working in the retail garden center business and I can tell you from personal experience that more people kill more plants by overwatering them than by underwatering them. A dry plant wilts and reminds you of its needs, but perks back up once you've watered it. A wet plant will only wilt, generally speaking, once it is beyond saving and its roots are in a rapid state of irreversible decline. If all else fails, stick your finger in the soil and see if it *feels* wet or dry. This may mean the difference between a plant living or dying.

2. Use less water by watering deeply. It seems counterintuitive that watering for a longer

period of time would use less water than watering for a shorter period of time, but in the long run, it's true! Watering deeply and thoroughly, saturating the soil and then letting it dry somewhat in between, will encourage roots to grow deep into the soil. The deeper the roots grow, the more efficiently they will use water and the less supplemental water they will need from you in the long run. Over the life of your landscape, this practice will end up saving you far more water than it uses.

3. Use less water by mulching properly. This does *not* mean use more mulch and pile it deep. Mulching properly means distributing an even layer of mulch across the surface of the soil and keeping it replenished as needed. What you choose to use for mulch is entirely up to you. Commercial wood products are fine, but the source of that wood is not always known and may contain chemicals. If you are a truly organic gardener, using your own compost, decaying leaves, straw, or mulch from a known source may be a better bet. A 2-inch layer of mulch spread evenly across the soil surface will reduce water loss by up to 20 percent and keep the soil temperature anywhere from 5 to 10 degrees cooler than unmulched soil.

4. Use less water by watering at the right time of day. Watering during the earliest morning hours is beneficial for several reasons. In the early hours before sunrise, the temperatures are at their lowest and winds calmest, so less water is lost through evaporation and more water reaches and stays on the ground where it can soak in to be used by the plants. Some estimates show that watering during the heat of the day causes up to 50 percent water loss to evaporation. Watering in the early morning hours also gives the leaves a chance to dry off during the day, helping to reduce disease outbreaks in the garden.

5. Use less water by truly learning about your irrigation system and how it functions. This doesn't mean just learning about the computerized clock that runs it, but also how much water is put out in a given zone in a given time. Place some aluminum pie tins around the garden (and the lawn, for that matter) and see how much water collects in each one in the amount of time each zone runs. You may be surprised! In some cases, you may be putting down more water than you thought you were and, in other cases, considerably less. By knowing the distribution of water in different zones, you can adjust your system accordingly and conserve a considerable amount of water over a period of time.

THE (ALMOST) CHEMICAL-FREE GARDEN

In the 1950s and 1960s, with amazing breakthroughs in chemistry and biochemistry that allowed for the creation of a dizzying array of "helpful" landscape and gardening products, spraying our lawns and gardens to control every insect and disease that appeared on the horizon became not just the popular, but the *expected* thing to do. Everyone was running out and buying this spray or that tonic to do everything from killing insects in their vegetable gardens to managing fungus in their lawns, not to mention the clouds of DDT that were released into the atmosphere and our water supply as mosquito control. The "perfect" home in the "perfect" subdivision was in vogue, with everything outdoors neat and tidy and trimmed and sprayed to excellence.

It took years for people to begin realizing the ill effects that this was having on the environment—and on *them*! And unfortunately, practices that take a generation or more to create also take a generation or more to eliminate, which meant that the "spray it and kill it" mind-set took until the 1990s to begin to diminish and well into the new millennium to actually be replaced by a broader section of the public with wiser alternatives.

Fortunately, the tide seems to have turned and much of the public (and especially the younger generation, which bodes well for all of us) has embraced the idea of the reduction of chemical use across the board, not just on our lawns and in our gardens, but in every aspect of our lives. This is not a concept that is new to experienced gardeners, but it is encouraging to see the general public embracing ideas that we have known about all along!

Watering deeply and thoroughly encourages deep, efficient root systems that can support lush growth and showy blooms.

What, then, can we do to perpetuate this stream of consciousness—of being as environmentally friendly as possible—in our own yards and gardens?

FIVE TIPS FOR REDUCING OR ELIMINATING CHEMICALS IN THE LANDSCAPE

1. Reduce the need for chemicals in your landscape by using the "Right Plant, Right Place" mantra. When you choose plants according to the growing conditions where they are to live in your yard and not just because you like the looks of them, you are doing yourself, your garden, and the environment a huge favor. While some may take this to mean growing native plants exclusively, this "Right Plant, Right Place" idea is not exclusive to growing native plants. It simply means to take a close look at your soil, the sun/shade conditions, availability (or lack) of water, the microclimate (discussed earlier in this book), and choose your plants wisely for a given location based on those criteria, wherever their native lands may be. As I've said before, not all non-native plants are bad and not all native plants are suitable for the garden. Can't we all just get along?

2. Reduce the need for chemicals in your landscape by *encouraging* your soil to be the living, breathing, dynamic, teeming-with-life organism it is. A nearly infinite and unimaginable number of living organisms reside in the soil in your garden. It is swarming with beneficial microscopic organisms that live together in harmony and work symbiotically for the greater good. Those healthy relationships between organisms so small it takes an electron microscope to see them are what allow us to grow healthy and beautiful lawns, flower gardens, vegetable gardens, and so much more. By reducing the amount of chemicals we apply to our landscapes (almost all of which enter your soil at some point), along with adding as much healthy organic matter as possible and maintaining healthy soil moisture levels, we create the best possible environment for the explosive growth of beneficial organisms. These organisms, in turn, boost the health and wellness of our plants, increase their pest and disease resistance and their ability to utilize available nutrients, and dramatically reduce the need for spraying pests or the addition of synthetic fertilizers.

3. Reduce the need for chemicals in your landscape by changing your outlook and being accepting of flaws and imperfections. None of us is perfect, so why do we expect perfection from our lawns and gardens? Much of it has to do with our need, as a species, to dominate and conquer. Yes, it's true. Gardening fulfills a deep-seated need in us to control our surroundings. With plants, we plant them, water them, feed them, spray them, prune them, stake them, and otherwise manipulate them to do our bidding— and they don't talk back. If they look poorly— or die—we simply replace them. But what if we could (and we can) overlook some minor flaws and imperfections. How much time, money, and energy would we save by simply changing our own values and expectations of our gardens? By using the suggestions in Step 2 and then slightly adjusting our expectations, we can nearly eliminate the need for the use of any harsh chemicals in our landscapes. Embrace the clover in the lawn. Accept a few holes in the hosta leaves or search out and plant the most slug-resistant, leathery-leaved varieties you can find. Or, find the most effective, earth-friendly way to control the slug population. By adjusting your own expectations, however slightly it may be, you will dramatically reduce the need for using toxic chemicals to control what, in the grand scheme of things, are minor imperfections.

4. Reduce the need for chemicals in your landscape by turning to natural pest and disease controls first. Not only is this a safer and sounder practice for the environment, it is a safer and sounder practice for *you*. By turning to natural controls first, you are reducing the risk to your own health of spraying hazardous chemicals. In turn, you are inflicting less damage on your soil, your groundwater, your plants—your landscape as a whole—and the many beneficial insects, mammals, and birds that reside there. As you reduce your chemical usage, the populations of

Spiders may seem scary, but the majority you find in the garden are quite harmless to humans and fill an extremely important niche in controlling insects that are destructive to the garden.

beneficial animals, fungi, bacteria, and more will increase exponentially. As this happens, the need for intervention by you will continue to be reduced. Your landscape will live in harmony with itself, and you will reap the benefits. This does not mean that all work will be eliminated. Simply that you can focus on more worthwhile tasks while nature works out its system of checks and balances.

5. Reduce the need for chemicals in your landscape by turning to natural and organic fertilizers first. What's the big deal about natural and organic fertilizers? Without getting into a too-scientific discussion, the basic differences between organic or natural fertilizers and synthetic ones are these: The nutrients in synthetic, man-made fertilizers are distributed into the soil by being attached to soluble salts. Have you ever used fertilizer to de-ice a sidewalk in the winter? It isn't the nutrients that are melting the ice, it's the salt. It's no different than putting down rock salt or the salty brines they use on highways. These soluble salts build up in the soil and when they become too highly concentrated, may begin killing off beneficial microorganisms. This interruption in the soil food web doesn't take long to take effect, and, as the microorganisms begin to die off, the larger organisms starve to death, literally "killing" your soil. Soluble salts also leach very quickly from the soil and carry the attached nutrients with them, so the nutrients in most chemical fertilizers are available for absorption for a very short period of time.

Natural and organic fertilizers, on the other hand, are derived from natural plant, animal, or mineral origins. They are not delivered by being attached to soluble salts, so they remain in the soil longer. They are also "digested" by other soil organisms *first* and *then* their nutrients become available to the plants. So by using natural and organic fertilizers, you are feeding both the soil's living organisms *and* your plants, and because the nutrients remain in the soil for a much longer period of time, you reduce the amount of product you need to apply and the frequency with which you need to apply it, ultimately reducing your overall chemical use quite dramatically.

COMPOST—A GARDENER'S "BLACK GOLD"

I have several gardening friends who own t-shirts that say "Compost Happens." Maybe some of you do too. One thing I know for sure is that compost doesn't just "happen." Well, it can. You can just pile the garden and yard debris up in a corner and wait a few years for it to break down into something usable, but that really isn't the efficient way to go about it. If you want a steady supply of the gardener's "black gold," you have to *make* it happen! Luckily, it's not that hard to do.

Now, some gardeners have fancy compost bins that are shaped like barrels and sit up on big stands, a handle on one end allowing you to give the whole apparatus a couple of good spins once a week or so to shake up the contents inside and encourage it to break down faster. Others have plastic bins that sit on the ground, their tops lifting off to add more raw material to the bin while a trap door opens in the front to allow access to the rich, black goodness that has collected at the bottom. Both of these systems, while impressive to look at, produce a relatively small amount of compost. Plenty to brew some compost tea or amend the occasional planting hole, but hardly enough compost to topdress a garden of any size. A friend of mine who is handy with tools has built himself a multi-bin compost

system out of recycled wooden pallets with various stages of compost decomposing in the five or so separate sections. Me? I have a pile. Fortunately, I live in the country, so having a big pile of decomposing garden debris isn't an eyesore (it's over in a far corner where you have to go looking for it) and it doesn't bother any of the neighbors because none of them live close enough to notice.

My garden is not especially large, but I am always amazed at the size of the debris pile that it can generate over the course of a growing season. I keep two separate piles going most of the time; one for grass clippings, green trimmings from the garden, and kitchen waste, and the other strictly for leaves as they drop in autumn. The former I do my best to layer like all of the books say to, with some green and some brown material included to keep the right balance of carbon to nitrogen. I sprinkle it with the hose occasionally to keep it damp and to keep those billions of microbes actively breaking it down into rich goodness, and, when I have the time, I turn it to keep it aerated and actively decomposing. The latter—the leaf pile—I just allow to sit and work on its own. I pile the oak leaves (I have three white oaks) into a long pile about 4 feet high as I rake leaves on the weekends in autumn. I sprinkle it down with water and throw a few handfuls of organic fertilizer in it to help feed the microbes and then I leave it alone. The following year I repeat. By the third year, the bottom two-thirds of the pile has turned to rich, black, coarse leaf mold, a product I cherish beyond all others, even more than compost. The worms love the leaf mold too. As I dig in with a shovel to scoop the rich, black goodness into the garden cart, the worms are writhing and wriggling as they try to escape. Some do, the escapees staying to help with decomposition, but just as many make their way to the garden where they will burrow into the soil, aerating it as they go and leaving behind valuable worm castings. Few things are more valuable to your garden's soil than fresh, living compost and rich, organic leaf mold.

A Monarch butterfly larva feeding on milkweed.

FIVE TIPS FOR MAKING GREAT COMPOST

1. If you want to make great compost, anything from the garden is fair game. It doesn't matter whether it is green (grass clippings, garden clippings, or kitchen waste) or brown (twigs and fallen leaves), almost anything that comes from the yard can be composted. There are only a handful of exceptions. Debris from diseased plants does not go in the compost pile. While a good compost pile will get nice and warm (sometimes even hot) on the inside, rarely does it get hot enough throughout the pile to kill off disease-causing pathogens, and having them in the compost could help to spread them throughout the garden later. It's best to remove diseased plant material from the property and throw it away. I also avoid fireplace ashes because of their extremely high alkalinity and twigs and branches that are larger in diameter than my little finger because it just takes too long for them to break down. I keep those in a separate pile to use as kindling in the fireplace in winter.

2. If you want to make great compost, layer your grass clippings (if you catch them) into your compost pile. They are a good source of natural nitrogen that will help feed the microbes that are doing the work of breaking down the garden debris into usable compost. Layers of fresh, green grass clippings between the brown layers of leaves, twigs, and dried plant material will ensure that microbial activity remains high and that the slower-to-decompose dry material breaks down efficiently. A good rule of thumb is about 20 percent grass clippings or green material to 80 percent brown material. Be cautious about collecting grass clippings from other sources if you're trying to maintain an organic garden. While it may be tempting to collect bags full of clippings from curbs and street corners in the neighborhood, you can never be sure what other lawns have been treated with and some chemicals have a long decomposition period (unaffected by the heat of a good compost pile) and may contaminate your compost and, eventually, your garden.

3. If you want to make great compost, don't forget the indoors. No, I'm not encouraging you to make compost indoors. Just don't forget all of the kitchen scraps and a variety of other items from around the house that are perfectly compostable. These include, but are not limited to, the obvious things like vegetable peelings and other fruit and vegetable scraps, coffee grounds, and egg shells, as well as some items you may not have considered, like napkins, paper towels, and the cardboard rolls they are rolled onto. What about from around the house? Have you ever considered composting things

Zebra swallowtail butterfly on butterfly weed (*Asclepias tuberosa*).

like newspaper, cotton rags, hair, fur, the contents of your paper shredder, or the dryer lint? What about toilet paper rolls and the vacuum bag? Had you considered the vacuum bag?! Things to avoid composting include any type of meat products, oils, grease, dairy products, or bones. They will attract a variety of scavengers, mostly rodents, and may also contribute harmful bacteria or other pathogens to the compost pile.

4. If you want to make great compost, keep your leaves. This is worth mentioning again in a point of its own. In the autumn, leaves are abundant, easy to manage, and—maybe best of all—free! All you have to do is rake or blow them as they fall. I have learned that the easiest way to collect the *enormous* quantity of leaves that fall from my three oaks is to lay a large tarp out on the lawn and blow the leaves up into it. Then, all I have to do is drag the tarp to the leaf pile and *voilà*—done. While using a gas-powered

blower may not seem the most eco-friendly thing in the world, the quick job it makes of leaf removal is worth it, and the valuable compost that comes out of a job well done makes up for it on the other side of the equation, in my estimation. Once the majority of leaves have been removed to their decomposition area and they aren't lying a foot deep in all of the beds and over the lawn, I simply blow the rest of the leaves out of the beds and run over them with the mower several times to mulch them into the lawn where they provide all-important organic matter and a source of food for the earthworms.

5. Now that you've made great compost, how about recycling some of those items from the house and garden that can't be composted? Use a chipper to break down larger tree branches and use the chips to topdress mulched pathways in the garden. Recycle plastic pots by taking them back to local nurseries who grow their own flowers, trees, and shrubs. They will gladly (usually) re-use them. If not, more recycling centers will now take black plastic and other types of plastic pots than ever before. Recycle old bricks as bed edging, broken concrete as stepping stones, or old windows as tops for a do-it-yourself cold frame. What about all of those wine bottles? They can be used to make a variety of decorative and beautiful art for the garden, as well as fun and funky bed edging. You are limited only by your imagination when it comes to re-using and recycling what otherwise might end up in the landfill.

GARDENING FOR WILDLIFE

Once you've jumped on this "Greener Ways to Garden" bandwagon, you'll find—even in the city—a vast increase in the amount of wildlife you find taking up residence in your garden. Birds and butterflies will make your garden their home. Honeybees and other beneficial pollinators will buzz from flower to flower, drinking nectar and collecting pollen, helping to ensure the next generation of garden flowers as they go. You may find that you have other garden residents as well—chipmunks, squirrels, rabbits, frogs, toads, lizards, and yes, even snakes! I will be the first to admit that I am not a big fan of snakes. It's not the snake itself, really, but their sneaky demeanor and their innate ability to surprise at the most inopportune moments. Once I'm over the initial shock, I'm fine. Usually. But the point is that all of these birds, insects, mammals, amphibians, and reptiles are all signs of a healthy, happy ecosystem. They are the end goal because when your soil is healthy and well taken care of, when your plants are growing happily, when all is right and in balance in the world that is your garden, all of these things live together in peace and harmony, one dependent on the other in the greater web of life.

Bumblebee on a thistle bloom.

GARDEN
LIKE A PRO

Like some of you, I have been gardening for most of my life. When I was three years old, I planted the seeds from a silver maple growing in my babysitter's front yard into the flower bed in front of her house, where those seeds promptly sprouted and grew. Forty years later, two of the resulting trees from my first foray into gardening still stand in my parents' yard a few miles away (although one may not be long for this world if the power company has a say). I have been gardening professionally since I was fourteen years old, when I started my first job at the nursery of some family friends near my hometown. A season has not gone by since that my hands have not been in the dirt. I've learned a lot of lessons over the years—some of them the hard way—about *how* to garden successfully and face the challenges that inevitably come along. Experienced gardeners know the best way to learn is from others, so I'd like to share some of those lessons with you.

When visitors come to my garden, one of the most frequently asked questions is, "How do you get your garden to be so lush and full of blooms?" I feed it. I feed the soil and I feed the plants. There are those who would argue that if you have the proper balance of organic matter and microbes in your soil, there is no need to fertilize. Most of us, me included, are not gardening under those kinds of ideal conditions. Also, I garden intensively and with a wide variety of species from around the world. The number of plants I expect my garden to support and the volume of beautiful foliage and blooms I expect it to produce often goes above and beyond what my soil will naturally sustain and so I lend my soil and its inhabitants a helping hand.

I have been on a steady trend away from the use of chemicals for close to twenty years, but when I moved to my current home in 2008 and began the process of clearing the larger part of the garden of weeds and of transplanting the plants that were struggling, one thing was immediately apparent: There was no life in the soil! After hours, days, and weeks worth of digging, I turned up nary an earthworm. Even the less desirable creatures—grub worms and the like—were almost non-existent. There simply was no visible life in the soil and I

had to wonder, if visible life was struggling, what about the life I couldn't see? Was this an indicator that the microbial life in the soil was just as inadequate? It became immediately apparent that not only were the plants struggling that were already growing there, but the soil itself must have been struggling too.

By incorporating compost, leaf mold, and other organic matter into every square inch I turned, the quality of the soil began to improve. The soil was becoming more friable, breaking up more easily and allowing the penetration of air, water, and nutrients. Within the first year I began digging up the occasional earthworm and by the end of the second, they became regular residents of the soil again. The return of visible life meant that the unseen microorganisms were also thriving. When the time came for planting, the products chosen for establishing new plants and for long-term growth and maintenance of those plants were selected as much for their ability to feed the soil and its inhabitants as for their benefits to the plants themselves. I continue to rely heavily on all-natural and organic fertilizers, root inoculants, and microbial soups to feed my garden and to keep its soil teeming with life.

THE SCIENCE OF FERTILIZER

Nearly all plants require three major and a number of minor nutrients, macronutrients and micronutrients in order to grow properly and eventually reproduce, whether by setting seed, producing spores, or propagating by other means. Most gardeners know the three macronutrients, nitrogen (N), phosphorous (P), and potassium (K) that plants need to grow: nitrogen to support the growth of stems and leaves; phosphorous to support active root growth, flowering, and fruit production; and potassium, which is essential for many of the metabolic processes within the plant, increasing the efficiency of a plant's biological systems and its tolerance to stress. The three major nutrients are used by plants at a relatively high rate and in some soils may be depleted fast enough that nature cannot keep up with the demand. This is where we often step in and assist with the addition of fertilizer.

Micronutrients are perhaps less familiar, but have no less importance. Iron, copper, zinc, and others all have very specific functions within the plant and, when not present, cause the chemical and biological processes inside the plant to be interrupted or to quit functioning altogether. Micronutrient deficiencies, except for iron deficiency, which is rather commonplace, don't often occur in the garden, as most micronutrients are required in very small quantities and are naturally present in great enough supply in the soil. When they do occur, it is more often an issue of improper soil pH that doesn't allow the roots to absorb the micronutrients than an actual deficiency of the micronutrients themselves.

How, then, do we best incorporate these necessary nutrients and beneficial microorganisms into our gardens?

COMPOST

Compost and leaf mold (decomposing leaves) both have nutrient value and do act, in some small way, as natural fertilizers. Whether or not this is enough to sustain suitable plant growth will depend in part on how intensively you garden, your expectations for your garden, and the quality of your soil to begin with. Regardless, compost and leaf mold are, or at least should be, the point at which we all start if for no other reason than their considerable benefits to the soil and the organisms living there.

COMPOST TEA

• If you want to take composting to the next level, once you have a good supply of compost in your pile you can make your own compost tea. Compost tea is a microbe-rich liquid "brewed" from your own compost, applied immediately to your plants and soil while it teems with microscopic life. Because you are creating this "tea" from your own compost, you are brewing microbes that already exist in your soil and will knowingly thrive there, enhancing your soil and, in turn, your garden's health and productivity.

MANURE

• Manure, like compost, does have some nutrient value. Typically, manures offer more nitrogen than other nutrients and even that will vary based on the animal and its diet. Nutrient content will also vary depending on whether you are using manure from the farm or commercial manure from your local garden center. Remember, when using farm "fresh" manure, that it *must* be well-composted before being applied to the garden or you risk burning your plants. A minimum of one year of composting and mellowing is recommended prior to your application in the garden.

COMMERCIAL MICROBIAL BREWS

• If going to the trouble of brewing your own compost tea isn't, well, your cup of tea (sorry!), many garden centers have water-soluble microbial brews that can be purchased ready to mix and use. One of my local garden centers has its own microbe and enzyme concoction that I have used many times through the years with excellent results. You simply purchase a bottle of each of the components, stir them up, allow them to brew and bubble for twenty-four hours, and apply. Check with your own local garden centers to see what products they might recommend, or perhaps they have a brew of their own.

COMMERCIAL FERTILIZERS

It seems that nearly every spring when I begin making my rounds at the local garden centers, a new all-natural or organic brand of fertilizer awaits my perusal. They are as different and varied as the plants themselves. My best advice is to try a variety of products and find those that suit your gardening style and, more importantly, give you the results you seek in your garden and in your soil. Each of us will have a different experience and each of us will come to rely on products that work the most efficiently and produce the best results in our own gardens.

~A LESSON FROM THE GARDEN~

BREW YOUR OWN COMPOST TEA

You'll need some inexpensive equipment to brew the best compost tea, but it's worth a bit of extra effort. Gather two 5-gallon buckets, a small aerator (the kind used for a small fish tank works well, if you have one sitting on a shelf) and its accompanying plastic tubing, a bit of sugar (to feed your microbes), some fresh water (dechlorinated if you live in the city or fill one bucket and let it sit for 24 hours), cheesecloth, and some twine. If you have a splitter valve (sometimes called a "gang valve") for your aerator to divide the airflow into more than one stream, it will enhance the quality of the end product, but is not a necessity.

Pick a location to set up your operation: a covered porch, garage, garden shed, or somewhere out of the direct sun and where the temperature is moderate. You'll also need access to an outlet for the pump. In the bottom of one 5-gallon bucket, add 3 inches of mature compost, burying the ends of the plastic tubing from the aerator under the compost. Add ½ cup white sugar to the compost and then fill your bucket with about 3½ gallons of water—from the hose if you have well water or from your other bucket if you have set water out to dechlorinate. Plug the aerator in and let your compost brew, stirring occasionally, for forty-eight hours.

When your compost tea has finished brewing, it is ready to use immediately. Use the twine to tie three layers of cheesecloth firmly over the top of your second bucket and slowly pour the contents of the tea bucket into the empty one, straining the solids out with the cheesecloth. The remaining solids can be added back to the compost pile to "seed" it with fresh new microbes and jumpstart its activity. The now clean tea can be applied directly to the garden, either as a foliar spray or as a soil drench. It should be used quickly, as the living microbes will begin to decline once you have removed their source of air. I use a hose sprayer, the kind you might apply liquid fertilizer with, set on its highest setting. This dilutes the tea down as it is being sprayed and allows me to cover more of the garden with one batch. It can be sprayed directly on the leaves of the plants as well as on the soil and is ideally done just before a good rain to help wash all of this microbial goodness down into the soil where it is needed most.

ALL-NATURAL VS. ORGANIC: IS THERE A DIFFERENCE?

Is there a difference between a garden product that is labeled "All Natural" vs. one that is labeled "Organic"? There is. Technically speaking—and I am paraphrasing to a great extent here—a product may not be labeled organic if it or any of its components have come in contact with chemicals that may be toxic or potentially harmful in nature. For example, one of my favorite all-natural fertilizers relies heavily on cottonseed meal as a source of nitrogen; because of the boll weevil, cotton requires a high level of chemical application to keep the weevils at bay, so fertilizers containing cotton byproducts like cottonseed meal cannot be certified organic unless the source was organically grown cotton. Many natural fertilizers also rely heavily on the use of blood meal, or dried animal blood, as a source of nutrients and, because of the high level of steroids and antibiotics used in commercial meat production, the same is true when it comes to fertilizers containing blood meal, bone meal, and other animal byproducts. There are products on the market, including fertilizers, pest controls, and others, that are certified organic. It is a personal choice as to how pure you want those products you use to be.

SOIL pH AND FERTILIZER

Every gardener should have a simple understanding of soil pH and its effect on plants and how they function. At the most basic level, pH is a measure of how acidic or alkaline your soil is. The pH scale ranges from 0 to 14, extremely acidic at the low end to extremely alkaline at the high end, with 7.0 being neutral. Generally speaking, soil pH may range from 4.5 to 9.0, with natural buffers in the soil keeping it from rising or falling too much above or below that range, although exceptions may occur. Most plants fall somewhere in the middle, preferring soils that are slightly acidic at pH 6.0 to slightly alkaline at pH 7.5. Nevertheless, there are plants that thrive well outside of those limits.

When soil pH fluctuates outside of a plant's acceptable range, problems can occur. Most commonly, improper soil pH causes nutrients to be bound within the soil, not allowing them to be assimilated by plants' roots and potentially leading to nutrient deficiencies within the plants themselves. This is most frequently recognized by stunted or contorted growth or by yellowing or other discoloration of the leaves.

When you are considering fertilizers, pH also plays an important role. Fertilizers intended for acid-loving plants like azaleas, camellias, and hollies not only feed the plants, but react with the soil in such a way as to help maintain its pH in the proper range for the health of those plants. The addition of lime and bone meal will cause an increase in the soil's pH and may be appropriate for plants, like most clematis, whose preferences are for a more alkaline soil environment.

When establishing any garden, it is always a good idea to have a basic soil test performed. It will provide you with valuable information about your existing soil, including its pH. Knowing your pH will give you an excellent starting point for refining the list of plants you wish to grow and will guide you in knowing which plants may struggle in your garden if they have a given pH range that will be difficult for you to provide. Azaleas, for instance, require acidic soil in order to thrive. In alkaline soil, they will be unable to draw iron from the soil, becoming sickened and yellow (iron chlorosis) over time, and may eventually die from this condition.

APHIDS

You can adjust pH through fertilization and amendment, but only to a certain degree, as soil has a tremendous buffering capacity and the pH will constantly readjust itself without regular treatment. If you live in a region where the soil pH is well above 7.0 and you have little hope of maintaining your soil's pH at 6.0 to 6.5 long-term, azaleas should, perhaps, be removed from your wish list. There are hundreds (possibly thousands) of beautiful plants to choose from that will thrive in whatever your conditions may be. Why bang your head repeatedly against a wall over a plant that continually struggles and brings the whole garden down with it?

GARDEN PESTS AND DISEASES

The first step in identifying any insect, disease, or other problem is observation. Gardeners are generally observant types and you *will* notice fairly soon if something is amiss with one of your prized plants: leaves chewed on or with holes in them; leaves puckered, curled, speckled, or spotted; discoloration of, abnormal and prolonged wilting of, or the partial or total loss of foliage. These and other signs indicate potential problems and warrant investigation.

INSECT PESTS AND THEIR CONTROL

Insects are one of the primary sources of damage to garden plants, including common invaders such as aphids, scale, and a variety of mites, as well as those that might be less familiar to the home gardener, like nematodes. The list certainly extends far beyond these few, but most of us find ourselves dealing with at least some of these offenders on a regular basis, while others may be only occasional distractions.

APHIDS

- Aphids are soft-bodied insects and may or may not have wings. They are very small, pear-shaped, and come in a variety of colors ranging from the common green form to gold, red, orange, brown, and even black. Aphids are most commonly found in some quantity, clustered together on succulent and soft new growth, especially in spring and early summer.

- **Control:** Aphids are one of the easier pests to control in the garden. For mild infestations, a strong spray of water every other day for one week will dislodge and disperse them. For more serious infestations, insecticidal soap or highly refined horticultural oil will eradicate them in an environmentally friendly way.

CATERPILLARS

- The first thing that should be mentioned of caterpillars is that there are both "good" and "bad" caterpillars where the garden is concerned, and caution should be used in their control, as many caterpillars are the immature forms of some of our most desirable garden inhabitants: butterflies. Common methods of controlling caterpillars do not distinguish between those that are pests and those that are not. Always use great care when spraying for caterpillars and carefully target the problem kinds.

- **Control:** For most leaf-eating caterpillars (which is the vast majority where garden pests are concerned), Bt (*Bacillus thuringiensis*) is an effective biological control. Bt is non-selective in its control of most caterpillars, so targeted spraying of undesirable species (tomato hornworms or cabbage loopers, for instance) is recommended. Spray only the plants where the problem caterpillars reside. Otherwise, you may find yourself eradicating those caterpillars that will turn into monarch, swallowtail, fritillary, and other desirable butterflies. Know a butterfly's larval host plants, learn to identify their caterpillars, and avoid spraying near host plants as much as possible, even with earth-friendly products.

NEMATODES

- In some parts of the South, nematodes are a prevalent and often serious challenge. The most common nematode is the root knot nematode that attacks a plant's roots, causing knotlike nodules to form and inhibiting root function, but there are also foliar nematodes, bulb nematodes, and others. Often, nematodes will be kept in check by the balance of nature, good nematodes, and other microorganisms keeping the problem types at bay. But on occasion, trouble arises.

- **Control:** Nematode control, particularly root knot nematode, is difficult, sometimes requiring fumigation of the soil if the outbreaks are particularly bad. Gardeners can take precautionary measures by regularly adding compost, leaf mold, and other organic matter to their soil, thereby feeding and increasing the number of desirable nematodes and other beneficial microbes that will naturally control the problem types. Soil solarization is also effective, sterilizing the soil by heating it under a layer of black or clear plastic (white plastic reflects too much heat and light and is rather ineffective in regard to solarization).

SCALE INSECTS

- Scale insects, like aphids, are attracted most often to succulent new growth where they attach themselves, secrete their waxy or hard protective covering, and proceed to suck the sap from the plants' leaves and stems. Often you will find them lined up along leaf veins, where they have maximum access to the sap flowing inside the plant, or attached directly to the stem of a plant where water and nutrients flow freely just under the surface. The most noticeable symptom of scale is the sticky secretion (honeydew) they leave behind. Almost always, if the leaves of your plants become sticky or covered in a black, sooty-appearing mold, scale is the culprit.

- **Control:** Scale can be a challenge to control. Scale insects secrete their own protective shell or waxy covering that repels water and chemicals and protects them from attack by beneficial predators. The best control for scale insects, short of using a toxic systemic insecticide, is by smothering them with applications of insecticidal soap or highly refined horticultural oil. Repeat applications are usually necessary, but with some persistence, oils and soaps will give good results.

SLUGS AND SNAILS

- In the interest of not creating a standalone category for mollusks, slugs and snails are being included here. When plants come under attack by slugs or snails, the most obvious symptoms are ragged (chewed on) leaf edges and erratic holes chewed directly through the leaf surface, often in between veins. Slugs and snails are most active overnight and take refuge in the cool

SLUGS ON LETTUCE LEAVES

environment of the mulch, under rocks, or at ground level around the base of a plant during the day.

- **Control:** As frustrating as they can be, slugs and snails are not difficult to control. The key is to start early in the season and to be persistent to keep them from breeding and creating a population explosion. Beer traps are extremely effective and can be as simple as placing shallow dishes of beer in places in the garden where slugs are a problem. Commercial slug baits are also effective methods of control, but many are extremely toxic to children, pets, and other animals. I prefer those that are iron-based and that, upon ingestion by the slug or snail, cause it to stop eating and wither away, all while being completely nontoxic to other living organisms.

SPIDER MITES

- There are numerous types of mites that can be nuisances in the garden, and, like nematodes and slugs before them, they don't technically fall into the insect category, but are best treated here anyway. The first sign of spider mites is pale green to near white stippling or speckling of the leaves, followed by visible white webbing if the infestation is severe enough. Spider mites thrive in hot, dry conditions and are especially prevalent during the hot summer months. Potted plants that dry out frequently are especially susceptible, but garden plants are certainly not immune.
- **Control:** Spider mites can be difficult to control, especially if the infestation is severe. Regular misting or spraying of infested plants with a strong spray of water can dislodge and disperse mites. Diatomaceous earth dusted onto the upper and undersides of leaves can also be very effective. It will wash off as the plants are watered or rained on and may need to be applied several times in the case of severe infestations. Insecticidal soaps and highly refined horticultural oils are also very effective in smothering mites, but care must be taken to saturate the undersides of the leaves where most mites reside, and it will almost certainly take multiple applications at regular intervals to arrive at total eradication.

COMMON DISEASES OF GARDEN PLANTS

Complete disease diagnosis is far beyond the scope of this book and, frankly, beyond the reaches of most home gardeners, even more experienced ones. Obvious diseases are easy enough for the gardener to diagnose and treat, but often, beyond the clearly visible signs of powdery mildew, rust, and various leaf spots, plant diseases require diagnosis and a recommended scope of treatment from someone better versed in the topic; a garden center professional or plant disease specialist with your local County Extension Service.

Plants are susceptible to a wide array of diseases that are not limited to fungal infections, but may also include bacterial diseases and viruses. Most are treatable, many curable. Unfortunately, a few are incurable and require the removal and destruction of infected plants. Prevention is often the best approach, avoiding infection of plants to begin with. This means keeping the garden well groomed, removing unnecessary leaf litter, mulching and watering properly, and pruning plants (especially trees and shrubs) to encourage airflow within the plant as well as around it. Practicing proper hygiene with your tools is essential: sterilize pruner blades, pruning saws, and other implements with rubbing alcohol to avoid spreading diseases from plant to plant. Included alongside diseases are a handful of cultural disorders stemming from environmental factors that may be disease-like in their appearance.

CONTROLLING FUNGAL AND BACTERIAL DISEASES

Where fungal and bacterial diseases are concerned, prevention is your first line of defense. Good cultural practices, including tidiness and cleanliness in the garden will keep them from spreading. Proper mulching will prevent fungal spores and bacteria from splashing onto plants by way of rain or irrigation, and proper spacing of plants will allow air for proper air circulation and the reduction of heat and humidity that many diseases thrive on. When necessary, fungicides—including those that are natural in origin and low in their toxicity—will prevent a broad spectrum of diseases if properly applied and several do double duty in eliminating bacterial diseases as well. Perhaps it is more prudent to cover the methods of control as opposed to the diseases themselves, as many products are broad in the spectrum of diseases, both fungal and bacterial, they will control.

BAKING SODA

- Baking soda is good for many things, but you may be surprised to learn of its effectiveness in the prevention of some of the more common fungal diseases in the garden. When mixed at a rate of 2 teaspoons per gallon of water and sprayed on both the upper and under surfaces of the leaf, baking soda will help to prevent outbreaks of powdery mildew and may have some effect on other forms of mildew as well. It is particularly effective when mixed with a highly refined horticultural oil to help it stick to the surface of the leaf.

COPPER-BASED FUNGICIDES

- There are a number of copper-based fungicides on the market, most of which use copper sulfate as their active ingredient to aid in the control of both fungal and bacterial diseases. These include powdery and downy mildews, early and late blights (especially prevalent on tomatoes), and various fungal and bacterial leaf spot diseases. Copper fungicides should not be applied during periods of cool, wet weather, as damage to plants may occur. Copper-based fungicides also show some effectiveness in treating root rot diseases when mixed according to label directions and used as a soil drench around a plant's roots.

HORTICULTURAL OILS

- There are a number of types of oil- or fat-based products on the market, most of which are used for the control of various types of insect pests. Some of these are what are referred to as dormant oils, which are heavy and must be applied only when plants are dormant and generally only to woody plants (trees or shrubs). When speaking of horticultural oils, these are highly refined and very light in their makeup and

are safe to be used on actively growing plants of all types. These highly refined oils, in addition to insect control, have shown some ability to ward off common leaf diseases like powdery mildew, rusts, and blackspot, most likely because they seal the surface of the leaf and germination of the fungal spores is prevented. Applications should be made early in the day, especially during the heat of summer.

SULFUR

- For many years, sulfur has been the fungicide of choice in my garden. I purchase it from my local garden center as a wettable powder, mixing it at a rate of 1 tablespoon per gallon of water and spray preventively, every two weeks, beginning in early spring and continuing throughout the growing season. I find it extremely effective against the most common diseases—blackspot, powdery mildew, rust (even daylily rust), and anthracnose. Like baking soda, I have found sulfur to be more effective when a small amount of highly refined horticultural oil or a spreader sticker is added to the solution to help it adhere to the foliage. Sulfur should not be applied when temperatures are over 80 degrees. During hot weather, I switch to copper fungicide.

VIRAL DISEASES

Viral diseases in the garden are the most difficult to treat. In fact, most have no effective treatment, and it is often best, if plants are diagnosed with a virus, to immediately remove and destroy the plant. Plants diagnosed with viral diseases should not be added to compost piles, as most compost piles do not generate enough heat to kill the pathogens and prevent them being reintroduced to the garden when the compost is distributed.

Prevention is a gardener's primary and sometimes only defense against the spread of viral diseases in the garden. Therein lies the importance of keeping tools clean and disinfected. Rose mosaic virus and rose rosette disease are frequently spread from plant to plant by way of contaminated pruning shears and deadheading scissors. Pruning a branch or deadheading a spent bloom from an infected rose and then pruning a branch from or deadheading a healthy rose is enough to spread the disease from the infected plant to the healthy plant.

ANIMAL PESTS IN THE GARDEN

Of all garden pests, animals are the most difficult to control. Most of them are quick on their feet. Many operate under cover of darkness. Some, like moles, voles, and chipmunks, spend part or all of their time doing their damage underground. For smaller animals, the best one can hope to do is trap them (live or not, depending on your stance on that issue) or, in some cases, repellents may be effective. For larger animals like deer, your only hope (aside from the most drastic measures) is to either bar them from the garden with a series of tall fences or repel them with an arsenal of homemade or commercial repellents. There is so much information available from resources dedicated to the control and eradication of animal pests that I feel it redundant to include the same material here. I can, however, offer some insight into how to bait your traps for the small- to medium-sized animals in order to trap and, when possible, relocate them. I've become rather proficient at it.

CHIPMUNKS

- Chipmunks cannot resist nuts. Peanuts will do, but they really love pecans. Pecans mixed with peanut butter and placed in a small live trap have been quite effective for me in the trapping and relocation of chipmunks. In the flower garden, chipmunks are not so bad, but they wreak havoc in the vegetable garden, eating (or even more frustrating, partially eating) fruits and vegetables just as they ripen for harvest. It is also the chipmunk runs that provide access underground for the voles, which are a serious problem if you have them.

GROUNDHOGS

- Yes, I've had groundhogs, too, and they simply can't resist fresh fruit. They are particularly fond of cantaloupe (technically not a fruit, I'm aware). The key is to bait them with slices of cantaloupe first—without the trap—and then when you have them hooked, add the trap (with

CHIPMUNK IN THE GARDEN

NATURAL PREDATORS

I do everything I can to encourage natural predators in my garden, from microbial predators that are "fed" and encouraged through the addition of compost, leaf mold, and other organic matter and then go on to help control undesirable microorganisms and nematodes, to insect predators that eat other insects, and even to larger animal predators that help control the rodent population.

While I understand their necessary role in my garden's ecosystem, I am admittedly not fond of snakes. I don't really have anything against them, personally. It's that element of surprise they bear. Why can't they be seen until you're near to stepping on or grabbing one? At any rate, I understand their necessity, and they are, admittedly, invaluable in controlling the mouse, vole, chipmunk, and baby rabbit population in my garden. So they are welcome—sort of.

In my garden, I also have a healthy population of birds of prey, which are most welcome and useful in controlling the field mice, voles, and rabbits. Coyotes also help maintain the rabbit and small rodent population at near-tolerable levels and, most recently, I had a bobcat sighting. Oh, that the bobcat would hang around! I could deliver it a smorgasbord of animal delights! (And I'm betting the deer would think twice about crossing the fence.)

At the time of this writing, I have had the first sighting of hoof prints in my garden in the several years I've lived here. I knew it was too good to last, but I'm still hoping against hope that it was only an errant youngster. I am surrounded by hundreds of acres of open fields and beautiful forests. There are much greater places to make your home, dear deer. To be safe, I have my bottle of deer repellent at the ready.

MOLEHILLS IN A ROW

the cantaloupe inside it, of course). They'll walk right in and the door will snap shut behind them. Mind their teeth when you are releasing them and be sure to take them several miles away or they will just be back.

MICE AND VOLES

- Unfortunately, I have not found live traps to be at all useful for either one, as both mice and voles are proficient escape artists. Standard mouse traps are much more effective and permanent. A combination of nuts and peanut butter is a sure-fire lure, as is trail mix or dried fruit. For voles, I find the end of their run (a hole in the ground leading down to their tunnels), bait the mouse trap, set it near the hole, and place an 8-inch diameter clay flowerpot over the top. This prevents other animals from getting caught in the trap.

RABBIT IN THE GARDEN

MOLES

- Live traps are also not effective against moles. Harpoon traps set in their active runs are effective and no mess, as the bodies remain underground. Recently, I have become fond of the poison "earth-worms" (they look more like rubber fishing lures) that are placed underground in the active runs to be eaten by the moles. They are out of sight from birds and other animals, targeting only the moles, and have proven quite effective.

RABBITS

- Rabbits can be effectively baited and trapped. It's the propensity with which they procreate that is the issue. Simply relocating them allows them to continue multiplying at a frenzied pace. Baby rabbits are the most destructive in the garden, as they scout about learning which plants are good to eat (by chewing them off and then leaving the unpalatable ones laying there shriveling). Fresh greens from the garden, a carrot or two, or even a handful of fresh clover will be enough to lure a rabbit into a live trap. The farther away you relocate them, the better.

I know this seems like a lot of information, but this is *how* I garden—the way it's done in the garden that so many of the photos in this book have come from. If you like what you see, the proof is in the pictures. When it comes to feeding my plants and my soil, controlling animal and insect pests, or treating disease, I do my best to use natural products that are going to be best for my garden, the environment, and for me. On the occasion when I do have to reach into the back of the cupboard for something more potent, I use it in the safest and most responsible way possible—and only when absolutely necessary. For forty years I have gardened and while I was educated in horticulture, my real gardening knowledge has been taught to me by the garden itself and through the trials, tribulations, and successes I have experienced there. I hope the lessons here and throughout the book will be useful in your own gardening endeavors.

ANNUALS &
BIENNIALS
for the South

Annual garden flowers are the workhorses of the Southern garden. In almost every season, annuals can be found filling the gaps between perennials and shrubs, offering up their colorful blooms or exotic foliage to knit the garden together into one cohesive and beautiful display. So what is an annual? By definition, an annual is a plant whose entire life cycle, from germination to flowering, setting seed and dying, occurs within one growing season. It does not have the ability to store energy and live through the winter to return the following year like perennials do. Annuals grow fast, bloom hard, procreate, and die young. You might say that annuals live life in the fast lane!

For all of their fast living, annuals work harder in the garden than any other plants. From the time they are planted in the spring until the time a hard freeze takes them out in autumn, annuals provide spectacular displays of flowers or may stop you in your tracks with the brightly colored and exotic-looking foliage. Annuals often fill what I call the "summer bloom gap"—those weeks from mid-July to late August when most of the main season perennials like daylilies, iris, and coneflowers have long since finished, but before the autumn show of asters, perennial sunflowers, and Japanese anemones begins. In the South, this can be a very long gap, but with annuals you can ensure that it is a time when the garden still looks its very best. Annuals can also fill those drab and dreary gray days of winter. Pansies, violas, ornamental cabbages and kales, snapdragons, and a variety of others will pay no heed to a few brief bouts with winter and charm us with their beauty while the rest of the garden lies in wait for spring.

Annuals can take on a broader definition in the garden than just the dictionary version. In northern gardens, plants like cannas, elephant ears, and dahlias are grown as annuals, but are reliable perennials for many of us living south of the Mason-Dixon line. Here, we may grow castor beans, mandevilla vines, and banana trees as annuals, but in subtropical and tropical climates, those are all long-lived perennials. In some cases, short-lived perennials, like some of the new hybrid coreopsis, are grown as annuals. Technically, they are perennial, but they flower so much and for so long, they literally bloom themselves to death after the first season. We're going to try to stick fairly close to the technical definition of an annual—a plant that grows, flowers, sets seed, and dies, all within the space of a few weeks or months and certainly within a single growing season.

"So what, then, is this biennial he speaks of?" you may wonder. I'm glad you asked. Annuals and biennials are not much different from one another, really, and some gardeners may not know the difference. A biennial, technically, is a plant that needs two seasons to grow to maturity and flower, but still dies after going to seed. It doesn't have the ability to return from its own roots or crown after the second year. Once it sets seed, in theory, it's done. One of our most popular biennials is the foxglove. Yes, there are some perennial foxgloves that will return each year, but the common foxglove—the one with the 4- to 6-foot spires of blooms in shades of pink, purple, yellow, or white—is a biennial. The first season it is in the ground, it grows a leafy green rosette that resembles a fuzzy cabbage plant, but it is not until the second season—after it has gone through a cold winter—that the magic happens, and its enchanting spires of flowers rise high into the late spring and early summer garden. Then, before dying, it sets seed to ensure that a new generation of seedlings will begin growing. These seedlings will overwinter to flower the following spring and early summer.

ANNUAL AND BIENNIAL DIVERSITY

Annuals and biennials are two of the most diverse groups of plants I know. With a little thought and planning, you can find an annual or biennial to fit almost any environment in your garden, be it full sun, full shade, heavy clay, loose sand, boggy wet, or desert dry. They range in color from the softest and most delicate pastels to the brashest and brightest jewel tones. Their form can be airy and wispy or daring and bold. The Victorians famously adapted annuals to highly stylized "carpet plantings" in complicated and artistic patterns, while the French took a loose and scattered cottage garden

GOMPHRENA & VERBENA

approach to annuals, mixing and mingling them in all shapes, forms, colors, and textures throughout their gardens.

I like annuals and biennials because they allow me the opportunity, as a gardener, to change my mind each season and plant different flowers in different places, experimenting with new and (hopefully) inspiring combinations. They also allow me the opportunity to amend my rather heavy clay soil often and to good effect. The very action of turning the soil once or twice each year, adding compost and manure, tilling in soil conditioner or at least digging it into the planting holes, has allowed me the opportunity to dramatically alter my soil in a reasonably short period of time. Five years ago, plants languished in heavily compacted, gummy clay. Today, with the blending in of organic matter once or twice yearly, my soil is, if not

exactly loose and friable, at least diggable. That's more than I can say for it when I moved in!

HAPPY, HEALTHY ANNUALS AND BIENNIALS

Annuals and biennials do require a certain amount of dedication, it's true. They are going to die eventually, and they are going to have to be replaced. That indicates a certain amount of work that you must be willing to do. You also have to be willing to go to the expense of purchasing a certain number of annuals and biennials each year and that is where many gardeners get hung up. They don't want to spend the money. I would argue the opposite and say that for the most part, annuals and biennials give you as much or more bang for your buck than a good many perennials. Most common annuals are a few dollars each, at most, and many are cheaper. What else can you buy for $4.00 and have it bring you six months of joy and happiness? A question to ponder the next time you're at the garden center.

Let's say you decide to make the investment. How do you keep your annuals and biennials happy, healthy, and giving you the biggest possible show in their brief, but spectacular life? First, you prepare your soil to get them off to the best possible start. This could mean amending and tilling larger, open beds to accommodate mass plantings of annuals, or it could mean digging individual holes in between other, more permanent, garden plants and adding soil amendments as you go. Either way, the more you amend, the greater the results you'll see from your annuals and biennials.

Our more common annuals and biennials like angelonia, cosmos, lantana, and foxglove are hungry plants and most of them (although some may be drought tolerant, once established) are equally as thirsty. There is probably no other group of plants that will respond to fertilizing and watering the way that annuals and biennials will. If lush, full, flower-laden beds and borders are what you're after, these plants will respond with gusto! A few, like globe amaranth and spider flower, will perform better in slightly leaner and drier soils where they'll have sturdier stems and be less rangy and likely to lodge, or fall over.

While I strive to add more perennials and shrubs to the garden each year, I will always find room for annuals and biennials no matter where I garden. Their beauty enhances the garden in every season, their flower power is second-to-none, and the fact that they do have a shelf life ensures that each year and sometimes each season, I get to change my mind, experiment with new plants and new combinations, and keep learning the lessons the garden has to teach.

Zinnias and copperleaf (a tropical) add a seasonal splash of color.

ANGELONIA
Angelonia angustifolia

Why It's Special—When it was introduced to the gardening public a little over a decade ago, angelonia took the gardening world by storm. Heat and humidity don't faze it, and it is virtually pest free. Color choices have now been expanded to include pastel shades, bicolors, and white, in addition to the original cobalt blue and purple.

How To Plant & Grow—Angelonia likes it warm, so wait until at least two weeks *after* the last frost to plant it in the garden. It will grow and develop very quickly once the soil and air temperatures have warmed.

Care & Problems—Deadhead spent flower spikes when they begin to look shabby by cutting two to three sets of leaves below the base of the spike. This will encourage multiple branching and profuse flowering. Angelonia expends a lot of energy on flowers, so supplemental feeding is essential.

Bloom Color—Cobalt blue, purple, lavender, pink, white, bicolors

Peak Season—Spring through fall

Mature Size (H × W)—10 in. to 2 ft. × 1 to 1½ ft.

Water Needs—Evenly moist soil

Good in Containers?—Yes. Excellent in containers.

BLUE SALVIA
Salvia farinacea

Why It's Special—Blue salvia is a perfect choice to mix into the perennial border where its violet-blue spires of bloom will add color throughout the summer. In warm climates, it may even act as a perennial for a few seasons. The variety 'Victoria' is most commonly available.

How to Plant & Grow—Blue salvia is best planted in spring, when it is commonly found in garden centers. While technically an annual, it may return reliably in warmer regions of the South for several years. When its crowns become woody and growth is weak, it's time to replace it.

Care & Problems—Salvias will languish if planted where the soil is poorly drained. In heavy clay soils, spade in 3 inches of pine-bark soil conditioner to help loosen the soil and improve drainage. Feed regularly to promote continual new growth and flowering, deadheading old flower spikes as they fade.

Bloom Color—Violet-blue, white, bicolor

Peak Season—Spring through fall

Mature Size (H x W)—1½ to 2 ft. × 1 to 1½ ft.

Water Needs—Drought tolerant, once established

Good In Containers?—Yes. Good as an upright filler.

BREAD SEED POPPY
Papaver somniferum

Why It's Special—The bread seed poppies are a large group of hybrids and selections whose habit is to reseed around the garden with wild abandon, popping up among other plants, flowering quickly, going to seed, and dying. That may not make them sound very desirable, but there is simply nothing like a garden full of poppies in full bloom.

How to Plant & Grow—It doesn't get any easier than planting bread seed poppies. Simply take the seeds out to the garden on a winter's day and sprinkle them on the ground where you want them to grow. It's even better if you have a dusting of snow and can sprinkle the tiny seeds into the snow, making it easy to see where they land.

Care & Problems—Poppies are completely care- and problem-free. Just be sure to snip a few seedpods, saving seeds to sprinkle around the garden for next year.

Bloom Color—A variety, but mostly in pink, red, orange, white shades

Peak Season—Spring

Mature Size (H x W)—2 to 3 ft. × 1 ft.

Water Needs—Natural rainfall will suffice

Good In Containers?—No. Best suited to the garden.

COLEUS
Solenostemon hybrids

Why It's Special—Coleus has long been the backbone of annual shade gardens, but in the past twenty years, thanks to much hybridizing and many new introductions, coleus can now be grown in nearly any setting from full sun to shade.

How to Plant & Grow—Coleus is tender and susceptible to late frost, so plant after the frost date has passed and when the soil has warmed enough to ensure the plants will take off and grow quickly. Coleus don't like to be dry. In containers, use potting soil with moisture crystals mixed in to help reduce water needs.

Care & Problems—Occasional pinching will keep plants full and bushy. Remove any flower buds as they appear to keep new growth fresh and attractive. Slugs and snails can be a problem on young plants, but can be controlled with a non-toxic, iron-based slug and snail bait.

Bloom Color—Grown for foliage

Peak Season—Late spring through fall

Mature Size (H x W)—2 to 4 ft. × 2 to 3 ft.

Water Needs—Consistently moist soil

Good In Containers?—Yes. Thrives in containers.

COSMOS
Cosmos bipinnatus

Why It's Special—Its ferny, airy leaves give this species a delicate look, but don't be deceived! Cosmos is a tough and enduring annual. A sister species, *Cosmos sulphureus*, is slightly smaller but just as tough and blooms in shades of golden yellow, orange, and scarlet. Both make excellent cut flowers.

How to Plant & Grow—Cosmos plants can be found in garden centers in spring, but are also easy to direct sow right where you want them to grow. If you purchase plants, be sure to gently break the rootball when you plant so that roots will grow deep into the soil to hold plants upright.

Care & Problems—When plants reach 18 to 24 inches tall, it may be helpful to pinch them hard to encourage them to branch and remain slightly shorter, which helps to prevent them from blowing over during rain and windstorms. Cosmos are rugged and basically pest free.

Bloom Color—Pink, magenta, crimson, white, lavender

Peak Season—Mid- to late summer

Mature Size (H xW)—4 to 6 ft. × 2 to 3 ft.

Water Needs—Drought tolerant, once established

Good In Containers?—No. Best in the garden.

DRAGON WING™ BEGONIA
Begonia x *hybrida* Dragon Wing™

Why It's Special—This outstanding and relatively new begonia will give you more bang for your buck in a part-sun to part-shade location than almost any other shade-tolerant annual. Large clusters of red or pink blooms appear throughout the summer and well-grown plants will stop visitors in their tracks.

How to Plant & Grow—Plant after danger of frost has passed. Dragon Wing™ begonias prefer rich, moist, well-drained soil and will grow to near-shrub-like proportions by summer's end, so give them room. They make excellent space fillers in partly shaded beds and borders.

Care & Problems—Plants won't develop fully in deep shade and flowering will be sparse, so be sure that plants receive at least some sun during the day. Water regularly and feed every two weeks with a water-soluble fertilizer to promote lush growth and flowering. Slugs and snails can occasionally be a problem in damp shade.

Bloom Color—Red or pink

Peak Season—Spring through fall

Mature Size (H x W)—2 to 2½ ft. × 2 ½ to 3 ft.

Water Needs—Evenly moist soil

Good In Containers?—Yes. Excellent in large containers.

FANFLOWER
Scaevola aemula

Why It's Special—Fanflower is a low-growing, trailing annual that produces a profusion of small, purple-blue, fan-shaped flowers from spring to frost. For a long season of bloom with minimal care, fanflower can't be beat, thriving in the heat and humidity of our Southern climate. New varieties are available with pink or white flowers.

How to Plant & Grow—Plant fanflower in the spring after the danger of frost has passed. Fanflower needs full to part sun and well-drained soil. Water as needed to keep plants from wilting for the first month after planting. Once established, plants are quite drought tolerant.

Care & Problems—Fertilize fanflower with a water-soluble, bloom-promoting fertilizer once a month. Plants may be leggy when they are first planted. Trimming back by half when they go in the ground will encourage fuller growth and more blooms. Water and fertilizer are essential to success.

Bloom Color—Violet-blue, pink, white

Peak Season—Spring through fall

Mature Size (H x W)—6 to 8 in. × 24 to 36 in.

Water Needs—Average to slightly dry

Good In Containers?—Yes. An excellent trailer.

FLOWERING TOBACCO
Nicotiana sylvestris

Why It's Special—*Nicotiana sylvestris* is a tall-growing, reseeding annual with large clusters of pendant white blooms that dangle from the top of the plant. In the evening, flowers are intoxicatingly fragrant and attract hummingbird moths to the garden.

How to Plant & Grow—Flowering tobacco is easily started from seed in early spring. Seeds are tiny and are sowed just on the surface of the soil, transplanted to larger pots and eventually to the garden. Small transplants will grow rapidly once in the ground and will flower in midsummer. In most gardens, once started, it will reseed itself from year to year.

Care & Problems—*Nicotiana* needs little care. Aphids may collect on tender new growth and can be treated with a stream of water from the hose or, for particularly bad infestations, insecticidal soap. Root rot can occur in heavy clay soils that stay too wet.

Bloom Color—White

Peak Season—Late spring to late summer

Mature Size (H x W)—4 to 5 ft. × 2 ft.

Water Needs—Evenly moist soil

Good In Containers?—No. This species is too tall.

FOXGLOVE
Digitalis purpureus

Why It's Special—Foxgloves are one of the most sought after of cottage garden plants, their tall spires of white, pink, purple, and soft yellow blooms rising above other denizens of the garden in late spring and early summer.

How to Plant & Grow—The trick to growing foxgloves successfully in the South is to start them from seed in late July or early August to have transplants ready to go in the ground by early autumn, where they will overwinter to bloom in spring. Foxgloves love good moisture and rich soil, but need good drainage in winter to prevent rotting.

Care & Problems—Foxgloves are mostly trouble free. The tallest varieties may require staking as their tall bloom spikes reach skyward. Stake early to keep plants growing straight and tall. Some plants may live for a year or two, but most will flower and die, leaving seed behind for the next generation.

Bloom Color—White, pink, purple, yellow

Peak Season—Late spring to early summer

Mature Size—3 to 6 ft. × 1 to 2 ft.

Water Needs—Moist, but well drained

Good in Containers?—No. Not suitable for containers.

GLOBE AMARANTH
Gomphrena globosa

Why It's Special—Globe amaranth ranks at or near the top of the list of low-maintenance garden flowers. Shorter varieties are excellent for edges and low borders, while the taller varieties are perfect for filling gaps in the perennial border.

How To Plant & Grow—Globe amaranth needs a sunny location and well-drained soil; even a dry spot in the garden will do. Take care not to set plants too deeply. Water regularly for the first two to three weeks until they're established.

Care & Problems—Globe amaranth thrives on neglect. Prune plants by one-third if they get leggy and feed very lightly to encourage new growth and flowering. Avoid poorly drained soils that lead to root rot. To dry the flowers, cut when the flowers are half open and hang them upside down using a clothespin to attach them to a hanger in a warm, dry garage or garden shed.

Bloom Color—White, lilac, purple, orange-red, salmon

Peak Season—Summer to fall

Mature Size (H x W)—10 to 24 in. × 10 to 24 in.

Water Needs—Drought tolerant

Good In Containers?— No. Better suited to beds.

LANTANA
Lantana camara

Why It's Special—Lantana provides a profusion of bright, cheerful blooms that last from planting time in spring all the way through a hard frost in autumn. Lantana is a favorite of hummingbirds, butterflies, and honeybees, and in warmer parts of the South it may be perennial.

How to Plant & Grow—Lantana likes it hot and sunny and even a few hours of shade will reduce flower production significantly. It is perfect for planters and container gardens but will need consistent watering since it's a rampant grower.

Care & Problems—Lantana is a flowering powerhouse and uses a lot of water and energy for this purpose. The more you feed and water, the higher your reward. Deadheading is not necessary, but occasional light pruning will help control the size of the plant. Some people find that the tiny hairs on the leaves irritate their skin, but this is nothing serious.

Bloom Color—Yellow, orange, red, pink, peach

Peak Season—Early summer to frost

Mature Size (H x W)—1 to 4 ft. × 2½ to 4 ft.

Water Needs—Drought tolerant, once established

Good In Containers?—Yes. Excellent container plant.

LOVE-IN-A-MIST
Nigella damascena

Why It's Special—Love-in-a-mist is an unusual, reseeding annual or biennial with foliage so narrow that the flowers seem to almost be floating in a hazy green mist, hence the name. Tougher than it looks, it thrives in full sun and will politely reseed itself in and among perennials and other annuals, always welcome, and never invasive.

How to Plant & Grow—Sowing seed in autumn is your best bet, scattering it into your garden beds and allowing it to come up naturally. Mark one or two places where you plant it so you can learn what the seedlings look like when they emerge, and avoid pulling them.

Care & Problems—Love-in-a-mist is as carefree, pest free, and problem free as plants come, as long as you don't mind its habit of seeding around. If seedlings come up too close to your most desirable plants, simply pull them out. There will be plenty of others to take their place.

Bloom Color—Lilac, lavender, pink, white

Peak Season—Late spring to midsummer

Mature Size (H x W)—12 in. × 12 in.

Water Needs—Drought tolerant

Good In Containers?—No. Better in beds.

MARIGOLD
Tagetes spp. and hybrids

Why It's Special—Marigolds have long been popular in gardens throughout the South. The bright flowers are sunny and warm and the single and semi-double types are very attractive to butterflies. The dwarf French marigolds are perfect for bedding or edging, while the larger African types blend nicely into perennial borders.

How to Plant & Grow—Plant seed or transplants in full sun in ordinary garden soil. Space the larger-growing African types 18 to 24 inches apart, while the dwarf French types need only be 10 to 12 inches apart. Feed regularly to keep plants growing and blooming.

Care & Problems—Remove spent blooms on a regular basis to promote continuous flowering. Taller varieties may need to be staked. Spider mites can be a problem during dry weather and if plants become stressed. Keeping the soil evenly moist and plants well fed and actively growing will help combat this problem.

Bloom Color—Yellow, gold, orange, red, bicolors

Peak Season—Early summer to frost

Mature Size (H x W)—10 in. to 3 ft. × 10 in. to 2 ft.

Water Needs—Regular, even moisture

Good In Containers?—Yes. Use dwarf varieties.

MELAMPODIUM
Melampodium paludosum

Why It's Special—Melampodium thrives in Southern heat and humidity and new varieties have been bred for compact habit and mildew resistance. Looking somewhat like tiny zinnias, their bright yellow flowers light up the summer garden.

How to Plant & Grow—Melampodium likes it hot and will languish if planted too early in the season, often developing root rot if planted in cold soil. Set out transplants after all danger of frost has passed and the soil has begun to warm. They will reward you ten-fold when planted in soil amended with compost and soil conditioner, growing robustly and flowering profusely.

Care & Problems—Melampodium requires little in the way of maintenance. Deadheading is not necessary, and the continual new growth covers spent blossoms, so plants always look clean and fresh. Melampodium responds very well to water and fertilizer, growing lush and full, and flowering until frost.

Bloom Color—Yellow

Peak Season—Early summer to frost

Mature Size (H x W)—1 to 2 ft. × 1 to 2 ft.

Water Needs—Drought tolerant, once established

Good In Containers?—Yes. Use dwarf varieties.

MEXICAN SUNFLOWER
Tithonia rotundifolia

Why It's Special—Some gardeners may balk at the size of this terrific annual, but its multitudes of brilliant orange daisies are worth making room for! Attractive to butterflies and hummingbirds, its large size isn't as hard to accommodate in garden design as you might think.

How to Plant & Grow—Plants can be found in some of the better garden centers in late spring, but Mexican sunflower is also very easy to grow from seed, sowing it directly where you want it to grow. It is not fussy about soil, but the better you treat it, the more it responds with growth and blooms.

Care & Problems—Staking may be necessary for very tall plants. A light application of all-purpose fertilizer twice during the growing season will keep the plants vigorous and blooming. The dwarf variety 'Fiesta del Sol' grows only 2 ½ feet tall and is excellent for small gardens.

Bloom Color—Brilliant orange

Peak Season—Midsummer to frost

Mature Size—2½ to 5 ft. × 2½ to 4 ft.

Water Needs—Thorough soaking once a week

Good In Containers?—Yes. 'Fiesta del Sol', a dwarf form, is good in containers.

MONEY PLANT
Lunaria rediviva

Why It's Special—Money plant is an old-fashioned biennial garden plant that I remember my grandmother growing in her garden. Seedlings germinate in late autumn, overwinter as small plants and then grow, flower, and set their silvery, coin-like seedpods the following spring and summer.

How to Plant & Grow—Sow seed in autumn and be sure to mark where you sow it to learn what the seedlings look like when they emerge. Most of the seed will sprout in autumn, but some may wait until spring. Those that sprout in autumn will flower the following spring while those that sprout in spring will wait for another winter to pass before they bloom.

Care & Problems—Money plant is care-free and only problematic if you don't like its propensity to seed itself around the garden. Seedlings are easily identifiable and easy to pull if you get too many.

Bloom Color—White, lavender, purple

Peak Season—Spring and early summer

Mature Size (H x W)—1 to 2 ft. × 1 ft.

Water Needs—Average moisture from spring rains.

Good In Containers?—No. Not well-suited to containers.

NARROW-LEAF ZINNIA
Zinnia angustifolia

Why It's Special—A much smaller plant with a different form and habit than what most of us call "zinnias," this special plant will thrive with minimal care in the heat and humidity of our Southern summers. The 1 ½-inch-wide blooms look like miniature daisies and are produced in great quantity from summer to frost.

How To Plant & Grow—Plant transplants into the garden once the soil has warmed thoroughly, not before late April or early May. Zinnias despise cold, wet soil and will languish and sometimes rot before getting established if the soil is not sufficiently warm.

Care & Problems—In early summer, after plants are well established and actively growing, a light shearing will produce fuller, bushier, more compact plants. Even though you'll be removing the flowers by doing this, plants will respond quickly and will be better than ever. Apply a liquid fertilizer every two weeks during the growing season.

Bloom Color—Orange, yellow, white

Peak Season—Early summer to frost

Mature Size (H x W)—6 to 12 in. × 12 to 15 in.

Water Needs—Average to evenly moist soil

Good In Containers?—Yes. A good filler plant.

NEW GUINEA IMPATIENS

Impatiens hawkeri hybrids

Why It's Special—New Guinea impatiens have always enjoyed a kind of mixed popularity. Not every variety was a robust grower and some simply languished through much of the summer. With the introduction of a new breed of New Guinea impatiens known as SunPatiens®, that has all changed. These tough, free-flowering plants have changed the New Guinea impatiens for the better.

How to Plant & Grow—Plant in full to part sun in rich, deep, well-amended soil. Impatiens will not thrive in compacted clay. Water and feed regularly throughout the growing season and New Guinea and SunPatiens® will reward you over and over.

Care & Problems—Rich, well-amended soil is a requirement. While they are more sun tolerant, New Guinea impatiens and their close relatives are just as thirsty and as hungry as any impatiens you've ever grown. Regular feeding will encourage robust growth and blooming.

Bloom Color—Red, orange, pink, fuchsia, purple, white, bicolors

Peak Season—Spring to frost

Mature Size (H x W)—I to 2 ft. × I to 2 ft.

Water Needs—Evenly moist soil

Good in Containers? —Yes. Excellent in containers, with irrigation.

PANSY

Viola x *wittrockiana*

Why It's Special—When it comes to brightening up the winter garden, few plants can hold a candle to the cheerful jewel-tone faces of pansies. When mixed with other cold-tolerant annuals like chard, kale, flowering cabbages, mustard, and others, pansies provide a stunning, colorful display through the dreariest months.

How to Plant & Grow—Pansies can be planted from mid-September through late fall, as soon as nighttime temperatures begin to moderate. The earlier you can plant them, the better established their roots will be and the more profusely they will flower through the winter.

Care & Problems—If plants begin to grow leggy, pinch them back by one-third to encourage bushy new growth from the base. Deadhead regularly for the first few weeks to encourage plants to get into a healthy bloom cycle. Mixing a slow-release fertilizer into the soil at planting time is very beneficial.

Bloom Color—All colors, pastels to jewel tones

Peak Season—Fall, winter, early spring

Mature Size (H x W)—6 to 8 in. × I0 to I2 in.

Water Needs—Regular, even moisture

Good In Containers?— Yes. Outstanding in containers.

PENTAS

Pentas lanceolata

Why It's Special—If it's multitudes of hummingbirds and butterflies you love in your summer garden, look no further than pentas to attract them in droves! Pentas thrive in the heat and humidity of Southern gardens, and new varieties flower profusely and continuously until frost.

How to Plant & Grow—Plant pentas in the garden or in containers after the danger of frost has passed. Pentas prefer full sun, but may appreciate some light afternoon shade in the hottest coastal areas. Deadheading, while not required on new hybrids, keeps them neat and tidy.

Care & Problems—Rabbits can be a problem for young plants. Repellent sprays may be helpful. While deadheading is not an absolute requirement, it is very helpful. Pentas are heavy feeders and respond well to liquid fertilizer applied once every two weeks throughout the growing season. Water deeply and thoroughly during periods of drought and hot weather.

Bloom Color—Red, pink, lavender, white

Peak Season—Midsummer to frost

Mature Size (H x W)—I to 2 ft. × I to 2 ft.

Water Needs—Moderate, even moisture

Good in Containers? —Yes. Perfect container plants.

SNAPDRAGON
Antirrhinum majus

Why It's Special—As a cool-season annual to join pansies, violas, ornamental kales, and others, snapdragons can't be beat. Their bright and cheerful colors complement those of many other winter-flowering plants, and in Zones 7b and warmer, snapdragons will flower right through the winter months.

How to Plant & Grow—Transplants can be set early in the spring and will even tolerate very light frosts—down to 30° or so if they are hardened off. They thrive in cool temperatures, and many gardeners like to plant them in early September to take advantage of the mild autumn months for a spectacular show.

Care & Problems—Aphids can be a problem on young plants or new growth of older plants. Control with insecticidal soap. Rich soil and good drainage are all snapdragons really need to thrive. Staking may be necessary for tall varieties.

Bloom Color—Shades of red, pink, yellow, purple, white

Peak Season—Spring to early summer, again in fall

Mature Size (H x W)—8 in. to 3 ft. 8 in. to 1 ft.

Water Needs—Evenly moist soil

Good In Containers?—Yes. Dwarf or medium varieties.

SPIDER FLOWER
Cleome hassleriana

Why It's Special—A favorite, old-fashioned garden flower, spider flower gets its common name from the long, wispy stamens that protrude noticeably from the blooms. Seedpods form after the blooms fall, providing further interest and ensuring that the garden will not be without spider flower for several years.

How to Plant & Grow—Cleome seeds germinate readily and grow strongly from direct-seeding in sunny, warm flowerbeds. Plants can also be bought in spring and planted in the garden after frost is passed. It is drought tolerant, once established.

Care & Problems—Little is needed in the way of care except for weed pulling. Plants that look ragged and worse for wear by midsummer should be pulled up and a second sowing of seed in late July will ensure a spectacular fall show. Spider mites can occasionally attack, but can be controlled with insecticidal soap.

Bloom Color—Shades of pink, lavender-purple, white

Peak Season—Midsummer, fall with second sowing

Mature Size (H × W)—2 to 5 ft. × 1½ to 2 ft.

Water Needs—Drought tolerant

Good in Containers?—No. Better in the garden.

SWEET POTATO VINE
Ipomoea batatas

Why It's Special—Few foliage plants can rival the brilliant color provided by sweet potato vine, and it's the perfect companion plant for both flower beds and containers. A sometimes rampant grower, newer selections are more compact and are easier to accommodate in both gardens and containers.

How to Plant & Grow—Plant sweet potato vines after the soil has warmed thoroughly in the spring. Late spring frosts may kill tender young plants and will definitely set them back. Sweet potato vine responds exceptionally well to water and fertilizer and will be lush, full, and possibly halfway to the neighbor's before you know it.

Care & Problems—Pruning is inevitable. Potato weevils and slugs may chew holes in the leaves and, while unsightly, this is not life-threatening. The fleshy roots can be dug and stored in a frost-free place to be replanted in the garden next spring.

Bloom Color—Grown for its foliage

Peak Season—Early summer through frost

Mature Size (H x W)—6 to 10 in. × 3 to 6 feet

Water Needs—Water deeply when plants wilt

Good In Containers?—Yes. Very good trailer/accent plant.

TORENIA
Torenia hybrids

Why It's Special—New cultivars have expanded the color range from beautiful blue into stunning combinations of gold, purple, white, and pink. Torenia comes in both mounding and spreading forms, so be sure to read the label if you need it to fulfill a specific function.

How to Plant & Grow—Torenia thrives in any average garden soil, but will respond particularly well to soil that has been thoroughly amended with compost or manure. It also thrives in commercial potting mixes, making it a great addition to pots and containers throughout the garden.

Care & Problems—Water regularly during hot, dry weather and keep beds mulched to help conserve moisture and suppress weeds. In containers, water as needed to keep plants from wilting and be prepared to feed at least twice a month to keep new growth and flowers coming all summer long. Occasional deadheading will keep plants from looking tired and spent.

Bloom Color—Blue, purple, pink, white, yellow

Peak Season—Early summer through frost

Mature Size (H x W)—8 to 12 in. × 12 to 18 in.

Water Needs—Evenly moist soil

Good in Containers?—Yes. Excellent in containers.

VIOLA
Viola x wittrockiana

Why It's Special—Violas are distinctly different enough from pansies, especially in hardiness and their ability to flower through the winter in colder regions of the South, that they deserve separate treatment. Pansies frequently go dormant when the coldest winter weather sets in and though they'll live, they may not wake back up and flower again until spring. Violas, however, may sulk when it's cold, but will continue right on flowering when the temperature rises again.

How to Plant & Grow—Plant violas in late September and early October to get them well established before winter arrives. Mix a slow-release fertilizer into the soil at planting time and watch your violas put on a spectacular cool-season show.

Care & Problems—If plants begin to grow leggy, which rarely happens with violas until it gets too warm in spring, pinch them back by one-third to encourage bushy new growth from the base.

Bloom Color—All colors, pastel to jewel tone

Peak Season—Fall, winter, early spring

Mature Size (H x W)—6 to 8 in. × 10 to 12 in.

Water Needs—Regular, even moisture

Good in Containers?—Yes. Outstanding in containers.

WHY PLANT ANNUALS?

Some gardeners look down their noses at annuals. They require yearly planting (too much work), you have to buy them every year (too much money), and you have to water, deadhead, and feed them regularly to keep them looking their best (too much maintenance). Annuals do require a certain amount of work and dedication, but in a Southern garden, annuals are the workhorses that carry our gardens through seasons where there otherwise might be little going on. Through the hottest months of the summer, annuals like lantana, angelonia, and pentas keep right on flowering without missing a beat. Through the coldest months of winter, pansies, violas, snapdragons, and others offer cheerful color on the grayest of days. All they ask of you is a well-prepared bed, to be planted in some good soil, organic fertilizer tilled in, and a little extra water until they're thoroughly rooted in and ready to grow. Then, they're going to do the heavy lifting and you're going to get all of the enjoyment!

PLANTING TIPS FOR ANNUALS

I use a lot of annuals in my garden each year. The following tips will help ensure you get the most out of your annuals, be it winter, summer, spring, or fall.

SCAEVOLA

1. If your plants are growing in plastic pots, moisten the soil before removing them from their pots. This will help them slide out without damaging the roots and ensure that plants are well hydrated before planting in the garden. Dry roots will stick to the inside of the pot and can be torn or damaged if they are pulled forcefully from their containers.

2. Never plant dry or wilted annuals before soaking and hydrating them well. Most annuals are grown in soilless mixes that are difficult to moisten once they dry out, and trying to dampen a dry rootball once it is planted in the ground is nearly impossible.

3. When planting annuals, most should be planted at the same level in the ground that they were growing in their pot. A few exceptions, like marigolds and cosmos, can be planted 1 to 2 inches deeper and they will root along their stems, forming stockier, healthier plants in the long run.

4. Some homeowners and nurseries grow annuals in peat pots or other types of biodegradable, plantable pots. If the rim of the pot is left sticking above the soil when planted in the ground, it will wick water out of the rootball of the plant, leaving the plant dry and struggling even if the surrounding garden soil is moist. Tear or cut the exposed pot rims off at soil level and lightly cover the edges with soil to prevent wicking.

5. Most annuals are heavy feeders and will respond splendidly to additional fertilizer. Organic or slow-release fertilizers that are low in nitrogen and high in phosphorous (often called "bloom boosters") can be mixed directly into the soil as you plant. Avoid high-nitrogen formulas that may cause lush growth at the expense of flowering.

6. After you've filled in around the rootball, firm the soil gently around the plant with your hands and water it. Too often I see gardeners *stomping* a plant into a hole with their foot. This is a bad idea with large plants and even worse for small annuals, as it only serves to compact the soil and create unkind growing conditions.

JANUARY

- January is a great month to get organized for seed starting. In warmer regions of the South, where planting season comes earlier, you may need to start seed soon. In colder parts of the South, you may have a few more weeks before you need to start your annuals, since you won't be able to plant them out until after the danger of frost has passed.

- Grow lights can be a helpful tool for starting seeds indoors, and they don't have to be fancy or expensive. Simple, fluorescent shop light fixtures are perfectly suited to the job, and special grow light bulbs are not necessary. Warm white and cool white fluorescent tubes, used in combination—most fixtures hold four bulbs, so use two of each—will provide the spectrum of light your seedlings need to grow well.

- To calculate a date for sowing seeds, choose a preferred planting date in the garden and count backward from there. For instance, if you want to plant your marigolds in the garden on April 15 and they need eight weeks to grow from seed, count backward by weeks starting at eight on April 15, until you get to zero, which lands you around February 18 as the date you need to start your marigold seeds. Make sure you count back to zero or you will short yourself a week of growing time. Now you know the approximate sowing date for seeds that need eight weeks to grow. You'll have to re-calculate for different numbers of weeks.

- Keep seedling trays evenly moist—but never wet—while seeds are germinating. Tender seedlings are susceptible to damping off that is most active when the soil is too wet. Damping off will become very obvious if seeds begin falling over at soil level and is difficult to control once it has started. Good air circulation and a light hand with the watering can is your best defense.

FEBRUARY

- By now you have probably sown at least some seeds and may have seedlings emerging. Water them carefully to avoid damping off and other root rot diseases. In colder areas, you may just be starting your seeds over the next few weeks. Refer to the example in January about how to calculate sowing dates based on when you want your seedlings ready for the garden.

- The last days of winter are a great time to begin planning the combinations of annuals you want to plant in the garden this summer. As your seedlings come up and begin to grow, you'll know which ones you're going to have the most of and which ones will be fewer in number. Make a few notes about which varieties you'll use where. You may change your mind later, but at least you'll have a place to start when the busy planting season arrives.

- If you are using grow lights to start your seedlings, remember they need to be close to the plants—only 4 to 6 inches from the tops of the leaves—to keep plants from stretching toward the light. Early on, you may need to lower the lights closer to the trays, raising them as needed as the seedlings grow taller.

- Continue watching for damping-off disease on young seedlings and water carefully. Remember that even though the soil surface may appear dry, there is still moisture underneath. Erring just slightly on the dry side will prevent most damping off and root rot of tender seedlings.

MARCH

- In warmer regions, garden centers will begin stocking annuals this month, while in cooler areas it may be April before the frost date passes and the garden centers are fully stocked. Before visiting the garden center, make a list of the kinds and quantities of annuals you need. There are plenty of distractions, but a list can be very helpful in keeping you on track.

- In much of the South, we have the advantage of having "in between" seasons early and late in the year—"in between" winter and spring and "in between" fall and winter. Cool-season annuals like snapdragons, alyssum, calendula, stock, and others make great container plants outdoors during this time when the days are beginning to get warmer, but nights are still chilly. They will only last until it gets hot, but sometimes you just need to get your hands in the soil.

- In warmer areas, you may have seedlings that need hardening off before planting outdoors. This process takes about ten days to do it properly, so plan accordingly. Start by moving seedlings outdoors on days that are warm enough by placing them in a shady spot for a few hours. Slowly acclimate them to more sun and more time outdoors until they are ready to go in the garden.

APRIL

- April gets us into the main part of the planting season across much of the South. In the upper South, it may still be chilly, so you'll have to be patient. Warm weather is coming! Even if your frost date is near (or has recently passed), keep an eye on the weather forecasts. We all know we can have unexpected cold weather throughout the month of April and need to be prepared.

- Warm-season annuals such as cosmos, gomphrena, marigolds, zinnias, and others can be planted in the garden beginning two to three weeks after the last frost date. Soil should feel warm to the touch before planting warm-season annuals.

- Tender annuals started indoors should gradually be hardened off before transplanting them to the garden. If you haven't already started this process, gradually expose young plants to outdoor light and weather conditions for seven to ten days before transplanting them to their permanent place in the garden. Sun and wind will quickly damage tender seedlings, so expose them to brighter light and more open areas gradually.

- Watch for aphids on annuals that have just been transplanted to the garden. They love tender new growth but can easily be washed away with a gentle spray from the garden hose.

MAY

- Many large-growing annuals like spider flower, sunflowers, zinnias, and Mexican sunflower can be sown directly in the garden when the soil is warm to the touch. They will often grow faster and more robustly when sown directly in the garden, since they don't like root disturbance and transplanting. If you've started some indoors, try also sowing some directly and see which ones grow better for you.

- Newly planted transplants should not be allowed to dry out. Check them daily for the first two to three weeks after planting, watering as necessary to keep them evenly moist so that roots grow quickly into the surrounding soil. Once established, you can water less frequently. Watering in early morning gives the foliage time to dry before the heat of the day and helps prevent fungal diseases.

- Every pest you can think of will be making its way through your garden now that the weather is sufficiently warm. Aphids, spider mites, whiteflies, and slugs and snails can all be problems. Insecticidal soaps work well for soft-bodied insects and iron-based slug and snail baits are non-toxic to birds, as well as curious pets and children.

JUNE

- It's not too late to plant annuals if you have spaces that still need filling up. Seeds are inexpensive and cosmos, cleome, Mexican sunflower, portulaca, sunflower, and zinnia can all be seeded directly into the garden even as the hotter days of summer arrive. They'll grow fast and bloom beautifully when the soil is warm and the sun is high.

- Pansies, violas, and other cool-season annuals should be long gone by now. If you haven't pulled them up yet, it's time to let them go. Pansies make excellent compost because they are so leafy and green. Composting them will allow them to have one more life in the garden by feeding the next generation.

- Fertilize your annuals this month, especially in sandy soils where nutrients leach out quickly. Annuals are heavy feeders and must have a continuous supply of nutrients to stay looking their best.

- By the end of the month, you will be into a regular watering routine both for gardens and pots. Avoid watering overhead, if at all possible, and you will be amazed at the reduction in powdery mildew and other foliage diseases. Not only does overhead watering wet the leaves and make conditions perfect for disease growth, it splashes fungal spores and bacteria from one plant to the next, infecting all of those in the vicinity.

JULY

- If you don't have an automatic irrigation system that will water your garden while you're on vacation, invest in a few inexpensive digital watering timers. By connecting hoses and sprinklers to these programmable timers while you're away, you can rest assured that the garden will be alive and well when you return.

- If you're traveling this month, search for public gardens wherever you're going and visit to find inspiration for your own garden. Home gardeners can't always do things on the grand scale that public gardens can, but you can always adapt the ideas to your own garden, no matter its size.

- In late July, consider sowing a second crop of warm-season annuals like cosmos, cleome, cutting zinnias, and others. Early crops will play out soon and it is a waste of time to coddle them and try to nurse them back to health when they have outlived their usefulness. A new, late summer sowing will ensure a bountiful harvest of blooms until frost.

- Deadheading is especially important this time of year to keep annuals growing and flowering. An extra shot of liquid fertilizer won't hurt them and will push annuals to continue growing and blooming vigorously through the heat and into cooler autumn weather.

- July is spider mite season. When the weather turns hot and dry, the spider mites thrive. Unnoticed and uncontrolled, they can wipe out a planting in no time. Caught early, spider mites can be controlled with regular applications of insecticidal soap, but severe infestations will require the use of miticides before they kill the plants they've infested.

AUGUST

- Fight the heat and humidity of August by getting up early and working in the garden in the morning hours. You can't neglect the garden entirely, even though the weather may not be the most pleasant. You'll be surprised at how much you can accomplish by doing thirty to sixty minutes of focused garden work each morning, and it will keep you out of the heat of the day.

- A final planting of marigold, zinnia, and cosmos seed can still be made this month and have enough time to grow and bloom before frost.

- If you want to grow flowering cabbage and kale or pansies and violas from seed for your fall garden, now is the time to get them started. It takes about eight to ten weeks from seed to plants that are ready to go in the ground. You can use the same method for determining your seed sowing date that was described back in January.

- Fungal leaf spot and powdery mildew love the heat and humidity of August. Be on the lookout and treat severe infestations with fungicide to prevent long-term damage to plants. Keeping water off the foliage will help prevent the development and spread of many fungal diseases.

SEPTEMBER

- Farmers' markets and garden centers will be loaded with transplants for cool-season greens starting this month. Try replacing some of your fading summer annuals with spectacular fall crops like kale, cabbage, mustard, and chard. Be adventurous! These plants have beautiful stems and leaves and bring a new dimension to the autumn garden. They also thrive in containers.

- If you have the advantage of having a greenhouse or sunroom, take cuttings of some favorite annuals to root now and overwinter as small plants wherever you have room for them. It's a great way to save favorite plants from year to year and small cuttings are easier to maintain than mature plants that take up half of the dining room!

- Summer annual weeds like crabgrass and goose grass have matured and are going to seed. Stay on top of weeding so that these pernicious pests don't have the chance to drop thousands of seeds that you will have to contend with next year.

OCTOBER

- Early October is a great time to set out foxglove transplants if they can be found at a local nursery or garden center or if you have grown your own from seed sowed in August. Days are warm, nights are cool and plants will establish quickly.

- Ornamental kale and cabbage and pansies need to be in the ground as soon as possible to give them at least six weeks to settle in and grow before cold temperatures arrive. If you are also planting bulbs, you may need to coordinate your bulb and annual planting at the same time so you're not digging up one to plant the other.

- If you have recently transplanted young seedlings to the garden, don't forget to water them, It's easy to forget that plants still need to be watered when the cooler days of autumn arrive. October is one of the driest months of the year across much of the South and watering newly planted annuals is important until they are well established.

- If you're planning to overwinter any annuals indoors, be sure to treat them thoroughly for spider mites and whiteflies before bringing them indoors. These pests can rapidly invade houseplants and are almost impossible to control safely indoors. Spray plants weekly with insecticidal soap for three to four weeks before bringing them in for the winter to kill as many pests as possible.

NOVEMBER

- As the season winds down, it's a great time to clean out the garden shed, clean up the tools, and make sure that everything is stored properly for the winter. If you've changed the oil in the lawnmower, old motor oil can be used to oil shovel blades, hoes, and metal rakes to keep them from rusting over the winter.

- As the leaves fall, garden cleanup becomes extremely important. Some trees will literally bury the garden in leaves and this may be detrimental to many plants, especially groundcovers, smaller perennials, and annuals. A deep cover of leaves will block light and keep moisture from reaching the ground. Leaves can also harbor insects and fungal spores and provide perfect cover for voles.

- Cold weather will arrive across most parts of the South by the end of this month. If you have any annuals that are still not in the ground, plant them immediately.

DECEMBER

- Pansies may go through a semi-dormant phase during the coldest weather, but will perk up fast as soon as temperatures return to above freezing. Violas, though, having smaller flowers, will continue blooming right on through all but the coldest weather.

- Take some time to sit down with your garden journal and recall things from the fall season that you want to remember in coming years. Doing this while it's still fresh in your memory will ensure you don't miss something important.

- You can lightly fertilize winter annuals—such as pansies, violas, and cabbage and kale—between bouts of cold winter weather. Fertilize at one-half the recommended rate so that you don't force too much soft, new growth that could be damaged by cold temperatures. The goal is to keep plants healthy without forcing them to flush tender new growth.

BULBS
for the South

Bulbs are some of the most versatile and adaptable plants for Southern gardens. There are hardy bulbs and tropical bulbs, bulbs for sun and bulbs for shade. There are bulbs that are grown for the flowers and a few that are grown strictly for their beautiful leaves. Some hail from dry, desert-like regions while others grow at the edges of ponds and streams. For nearly every condition in the garden, you can find a bulb that will thrive there.

WHAT IS A BULB?

Gardeners tend to lump any plant that grows from an underground storage organ into the "bulb" category, and, for practical purposes, it's perfectly fine. But this isn't completely accurate. True bulbs, such as tulips and daffodils, have fleshy leaf scales that surround and protect a tiny and dormant, but completely formed, plant inside. Crocus and gladiolus grow from modified stems called corms, while the modified stems of bearded irises are called rhizomes. Tubers and tuberous roots are modified roots like you see on caladiums or dahlias. These storage organs stockpile food reserves from season to season, giving bulbs the ability to perennialize in the garden or to be stored and replanted the following spring.

PLANTING SPRING-FLOWERING BULBS

Nothing beats tulips and daffodils when it comes to the popularity of spring-flowering bulbs. Running a close second would be bulbs such as the intoxicatingly fragrant Dutch hyacinths, crocus, grape hyacinths, various kinds of iris, fritillarias, anemones, and others. All of these bulbs whose flowers grace our gardens from late winter through spring must be planted in the autumn to bloom the following spring. Almost all spring-flowering bulbs require a cold period of dormancy during the winter in order for their roots to grow and for certain chemical changes to happen inside the bulb before they can grow and bloom. Sometimes this presents a challenge in Southern gardens since we don't always have cold winters and without this cold period of at least three months, you'll likely see mixed results.

For gardeners in Zone 8 and warmer, it may be necessary to refrigerate your bulbs prior to planting them to help them experience "winter." In some cases, you may be able to order your bulbs pre-chilled, meaning that the supplier has already held the bulbs in cold storage for you, and they are ready to plant. Otherwise, you'll need to chill them yourself. This can be done by placing them in the crisper drawer of the refrigerator, but be sure to keep ripening fruit, like apples, away from your bulbs. The ethylene gas that ripening fruit gives off can actually kill the flower buds that are lying dormant deep inside your bulbs.

Planting depth can also affect how well your bulbs perform in the garden. As a general rule, most bulbs should be planted at a depth that is equal to about three times their diameter. So, a large daffodil bulb that might be as large as 2½ to 3 inches in diameter should be planted at least 6 inches deep and could be placed closer to 8 inches deep and still grow just fine. Smaller bulbs, such as crocus and muscari, are planted anywhere from 2 to 4 inches deep depending on the size of the bulb.

Note that the planting depth for bulbs is measured from the top of the planting hole (ground level) to the bottom of the planting hole. That is, in a hole 8 inches deep, the *bottom* of the bulb sits at 8 inches while the top may only be covered with 6 inches of soil. Not planting bulbs deep enough can contribute to various problems including making them easier for voles and chipmunks to get to, heaving out of the ground during winter's freeze-thaw cycle, and emerging from the ground too early in the spring and getting frozen in early spring frosts. Deep planting also keeps bulbs like tulips in cooler and drier soil during the summer while they are dormant, which is almost as important as them getting the cold temperatures they need during winter.

THINKING BEYOND SPRING

While tulips and daffodils may still rank at the top of popularity polls, flower bulbs are not just spring bloomers. Throughout the South, bulbs can flower twelve months of the year, depending on the species, extending the season well beyond Easter and into summer, autumn, and even winter. Indulge yourself with the wonderful woodland varieties like surprise lilies, autumn crocus, and hardy cyclamen. For vertical accents, scatter a few gladiolus and crocosmia bulbs in a sunny perennial border and be sure to include some Oriental lilies for their spectacular flowers, exquisite perfume, and stately presence in the garden.

With some bulbs, their foliage makes as big a statement as their flowers, and a few, like caladiums, are grown for their foliage alone. The bold leaves of cannas provide an exclamation point in open borders even when not in bloom, while caladiums brighten up the shadows under a majestic shade tree.

Dahlias flower repeatedly throughout the season, and you'll find that the best blooms come during the cooler days of autumn when colors intensify and the size of the blooms, especially the dinner plate types, is truly astounding. Joining the dahlias in these late days of summer and autumn are the rain lilies, whose blooms will suddenly surprise you within just a day or two of a passing thunderstorm after lying in wait for just a little moisture to spur them from their summer nap. Remontant (reblooming) iris will also begin flowering again in early autumn and continue their show until almost Thanksgiving in mild climates.

The hardy cyclamen have a tough constitution that belies their diminutive size and delicate appearance. These bulbs begin emerging and flowering in autumn and, depending on the species, will continue to flower right through the winter months. Their beautiful silver-and-green mottled foliage is an added bonus and remains even through the coldest winter days! Cyclamen will also reseed where they are happy, creating magnificent carpets of color across the woodland floor.

BULBS ARE IN FOR THE LONG HAUL

Aside from tulips and a very small handful of others, bulbs are going to be in your garden for the long haul. The best varieties will be reliable perennials that will increase in size and number, producing bigger clumps or patches and more blooms with each passing year. There are a few steps you can take to help your bulbs reach their fullest potential.

People have commonly used bone meal at planting time, but this is no longer recommended since bone meal attracts vermin to the garden and may be a health hazard. There is nothing more discouraging than to spend a day planting bulbs in holes laden with bone meal, only to wake the next morning and find that every dog in the neighborhood has spent the night methodically digging them all up! I feed my bulbs twice each year: once in late autumn, when roots are forming, and again in late winter or very early spring, just as the green shoots push through the soil. Fertilizers specially formulated for bulbs will help to ensure their yearly flowering and an increase in size and number each season.

Summer-flowering bulbs, like calla lilies and gladiolus, also benefit from regular feeding. Feed new bulbs by incorporating the fertilizer into the soil as you plant them in the spring. Established clumps can be fed just as they break through the soil. Bulbs that flower all summer, like dahlias and cannas, will benefit from occasional feedings throughout the growing season, since flowering almost continually requires so much energy.

THE CRITTER CURSE

Few things are more disappointing than going out one morning and finding that the bulbs you worked so hard at planting last fall have been eaten by some marauding varmint! Browsing deer rummaging through a tulip bed at peak bloom brings out the very worst response in most of us, while voles can wipe out entire plantings of bulbs before you even know they've been there! Tulips, lilies, and others that deer find desirable can be protected through regular spraying of deer repellent products. Consult your local garden center to find which ones work best in your area. For voles, try using a generous quantity of sharp gravel, like turkey grit, in your planting holes. Voles don't like to dig through the sharp edges, and a good dose of gravel also helps with drainage, which is always an advantage with bulbs.

AGAPANTHUS
Agapanthus hybrids

Why It's Special—Agapanthus has an enormous fleshy root system that stores water and energy in much the same way bulbs do, and its green straplike leaves resemble amaryllis. In late spring and summer, the dramatic blooms comprised of hundreds of small, bell-shaped flowers in heads 8 to 10 inches or more rise on tall, reedlike stems hovering well above the foliage.

How to Plant & Grow—Agapanthus prefers rich, deep, well-drained soil. During the growing season, it needs regular watering and feeding to keep it growing vigorously and flowering well. In winter, when dormant, it can dry out thoroughly between watering.

Care & Problems—In warmer regions of the South, there are several forms of agapanthus that will flourish year-round in the garden. In colder parts of the South, agapanthus makes an outstanding container plant and is easily overwintered in a frost-free garden shed or garage with one or two windows for natural light.

Hardiness—Zones 7b to 10

Color—Violet-blue, white

Peak Season—Late spring to summer

Mature Size (H x W)—2 to 4 ft. × 2 to 3 ft.

Water Needs—Moist in summer, dry in winter

ALLIUM, DRUMSTICK
Allium sphaerocephalon

Why It's Special—Drumstick allium is a fast-growing, reliable, and pest-free bulb with onionlike leaves and small globes of purple flowers borne on tall, wiry stems in summer. It will multiply rapidly, putting on a more impressive show in the garden with each passing summer.

How to Plant & Grow—Drumstick allium grows from bulbs that resemble garlic or small onions (they are closely related). Plant in loose, well-drained soil in small groups of five or six bulbs per hole to get the best show. Bulbs will multiply quickly, forming impressive clumps.

Care & Problems—Being a member of the onion family, drumstick allium is relatively pest free. It prefers well-drained soil, but is quite tolerant of heavier clay, as long as it is not waterlogged in winter.

Hardiness—Zones 4 to 8

Color—Purple

Peak Season—Early summer

Mature Size (H x W)—2 ½ ft. × 1 ft.

Water Needs—Average to slightly dry

ALLIUM, GIANT
Allium giganteum

Why It's Special—Few flowers are more impressive than a well-grown giant allium, its 6-inch globe-shaped blooms comprised of thousands of tiny, individual flowers supported atop a sturdy, 3-foot stalk. Grouping several bulbs together in close proximity will make a showstopping display in late spring to early summer.

How to Plant & Grow—Giant allium prefers leaner, drier, well-drained soils. Heavy clay that stays wet, especially in winter, is not to its liking. Plant bulbs 4 to 6 inches deep in very well-amended soil in autumn, when you are adding tulips, daffodils, and other bulbs to the garden. Leaves will come up almost immediately and overwinter until spring. Bulbs go dormant in summer.

Care & Problems—Alliums are nearly care-free. Their biggest enemy is poorly drained clay soil, which may cause bulbs to rot. Few animal pests bother them, since they are in the onion family.

Hardiness—Zones 5 to 8

Color—Purple

Peak Season—Late spring

Mature Size (H x W)—3 ft. × 1 ft., in bloom

Water Needs—Moist in spring, dry the rest of the year

AMARYLLIS
Hippeastrum spp. and hybrids

Why It's Special—Known for their indoor houseplant Christmastime blooms, amaryllis also make an excellent garden bulb in hardiness Zone 7 and warmer. Amaryllis can be added to the perennial border, where they will form large clumps and produce extraordinary clusters of flowers each year. Bulbs that were forced for Christmas will resume their normal springtime bloom in the garden.

How to Plant & Grow—Amaryllis that were forced for Christmas should be grown indoors until spring and planted out after the last frost. Prepare the soil deeply and amend thoroughly with compost or other organic matter. Bulbs should be planted so that the tip of the bulb, is about 2 inches below the soil surface.

Care & Problems—When bloom stalks emerge and active growth begins, an application of compost or fertilizer is beneficial. Water regularly during dry spells to keep the bulbs growing actively throughout the summer.

Hardiness—Zone 7 (with protection) to 10

Color—White, pink, red, salmon, orange, striped

Peak Season—Flowers in spring and early summer

Mature Size (H x W)—2 ft. × 1 ft.

Water Needs—Water regularly when dry

AZTEC LILY
Sprekelia formosissima

Why It's Special—Aztec lily is a close relative of our Christmas amaryllis that has become a popular passalong plant in the Deep South and makes an exceptional potted plant where it is too cold for it to grow outdoors year-round. It's butterflylike red flowers appear from late spring to early summer, depending on your region and how much rainfall you receive.

How to Plant & Grow—Aztec lily prefers regions with dry winters or, in wetter areas, to be planted in well-draining sandy or gravelly soil or even on a slope. If not, bulbs may rot. Bulbs can be planted either in early spring or autumn with their tips just below the soil surface.

Care & Problems—Hailing from Mexico, the Aztec lily is care-free and extremely drought tolerant. Its biggest enemies are heavy clay soil and winter moisture. The two combined mean almost certain death, but with excellent drainage, the Aztec lily will live for years, multiplying and becoming more spectacular with age.

Hardiness—Zones 8 to 10

Colors—Deep red

Peak Season—Late spring to early summer

Mature Size (H x W)—12 in. × 12 in., in bloom

Water Needs—Very drought tolerant, once established

BUTTERFLY GINGER
Hedychium spp. and hybrids

Why It's Special—Most butterfly gingers are not for small gardens, but for gardeners who have the room. Few flowers are as exotically beautiful or fragrant. The moth- or butterflylike flowers appear from large, pinecone-shaped buds at the ends of the stems in late summer through late autumn. *Hedychium coronarium*, the white butterfly ginger, is easy-to-grow and readily available.

How to Plant & Grow—Plant in spring when the soil is warm to give butterfly gingers—which are subtropical and tropical species—the opportunity to get established during the hot and humid summer months. They prefer deep, rich, evenly moist to very moist soil.

Care & Problems—Avoid heavy clay soils that remain wet in winter unless they are planted on a slope, for drainage purposes. There are many species and hybrids and their hardiness varies. A little research on the front end will ensure that you purchase varieties that will grow well in your garden.

Hardiness—Zones 7 to 10, depending on variety

Color—White, pink, orange, yellow

Peak Season—Late summer to frost

Mature Size (H x W)—4 to 10 ft. × 4 to 10 ft.

Water Needs—Evenly moist to very moist; well drained in winter

CALADIUM
Caladium bicolor

Why It's Special—Caladiums can be grouped into the "fancy-leaved" varieties, with heart-shaped leaves and the "strap-leaved" varieties whose leaves are arrow shaped, thicker, and more leathery. The strap-leaved varieties are more sun tolerant and work well in the brighter areas of the garden.

How to Plant & Grow—Caladiums should not be planted outdoors until nighttime temperatures remain above 60° (preferably warmer) and the soil is warm to the touch. In cold soil they will rot, especially if there is a stretch of wet weather. Many will grow in sun or shade if you plant the dormant tubers and allow the leaves to acclimate to their environment as they emerge.

Care & Problems—Spray with liquid repellent if deer become a problem. Slugs and snails can be controlled with non-toxic slug baits. Tubers can be dug in autumn, dried, and stored for the following year.

Hardiness—Grown as annuals

Color—Green, white, pink, rose, red

Peak Season—Late spring through fall

Mature Size (H x W)—10 to 24 in. × 10 to 24 in.

Water Needs—Keep soil evenly moist

CALLA LILY
Zantedeschia spp. and hybrids

Why It's Special—Few flowers match the elegance and beauty of calla lilies. Upright stems carry large, blade-shaped leaves, and the unique, funnel-shaped blooms emerge just above the foliage. *Zantedeschia aethiopica*, giant white calla, will grow in standing water at a pond's edge, while smaller, more colorful forms are perfectly suited to the garden. They make exceptional cut flowers.

How to Plant & Grow—Calla lilies grow from a relatively large tuber and can be bought dormant in early spring with other flowering bulbs, or they can be purchased as flowering potted plants and added to the garden already growing. Most varieties thrive in part sun, but will grow in full sun with plenty of moisture at their roots.

Care & Problems—Calla lilies are relatively care-free. In most of the South, they will perennialize and come back bigger, stronger, and more beautiful each year.

Hardiness—Zones 7 (6 with protection) to 10

Color—White, yellow, pink, maroon, blends

Peak Season—Early to midsummer

Mature Size (H x W)—1 to 4 ft. × 1 to 4 ft.

Water Needs—Evenly moist

CAMASSIA
Camassia leichtlinii

Why It's Special—Camassia's upright growth habit makes it a perfect bulb for tucking in between other garden plants. Its blue or white flowers are borne on tall spires from late spring to early summer. Leaves are slender and unobtrusive, blending neatly into beds and borders. *Camassia scilloides* is native east of the Mississippi.

How to Plant & Grow—Camassia should be planted in autumn at the same time as tulips, daffodils, and other spring-flowering bulbs. They prefer full to part sun in rich, loose, well-drained soil. Where native, they are commonly found growing in meadows or at woodland edges.

Care & Problems—Camassia is an easy-to-grow and care-free bulb. Basal rot can occur in cold, wet clay soils that are poorly drained. Bulbs may become crowded and flowering may diminish after several years. Dig and divide to reinvigorate them.

Hardiness—Zones 5 to 8

Color—Blue, white

Peak Season—Late spring to early summer

Mature Size (H x W)—1 to 2 ft. × 1 ft.

Water Needs—Drought tolerant, once established

CANNA
Canna spp. and hybrids

Why It's Special—Once relegated to mass plantings along roadsides and in city parks, cannas have now become stars in the garden with their bold, often colorful tropical foliage and flowers that appear from early summer until frost. A few plants give you more bang for your buck!

How to Plant & Grow—Cannas grow quickly from deeply rooted rhizomes that can spread to form large clumps over time. Divide every three years to keep them in-bounds. Dormant rhizomes can be planted in spring, 3 to 4 inches deep in rich, moist garden soil. Plants can also be purchased, potted and growing, in spring and summer.

Care & Problems—In the wild, cannas are found growing near the edges of ponds, lakes, and streams, and while they don't need standing water, they appreciate consistent moisture. Regular feeding will help keep them looking their best. Japanese beetles and leafrollers can be problems in some areas, but these are treatable.

Hardiness—Zone 7 to 10

Color—Red, yellow, orange, pink, bicolors

Peak Season—Early summer to frost

Mature Size (H x W)—2 to 6 ft. × 2 to 4 ft.

Water Needs—Regular moisture required

CAROLINA SPIDERLILY
Hymenocallis caroliniana

Why It's Special—This beautiful native bulb grows in lowlands in river bottoms and along stream banks. Its amaryllislike foliage emerges in spring, followed by the white, spidery blooms in late summer. The native species is available from some native plant specialty nurseries. Many other species that are just as beautiful are widely available through bulb suppliers.

How to Plant & Grow—Carolina spiderlilies likes rich, organic, damp soil and can often be found growing in large quantities in low wetlands. They adapt readily to garden life as long as the soil is prepared with compost. In the wild, it is found growing in part-to-full sun.

Care & Problems—Spiderlilies, in general, are easy and care-free plants. The varieties most commonly offered are non-native, but they make excellent garden plants and have no propensity to be invasive. **Note:** Native wildflowers should never be dug from the wild. Seek out native plant specialists who offer nursery-grown stock.

Hardiness—Zones 5 to 8

Color—White

Peak Season—Late summer

Mature Size (H x W)—1½ ft. × 1 ft.

Water Needs—Loves damp areas

CLIVIA
Clivia miniata

Why It's Special—Clivia is a close relative of many bulbs, but doesn't have an actual underground storage organ. Its thick, ropelike roots store water and nutrients. From spring through summer it is adorned with enormous heads of orange or yellow flowers on stems that reach just above the foliage.

How to Plant & Grow—Clivia are not hardy except in the Deep South, but make excellent container specimens and are easy houseplants where they are not hardy. Summer them outdoors in a shady location. Water and feed regularly. Winter in a bright, cool location indoors and allow to rest. **Important:** Clivia do not require any water *at all* from November 1 until early March. They will remain green, but are dormant in winter.

Care & Problems—Mealybugs can be a problem in winter indoors. Treat plants with rubbing alcohol or insecticidal soap. Plants that are not kept dry during the winter may bloom down in the leaves come spring.

Hardiness—Zones 9 to 10

Color—Orange, yellow

Peak Season—Spring

Mature Size (H x W)—2 ft. × 2 ft.

Water Needs—Moist in summer, very dry in winter

COLCHICUM
Colchicum autumnale

Why It's Special—Called "autumn crocus" because their flowers look similar to crocus, colchicum provide a spectacular fall display in September and October, just as the nights begin to cool and we begin to feel some relief from summer temperatures.

How to Plant & Grow—Bulbs will be shipped or available in garden centers in late summer at the proper time to plant. It is not uncommon for the flowers to emerge from the bulbs before they are even planted. Colchicum should be planted 2 to 3 inches deep and 6 inches apart in thoroughly amended garden soil. They are perfect for woodland gardens, where winter and early spring sunshine will reach their leaves; drier summers help to cure the bulbs.

Care & Problems—The leaves will begin to emerge immediately after the bulbs flower and will remain green throughout the winter and spring. Foliage should not be removed until it has turned yellow and begun to die in late spring or early summer.

Hardiness—Zone 4 to 8

Color—White, pink, rose, lilac, purple

Peak Season—September to November

Mature Size (H x W)—6 to 10 in. x 12 to 18 in.

Water Needs—Low

CRINUM
Crinum spp. and hybrids

Why It's Special—Old-fashioned Southern passalong plants, crinum lilies have graced farms and homesteads throughout the South for generations. Like cannas, crinums have experienced a garden renaissance of late, and the conservation of antique varieties along with the introduction of newer and hardier hybrids has only helped their cause.

How to Plant & Grow—Crinum bulbs are large, requiring a deeply dug planting hole a minimum of 1 foot deep by 1½ feet wide. Soil should be thoroughly amended with large quantities of compost or other organic matter. Space the bulbs 2 feet apart, planting each with its long neck prominently visible aboveground.

Care & Problems—Crinums have no serious pests or diseases. Newly planted crinums will need a season or two to establish. Fertilize established clumps with a bulb booster fertilizer in mid-May of each year. Deadheading as the flowers fade will help keep them blooming.

Hardiness—Zone 7b to 10 (some are hardier)

Color—White, shades of pink, bicolors

Peak Season—Summer

Mature Size (H x W)—1½ to 3 ft. × 1½ to 3 ft.

Water Needs—Evenly moist

CROCOSMIA
Crocosmia spp. and hybrids

Why It's Special—Crocosmia opens its showy flowers atop tall, wand-like stems in midsummer. Spear-like foliage, in shades of green to slightly bronze, offers an excellent vertical accent when not in bloom. Fiery red 'Lucifer' is the most popular, but new hybrids have expanded the range of colors into glowing apricots, bronzes, yellow, and bicolors.

How to Plant & Grow—Crocosmia grows from small corms similar to crocus, and gardeners are often surprised that such a robust and profusely flowering plant can come from such a small corm. Dormant corms can be planted in spring about 3 inches deep and 5 inches apart. Growing plants can be purchased at garden centers for planting anytime during the growing season. They prefer well-drained, humusy, fertile soil in full sun.

Care & Problems—Spider mites can be a problem, especially in hot, dry weather. Spraying may be necessary for control. Regular summer watering is a must.

Hardiness—Zones 6 to 10

Color—Red, orange, yellow, apricot, blends

Peak Season—Mid to late summer

Mature Size (H x W)—18 to 36 in. × 18 to 36 in.

Water Needs—Keep the soil evenly moist

CROCUS
Crocus tommasinianus

Why It's Special—*Crocus tommasinianus*, called "tommies" for short, are some of the very first crocus to flower at the end of winter. Often, they'll be in full bloom as early as late January to mid-February, depending on your location. Where happy, they will reseed and establish enormous drifts, making them especially suited for planting in lawns.

How to Plant & Grow—Plant crocus in autumn along with tulips, daffodils, and other spring-flowering bulbs. Crocus corms are small and only need to be planted about 1 ½ to 2 inches deep, making them easy to naturalize in large quantities through lawns and woodlands. Avoid mowing lawn areas, if possible, for 4 to 6 weeks after flowering to ensure they have time to set seed.

Care & Problems—*Crocus tommasinianus* is recommended for Southern gardens because it is less palatable to chipmunks and squirrels and better suited to our warmer winters.

Hardiness—Zone 3 to 8

Color—Lavender, pink, white

Peak Season—Late winter

Mature Size (H x W)—4 in. × 4 in.

Water Needs—Drought tolerant, summer dormant

CYCLAMEN
Cyclamen hederifolium

Why It's Special—Hardy cyclamen bring color and interest to the garden at a time of year when it's needed most.*Cyclamen hederifolium* flowers in mid- to late autumn with beautiful silver-and-green mottled foliage providing interest from winter into spring. *C. coum* flowers in the winter months provide a stunning show from November through February, also followed by green-and-silver leaves.

How to Plant & Grow—Cyclamen are perfect in woodland shade gardens. They are summer dormant, so mark their locations to avoid accidentally digging them up while weeding or planting other plants. Cyclamen should be planted in humusy, woodland soils with the tops of their tubers right at soil level, just barely covered, if at all.

Care & Problems—Cyclamen will re-seed themselves where they are happy and may eventually form spectacular carpets of color in the garden. This is welcome and not problematic. Chipmunks and voles may dig and/or eat the tubers.

Hardiness—Zones 5 to 8

Color—White, pale pink to deep fuchsia

Peak Season—Fall and winter

Mature Size (H x W)—4 to 6 in. × 8 to 12 in.

Water Needs—Rarely needed

DAHLIA
Dahlia × hybrida

Why It's Special—This spectacular tender perennial has flowers in more colors, sizes, and forms than almost any other garden plant. Dahlias come in nearly every color but true blue, and the flowers can range in size from those as small as a nickel to the stunning "dinner plate" types whose blooms may exceed 12 inches across!

How to Plant & Grow—Dormant tubers may be planted in April, 2 to 3 inches deep in rich, well-amended garden soil, or growing plants can be found in garden centers in spring. Dahlias need regular water and fertilizer throughout the growing season. In mid-July, cut plants back hard, fertilize and water well, and they will resprout to put on a spectacular display of flowers during the cooler autumn months.

Care & Problems—Staking will be necessary for taller varieties, and, while they do like moisture, waterlogged soils may cause stem rot.

Hardiness—Zones 6b to 9

Color—Every color except true blue, as well as bicolors and blends

Peak Season—Summer to fall

Mature Size (H x W)—1 to 7 ft. × 1 to 4 ft.

Water Needs—Regular water throughout the growing season

EUROPEAN WOOD ANEMONE

Anemone nemorosa

Why It's Special—Wood anemone is a low-growing, groundcoverlike spring wildflower found in European woodlands and is very well adapted to Southern gardens. It grows from small, twiglike rhizomes that creep along just under the soil surface forming impressive and beautiful patches over time.

How to Plant & Grow—Wood anemone is planted in the fall, along with grape hyacinths, crocus, and other small bulbs. Its delicate, twiggy rhizomes should be planted about 1 inch deep in very well-prepared, loose, rich soil like you would find on the forest floor. If you do well with hostas, coral bells, and ferns, wood anemone will be right at home.

Care & Problems—Wood anemone is summer dormant, so account for that when you plant it. It is perfect for creeping in and around other perennials where it won't be missed when its leaves die down. Mark its location so it doesn't accidentally get dug up.

Hardiness—Zones 4 to 8

Color—Blue, purple, pink, white

Peak Season—Spring

Mature Size (H x W)—6 to 10 in. × 2 ft.

Water Needs—Moist when growing

GLADIOLUS, BYZANTINE

Gladiolus communis ssp. byzantinus

Why It's Special—A popular passalong plant in the South, Byzantine gladiolus forms large colonies over time and, when in full bloom, its dramatic magenta-colored blooms will draw attention over a long distance. Enormous stands can be found on old farmsteads across the South.

How to Plant & Grow—Byzantine gladiolus grows from small corms (never the size of the giant hybrid gladiolus) that should be planted about 2 inches below the soil surface for larger corms, slightly shallower for smaller ones. Full sun and maybe some light staking are needed to keep plants standing upright.

Care & Problems—Relatively care-free, their only real requirements are full sun and good winter drainage. Voles can be a problem in winter months as they burrow and forage for food. Foliage will be dormant by late summer, so mark their location to keep from digging them up accidentally.

Hardiness—Zones 7 to 9

Color—Magenta purple

Peak Season—Late spring to early summer

Mature Size (H × W)—2 ft. × 2 ft.

Water Needs—Drought tolerant, once established

GRAPE HYACINTH

Muscari spp. and hybrids

Why It's Special—Muscari, also known as grape hyacinths, are old-fashioned bulbs that many of us remember our mothers and grandmothers growing when we were children. They are easy, tough perennials that will multiply quickly and are excellent for naturalizing in lawns. Purple, grapelike clusters of blooms appear in February or March, depending on where in the South you reside.

How to Plant & Grow—Plant muscari in autumn, 2 to 3 inches deep in amended garden soil. Fertilize after flowering to encourage the bulbs to multiply and form clumps and colonies. A useful "trick" is to plant a few grape hyacinths where you plant tulips, daffodils, and other dormant bulbs. The grape hyacinths will sprout almost immediately, and their leaves will remind you where you have planted other bulbs.

Care & Problems—Voles, squirrels, and chipmunks can be occasional problems. If old clumps seem to flower less, dig and divide to reinvigorate them.

Hardiness—Zones 3 to 8

Color—Purple, blue, yellow, white

Peak Season—Early to mid-spring

Mature Size (H x W)—6 to 8 in. × 6 to 8 in.

Water Needs—Regular moisture when growing

HYACINTH
Hyacinthus orientalis

Why It's Special—Hyacinths are grown for one reason: their beautiful and fragrant blooms. My mother and grandmother had hyacinths in the garden when I was a child and their fragrance immediately takes me back. Short spikes of densely packed blooms last for about 2 weeks in the spring garden—a short but most welcome appearance.

How to Plant & Grow—Hyacinths are planted in autumn along with crocus, grape hyacinths, daffodils, and other spring-flowering bulbs. Buy the largest bulbs you can find, since they will produce the largest and most impressive blooms come spring. Hyacinths are heavy feeders and a twice-yearly application of fertilizer, once in autumn and once in early spring, will keep them robust.

Care & Problems—Hyacinths are pest free. Some people are allergic to the bulbs and may break out in a rash from handling them. It may be best to wear gloves when handling hyacinths, just in case.

Hardiness—Zones 3 to 8

Color—Purple, blue, pink, white, yellow

Peak Season—Early spring

Mature Size (H x W)—8 in. × 6 in.

Water Needs—Moist while growing, dry when dormant

IRIS, BEARDED
Iris x hybrida

Why It's Special—Bearded iris are tough, easy, and showy garden perennials that bloom in a rainbow of colors. There are several classifications from standard bearded, reaching 36 to 40 inches tall in bloom down to dwarf bearded, flowering at only 6 to 8 inches tall. Some are exceptionally fragrant.

How to Plant & Grow—Bearded iris form thick, creeping rhizomes, which should be planted just at the soil surface in neutral-to-alkaline soil. Adding lime may be needed in acidic soils. Iris should be fed every spring as the leaves emerge to encourage vigorous growth and heavy flowering.

Care & Problems—Division every three to four years is needed to keep plants actively growing and blooming. Iris borers can be treated by spraying the foliage and the exposed rhizomes regularly in early spring. Division and transplanting are done in late summer when plants are dormant.

Hardiness—Zone 3 to 10

Color—White, yellow, apricot, rose, maroon, blue, lavender, purple, bicolors

Peak Season—Spring to early summer, some re-bloom in autumn

Mature Size (H x W)—6 to 40 in. × 15 to 40 in.

Water Needs—Drought tolerant once established

LILY
Lilium spp. and hybrids

Why It's Special—Lilies are grown for their exquisite flowers and heavenly fragrance and come in a wide variety of sizes, shapes, and colors. Most of the hybrids are easy-to-grow garden plants and some may bear as many as forty to fifty flowers per stalk!

How to Plant & Grow—Lily bulbs can be as large as baseballs and should be plump and firm when you buy them. Soil for lilies should be deeply dug and generously amended before planting. Large bulbs should be planted 8 inches deep, smaller ones 4 to 6 inches.

Care & Problems—Lilies like their head in the sun and feet in the shade, so they're perfect to mix into perennial borders where surrounding plants will help shade and cool their roots. Unfortunately, deer love lilies! Voles can be a problem, and taller varieties need staking. Fertilize yearly in early spring.

Hardiness—Zones 4 to 9

Color—White, pink, red, yellow, orange, blends

Peak Season—Early summer to early fall

Mature Size (H x W)—1½ to 7 ft. × 1½ to 4 ft. (clump size, when mature)

Water Needs—Even moisture year-round

LILY, PHILIPPINE
Lilium formosanum

Why It's Special—Philippine lily is especially well-suited to Southern gardens, thriving in the heat and humidity of our climate. Its pristine white, trumpet-shaped blooms are borne on tall stems in late summer after many other lilies have finished. Large, ornamental seedpods form on the tall, candelabralike stems when flowering is done, extending the season of interest well into autumn.

How to Plant & Grow—Philippine lily is commonly grown from seed and is the only lily to be produced commercially in this way. It is unique in that it will frequently flower its first year. Philippine lily prefers full sun in deep, rich, well-drained soil and should be planted where it can be left undisturbed to grow into an impressive specimen.

Care & Problems—The stems of Philippine lily are usually quite sturdy, but on windy sites, it may need staking to keep it upright when it's in full bloom. Fertilize yearly in early spring.

Hardiness—Zones 6 to 9

Color—White

Peak Season—Late summer

Mature Size (H x W)—5 to 6 ft. × 2 to 3 ft.

Water Needs—Average

NARCISSUS
Narcissus spp. and hybrids

Why It's Special—When it comes to tried-and-true garden bulbs, perhaps none is as tried-and-true as the narcissus. Also known as daffodils, jonquils, and in the South, "buttercups," the narcissus is a perennial performer and by planting early, late, and midseason varieties you'll have blooms from February to April.

How to Plant & Grow—Narcissus have a reputation for being tough and indestructible. However, digging generous holes and amending soil well when planting new bulbs gets them off to the best start. Planting depth will vary with the size of the bulbs, and groups or clumps of ten bulbs or more will give the best effect in the garden.

Care & Problems—Daffodil bulbs are untouched by deer, voles, chipmunks, and so forth. Foliage should be allowed to yellow completely after flowering before cutting it back or you will weaken the bulb for the following year. Fertilize yearly in early spring just as growth begins.

Hardiness—Zones 3 to 8

Color—White, yellow, gold, orange, combinations

Peak Season—Spring

Mature Size (H x W)—4 to 20 in. × 6 to 18 in.

Water Needs—Low, once established

PINEAPPLE LILY
Eucomis spp. and hybrids

Why It's Special—Pineapple lily has become a popular Southern garden plant in recent years for its unusual blooms that are long, slender spires composed of many smaller flowers. At the top of each flower stalk is a small "knot" of leaves that resembles the topknot of a pineapple, hence the plant's name. Some varieties have leaves in shades of purple-maroon, adding further interest in the garden.

How to Plant & Grow—Pineapple lilies are easy to grow in Southern gardens. Plant bulbs in spring (either dormant or already growing) to ensure the plants become well established before going through winter. They prefer adequate moisture while they are in active growth, and I have found good success with them, even in my heavy clay soil.

Care & Problems—Pineapple lilies are relatively pest free. Blooms may become top heavy and fall over, but are difficult to stake since they come from the center of the plant.

Hardiness—Zones 7a to 10

Color—Cream to pink

Peak Season—Early to midsummer

Mature Size (H x W)—1 to 3 ft. × 1 to 2 ft.

Water Needs—Evenly moist while growing

RAIN LILY
Zephyranthes spp. and hybrids

Why It's Special—The tough and durable rain lily provides a beautiful and surprising show in late summer and early fall. The leaves sprout in spring at the same time as many other bulbs, but the rain lily waits to flower until the last days of summer when a passing thunderstorm provides just enough moisture to cause them to suddenly burst into bloom—often overnight!

How to Plant & Grow—Many rain lilies are native to the arid lands of Mexico and Central America where the soils are gritty and very well drained. They will benefit from the addition of coarse sand, turkey grit, or small crushed gravel to help improve drainage, especially in clay soils. Once established, they require little care.

Care & Problems—Rain lilies have few pest or disease problems. A topdressing of compost once a year will help keep them healthy and well fed.

Hardiness—Zones 7 to 10

Color—White, pink, yellow, new hybrids in sunset colors

Peak Season—Late summer to early autumn

Mature Size (H x W)—8 to 14 in. × 8 to 14 in.

Water Needs—Low, once established

SPANISH BLUEBELL
Hyacinthoides hispanica

Why It's Special—Spanish bluebell is one of the few bulbs that will truly thrive in a woodland setting, not minding the shade of overhead trees or competition from roots. In spring, 12- to 16-inch-tall spires of hyacinth-like blossoms appear in shades of blue, white, and occasionally pink. In most gardens, it will self-sow and naturalize freely, forming spectacular patches over time.

How to Plant & Grow—Plant bulbs in autumn in well-prepared soil that is moist and fertile. A topdressing of slow-release bulb fertilizer each fall will benefit the bulbs as the roots begin to grow in late fall and winter. Deadheading is not necessary, especially if reseeding is desired; the foliage should be allowed to die down naturally. Cutting the leaves off prematurely will weaken the bulbs for the following season.

Care & Problems—No serious pests or diseases, although deer may nibble. They usually stop after a bite or two.

Hardiness—Zones 5 to 8

Color—Blue, purple, white, pink

Peak Season—Mid-spring

Mature Size (H x W)—12 to 16 in. × 12 to 16 in.

Water Needs—Regular moisture while growing, drier when dormant

STARFLOWER
Ipheion uniflorum

Why It's Special—Starflower is a lesser-known bulb that deserves to be more widely grown in Southern gardens. Its cheerful, star-shaped blooms first appear in early spring with new buds and blooms continuing to open for several weeks. It is one of the longest-flowering bulbs in the garden. The variety 'Rolf Fiedler' is especially beautiful, with flowers of azure blue.

How to Plant & Grow—Starflower bulbs are small and should be planted in well-prepared garden soil about 2 inches deep. They are also excellent for naturalizing both in lawns and woodlands. They make beautiful miniature cut flowers in tiny vases and will last several days. They are summer dormant, so be sure not to damage them while planting or weeding.

Care & Problems—Starflower is a care-free bulb that will reseed itself where happy. If naturalized in lawns, be sure to mow high until the foliage has died down in order to feed the bulbs for the next year.

Hardiness—Zones 6 to 8

Color—Azure blue, pink, white

Peak Season—Spring

Mature Size (H x W)—6 in. × 8 in.

Water Needs—Moderate while actively growing

SURPRISE LILY

Lycoris spp. and hybrids

☀ ☀ ☀

Why It's Special—Lycoris species are also commonly known as "surprise lilies," "magic lilies," "spider lilies," and "naked ladies." These common names come from the fact that their blooms emerge suddenly and without warning in late summer and fall and are borne atop bare stems.

How to Plant & Grow—Plant surprise lilies 3 to 5 inches deep in well-amended garden soil. Don't be surprised if some species put up leaves in autumn while others wait for spring. This is normal. Lycoris perform well in woodland gardens since they are up and growing while the trees are bare and the sun is shining down, but they also mingle well in perennial borders.

Care & Problems—Surprise lilies are generally pest free. Basal rot can occur in winter in cold, wet clay; drainage is important. Over time they will slowly form offsets and the clumps will grow larger and more spectacular with each passing year.

Hardiness—Zones 5 to 9

Color—Pink, white, lavender, yellow, orange, red

Peak Season—Late summer to fall

Mature Size (H x W)—15 to 24 in. × 12 to 24 in.

Water Needs—Low, once established

TUBEROSE
Polianthes tuberosa

☀ ☀

Why It's Special—Tuberose is grown for its creamy white flowers whose sweet, intoxicating fragrance makes it especially popular as a cut flower, as well as in the garden. Laden with nectar, the flowers are favorites of hummingbirds, honeybees, and other beneficial insects. 'The Pearl' is a unique, double-flowered form.

How to Plant & Grow—Tuberoses need exceptionally well-drained soil if you want them to come back from year to year. Heavy clay will cause basal rot during the cold, wet winter months. Adding 1 to 2 inches of gravel or turkey grit to the bottom of the planting hole will help ensure the drainage these bulbs need. Given good drainage and full sun, they are otherwise undemanding.

Care & Problems—Tuberoses have few problems, although deer may graze the foliage and may nip the tops off the bloom stalks as they emerge, which can be very frustrating. Commercial deer repellent sprays are effective controls if applied regularly.

Hardiness—Zones 7 to 10

Color—White

Peak Season—Early summer

Mature Size (H x W)—2 ft. × 1 ft.

Water Needs—Average

TULIP
Tulipa spp. and hybrids

☀

Why It's Special—Tulips are one of the most widely known and loved of all spring-flowering bulbs. In the South, they are usually grown as annuals, since our heavy clay soils are not to their liking. Even so, a few tulips planted throughout the garden are a sure sign that spring is at its peak!

How to Plant & Grow—Tulips need cold weather in order to bloom. In parts of the South that don't experience much winter, tulip bulbs should be refrigerated for six weeks before planting outdoors. Planting deep—at least 6 to 8 inches—also keeps the bulbs drier in summer and encourages them to be more perennial in the garden.

Care & Problems—Voles are particularly enamored with tulip bulbs. Deep planting helps keep the bulbs out of harm's way. Deer are also destructive to tulips when they emerge in spring.

Hardiness—Zones 3 to 7

Color—Nearly every color, blend, and pattern imaginable

Peak Season—Early to late spring

Mature Size (H x W)—6 to 30 in. × 6 to 10 in.

Water Needs—Evenly moist while growing, drier when dormant

FORCING BULBS

Forcing bulbs, or making them flower outside of their normal season, is a fun and rewarding way to enjoy their beauty indoors during the cold and gray months of winter. While many books suggest forcing tulips and daffodils, this can be labor intensive and time consuming and sometimes results are mixed, at best. They are worth a try, certainly, but for first-time bulb forcers, you may find more success with smaller bulbs such as crocus, grape hyacinth, Spanish bluebell, and starflower. If you want to try your hand at daffodils, look for miniature varieties like 'Tête-à-Tête', which are much easier to manage indoors. Forcing bulbs is not difficult, but it does require a certain amount of dedication and space, especially during the "winter" you will be required to provide for them in your refrigerator!

STEP-BY-STEP BULB FORCING

First, you'll need to decide early in the season which bulbs you want to try to force, and buy them as

NARCISSUS

soon as they are available. If you are ordering from a mail-order source (they usually have bulbs long before garden centers put them out for sale), indicate on your order which bulbs you want to force and ask them to ship those to you as soon as they are available. Your bulbs have to have a "winter" before they'll grow, so you'll need to pot them early in the season in order to give them enough time to root before they begin growing.

Once your bulbs arrive, you're ready to get started. It may seem early to be potting them, but remember they'll need about three months of "winter," so planting in mid-September to early October means they won't be ready to come out of the refrigerator until mid-December to early January, or later.

1. Select pots for growing bulbs. Low, shallow pots work well, since smaller bulbs don't have deep roots, plus they'll look more in scale when they're in bloom. "Bulb pans" are pots that are made especially for forcing bulbs and their height is equal to half of their diameter, so a pot 8 inches in diameter is 4 inches tall.

2. Select a good, lightweight commercial potting mix that is moisture retentive, but well drained. Avoid using garden soil or even bagged topsoil. It will become compacted and bricklike in a pot, stunting growth or even rotting your bulbs.

3. Fill your pots about halfway with soil for larger bulbs, two-thirds full for smaller bulbs, and place the bulbs close together but not touching. Continue filling the pots with soil to cover the bulbs. Bulbs with pointed tops, like daffodils, may have the tips of the bulbs slightly exposed, but that's okay. They'll still grow.

4. Once your bulbs are planted, water the pots thoroughly until the soil is saturated all the way through. Then, let them sit and drain until no more water is coming out of the bottom. The soil may have settled, so fill in as needed to bring it up to level again and dampen any dry soil you have added.

5. Now it's time to give your bulbs "winter." Make room in the refrigerator (a spare refrigerator in

the garage works perfectly for this) and slide the potted bulbs in on one of the shelves. Pots can sit toward the back so that food can sit toward the front and you don't have to constantly move things around. Your potted bulbs will have to stay in the refrigerator for a minimum of 10 weeks and 12 would be better, so plan accordingly. Check periodically to see if pots are drying out and water as needed.

6. After approximately three months of "winter" in the refrigerator, you can begin pulling pots out of the refrigerator and setting them in cool but sunny windows. They will quickly begin to grow and in a few days to a few weeks, you should be enjoying beautiful spring blooms in the middle of winter.

Don't take all of your pots out of the refrigerator at once. Start one or two growing at a time and leave the others to pull out a week or ten days later, in succession. That way, you'll have one or two pots blooming while others are just starting to grow. By the time the first have finished flowering, the next batch will be starting to bloom and your show will be extended from just a week or two to several weeks or even a couple of months.

As your bulbs begin to grow, turn the pots a little bit each day to keep them from leaning toward the light. If you've chosen to try tulips and large daffodils, you may have to stake them as they grow to keep them from flopping. Smaller bulbs should be fine on their own.

If you wait until after the last freeze, most forced bulbs—except for tulips—can be planted in the garden. During their time indoors, keep them in bright sunlight and fertilize them with a water-soluble houseplant fertilizer. Wait until no more hard freezes are in the forecast, since forced bulb foliage will be soft and tender, then plant them in the garden where you want them to bloom next year. Forcing is hard on bulbs and those you plant in the garden may take an extra year to recover and start blooming again, but most bulbs will eventually regain their strength and fall into a regular cycle again.

Crocuses are one of the easier bulbs to force to grow in pots.

JANUARY

- If you have bulbs such as dahlias, caladiums, cannas, or tuberoses that you have stored over the winter, check on them periodically. Discard any that show signs of rot and be sure that the peat moss, perlite, or sawdust you have used is dry to the touch. It will have *just* enough moisture in it, even if it feels dry, to keep stored bulbs from shriveling up, but the bulbs have no need for actual moisture during this time.

- Check the mulch where you have bulbs planted outdoors. If you see digging, you could have a chipmunk or vole problem. If so, consider laying some hardware cloth over the ground where bulbs are planted to help deter digging.

- If you are chilling potted tulips, daffodils, and so forth to force for indoor blooms, be sure to water occasionally to maintain moisture at their roots. Once the green shoots are 2 to 3 inches tall, you can begin bringing pots in a few at a time to flower indoors.

FEBRUARY

- Resist spring-flowering bulbs at local garden centers that have been put on clearance. Since winter is almost over, the bulbs will not get the chilling they need and those who suggest that the bulbs will just sit in the ground and wait to come up the following year are probably not being completely honest.

- It is still safe to purchase paper-white narcissus and amaryllis bulbs for forcing indoors if retailers still have them for sale. Bulbs should be firm and plump with no mushy spots. If they're not, avoid them.

- The earliest daffodils, crocus, winter aconites, and other bulbs will be flowering this month. Be sure to leave their foliage up for at least 6 weeks after they finish flowering to feed the bulbs for next year's display. Otherwise, they may not flower the following year.

- Daffodils make nice tabletop bouquets, but their sap can be harmful to other cut flowers, causing them to lose their petals prematurely. Condition daffodils in a separate container of water for a day before adding them to bouquets.

MARCH

- Spring-flowering bulbs can be fertilized as their new growth emerges from the ground up until the time they are about 4 to 6 inches tall. Roots will still be actively taking up nutrients at this time. After they finish flowering, bulbs begin going dormant and roots begin dying off, so feeding them then is not beneficial.

- Snip off the spent blooms of spring-flowering bulbs to prevent seedpods from forming unless they are varieties you want to have naturalize in the lawn or garden. Deadheading small bulbs like crocus, anemones, and snowdrops is unnecessary. It can be beneficial for larger bulbs, like daffodils. If you expect them to repeat their show next spring, allow leaves to mature and die naturally before removing.

- If weeds occur in bulb beds, pull them by hand so you don't risk cutting, stabbing, or digging up the bulbs.

- To control botrytis (gray mold), which can affect some bulbs while they are in bloom, collect and discard faded flowers. Fungicides can be applied at the first sign of disease. Provide good air movement by not overcrowding the plants.

APRIL

- Walk the garden several times while your bulbs are in bloom and make notes in your garden journal about which varieties performed the best this year and which varieties may need to be fed, transplanted or, if they just aren't happy in your garden, removed. There is nothing wrong with removing plants that don't meet your expectations.

- In warmer areas, summer-flowering bulbs such as crocosmia, dahlia, and gladiolus can be planted after the threat of freezing temperatures has passed. In cooler areas, you may want to wait until early May, when the soil has warmed sufficiently.

- Cannas and dahlias can be dug and divided now. The best time to do this is after the eyes have sprouted but before they have grown more than an inch. Stake dahlia tubers as you are replanting so you can insert the stake without skewering the tuber.

- Plant gladiolus corms every two weeks until July to create a continuous succession of flowers. Plant the corms at least 4 inches deep to stabilize them as they produce their long flower stalks. Insert stakes as you plant to avoid skewering corms later.

MAY

- The foliage of most spring-flowering bulbs will be disappearing this month. An easy way to fill the gaps left behind is to sow seeds of annuals like zinnias, marigolds, or cleome (spider flower) right over the tops of the bulbs. The plants will grow right in place without having to dig and disturb the bulbs.

- If you still have bulbs that were stored over the winter, now is the time to get them in the ground. Only plant bulbs that are still firm to the touch and don't have any brown or mushy spots on them. If there are any that are questionable, discard them.

- Plant caladium bulbs when soil temperature reaches 70 degrees or warmer. The soil should feel warm to the touch or it's still too cold to plant caladiums. Tubers may rot in cold soil if planted too early.

- Lightly fertilize newly planted summer-flowering bulbs such as cannas, dahlias, and so forth when their shoots emerge, using a slow-release fertilizer. Water thoroughly afterwards.

JUNE

- The leaves of the latest daffodils and other bulbs should be dormant or at least turning yellow by now. They can be cut off at ground level. Dig, divide, and replant any crowded bulbs that have declined and produced few, if any, flowers.

- Pests to watch for include aphids, spider mites, thrips, and Japanese beetles. Handpick Japanese beetles (they love cannas!) and discard them into a jar of soapy water. Neem oil can be applied to the leaves to reduce feeding by the adults.

- Watch for powdery mildew and leaf spot diseases on dahlias. Proper spacing and good air circulation will help to prevent fungal infestations, but spraying may be necessary for severe outbreaks.

- Hand-pull weeds when they are young and easier to remove. Suppress them with a shallow layer of compost. Another way of handling weeds is to plant companion plants among your bulbs whose leaves will shade the soil and deprive the young weeds of sunlight.

JULY

- Now is the time to take advantage of early-order discounts from mail-order bulb distributors. Some bulbs may be available in limited quantities, and you want to be first in line to ensure that you get the varieties you want.

- Watch for leafroller larvae on cannas. These caterpillars will chew and roll the leaves, making plants unsightly and occasionally will curb growth and flowering. Bt (*Bacillus thuringiensis*) sprays are safe and effective. Also keep an eye out for spider mites on bulbs like crocosmia and gladiolus.

- If you have bulbs such as caladiums or tuberous begonias growing in pots, don't forget to feed them. Constant watering leaches nutrients from the soil and container plants rely on you to replenish those nutrients.

- Continue securing and tying in tall dahlias, lilies, and gladiolus to the stakes you have already provided them. Staking early will help keep plants from falling over later on.

AUGUST

- August is the month to divide bearded iris. They are dormant now and will settle back into the garden quickly, ready to root out as cooler weather arrives.

- If you notice small holes in your iris rhizomes as you divide, you may have iris borers. The rhizomes can be soaked overnight in a solution of Neem oil to help control. Severely infested rhizomes should be discarded. For minor infestations, small sections of rhizomes can simply be cut away. Dust with sulfur before replanting to help prevent fungal diseases.

- Spider mites are especially troublesome during the hot, dry weather of this month. Regular applications of highly refined horticultural oils applied only during the coolest parts of the day will help to smother them. Keep a close eye on dahlias and crocosmia, since spider mites love them.

- Don't let the weeds get the best of you this month. They're thriving while we're wilting in the heat, but be persistent and your efforts will pay off.

SEPTEMBER

- As you make plans to visit a garden center to purchase spring-flowering bulbs, remember that "bigger is better" when it comes to bulbs. Bigger bulbs produce bigger blossoms. Stay away from soft, mushy, moldy, or heavily bruised bulbs.

- Some bulbs, such as tulips and daffodils, have a brown, papery tunic covering the bulbs. This often comes off, especially with tulips, but is of no concern as long as the bulb underneath is plump, white, and free from bruising or damage.

- If bulbs need to be stored after you get them home or when they arrive in the mail, a cool garage, cellar, or basement is ideal. Avoid storing bulbs in the refrigerator, as the natural ethylene gas that is given off by fruits and vegetables as they ripen can be detrimental to flower bulbs.

- If you have purchased or ordered fall-flowering bulbs, such as saffron crocus, colchicum, or *Lycoris*, be sure to plant them as soon as possible after their arrival. They will begin growing almost immediately.

OCTOBER

- Cut back lily stalks to soil level after they have turned yellow. The same applies to other summer-flowering bulbs, like crocosmia, gladiolus, and caladiums, once their foliage has yellowed or withered.

- If you have any bulbs that are not hardy enough to live over the winter where you live, dig them as their foliage begins to yellow or die down, brush as much dirt as possible off them and leave them in a warm, dry place to dry for several days before storing them in a cool, dry, and frost-free location for the winter.

- Dusting your bulbs lightly with sulfur before you store them will help to prevent botrytis, soft rots, and other fungal diseases that may cause bulbs to rot while they are being stored. Mesh onion bags work well for storing bulbs, as they allow for good air circulation that also helps to prevent rotting in storage.

- Spring weeds will be germinating with gusto this month. Be careful when weeding and keep an eye out for the emerging fall foliage of bulbs, like some varieties of surprise lilies, muscari, starflower, and others. They all have winter foliage that will emerge in autumn.

NOVEMBER

- Minor bulbs are excellent for naturalizing in lawns and natural areas around your property. Randomly scatter crocuses, miniature daffodils, grape hyacinths, snowdrops, and anemones, and plant them where they fall. Over time, they will create magnificent drifts.

- November is the time to plant spring-blooming anemones, crocus, daffodils, scillas, snowdrops, and others across most of the South. In cooler areas, tulips can also be planted now, but in warmer areas you'll need to keep them refrigerated a few more weeks. Use a good bulb fertilizer tilled into the beds or added to the planting holes as you plant.

- Clean up and remove old, dried iris leaves, stems, and other debris in the fall to help eliminate overwintering eggs or iris borers. General cleanup of garden debris is a good idea at this time to prevent overwintering of insects and diseases from this year's garden.

- Fertilize new and established beds with a slow-release nitrogen fertilizer. Don't wait until spring, because the bulbs are producing roots and foraging for nutrients now.

DECEMBER

- Have soil samples taken from your beds if you have not done this in the past two or three years. Since lime can take up to six months to react and increase the soil pH, the sooner you have your soil tested, the sooner you can apply lime to your beds if necessary.

- Mice may get into outdoor bulb beds or cold frames. Use hardware cloth to keep them out. Voles, also called meadow or field mice, can feed on a wide variety of plants, including your bulbs. Nothing is more disheartening than to retrieve pots of bulbs to bring indoors for forcing and find that the bulbs have all been eaten!

- Paper-white narcissus are winter-blooming tender bulbs that can be forced without having to expose them to cool temperatures. They are great fun for children to grow because they are easy and fast. You can even measure how much they've grown overnight once they begin to sprout.

Roots will grow out of the basal plate at the bottom of bulbs. Make sure this basal plate is down when you plant the bulb or corm.

EDIBLES
for the South

There are few types of gardening that are more rewarding than vegetable gardening. Planting and nurturing small plants, seeds, cuttings, or bulbs and, in a relatively short period of time, harvesting your own fresh crop of tomatoes, peppers, or sweet corn or serving up a salad whose ingredients were all grown just a few feet from the back door is something that every gardener can be proud of. Today's creative and inventive gardeners have taken vegetables from being relegated to the far corner of the back yard to front yard "edible landscapes" and welcome and beautiful members of perennial beds and flower borders. No longer are we hiding our vegetables from public view. Instead, they're taking center stage and encouraging friends and neighbors to grow them too.

PICKING THE PERFECT SITE

Vegetables love sun and will produce the most abundant harvest when they receive 8 to 10 hours of direct sun each day. A few vegetables may tolerate a little light shade, but generally speaking, the heavier the shade, the lighter the yield. Vegetable gardens and trees just don't mix. Even if your garden is on the south side of a tree so that it is not being shaded, tree roots will quickly invade your vegetable garden in search of the water and fertilizer you are regularly applying to keep your vegetables happy and healthy. Vegetables won't stand a chance against the roots of a 70-foot-tall shade tree. Choosing a site with a nearby water source will also make gardening easier for you in those inevitable dry spells.

PREPARING YOUR VEGETABLE GARDEN SOIL

The most important step in creating any garden, especially a vegetable garden, is the proper preparation of the soil. Most of our common vegetables are heavy-drinking, heavy-feeding annual plants that grow, flower, and set fruit and/or seed in a single season. Every dollar you invest and every hour you spend plowing, amending, and tilling the soil will reward you ten times over when harvest time arrives.

The first step when building a new vegetable garden from scratch is to kill existing grasses and weeds. There will be no shortage of new weeds that appear on their own, so starting with a clean slate will at least give you a head start. You may choose to plow the weeds under and then till the ground thoroughly, hoe them out, or kill them with herbicides. Glyphosate is a nonselective herbicide that will clear the ground quickly and effectively. However, if you want to be truly organic about your approach, you should steer clear of chemical weed killers. In that case, you'll have to resort to other methods—frequent tilling, hand weeding, and so forth—to control the weeds. Solarizing the ground by stretching black plastic over the area in midsummer when temperatures are highest will kill existing weeds as well as their seeds. You have to plan ahead, killing weeds in the hottest part of the summer a season *ahead* of when you want to plant, but solarizing is very effective.

Zucchini is an easy and bountiful crop to grow.

Mulching around your vegetables will help keep the weeds down, and also keep the roots cooler.

TO PLOW OR NOT TO PLOW

Gardeners frequently debate the points of plowing the garden versus just tilling it. My preference, and the practice I have followed for many years, is to plow deeply each fall and let the garden fallow over the winter, tilling in spring. I leave a small section unplowed in autumn for growing fall and winter crops. Plowing in the fall and tilling each spring gives me the opportunity to add soil amendments, such as compost, well-rotted manure (aged at least one year), and rotted leaves, incorporating them thoroughly into the soil. Each spring I add as much of those ingredients to the garden as I can get my hands on or afford to buy. It keeps all of the good microorganisms in my soil thriving, which in turn keeps the bad ones at bay.

Building a healthy soil environment may be more important in a vegetable plot than almost anywhere else in your landscape because vegetable gardens are cropped very intensively. Here, we are not thinking about long-term plantings or about having the advantage of time. In the vegetable garden, we need results right away!

PLANTING AND CARE OF VEGETABLES

WHEN SHOULD I PLANT MY VEGETABLES?

Part of the answer to that question depends on the kinds of vegetables you want to grow. Will you grow mostly warm-season vegetables like tomatoes, eggplants, peppers, and squash? Or do you like cool-season vegetables like lettuce, spinach, peas, and carrots? If you're like most gardeners, you'll grow some of each and get as much out of your vegetable garden each season as possible. For warm-season crops, you'll want to look at two things: the last average frost date in your area and the soil temperature. Most warm-season crops need warm soil to really thrive, so even if your last frost date is April 15, if the soil temperature hasn't reached at least 65 degrees or warmer, it won't do you any good to plant warm-season crops. They'll just flounder until the soil warms sufficiently. Likewise, it won't do you any good at all to plant a spinach crop in the heat of the summer. It will just languish and probably die, if the seed germinates at all.

Timing is everything in the vegetable garden, and, while it may seem daunting at first, it's really quite simple, and you'll be a pro in no time.

PROPER PLANTING TECHNIQUES

Vegetables are commonly planted either in rows or hills. We all know what a row is—a long, straight, narrow planting with seeds laid in single file in a shallow trench. Vegetables such as beans, corn, peas, okra, and others are more often grown in rows. Hills are just what they sound like—a low mound, raised slightly above the surrounding soil level for vining plants like cucumbers, squash, pumpkins, and melons. Hills are spaced widely enough to allow the plants growing in them to spread across the ground. Still other plants may be planted in individual planting holes. I plant all of my tomatoes, peppers, and eggplants that way. Each one gets its own thoroughly prepared and amended planting hole within the larger garden whose soil also has been thoroughly prepared and amended. This may seem like overkill, but it gets results.

Plant transplants you have grown or bought into your well-prepared soil. I like to use a water-soluble root stimulator when I'm planting tomato, pepper, and other transplants. For seeds, create rows or hills with a hoe and then plant the seeds at the depth indicated on the seed packet. Keep newly planted seedlings evenly moist until they have sprouted and are growing vigorously. Don't waterlog them, but don't let them dry out during this time.

VEGETABLES NEED WATER

Most vegetable crops need at least 1 inch of water per week. If you are not receiving regular rainfall in your area, it will be up to you to make up for Mother Nature's shortcomings. As summer progresses and plants grow larger, they will likely need more water to keep plants healthy and growing. It is important not to let plants wilt severely once fruit has begun to set or the plant may "shed" some of its crop in order to protect itself and reduce the stress from drying out. This is Mother Nature's way of taking care of the plants and ensuring good crops each year and is especially true for plants like tomatoes, peppers, and eggplants. Uneven watering will also cause tomatoes to crack.

MULCHING YOUR VEGETABLES

Mulches help control weeds, conserve water, cool the soil in summer, and keep fruit from coming into direct contact with the soil, which can cause rot. Organic mulches include leaves, grass clippings, and compost, as well as clean wheat straw and hay. These materials also decompose over the season, adding valuable organic matter to the soil and recycling the nutrients. Adding organic matter is the primary means of improving soil tilth. Organic mulches help cool the soil, so apply them after the soil has warmed sufficiently in spring and the plants are growing well. At the end of the season, till them to improve the soil.

FERTILIZING YOUR VEGETABLES

I primarily use organic fertilizers in my vegetable garden. They are usually milder formulations that won't burn tender roots and many are slow release in nature, meaning they last for a long time once you apply them. About midseason, after the plants have become well developed, another application of fertilizer may be beneficial. Water all fertilizers in thoroughly, after application, to wash fertilizer off the plants and to activate it in the soil. Water-soluble fertilizers can also be used, applying them according to package directions.

ASPARAGUS
Asparagus officinalis

Why It's Special—Asparagus is a perennial vegetable that can be grown successfully throughout the upper and mid-South and into the deeper South, through Zone 8. Its tasty green spears breaking through the soil is one of the most anticipated events in the spring vegetable garden.

How to Plant & Grow—Asparagus is grown from bare-root crowns that are planted in early spring. It is best grown in broad beds, deeply dug and well prepared with compost. Within the prepared bed, dig a broad, shallow trench about 6 inches deep and 15 inches wide, the length of the bed. Set the plants in the trench about 1 foot apart with the buds pointing up, spreading the roots in a uniform pattern around each crown. Cover the crowns with 3 inches of soil. You'll have some soil left. Leave it in place and after the asparagus goes dormant in the fall and has been cut back, rake the extra soil over the trench until the bed has been raked smooth.

Care & Problems—In the first year, the plants will produce weak, spindly growth. In year two, growth will be stronger and in year three, you can harvest the first few spears. Harvest only one-third to one-half of the spears each year, leaving the rest to feed the roots for next year. Asparagus is tough and problem free, once established.

Harvest & Best Selections—'Jersey Giant', 'Jersey Knight', and 'Jersey Prince' are male selections that are productive.

BEAN, GREEN
Phaseolus vulgaris

Why It's Special—Beans may be the most diverse garden vegetables ranking second only to tomatoes in popularity. Common beans are probably native to South America and were grown there for centuries before Europeans began growing them. All beans are members of the legume family, with the ability to fix their own nitrogen. Green beans are one of the richest in nutrients of all vegetables, being high in vitamins A, C, and K, as well as potassium, calcium, iron, and dietary fiber.

How to Plant & Grow—Beans require full sun and warm, well-drained soil. Sow seeds of bush beans 2 to 3 inches apart, and cover them with 1 inch of soil. Sow seeds of pole beans 6 inches apart in rows along a fence or trellis, or sow them in hills of six seeds around poles set 3 feet apart; then cover the seeds with 1 inch of soil.

Care & Problems—Beans require little care except regular weeding and adequate water if the weather is dry. Organic insecticides will help control numerous bean leaf beetles, which will eat holes in the leaves. Plant disease-resistant varieties and avoid working in the beans when they are wet to help prevent disease outbreaks.

Harvest & Best Selections—Popular snap beans include 'Blue Lake', 'Contender', and 'Kentucky Wonder'. Harvest snap beans when they are no larger in diameter than a pencil to ensure that they are crisp and tender.

BEAN, LIMA
Phaseolus lanatus

Why It's Special—Lima beans, certain varieties of which are called "butter beans," are probably more popular in the South than almost anywhere else in the United States. Native to South America, lima beans thrive in the heat and humidity of our summers and will bear enormous crops of delicious beans.

How to Plant & Grow—Beans require full sun and warm, well-drained soil. Sow seeds of bush beans 2 to 3 inches apart and 1 inch deep in rows 2 feet apart. Some varieties of lima beans are what are known as "half runners," which means that they won't climb like a pole bean, but do send out long, semi-running stems that may reach 2 to 3 feet long or tall. Some support for the plants will be beneficial to keep them from flopping over and the beans lying on the ground.

Care & Problems—Beans require little care except regular weeding and adequate water if the weather is dry. Applying an organic insecticide will control numerous bean leaf beetles, which will eat holes in the leaves. Plant disease-resistant varieties and avoid working in the beans when they are wet to help prevent disease outbreaks.

Harvest & Best Selections—'Fordhook' is still one of the most popular lima beans, harvested when the seeds begin to fill the pods. Butter beans and lima beans are the same thing, but butter beans are smaller, harvested before the pods fill out.

BEET
Beta vulgaris

Why It's Special—Beets, while perhaps not the favorite of many, are extremely versatile and nutritious. Beet tops, or greens, have become extremely popular in mixes of salad greens and are very high in vitamins A and C, as well as being a good source of iron and calcium. The roots are also highly nutritious and can be very tasty when roasted or pickled if you're not a fan of them prepared in the traditional boiled way (and I don't blame you).

How to Plant & Grow—Beets are a cool-season crop and are best sown in early spring, up to four weeks before the last frost date. Beets need full sun and well-prepared loamy soil that is slightly alkaline. Beets, like other root crops, grow best in loose, very well-amended soil. Heavy clay may restrict root development.

Care & Problems—Beets require little care, although seedlings will need to be thinned as they grow. You can sow fairly thickly and pull seedlings to use as greens until the remaining plants are spaced at 3 inches to allow roots to develop.

Harvest & Best Selections—Harvest tops when they are 4 to 6 inches high, and use them as you would use spinach, fresh or sautéed. Harvest roots when they are 1½ to 2 inches in diameter. Beets allowed to grow more than 3 inches in diameter will be tough and woody. 'Detroit Dark Red' and 'Bulls Blood' are both popular varieties.

BROCCOLI
Brassica oleracea var. *italica*

Why It's Special—Grown for its large heads of green flower buds, broccoli is harvested while the buds are still very tight and before the flowers begin to open. After the main head is harvested, the plants may produce side shoots of smaller broccoli spears that can be harvested for several more weeks. Broccoli is extremely high in vitamins A and C, as well as being a good source of calcium and iron.

How to Plant & Grow—Broccoli loves cool weather and should be planted early and harvested before hot weather arrives. For the earliest production, start with transplants. Since the broccoli will be harvested and out of the garden by midsummer, plan to replace it with a second crop. For a fall crop, set transplants in the garden between mid-August and early September. In mild fall weather broccoli may last beyond Thanksgiving.

Care & Problems—Broccoli requires very little care to produce a crop. For the highest quality, moist soil is needed to keep the plants vigorous and growing. Cabbage looper caterpillars can be a problem on broccoli, but are easily controlled with Bt (*Bacillus thuringiensis*), an organic spray.

Harvest & Best Selections—Harvest the heads with a sharp knife, leaving about 6 inches of stem attached, while still compact and before the flower buds open. Allow side shoots to develop for steady production. Some varieties are 'Green Comet', 'Premium Crop', and 'Romanesque'.

BRUSSELS SPROUTS
Brassica oleracea var. *gemmifera*

Why It's Special—Named for the city in Belgium where they first attained popularity, Brussels sprouts have been grown there since the early 1300s. Brussels sprouts are grown for the cabbagelike buds that develop around the stems, near the leaf bases. If you think you don't like Brussels sprouts, try pan or oven roasting them, drizzling them with olive oil, a splash of balsamic vinegar, and topping with a sprinkle of Parmesan cheese.

How to Plant & Grow—The very best Brussels sprouts will be harvested in late autumn after two or three light frosts. Transplants can be planted in the garden in mid-August, needing about 100 days from planting in the garden to harvest. If starting them from seed, start the seeds four to six weeks before you want to plant them in the garden.

Care & Problems—Brussels sprouts will need very well-prepared soil and adequate moisture to get them off to a good start. Use a mild, organic fertilizer at planting time and sidedress the plants again when they are about 1 foot tall.

Harvest & Best Selections—Pick or cut the sprouts when they are 1 to 1½ inches in diameter, harvesting only what you need and "storing" the rest right on the plants. These very cold-hardy plants can last all winter in many Southern gardens where winters are mild. 'Jade Cross' is one of the most popular varieties.

CABBAGE
Brassica oleracea var. *capitata*

Why It's Special—Cabbage is one of the most nutritious of leafy green vegetables. It is an excellent source of vitamin A, extremely high in vitamin C, and also provides high levels of calcium, iron, and dietary fiber. It retains the most nutrients when steamed or sautéed, rather than boiling and overcooking it.

How to Plant & Grow—Cabbage is a cool-weather plant that can be grown either in spring or fall. Transplants will be available at garden centers at the right time to plant and should have a good color and be compact and pest free. Spring-planted cabbage will be harvested and out of the garden by midsummer, so plan to replace it with a second crop, such as beans, that will thrive in summer weather.

Care & Problems—Plant cabbage transplants in rows, with 18 inches between plants and at least 24 inches between rows. Plant them at the same depth they were growing in their pots and water them with a water-soluble starter fertilizer. Keep the soil evenly moist to keep plants growing vigorously and fertilize the plants with an all-purpose fertilizer when the plants are about 12 inches across. Cabbage worms can be treated with the organic spray Bt (*Bacillus thuringiensis*) to control them.

Harvest & Best Selections—Harvest heads when they feel very firm, then pull and compost the plants. Popular varieties include 'Ruby Perfection', 'Savoy King', and 'Early Jersey Wakefield'.

CARROT
Daucus carota var. *sativus*

Why It's Special—Carrots have not always been a common part of our diet, but since the 1800s, they have been popular in America, partly because they stored well through long winters and were the highest source of vitamin A that settlers could eat.

How to Plant & Grow—Sow seeds as soon as the soil is workable in the spring. Light frosts will not harm them. Sow several batches of seed, two weeks apart, to harvest over a period of weeks in late spring and early summer. Carrots that develop in summer's heat will be woody and tasteless. Carrots require deeply prepared, well-drained soil that is high in organic matter. Short-rooted or round varieties are best in the heavier clay soils of the South.

Care & Problems—Keep seedling rows well weeded, as weeds will compete for much-needed moisture and nutrients. Thin seedlings when they are about 3 inches tall so there is at least 2 inches between plants. It's hard for some gardeners to thin, but it is very important for root crops so they will develop properly.

Harvest & Best Selections—Harvest carrots when they are no more than 1 inch in diameter. Staggered spring plantings will continue to produce for up to six weeks. Summer sowings for fall carrot crops can be left in the ground and harvested right through winter. Mulch them deeply with clean straw so the ground doesn't freeze.

CAULIFLOWER
Brassica oleracea var. *botrytis*

Why It's Special—If there is such a thing as a high maintenance vegetable, cauliflower is it. Unlike its other cabbage family cousins, cauliflower is known for being a little on the persnickety side. That said, homegrown cauliflower, as with most vegetables, is far superior to what you buy in the store.

How to Plant & Grow—Cauliflower is less tolerant of temperature extremes than its close cousin, broccoli, and is also not as tolerant of drying out. It can be grown for both spring and fall harvests. For the best success, use transplants instead of sowing seeds. Cauliflower prefers deeply prepared, well-drained soil; good drainage is essential. Space plants 18 inches apart in rows 36 inches apart.

Care & Problems—Cauliflower must grow vigorously from seeding to harvest and should be kept evenly moist. When plants are about half grown (8 to 12 inches tall), fertilize them with nitrogen to stimulate continuing vigorous growth. When heads are about 3 inches in diameter, lift the leaves over the heads to shade them, and tie them up with twine, rubber bands, or a couple of clothespins to blanch them. Self-blanching varieties produce upright leaves that shade the heads and don't require tying.

Harvest & Best Selections—Cut heads, leaving a few green leaves to protect them. Cauliflower does not store well, so use it as you harvest or freeze it. 'Snow Crown' and 'Self Blanch' are popular varieties.

COLLARDS
Brassica oleracea var. *acephala*

Why It's Special—A cool-season leafy vegetable, collards are members of the cabbage family. Collards tolerate warm and cold temperatures better than cabbage or cauliflower do. It is an important vegetable in the South where it is used as a leafy green, prepared in the same ways as turnip and mustard greens.

How to Plant & Grow—The best collards grow during the mild days and cool nights of autumn. Seed can be sown directly in the garden in late summer and with mild fall weather you can harvest them until well after Thanksgiving. In the warmest parts of the South, collards will grow all winter.

Care & Problems—Collards need adequate water to grow and develop to perfection, at least 1 inch per week. Some pests and diseases can be problems. Control infestations of cabbage worms with Bt (*Bacillus thuringiensis*) and use a copper-based fungicide to help prevent various leaf spot diseases. Spacing is important for collards. Thin plants to 12 inches apart when seedlings are 6 inches high, using those pulled as young greens, perfect for sautéeing. Allow the remaining plants to mature.

Harvest & Best Selections—Harvest collards either by cutting outer leaves as they reach full size or by cutting the entire plant at the soil line. 'Hi Crop' and 'Champion Long Standing' are popular varieties. Some gardeners like to blanch the inner leaves by tying the outermost leaves together at the top of the plant.

CUCUMBER
Cucumis sativus

Why It's Special—Cucumbers are vine crops that are closely related to squashes, pumpkins, and melons. They thrive in the warm summer season, growing quickly and producing prolifically. Bush types take up less space and can even be grown in pots, but also bear smaller quantities of fruit.

How to Plant & Grow—Cucumbers need warm weather to thrive and may rot if the weather is cool and wet, so don't be in a hurry to plant them too early in the spring. Cucumbers resent root disturbance and will grow best when seed is sown directly in the garden. Growing vining types on trellises or supports will save space and produce long, straight fruit.

Care & Problems—Cucumbers are thirsty plants and should be kept evenly moist from the time they sprout. Cucumber beetles are serious threats that spread bacterial wilt that will kill the plants about the time they begin to produce fruit. As soon as seeds germinate in the garden, use row covers over the plants, being sure to tuck in the edges and ends to keep out the beetles. Covers can be removed when plants begin to vine to ensure pollination and fruiting.

Harvest & Best Selections—Harvest cucumbers when they have reached a mature size for the chosen variety. Standard cucumbers are 6 to 8 inches long. Burpless types may be up to 1 foot long and pickling types are 2 to 6 inches long at maturity.

EGGPLANT
Solanum melongena var. *esculentum*

Why It's Special—Eggplant is a member of the nightshade family like its cousins, tomatoes, potatoes, and peppers. Eggplant is naturally low in sodium and high in vitamins A and K, as well as B6 and dietary fiber. It can be sautéed, grilled, fried, or baked and is an excellent substitute for lasagna noodles if thinly sliced.

How to Plant & Grow—Eggplants are very sensitive to cold weather and cold soil. They need warm weather to develop and may rot off when the weather is cool and wet. Transplants are the easiest way to start and can be planted around May 1. Earlier planting is possible in the warmest parts of the South.

Care & Problems—After they are established, eggplants are somewhat drought tolerant, but will grow and fruit best with at least 1 inch of water per week. When the plants are half-grown (about 12 inches high), side-dress them with a bloom-booster fertilizer. Flea beetles will make small holes in the leaves, and a severe infestation can reduce yield. Control outbreaks with a natural insecticide.

Harvest & Best Selections—Eggplants come in a variety of shapes and sizes and are best when young. Overly mature fruit will be spongy, seedy, and bitter. Cut the stem with pruning shears or a sharp knife instead of tearing off. 'Black Beauty' and 'Rosa Bianca' are two of the best varieties.

GARLIC
Allium sativum

Why It's Special—Garlic is a hardy perennial bulb that consists of a cluster of small bulblets called cloves, covered in a protective, papery skin. Garlic is touted as a reducer of high blood pressure and heart disease. Garlic can be roasted in the oven to mellow its flavor and is commonly added to Greek and Italian dishes. Its flavor also reduces the need for salt.

How to Plant & Grow—Plant garlic in autumn to harvest the following summer. Garlic prefers to grow in full sun and well-prepared, well-drained soil. Heavy, compacted clay will result in lower production. Garlic is started by separating the individual cloves from the bulb. Plant individual cloves 2 inches deep and 4 inches apart in rows 1 foot apart.

Care & Problems—Garlic may send up small leaves in autumn, overwintering and doing most of its growing the following spring and summer. Keep water- and nutrient-hogging weeds out of the garlic rows with regular weeding from planting time to harvest.

Harvest & Best Selections—Garlic begins to bulb when the days are longest in June. The larger the plants at that time, the larger the bulbs will be, so it is important to keep the plants growing. Harvest the garlic as soon as most of the leaves have turned yellow, usually in midsummer. There are many varieties of garlic. Try several to experience the wide range of types and flavors.

KALE
Brassica oleracea var. *acephala*

Why It's Special—Kale, once relegated to health food stores, has become a mainstream and popular vegetable. It is one of the healthiest greens you can eat, with tremendous amounts of vitamins A and C, as well as being very high in iron, calcium, dietary fiber, and a host of other nutrients.

How to Plant & Grow—Kale is extremely cold hardy and is best in the South as a fall and winter crop. Seed can be sowed in late summer to mature in autumn and early winter, or transplants can be planted in early autumn. The best varieties, in warmer parts of the South, will grow right through the winter with little or no protection from the cold. Kale grows best in rich, well-prepared soil that is high in organic matter. Keep it well watered and fed when young to keep it actively growing before cold weather sets in.

Care & Problems—Because it is at its peak during the cooler days of autumn and the cold days of winter, pests are rarely a problem. Rabbits may eat seedlings and young plants, so protect them accordingly from the little nibblers.

Harvest & Best Selections—Harvest kale by cutting the lowest leaves on the plant and letting the crowns continue to grow. 'Laciniato' or "dinosaur kale" is especially good and extremely cold hardy. It is the Italian kale that is used in the traditional Tuscan stew called ribollita.

LEEKS
Allium ampeloprasum

Why It's Special—Native to the Mediterranean region, leeks have been cultivated for thousands of years. They are the milder and smoother flavored cousins of onions, chives, and garlic. It is the cylindrical, white base of the plant that is typically used in cooking, although the smaller and more tender leaves can also be used to flavor soups and stews. Like their onion and garlic cousins, leeks are reportedly good for lowering blood pressure and reducing heart disease.

How to Plant & Grow—For the earliest production, start seed indoors six to eight weeks before planting outdoors in early spring. Leeks require deeply prepared, thoroughly amended, well-drained soil and usually require 100 or more days to mature. Spade or rototill the soil to a depth of at least 6 inches. Plant in rows with 4 inches between plants and 12 to 18 inches between rows.

Care & Problems—As the plants begin to grow, blanch the lower parts of the stems by gently hilling soil up on the stems of the plants to just below the bottom leaf. Continue hilling as plants grow to get a long white base. Leeks have few pests.

Harvest & Best Selections—Harvest leeks when the bases of the stems are about 1 inch in diameter. Dig only what you need because the plants store well in the ground and continue to increase in size. 'Alaska', 'Broad London', and 'Titan' are popular varieties.

LETTUCE
Lactuca sativa

Why It's Special—No other salad crop is grown or used in such large quantities as lettuce, which has become an essential part of our diet. Lettuce is a cool-weather crop that can be grown in spring or fall, but will quickly become bitter and bolt when hot weather arrives.

How to Plant & Grow—Sow seeds of leaf lettuce varieties directly in the garden as early as the soil can be worked. Since the lettuce will be harvested by midsummer, plan to replace it with a second crop. Bibb or butter crunch-type lettuces can be grown successfully in the South, but head lettuces are not well suited to our climate.

Care & Problems—Excellent drainage is a requirement for lettuce. It thrives with lots of water for vigorous growth, but resents having its roots in waterlogged soil. Keep the seedbed evenly moist after planting. Lettuce seed is tiny and can dry out quickly. Lettuce is almost all water and keeping it moist throughout its growth is beneficial.

Harvest & Best Selections—Harvest leaf lettuce by snipping off the outer leaves as soon as they are large enough for your use. Leave the plants intact so they continue producing over several weeks. Harvest Bibb or butter crunch-type lettuces when the heads are full size. 'Butter Crunch' (an actual variety) and 'Black-seeded Simpson' are two of the most popular and easily grown varieties.

MUSKMELON
Cucumis melo var. *reticulatus*

Why It's Special—Muskmelons are vine crops, closely related to cucumbers, squashes, and pumpkins. These hot-weather plants with sweet, juicy fruit are commonly called "cantaloupes." Like most vine crops, muskmelons can occupy a lot of room. One way to use less space is to grow them on trellises, as long as you can support the heavy fruit as it grows.

How to Plant & Grow—Muskmelons need warm soil to thrive and grow and may rot if weather is cool and wet. Don't be in a rush to plant them. Sow seeds 1 inch deep in hills about 36 inches apart. Muskmelon resents transplanting and will grow best if sown directly in the garden where you want it to grow.

Care & Problems—As soon as muskmelon seedlings emerge, protect them from cucumber beetles. Cucumber beetles not only eat the plants but also infect them with bacterial wilt that will kill the plants about the time they begin to produce fruit. Apply an organic insecticide or use row covers to keep the beetles out.

Harvest & Best Selections—For the best quality and sweetness, leave melons on the vine until they are fully ripe. The rind will change from green to tan between the netting, and a ripe melon will smell sweet. Muskmelons do not continue to ripen once they are picked. They will become softer, but not sweeter. 'Honeybush' and 'Jenny Lind' are both tried-and-true varieties.

MUSTARD
Brassica juncea

Why It's Special—Mustard, like its cousins turnips and collards, is grown for its large, cold-tolerant leafy greens that are popular throughout the South. Mustard has a more pungent flavor than collards or turnips and if grown in too dry soil or in too much heat, may become hot to the point of being nearly inedible. Mustard is extremely high in vitamins A and C, as well as fiber. It is also a good source of iron and calcium, as well as being a good source of vegetable protein.

How to Plant & Grow—Sow mustard seed in late summer or early autumn to harvest crops in late autumn and, in the mildest parts of the South, throughout winter and into early spring. By late spring, as the weather begins to warm, mustard will bolt, flower, and go to seed. It will sometimes reseed itself to naturalize in the garden and come back each year.

Care & Problems—Rabbits can be a problem on young seedlings and deer may graze it also. Other than some nibbling, mustard is quite care-free and easy to grow.

Harvest & Best Selections—Begin harvesting mustard when plants are 6 inches tall by removing some plants entirely to leave at least 6 to 8 inches of space between other plants in the row. Young leaves can be used raw in salads or sautéed like spinach. There are both red leaf and green leaf varieties of mustard.

OKRA
Abelmoschus esculentus

Why It's Special—Okra is a relative of the popular garden flowers hollyhock and hibiscus. It is grown for its lightly fuzzy green or red pods that are used to thicken soups and stews and to cook as vegetables. Perhaps its most famous application in the South is its use in traditional gumbo.

How to Plant & Grow—Okra likes it hot and should be planted after soil is warm to the touch. Seeds will not germinate in cool soil. Sow okra seed directly in the garden, waiting until at least a week after the last frost. Stagger two to three sowings about two weeks apart to harvest well into fall. Fertilize when plants are 6 inches tall with an organic bloom booster-type fertilizer to encourage heavy pod set.

Care & Problems—Okra needs little care to produce a good crop. Provide 1 inch of water per week and keep competitive weeds removed since they will steal water and nutrients from the plants. Grasshoppers may nibble the foliage, but they are generally not destructive.

Harvest & Best Selections—Harvest the pods when they are about 3 inches long and still tender. Use a knife or shears and harvest every two days. Okra pods grow amazingly fast and can go from perfect to overgrown almost overnight. If you miss some pods, remove them so plants don't set seed and will continue producing. Popular selections include 'Clemson Spineless', 'Dwarf Green Longpod', and 'Burgundy'.

ONION
Allium cepa

Why It's Special—Onions are members of the lily family and their ornamental cousins, the alliums, are grown for the beautiful blooms. Onions, on the other hand, are grown for their flavorful stems and bulbs. Onions, like their cousins garlic, leeks, and chives, are considered good for lowering blood pressure and reducing heart disease.

How to Plant & Grow—Onions are completely hardy and can be planted as soon as the soil can be worked in spring. Start them from seed sown directly in the garden, from seedling transplants, or from onion sets. For transplants and sets, place plants about 2 inches deep. Sow seeds according to packet instructions.

Care & Problems—Onions are shallowly rooted, so be careful as you hoe or pull weeds. Try to get as much top growth as possible by the first day of summer. Bulbs begin to form when the days reach about 15 hours in length, and the size of the dry onions is determined by the size of the tops. Keep onions watered until their tops begin to die in mid to late summer.

Harvest & Best Selections—Harvest green onions when the stems are pencil-sized. As tops begin to yellow in midsummer allow the plants to die completely before harvesting. 'Sweet Spanish' and 'White Portugal' are two of the most popular varieties. 'Granex' is grown in Georgia and sold as "Vidalia" in supermarkets.

PEAS
Pisum sativum var. *sativum*

Why It's Special—Peas are decidedly cool-weather plants, intolerant of Southern heat and humidity. As soon as the weather warms up, production ceases and the vines quickly turn brown. But peas lose their flavor quickly after harvest and are one of the best choices for growing in the home garden to get the absolute best quality.

How to Plant & Grow—Sow peas in the garden as soon as the soil can be worked in spring. In the South, planting between Valentine's Day and St. Patrick's Day is common. Seeds germinate when soil temperatures reach about 45°. By preparing the soil in the fall, you can sow the seeds at the earliest opportunity in the spring without having to wait to till the soil. Fall crops can be sown in September.

Care & Problems—Bush peas are self-supporting. Placing vining types on a support of some kind conserves space, makes picking easier, and keeps the peas from getting muddy every time it rains. Rabbits will wreak havoc on young peas. Nothing is more frustrating than going out one morning and finding that your entire crop has been eaten overnight.

Harvest & Best Selections—Harvest English or garden peas when they are full sized and before the seeds begin to dry. Pods should be green, not yet turning tan. Harvest sugar pod peas (*Pisum sativum* var. *macrocarpon*, also called snap peas) when the pods are fully formed, but before seeds begin to develop.

PEPPER, HOT
Capsicum annuum and *C. frutescens*

Why It's Special—Hot peppers are the special ingredients in foods from many cultures that impart smoky flavor and heat. Be aware that some of the oils in some hot peppers are so volatile that they can burn tender skin around the mouth and eyes; use some caution when harvesting and working with the fruit. Some may even require gloves.

How to Plant & Grow—Peppers thrive in our hot and humid Southern summers. Plant peppers in well-drained soil in full sun. Wait until the soil is very warm to the touch or plants will just sit there and do nothing. Plant pepper transplants at the same depth they were growing in the containers. Firm the soil gently around each plant, and water with 1 quart of transplant starter fertilizer mixed according to directions on the package.

Care & Problems—Use insecticidal soap to combat aphids and mites; apply organic insecticides to cope with caterpillars and beetles. Keep peppers well watered to get the biggest crop.

Harvest & Best Selections—Hot peppers can be harvested green or allowed to ripen and turn color. After ripening, the flavors improve and the amount of "heat" may change depending on the variety. Cutting the peppers with a sharp knife or shears is a better method than pulling them off, which may break the plants. 'Ancho', 'Habanero', 'Hungarian Wax', and 'Tam Jalapeno' are all popular selections with varying degrees of heat.

PEPPER, SWEET
Capsicum annuum

Why It's Special—Sweet peppers are native to the tropics and are perfectly suited to the hot and humid summers in the South. Some of the most popular are the sweet bell peppers. Like their tomato cousins, green peppers are immature fruits. As the peppers mature, they will turn red, purple, yellow, or orange, depending on the variety.

How to Plant & Grow—Peppers are warm-weather plants. Planting too early is an effort in futility, since plants will sit there and do nothing. Plant peppers in a well-drained part of the garden in full sun. Plant the pepper plants at the same depth they were growing in the containers. Firm the soil around each plant, and water it with 1 quart of transplant starter fertilizer mixed according to directions on the package.

Care & Problems—Blossom-end rot may appear as a brown spot on the bottom of a pepper. Poor growing conditions, such as cold or wet weather—not disease—cause blossom-end rot. Use insecticidal soap to combat aphids and mites; apply organic insecticide to eradicate caterpillars and beetles.

Harvest & Best Selections—Bell peppers can be harvested green or allowed to ripen and turn color. After ripening, the flavors improve. Cutting the peppers with a sharp knife or shears is a better method than pulling them off, which may break the plants. 'California Wonder' and 'Big Bertha' are excellent cultivars.

POTATO
Solanum tuberosum

Why It's Special—Potatoes are most commonly associated with Ireland and, in the United States, Idaho, but did you know that potatoes actually originated in the high country of South America and were cultivated by the Incas? Their cultivation and consumption goes back thousands of years.

How to Plant & Grow—Potatoes are started from pieces of seed potatoes. Seed potatoes can be purchased at garden centers in late winter and early spring. Cut these into smaller pieces, each with two or three eyes and let them dry for forty-eight hours before planting in the garden. Plant potatoes in trenches 8 to 10 inches deep, covering seed pieces with 3 inches of soil and leaving 4 or 5 inches to continue filling in around the stems as plants grow.

Care & Problems—When sprouts are 6 inches high, begin filling the trench around them, being careful not to injure the roots. The hills eventually should be about 6 inches high and 1 foot wide. Hilling keeps the potatoes covered, keeps the soil loose, and helps to reduce weeds that compete for water and nutrients.

Harvest & Best Selections—Harvest new potatoes when the first flowers on the potatoes appear, usually about ten weeks after planting. When vines begin to yellow, mature potatoes are ready to harvest. Carefully lift them with a fork or spade. Spread the potatoes on the ground and let them dry for a day. Do not wash them or they will not keep.

PUMPKIN
Cucurbita pepo

Why It's Special—Pumpkins make popular autumn decorations, but many people grow these warm-season vining crops for their flesh for pumpkin pies and their tasty and healthy seeds for roasting. Pumpkins are just one variety of winter squash, which also includes butternut, acorn, Hubbard, and a variety of others.

How to Plant & Grow—There is no need to get pumpkins into the garden very early. They need warm weather to develop and may rot if the weather is cool and wet. Pumpkins prefer full sun and need a location with well-drained soil. Pumpkins, even small varieties, make huge vines, so allow them plenty of room to spread.

Care & Problems—Pumpkins are very hungry and thirsty plants, especially once fruit set begins in midsummer. They will need a bare minimum of 1 inch of water per week throughout the growing season. Pumpkins are susceptible to attack by squash vine borers, which are the larvae of bee-like moths that lay eggs on the bases of the plants. Control these insects by applying an organic insecticide to the stems of the plants every two weeks throughout the growing season.

Harvest & Best Selections—Harvest pumpkins when they have no green on them. Cut the handles 3 to 4 inches long using a pair of shears to avoid breaking them. 'Howden', 'Connecticut Field', and 'Jack-Be-Little' are proven performers. 'Rouge Vif d'Etampes' is a French heirloom also known as the "Cinderalla" pumpkin.

RADISH
Raphanus sativus

Why It's Special—Radishes are fast-growing, cool-weather vegetables, many maturing in as little as forty-five to fifty days after sowing. They grow any place they can have some sun and moist, fertile garden soil. They can also be grown very successfully in pots and window boxes, harvested before it's time to plant summer flowers. Fresh radishes make hors d'oeuvres, tasty garnishes, or additions to salads.

How to Plant & Grow—Radishes can be planted in very early spring by sowing seeds directly in the garden as soon as the soil is dry enough to be worked, even February or March in warmer parts of the South. Fall crops can be sown from late summer to early autumn. Sow seeds thinly and cover very lightly, keeping moist until they germinate. Thin seedlings to 2 to 3 inches apart as plants mature.

Care & Problems—Radishes are not labor-intensive plants. Pull weeds carefully while the seedlings are small, so they don't compete with the radishes for water and nutrients. Keep the plants growing because radishes that develop slowly will be hot and pithy (soft and mealy).

Harvest & Best Selections—Harvest spring radishes at about 1 inch in size and winter radishes before they reach 2 inches. Radishes bolt in hot weather and send up seed stalks. Radishes come in both round and long forms. Popular round varieties include 'Cherry Belle', 'Easter Egg', and 'Early Scarlet Globe'. Long varieties include 'French Breakfast' and 'Icicle'.

SPINACH
Spinacia oleracea

Why It's Special—Spinach is another leafy green that gardeners have cultivated for centuries as both a leafy green and a cooked vegetable. Spinach is an extremely versatile green, great for use in salads, quiches, pizzas, crepes, and omelets, and a variety of other creative dishes. Spinach is a cool-weather crop that can be grown in spring or fall.

How to Plant & Grow—Sow seed in the garden as early as the soil can be worked. Spinach must be planted and harvested before hot weather arrives. In hot weather, spinach sends up a seed stalk (bolts), and the quality quickly deteriorates. Unless you want lots of spinach at one time, however, make multiple plantings to spread out the harvest.

Care & Problems—Spinach will grow best when it is evenly moist and not allowed to dry out severely. Spinach plants are shallowly rooted and easily uprooted, so weed carefully so you don't accidentally uproot small plants. Aphids love spring spinach, but can be controlled with a gentle but direct spray of water.

Harvest & Best Selections—Harvest spinach by snipping off outer leaves as soon as they are large enough to use. When plants are large enough to harvest, cut every other one, leaving more room for the others. As soon as the plants begin to bolt, harvest all that remain before they deteriorate. 'Bloomsdale' is still the standard against which all other spinach is tested.

SQUASH
Cucurbita spp.

Why It's Special—Squashes are warm-season vine crops with flavorful flesh. The many types are divided into summer squashes, grown for the immature fruit, and winter squashes, which are harvested after their skins thicken and they mature. Summer squash are often more compact plants and better suited to smaller gardens.

How to Plant & Grow—Don't be in a hurry to get your squash seed planted in spring. The plants need very warm soil to develop and may rot if soil is cool and wet. Sow seed directly in the garden where you want them, as they resent transplanting and thin hills to the three strongest seedlings once the first true leaves appear.

Care & Problems—Squash require lots of water and fertilizer after they set fruit, so be prepared to water if natural rainfall does not occur. Fertilize with an organic bloom booster fertilizer when the vines have almost covered the ground to promote heavy fruiting. All squash are susceptible to attack by squash vine borers. Control these insects by applying organic insecticide to the stems of the plants when the plants begin to vine and then every two weeks during the season.

Harvest & Best Selections—Harvest summer squashes while they are still immature for immediate use and winter squashes after they have completely matured for fall and winter storage. 'Yellow Crookneck' and 'Pattypan' are popular summer squash. Winter varieties include 'Butternut', 'Acorn', and 'Hubbard'.

SWEET CORN
Zea mays var. *rugosa*

Why It's Special—Few of us gardeners can resist the temptation that is fresh, home-grown sweet corn. It is a time- and space-consuming vegetable to grow, but there simply is no comparison between sweet corn grown in the home garden and commercially grown corn. Sugars begin to break down in sweet corn as soon as it is harvested, so harvest ears as needed and cook them right away for the ultimate flavor and sweetness.

How to Plant & Grow—Sweet corn needs full sun, good drainage, and lots of room. Begin sowing seed when soil feels warm to the touch and continue every two weeks until midsummer to prolong harvest later into the season. Sow seed 1 inch deep in well-warmed soil, spaced 9 inches apart in the rows with 24 to 36 inches between rows. Plant two or more rows of each variety side by side to ensure good pollination.

Care & Problems—Water is extremely important at all stages of growth, but especially when plants begin to tassel and silk, since pollination takes place during this time. It continues to be important as the ears develop, with plants needing at least 1 inch of water per week to keep the ears developing and filling out.

Harvest & Best Selections— 'Silver Queen' is one of the most popular varieties, but many other worthy varieties exist. Harvest when silks have turned completely brown and the kernels are full and plump.

SWISS CHARD
Beta vulgaris var. *cicla*

Why It's Special—Chard is only slightly different from beets, the difference being that it has been bred for leaves at the expense of the bulbous roots. Grown as a summer green, it is prepared like spinach, while the attractive colorful stalks of red and yellow also can be prepared and used like asparagus, eaten raw or cooked.

How to Plant & Grow—Sow seeds directly in the garden or set out transplants at the frost-free date. A spring planting will produce all summer if harvested regularly. As soon as the seedlings are large enough to handle, thin them to 4 to 6 inches apart. If you wait until the seedlings are about 6 inches tall, you can cook the thinned seedlings as greens.

Care & Problems—Chard needs 1 inch of water per week to keep it actively growing and leaves tender. These plants are very susceptible to leaf miner damage. Protect the plants by covering them with floating row covers made of lightweight fabric. Chard is susceptible to several fungal leaf spot diseases. Avoid harvesting or weeding while plants are wet to reduce the spread of spores.

Harvest & Best Selections—Harvest leaves when they are young and tender, about 12 inches long. Cut the most mature (outer) leaves 1 inch above the ground, being careful not to injure the remaining leaves to harvest continually for several weeks or months. 'Bright Lights', 'Ruby', and 'Fordhook' are popular varieties.

TOMATO
Lycopersicon lycopersicum

Why It's Special—Tomatoes are the most popular garden vegetable in the United States. The flavor of a newly picked red tomato from your garden is second-to-none.

How to Plant & Grow—Tomatoes are tender plants that should not be planted out until all danger of frost has passed and the soil is warm to the touch. Plants may rot in cold soil if planted too early in the season. Full sun and rich, well-prepared soil will give you vigorous growth and large quantities of tomatoes. Feed monthly with tomato fertilizer.

Care & Problems—Sturdy cages can be made from concrete reinforcing wire and will support plants during the season. Plants can also be staked, but this is much more labor intensive, as continuous tying is required to keep the plants from sprawling on the ground and keeping fruit from rotting. Plant disease-resistant varieties to eliminate verticillium and fusarium wilts and yellows. Control foliar diseases with copper fungicide. Use insecticidal soap on aphids and mites and Bt (*Bacillus thuringiensis*) for tomato hornworm.

Harvest & Best Selections—Selecting varieties to grow in your garden can be quite a challenge. Tomatoes are offered in a wide range of sizes, shapes, colors, growth habits, and maturity dates. Garden centers carry varieties that are best suited to your area. 'Better Boy', 'Burpee's Big Boy', and 'Beefsteak' are time-tested winners in most climates.

WATERMELON
Citrullus lanatus

Why It's Special—Watermelon is one of those strange plants that is hard to classify. A cousin to squash and gourds, it is sweet like a fruit and doesn't bear much resemblance to a squash or a gourd. Watermelons need a long, hot season to develop. If you are short on space, look for bush-type watermelons whose vines are compact and take up little space.

How to Plant & Grow—Watermelons like it hot and need warm soil to develop. They may develop root or stem rot if weather is cool and wet. Watermelons resent root disturbance, and it is best to sow them directly in the garden where you want them to grow.

Care & Problems—Cucumber beetles can damage the leaves and scar the stems. Use an organic insecticide to eliminate the beetles, or cover the plants with cloth row covers as soon as they emerge. When flowers appear, remove the row covers so that pollinators can reach the blooms.

Harvest & Best Selections—The most reliable way to check for ripeness is to look at the color of the bottom where the melon is lying on the ground. It should be a good yellow color, and the little curlicue where the melon attaches to the stem should be dry. The skin becomes dull, rough, and hardened sufficiently that you cannot cut into it with your fingernail. Popular varieties include 'Sugar Baby', 'Crimson Sweet', and 'Charleston Grey'.

ZUCCHINI
Cucurbita spp.

Why It's Special—Zucchini is the most prolific of all summer squash. A few hills will produce more than enough for a family of four and most of their friends and neighbors! Zucchini also makes a great choice for a child's garden because it is an almost guaranteed success.

How to Plant & Grow—Like all squash, zucchini likes it warm. Don't be in a hurry to plant your zucchini in the spring. Wait until the soil is comfortably warm to the touch. The easiest way to plant is to create a low mound (hill) and then plant three to five seeds about 6 inches apart in the top of the mound. Allow at least 5 feet of space per hill at maturity.

Care & Problems—Zucchini requires plenty of water while it is actively growing. Squash beetles can be a problem, as they can on all squash, and can be controlled with applications of an organic insecticide every two weeks from the time the seed germinates. Plants that suddenly collapse should be removed immediately to keep wilt diseases from passing from plant to plant. Do not compost diseased plants.

Harvest & Best Selections—One of the most common mistakes people make is leaving zucchini on the vine too long. Harvest when they are 6 to 8 inches long and not more than 1½ to 2 inches in diameter. This will keep the vines producing throughout the summer.

JANUARY

- January is the perfect time to plan the upcoming season's vegetable garden. In the warmest parts of the South, cool-season vegetables can be planted beginning in late January. Gardeners in cooler regions may need to get seed of tomatoes, peppers, eggplant, and so forth started soon, depending on where you live, to have transplants ready to go in the garden at the proper time.

- To make the most of your vegetable garden space, consider growing vining and sprawling plants, such as cucumbers, melons, pole beans, and indeterminate tomatoes, on trellises, nets, strings, or poles. These crops can be grown effectively in or on tomato cages made from concrete reinforcing wire, and the cold days of winter are the perfect time to make them, taking advantage of working in a garage or workshop during the coldest months of the year.

- In the warmest regions of the South, you may be able to grow spinach, lettuce, cabbage, broccoli, and other cool- or cold-season crops right through the winter. Most of us are not that fortunate, but we can make up for it with simple cloth or plastic row covers that will protect plants against winter's chill.

FEBRUARY

- When the soil can be worked, turn under the cover crops planted last fall. Till the soil to a depth of 8 to 12 inches. Never work the soil when it is wet—working wet soils destroys the structure and makes the soil hard, compacted, and unproductive.

- Tomatoes, peppers, and eggplants need six to eight weeks to grow into large enough transplants for planting in the garden. If you can plant outdoors in your area by early to mid-April, you will need to start seed indoors this month to have plants up to size and hardened off to go outdoors at the proper planting time. In cooler regions, you may not need to start seed until March.

- In warmer regions of the South, gardeners can plant hardened-off vegetable transplants of broccoli, cabbage, and cauliflower this month. Potatoes can be planted near the end of the month, as can the seed of cool-weather crops like lettuce, spinach, peas, and others. Onion sets and leek transplants can be set out at the end of the month.

MARCH

- If you are serious about growing vegetables, plan to start a journal this month. In it, document your observations, thoughts, and plans for your vegetable garden. List the seed of the vegetables you've sown indoors and what, if any, you have planted outdoors. Include the names of seed companies, plant name, variety, planting date, and harvest date. Also record daily temperature highs and lows, as well as any major deviations in the weather pattern—extreme heat for the season or exceptionally cold lows.

- Basil, chives, parsley, summer savory, and sweet marjoram can be started indoors this month for planting as companions into the vegetable garden this summer. To encourage parsley seeds to sprout more rapidly, soften the seeds by soaking them overnight in warm water.

- In the Deep South, after the last freeze, set out eggplant, onion, pepper, and tomato plants. Sow seeds of butter beans (lima beans), pole beans, snap beans, sweet corn, summer squash, and watermelon directly in the garden where you want them to grow.

- In the Upper and Mid-South, plant asparagus crowns before new growth emerges from the buds. Set out transplants of broccoli, cabbage, and cauliflower as well, up to four weeks before the last spring freeze. Sow seeds of carrots, lettuce (leaf and head), garden peas, mustard, radishes, rutabaga, and spinach. Mountain gardeners can sow mustard, garden peas, radishes, spinach, and turnips.

APRIL

- In the Deep South, after the last freeze, sow all types of beans, corn, cucumbers, and Southern peas. Avoid planting okra seeds too early. The soil temperature should be above 75 degrees; soak okra seed overnight before planting in the garden.

- Plant determinate, bush-type tomatoes for canning or preserving so the fruit will ripen all at once, all within a week or two of each other. This keeps you from having to string canning out over an entire season. For vine-ripened tomatoes, plant indeterminate tomatoes that have an extended fruiting period; they vine, flower, and fruit all the way up to the first frost.

- To keep the cauliflower curds pure white, loosely tie the long outside leaves onto the flat, open head when it is 1 to 2 inches across. Hold the leaves together with a rubber band until the head is ready for harvesting. This process is called blanching.

- Root crops must be thinned, no matter how ruthless this practice seems. If you don't, their roots won't develop well and tops will get so full and lush that plants may choke each other out. Thin beets, carrots, onions, Swiss chard, and turnips so you can get three fingers between individual plants.

MAY

- Sow warm-weather vegetables, such as beans, cucumber, okra, and Southern peas in the Upper and Mid-South this month. Extend your sweet corn harvest by planting successive crops when the previous crop has three to four leaves, or plant early-, mid-, and late-maturing varieties all at the same time.

- Harvest broccoli when the florets are still tight and green. After harvesting the main head, broccoli will put out smaller-sized heads from the side shoots. Pick cauliflower before the curds begin to separate, and cabbage before it bolts (blooms). Pick green, sugar snap, and snow peas every couple of days to keep more coming.

- Water deeply, keeping the leaves of your vegetables dry. This keeps roots working their way deep into the soil in search of water and nutrients, making them tougher and better able to survive dry periods during the coming summer. Invest in soaker hoses or drip irrigation.

- Be on the lookout for pest and disease problems in your vegetables as summer approaches. Aphids are very active this time of year and Japanese beetles will be hatching in just a few weeks. Consult your local garden center or your County Extension Service for effective and safe methods of control.

JUNE

- If you've planted more than you can use (don't worry, we all do it!), share your bountiful harvests with friends and neighbors. What about your community? Make plans to share your excess vegetables with your community soup kitchen or food bank.

- In the Upper South, gardeners still have time to plant summer crops such as beans, cucumbers, okra, pumpkins, Southern peas, squash, and a last planting of sweet corn. Also, set out transplants of pepper, tomatoes, and sweet potato slips. This may seem late, but there is no point in planting them before the soil is thoroughly warm. They will just sit there and, if the soil is cold and wet, may rot.

- In the Deep South, you may be harvesting beans, cucumbers, okra, and squash beginning this month. These crops mature very quickly and will need to be checked daily and harvested regularly to keep the plants producing. Pick cucumbers when the fruits are small and before they turn yellow.

JULY

- Start planning your fall garden. Choose early-maturing vegetables when you can. Sow beans, cucumbers, or even short-season corn. They will replace those early vegetables you harvested this month and will be ready to pick before freezing weather comes.

- Gardeners in the Upper and Mid-South can start seeds of Brussels sprouts, broccoli, cabbage, and cauliflower for the fall garden. Sow seed indoors or in a partly shaded area outdoors, in pots where plants can grow until they are large enough to harden off and plant in the garden.

- Sow pumpkins now for a perfect crop at Halloween.

- Be ready to water the vegetable garden this month. Vegetables will need a minimum of 1 inch of water, possibly more if the summer is especially hot, sunny, and dry.

- Help to restore and replenish the life in your soil before planting your fall crops by working in fresh compost or manure. Do not fertilize drought-stressed plants. Wait until after watering or rainfall and the plants' leaves have dried off to fertilize or you risk burning their roots.

AUGUST

- As you update your garden journal, note the vegetables and herbs that didn't live up to expectations and those that exceeded them. Make a note of insect and disease problems. In your plans for next year's garden, focus on varieties that performed well for you or that you have noticed did well in other gardens.

- Garlic can be planted as early as the end of August for a harvest early next summer. If temperatures are still extremely hot, you can wait until September or even October, and the garlic will have plenty of time to root out and get established before winter.

- In the Upper and Mid-South, plant greens, such as kale, mustard, and turnips in intervals now and next month to lengthen the harvest season.

- Hardy crops like cabbage, cauliflower, and collards can be planted now. Count back from your area's average first frost date the number of days the particular variety requires to mature; plant at the appropriate time. If your first average frost date is October 31 and your crop needs 60 days to mature, you will need to plant approximately August 31 to beat the frost in an average year.

Garlic cloves should be planted at the end of the growing season for harvest during the next summer.

SEPTEMBER

- September is a good month to begin tidying up the garden and taking steps to build up the soil for next spring. Certain insects and diseases overwinter in plant debris. Clean up garden debris and add it to the compost pile as you go. Remember to keep a balance between brown, dry material and green material in your compost pile so it will decompose quickly.

- Cover crops or "green manures" are planted in autumn, grow throughout the winter, and are turned under in the spring to improve soil fertility and structure. Try cover cropping for a few years and see the incredible difference in the quality and texture of your soil.

- In much of the South, short-term crops like beets, carrots, kale, lettuce, spinach, turnips, and radishes can still be planted for fall (and in some cases, winter) harvest.

- Dig sweet potatoes before frost, being careful to avoid bruises and scrapes. Cure them for two or three weeks in the warmest room in the house to toughen the skin. Store them where it is cool and dark. If any get knicked or bruised while digging, go ahead and cook them. They won't store well at all if they have been cut or bruised.

OCTOBER

- If you haven't planted garlic yet, get it in the ground right away. It will need a few weeks in warm soil to get rooted before cold weather arrives. Garlic is very hardy and will live right through winter's cold weather, growing rapidly in spring and forming bulbs underground for harvest next summer.

- Extend the gardening season well into the winter in colder regions by building cold frames that can be placed in the garden in winter. Lettuce, radish, and spinach can all be grown in cold frames and in all but the very coldest parts of the South will give you fresh greens all winter long.

- In warmer areas, onions can also be planted now. Be sure to plant short-day varieties that will thrive in the shorter days of winter with less daylight. Onions grow best in loamy or sandy soils where their bulbs can expand, becoming large and round. Compacted clay soils are less suitable.

- Harvest gourds, pumpkins, and winter squash after the first or second light frost. To store pumpkins, pick only solid, mature pumpkins of a deep orange color. Use the same philosophy when harvesting winter squash. Be sure they are as mature as possible to increase their winter shelf life.

NOVEMBER

- Drain and store water hoses to extend their lives and bring in your rain gauge to avoid freeze damage or breakage. Protect your investment in garden tools by cleaning them thoroughly and oiling their blades and other metal parts with used motor oil (old lawn mower oil is perfect) to protect them from moisture and rust. Repair or replace broken tools.

- It may seem like an odd suggestion, but plan now for spring planting. As soon as seed flats and pots are emptied of fall transplants, wash and sterilize them using a 10 percent solution of household bleach in water and dry them thoroughly before storing for winter.

- A 4- to 6-inch mulch of clean wheat straw, hay, or shredded leaves over the tops of carrots, turnips, and other root vegetables will help protect against freezing. Throughout the South, you can leave these crops in the ground all winter long and dig them as you need them. Carrots will become amazingly sweet when exposed to cold winter weather.

DECEMBER

- Finish organizing all of your journal notes from your gardening year. Garden journals are valuable tools as you begin planning for next year's vegetable garden. Your notes will remind you of what your biggest successes were, as well as those vegetables you might want to consider replacing with varieties that will perform better in your location.

- If you have added cold frames to your garden, you can continue sowing greens like lettuce and spinach right through the winter months. A good cold frame will offer plenty of protection, even during the coldest weather, and it is a real treat to have fresh, homegrown greens during the winter months.

- Think about your gardening Christmas list. Are there new tools you would like to have to make life in the garden a little easier next season? Do you have a favorite local nursery or garden center or a favorite mail order or online nursery where you like to buy seeds, transplants, fertilizers, and such? Ask for gift certificates for your favorite places to shop!

GROUNDCOVERS
for the South

Almost any low-growing plant has the potential to be a groundcover, but for gardeners it usually means a plant that has the ability to spread on its own and cover the soil's surface. Groundcovers can have several means of spreading. Some may spread underground by modified roots or stems, while others may spread across the surface of the soil by the same methods. Still others may send out short runners aboveground with a baby plant attached to the end. When that baby plant lands on the soil a few inches away from the mother plant, it roots and forms a new plant, which then does the same. Plants that don't spread in the traditional way can also be used as groundcovers when planted *en masse*. Lenten roses (*Helleborus* species, included in the Perennials chapter), for instance, are strictly clump forming, but will reseed themselves into large, groundcovering masses even though they lack runners of any kind.

Although we don't think of them as ground-covers, lawns are probably the most prevalent groundcover in the country. They do exactly what we expect of an ornamental groundcover by protecting the soil from erosion, providing a green backdrop for the rest of our landscape, and creating open, uncluttered areas where our eyes and minds can occasionally stop and rest. Ornamental groundcovers can be used in exactly the same way and with the same effect.

WHY PLANT GROUNDCOVERS?

Groundcovers have many uses in the landscape and garden, and the best types perform multiple functions. They are the workhorses of the landscape. In the best planned landscapes and gardens, groundcovers pick up where the lawn leaves off. After lawns, they create the lowest level of understory planting and provide "feet" to all of the other trees, shrubs, and flowering plants in your yard. They create boundaries between mowed lawns and landscaped beds, defining edges and filling voids that might otherwise be left to mulch. Too often, they are seen as utilitarian and unimportant—simply as space fillers instead of as an important part of the overall picture.

Groundcovers do provide a function and service in the landscape beyond aesthetics. They can be used to slow water movement across the soil's surface, or deep-rooted types may help to anchor the soil on steep slopes or where strong winds prevail. Many will choke out unwanted weeds, reducing maintenance. Some, like St. John's wort, creeping phlox, and moss phlox provide spectacular displays of flowers at certain times of the year, while others provide year-round interest with their evergreen leaves. Many groundcovers make great cover for favorite bulbs like crocus, daffodils, Spanish bluebells, and many others. When planted among groundcovers, the bulbs' foliage can be allowed to die naturally, feeding and building the bulbs' size and quantity for the following year without being obtrusive and unattractive.

GROUNDCOVERS INSTEAD OF LAWNS

What about replacing your lawn with a groundcover? In theory, replacing lawns with groundcovers is a great idea and many gardeners have done it with resounding success. There are tradeoffs, though. Most groundcovers will not have the highly manicured, "formal" appearance of what a lawn should be in the American homeowner's mind. Trading lawns for groundcovers means trading formality for informality and manicured for neat, but naturalistic effect. Aside from appearance, there is the issue of traffic. Almost no groundcover will take the abuse that we give our lawns—heavy foot traffic during a Fourth of July barbecue, neighborhood kids playing soccer, or the repairman driving his truck to the back of the house to fix a leaking gutter. Lawns will recover from this type of abuse in a matter of days or maybe a few weeks, at most. Groundcovers, depending on their growth habit and speed, may take weeks, months, or, in severe cases, more than a year to recover.

On the other hand, the average American homeowner pours more time, money, water, and chemicals into maintaining a perfect lawn than they do any other part of their landscape. Groundcovers can eliminate a large part of that when chosen wisely and maintained well. Once established, a well-chosen groundcover requires little supplemental irrigation and feeding, only occasional maintenance (and certainly not weekly or twice-weekly mowing!), and little in the way of spraying for insects and disease. Groundcovers are more costly to establish on the front end than lawns, but the long-term benefits and reduced maintenance will more than make up for the investment.

GROUNDCOVERS FOR PROBLEM AREAS

Sometimes, function takes precedence over beauty. A steep bank requires a deeply rooted groundcover to stabilize the soil and keep it from washing away. A street curb needs a tough plant that will tolerate occasional foot traffic, the pollution from car exhaust, and the garbage man rolling the trash and recycling cans back and forth through it each week on collection day. Perhaps a shallow drainage swale between your property and the neighbors' carries water after a heavy rain, but otherwise remains relatively dry. In these cases, the more aggressive a groundcover is the more abuse it will take and the better it may be for helping to stabilize areas with potential erosion or other problems.

A WORD ON BEHAVIOR

Some gardeners are afraid of groundcovers because they think of them as being aggressive thugs that will take over the garden, running amok through the beds, choking out neighboring and less vigorous plants or, in the case of vining groundcovers, climbing walls, buildings, and trees. This is a legitimate concern. Some groundcovers do have the ability to be all of these things and more. English ivy, purple wintercreeper, snow-on-the-mountain, dwarf bamboo, and many others can be aggressive and problematic. Choosing wisely, then, becomes even more important. In many cases, unfettered aggression is exactly what a site requires to keep it from eroding, and this is a primary, practical function of many groundcovers. Aesthetics are a different choice. Keep this firmly in mind as you choose which groundcovers to include in your landscape and groundcovers will become some of your best, maintenance-reducing friends.

St. John's wort is native to the Southeast United States and provides bright yellow flowers in the early summer.

AJUGA
Ajuga reptans

Why It's Special—Ajuga provides colorful foliage in shades of dark, bronzy green to purple that forms the perfect groundcover under larger perennials like hostas, Solomon's seal, ferns, and other shade-loving plants. In early spring, usually when the tulips and daffodils are in bloom, its spires of bright blue flowers are laden with honeybees and other beneficial pollinators.

How to Plant & Grow—Ajuga may be found by the flat in many garden centers in small pots or even six-packs that allow gardeners to buy in quantity and get some immediate bang for their buck. In the South, ajuga is particularly easy to establish during the warm days and cool nights of autumn. Moisture in the summertime is essential to keep it looking its best.

Care & Problems—If you notice patches of ajuga suddenly turning brown and dying, it may be infected by a fungus called Rhizoctonia. Infected areas can be raked clean and will usually fill back in on their own in a short period of time, or you can dig small plugs from healthy areas and replant. Particularly bad outbreaks can be treated with copper fungicide.

Foliage Color—Purple, bronze, variegated

Flowers—Blue, in spring

Hardiness—Zones 4b to 9a

Texture—Medium

Water Needs—Evenly moist soil is best

ASIAN JASMINE
Trachelospermum asiaticum

Why It's Special—A close cousin to the flowering Confederate jasmine vine that has become a staple in many Southern gardens, Asian jasmine is better suited to life as a groundcover. Its evergreen leaves and creeping stems form a dense mat that is almost impervious to weeds. Beautiful variegated forms bear leaves in shades of copper, gold, orange, pink, and white.

How to Plant & Grow—Asian jasmine can be planted in spring, summer, or fall and is usually found in sizes ranging from 4-inch to 1-gallon pots. Smaller plants can be planted 2 feet on center or larger plants up to 3 feet on center and will begin filling in nicely with just one or two seasons' growth. Once established, edging beds a few times each year will keep runners in check.

Care & Problems—Once established, Asian jasmine is a tough and forgiving groundcover. It does not attach itself to tree trunks, walls, or other surfaces, but may grow upward through the branches of shrubs or low-branched trees. It may be tender and require protection north of Zone 7.

Foliage Color—Dark green, with gold, orange, cream, white, or pink variegation

Flowers—White and fragrant, borne in early spring

Hardiness—Zones 7 to 11

Texture—Fine

Water Needs—Somewhat drought tolerant, once established

CAST-IRON PLANT
Aspidistra elatior

Why It's Special—For tough places in deep shade, the name cast-iron plant tells you almost everything you need to know about this plant. Although it is taller than what most of us might consider a typical "groundcover"—it certainly doesn't hug the ground—it does spread by underground rhizomes and forms dense masses of foliage in the most challenging parts of the yard. Variegated forms can add even further interest, and it is very competitive with tree roots.

How to Plant & Grow—Cast-iron plant can be planted anytime that it is actively growing, from spring through fall. Keep the soil moist until plants are established, and then they will be able to tolerate nearly anything Mother Nature dishes out. Occasional water during drought will keep plants from looking bedraggled.

Care & Problems—Fertilize with a slow-release fertilizer in early spring, just before new growth begins. If large stands become disheveled-looking, they can be cut to the ground in early spring for complete rejuvenation.

Foliage Color—Green or variegated

Flowers—Cream to maroon, at ground level

Hardiness—Zones 7a to 10

Texture—Bold

Water Needs—Drought tolerant, once established

CHINESE GINGER
Asarum splendens

Why It's Special—Chinese ginger is an attractive and well-behaved evergreen groundcover. Its heart-shaped leaves are deep green, often heavily and beautifully marked with silver. It spreads slowly by underground runners, forming a dense, evergreen mat. The curious flowers appear at ground level, under the leaves, in early spring and are pollinated by ants and other crawling insects.

How to Plant & Grow—Chinese ginger is typically available in 4-inch or 1-gallon pots and should be planted 18 inches on center for smaller plants or 24 inches on center for larger specimens. It will be lush and beautiful in soil that is well amended with compost and well drained. Irrigation during times of drought will keep it looking its best. Old foliage typically dies unnoticed and does not require cutting back or removal.

Care & Problems—Voles may be a problem in winters when food is scarce. Often, they don't actually eat the ginger itself, but damage it with their burrowing since its rhizomes are just under the soil surface. Too much sun, especially in summer, may burn the leaves or cause them to turn a sickly yellow-green.

Foliage Color—Deep green, marked in silver

Flowers—Maroon-purple, under the leaves

Hardiness—Zones 6 to 9

Texture—Medium

Water Needs—Moist to slightly dry

CREEPING JENNY
Lysimachia nummularia 'Aurea'

Why It's Special—For brightening up the ground under a high tree canopy or along a partly shaded walkway, the golden form of creeping Jenny is like a ray of sunshine. Forming impenetrable mats of stems and leaves. It will wind and creep its way around and through larger plants and is especially effective when paired with darker-leaved plants like coral bells, ajuga, or black mondo grass.

How to Plant & Grow—Creeping Jenny is best planted in early spring in rich, evenly moist soil. While it can be quite drought tolerant once established, leaves may turn brown around the edges if it gets too dry. Part sun to part shade will suit it best, although without *some* sun, its golden color may be less intense. It makes an excellent "spiller" for the edges of large pots and containers.

Care & Problems—This easy-to-grow plant has few problems. Its one need is that it does need some moisture to look its best. When grown between stepping-stones or as a lawn substitute, it may need an occasional grooming or mowing to tidy it up and rejuvenate it.

Foliage Color—Golden yellow to chartreuse

Flowers—Yellow, but insignificant

Hardiness—Zones 3 to 9

Texture—Fine

Water Needs—Slightly moist to wet

CREEPING JUNIPER
Juniperus horizontalis

Why It's Special—If a tough and resilient groundcover is what you need for a slope or other full sun area of the yard, creeping juniper fits the bill. Foliage color can range from deep green to a lighter, minty green to steely blue, and some varieties will take on a purplish hue when temperatures turn cold. Height can range from 3 inches to 18 inches, depending on the variety.

How to Plant & Grow—Creeping juniper is best planted in early spring or in autumn. Spring-planted plants will need occasional watering during their first summer. Fall planting allows them to take advantage of late autumn and winter moisture. Once established, it will be one of the toughest, most forgiving groundcovers you can grow.

Care & Problems—One of the biggest challenges with creeping junipers is keeping invasive grasses, like Bermudagrass, from creeping in and taking over. If this happens, there are some selective herbicides that can be used on Bermudagrass without harming your junipers, but you need to consult a local garden center professional to be certain you are buying the right product.

Foliage Color—Deep green to blue

Flowers—None significant

Hardiness—Zones 3a to Zone 9a

Texture—Fine

Water Needs—Drought tolerant, once established

CREEPING PHLOX
Phlox stolonifera

Why It's Special—Creeping phlox is an often overlooked wildflower that forms a superb groundcover in the woodland garden. Delicate and noninvasive, it will blend and mix well with other shrubs, perennials, and wildflowers. Small heads of flowers rise above the flat, ground-hugging leaves in early spring, providing a spectacular show for about a month.

How to Plant & Grow—Creeping phlox prefers loose, woodland soil. Its roots are shallow and heavy compaction will not suit it long term. It is generally found in bloom in 4-inch or 1-gallon pots in the spring with other cultivated wildflowers. It is best for natural gardens where it can show off in the spring and become a part of the woodland backdrop for the year.

Care & Problems—Creeping phlox is relatively care-free, once established. It has a very shallow root system so evenly moist soil or regular irrigation will suit it best. Its biggest enemies are voles, chipmunks, and squirrels that insist on digging through and uprooting it. Severe drought may cause sections to die out, but they will rebound over time.

Foliage Color—Green

Flowers—Light blue, lavender, pink, white

Hardiness—Zones 5 to 8

Texture—Fine

Water Needs—Evenly moist

HARDY VERBENA
Verbena x hybrida

Why It's Special—The semi-evergreen verbenas have risen to stardom as flowering groundcovers since the introduction of 'Homestead Purple' by Dr. Allan Armitage of the University of Georgia. Today, these hardy, heat- and humidity-loving perennial groundcovers come in a wide range of varieties and colors. They also attract beneficial pollinators and other insects.

How to Plant & Grow—Plant hybrid verbena from early spring through early summer. Verbena likes a warm, sunny location where it will spread and flower continuously. While good drainage is important, especially in winter, it is also important to keep the plant watered after planting until well established. Deadheading is required to keep plants blooming.

Care & Problems—Although not truly evergreen, it is helpful to leave the old stems and leaves intact through the winter for protection. Plants can be cut back in early spring and will resprout and grow quickly from the base when warm weather returns. Spider mites can be a problem in hot, dry conditions and are best treated with highly refined horticultural oil sprays.

Foliage Color—Deep green, semi-evergreen

Flower Color—Purple, lavender, pink, red, white

Hardiness—Zones 6a (with protection) to 9b

Texture—Fine

Water Needs—Drought tolerant

JAPANESE ARDISIA
Ardisia japonica

Why It's Special—Japanese ardisia, or marlberry, is an unusual and attractive evergreen groundcover whose shiny, leathery, dark green leaves are heavily scalloped around the edges. In spring, ½-inch white flowers appear in small clusters followed by red fruit that persists from autumn into winter. While not commonly grown in the South, impressive stands are occasionally found; the plant deserves to be more widely grown.

How to Plant & Grow—Japanese ardisia is a woodland plant and so prefers the kind of loose, rich soil found on the woodland floor. It fares best in shady areas where larger, overhead plants help to cool the soil in summer, where it will grow slowly into dense mats, requiring no cutting back or other maintenance. It must have moisture.

Care & Problems—Ardisia is not drought tolerant and will quickly decline if planted in the far reaches of the woodland and forgotten about. Regular irrigation, especially during the hot and dry summer months, is highly beneficial. Ardisia is not tolerant of foot traffic, so is not suited to planting between steppingstones or in areas where gardeners or pets may wander.

Foliage Color—Dark green

Flowers—White

Hardiness—Zones 7 to 9

Texture—Medium

Water Needs—Evenly moist

LILY-OF-THE-VALLEY
Convallaria majalis

Why It's Special—Lily-of-the-valley is one of the plants that many of us remember from our childhoods thanks to its fragrant white bells perfuming the air in spring. Many gardeners consider it difficult to grow in the South, but in Zones 6 and 7, I have found it will thrive. One especially attractive form, 'Fernwood's Golden Slippers', emerges with golden yellow leaves in spring before turning green for the summer and thrives even into Zone 8 in the Raleigh, North Carolina, area.

How to Plant & Grow—Lily-of-the-valley is frequently available by the flat, in pots as small as 2 inches, so that it can be planted out on 12-inch centers to grow and fill in. It can be slow and may take a season or two to spread, so planting closer is more effective than spacing far apart. While it is tolerant of poor soil and can be amazing drought tolerant once fully established, richer soils that are slightly to evenly moist will encourage faster growth and more profuse flowering.

Care & Problems—It's care-free, once established; its only problem is that most varieties are not especially heat tolerant.

Foliage Color—Green, with golden and variegated forms available

Flowers—White, occasionally pale pink

Hardiness—Zones 2 to 7

Texture—Medium

Water Needs—Moderate, although drought tolerant once established

LIRIOPE
Liriope muscari

Why It's Special—If "indestructible" is what you need in a groundcover, look no further. Some would argue that liriope, or monkey grass, is too overplanted to even be recommended, but all things have a reason and the reason for monkey grass is that it is one of the lowest maintenance groundcovers in existence. Low-growing, evergreen, and slowly spreading, it is a true workhorse in the landscape.

How to Plant & Grow—Liriope can be planted anytime the ground is not frozen. It will thrive in almost any soil conditions, but planted in good, well-amended garden soil, plants will respond with dramatic results. Their vigorous root systems are often potbound, so scoring the rootball with a knife will help roots branch out into the surrounding soil.

Care & Problems—In late winter, before new spring growth emerges, remove old foliage down to within 3 inches of the ground. Within a few weeks, new growth will sprout and plants will look neat and tidy. Voles may do occasional damage in winter as they seek out food and shelter.

Foliage Color—Deep green or variegated yellow-white

Bloom Color—Purple or white

Hardiness—Zones 6a to 9b

Texture—Fine

Water Needs—Moderate, but drought tolerant once established

MONDO GRASS
Ophiopogon japonicus

Why It's Special—Mondo grass is similar to the ever-popular liriope, or monkey grass, but is generally finer and more grass-like in texture. There are numerous varieties available that offer many more options in height, foliage color, and texture. For impact in a part shade area, consider *Ophiopogon planiscapus* 'Nigrescens', with almost solid black foliage.

How to Plant & Grow—Mondo grass is best planted in spring or summer, giving it ample time to settle in before winter. It prefers moist, well-amended soil in part sun to full shade. Most selections will tolerate full sun if well irrigated, but may show some sunburn or tip burn during the hottest and driest months of the year.

Care & Problems—Once established, mondo grass is fairly care-free. Taller varieties can be cut back in late winter, the same as for liriope, but the dwarf varieties, which may reach only 1 to 2 inches tall, require almost no maintenance at all. Voles can occasionally be a problem. Consult your local garden centers for methods of control.

Foliage Color—Dark green, green and white, black

Flower Color—Lavender-purple

Hardiness—Zones 6b to 9b

Texture—Fine to very fine

Water Needs—Moderate, not as drought tolerant as liriope

MOSS PHLOX
Phlox subulata

Why It's Special—Moss phlox is also called "creeping phlox" like its cousin, *Phlox stolonifera*. While they are both low growing and their blooms are similar in shape and color, the similarities end there. Moss phlox prefers full sun and while it doesn't mind moisture, good drainage is a must. Growing only 4 to 6 inches tall, it flowers profusely for about one month in early spring and its tiny, lightly prickly leaves form an attractive evergreen groundcover for the remainder of the year. It's excellent on steep, sunny slopes and banks.

How to Plant & Grow—Moss phlox is usually found in garden centers in early spring just as it begins to bloom. Buy it when you find it, as many places won't stock it once its flowering season is over. Planting in early spring will ensure that spring rains get it well established before the heat of summer. Once established, it is extremely drought tolerant.

Care & Problems—Voles can occasionally be a problem as they tunnel through patches eating stems and roots along the way. Otherwise, moss phlox is nearly problem-free.

Foliage Color—Green

Flowers—Light blue, pink, white

Hardiness—Zones 3 to 9

Texture—Very fine

Water Needs—Moderate, but drought tolerant once established

PACHYSANDRA
Pachysandra terminalis

Why It's Special—Pachysandra is one of the finest of all shade-loving evergreen groundcovers with veined, oval leaves, 2 to 4 inches in length and growing in whorled clusters at the top of upright stems. It will thrive in the shade of oaks and pine where grass is nearly impossible to grow and will even tolerate the dense shade and root competition of Southern magnolia.

How to Plant & Grow—For best results, set out potted pachysandra in spring or early fall, avoiding the hottest and driest months of the summer. Partial to full shade in rich, moist, organically enriched soils suit it best. A 1-inch layer of mulch over the soil after planting will help to conserve moisture and will encourage rapid growth of stolons and fast coverage.

Care & Problems—Pachysandra is a neat and tidy groundcover whose only maintenance need is occasional edging to keep it from creeping out of bounds. Occasionally, dead circular patches occur on the leaves—a disease known as *Volutella*. This disease is most prevalent where pachysandra is under stress from too much sun.

Foliage Color—Deep, lustrous green

Bloom Color—White

Hardiness—Zones 5b to 8b

Texture—Medium

Water Needs—Moderate

ST. JOHN'S WORT
Hypericum calycinum

Why It's Special—Several species of St. John's wort are native to the southeastern United States. Most are shrubby in habit, but a few, like *Hypericum calycinum*, make excellent groundcovers. This species is semi-evergreen and in very cold years may shed its leaves. However, in most years it will retain half or more of its foliage through the winter. Bright, cheerful yellow flowers appear profusely in early summer and sporadically into autumn.

How to Plant & Grow—St. John's wort is best planted in spring or early summer, taking care to keep it watered well through its first growing season. Once established, most species are quite tough and will even grow in thin, rocky soils. Fertilize in early spring as new growth begins.

Care & Problems—In wet soil or under heavy irrigation, a variety of stem and root diseases can be problems. Often, these diseases spread quickly and are difficult to control. Good drainage is essential and, once established, additional water is unnecessary unless you're experiencing drought conditions. Flowering occurs on new growth, and groundcover types can be trimmed to within 2 to 3 inches of the soil in early spring.

Foliage Color—Olive green

Bloom Color—Bright yellow

Hardiness—Zones 5a to 9

Texture—Medium

Water Needs—Dry to moderate, well-drained

JANUARY

- As the gardening catalogs arrive this month, scan them for new and unique groundcovers that might make good additions to your garden or landscape. Do you have troublesome areas that might be improved by the addition of a tough groundcover? Could your garden beds benefit from another layer of plants to add more interest?

- In the Deep South and most coastal areas, groundcovers can be planted as long as the soil can be worked. While the tops of the plants may be dormant, roots are growing actively and can use winter's moisture to get established before summer arrives.

- Water fall-planted groundcovers, especially evergreen types, if the soil is dry. Winter desiccation can be very detrimental to newly planted groundcovers.

- As groundcovers are settling in, apply a 1-inch layer of mulch to help suppress weeds. Winter weeds are actively growing now and can quickly take over newly planted beds.

FEBRUARY

- For heavily shaded areas where grass won't grow, shade-loving groundcovers are an excellent alternative. Pachysandra and Japanese ardisia are especially shade tolerant.

- Keep an eye on water needs this month, especially for evergreen groundcovers. Evergreen plants continue to lose water through their leaves, even when it's cold outside, and may need water if rain or snowfall doesn't occur.

- Fertilize groundcovers just as they begin growing. In warmer areas, February is a good month to do this, but in cooler areas, you'll need to wait until March. A soil test can help determine exactly what your fertilizer needs are.

- Cut liriope, or monkey grass, back to within 3 to 4 inches of the ground using a string trimmer or, for large areas, use a push mower *if* it will raise to a height of at least 3 inches. Otherwise, you may cut into the crowns of the plants.

MARCH

- When considering groundcovers to add to your landscape, look at options that have more than one attribute. Having evergreen foliage is always an advantage, but being able to enjoy flowers in spring or summer or berries in autumn adds another season of interest.

- For much of the South, gardening and planting season is off to a good start now and planting can begin in earnest. Container-grown groundcovers can be planted this month. Look for healthy, robust plants that look fresh and new and not like they were left over from last fall.

- If you haven't cut your liriope yet, your window of time is closing very quickly. If you don't get it done by early March, you run the risk of cutting off new growth as it begins to sprout. This will leave brown tips on the new growth, which won't hurt the plants but isn't very attractive.

APRIL

- For design purposes, consider groundcovers to help unify your home and landscape. From a distance, groundcovers will provide "feet" for the rest of your landscaping and give a polished, finished look to your design.

- April is prime planting season throughout most of the South. Garden centers are fully stocked and plants are vigorous and fresh from the grower. Soil and air temperatures have warmed, and plants are actively growing and will establish quickly.

- Continue to keep weeds under control in groundcover beds that have not filled in completely. Groundcovers are in their most active growth phase now and competition from weeds will be detrimental.

- Fertilizing your groundcovers is beneficial while they are in the most active stage of their growth. Organic fertilizers release their nutrients slowly over a period of several weeks when the plants need them the most.

MAY

- Groundcovers make excellent alternatives to lawns in areas where there is too much shade for grass to be successful. Replacing lawn with groundcover in these areas will reduce maintenance.

- If you have borders of liriope that are beginning to widen and encroach on the other plants, now is the perfect time to divide and replant to get it back "in-bounds." Simply use a sturdy shovel to dig the unwanted liriope, narrowing the band or border back to a desirable width.

- Is a little extra mulch needed in groundcover beds that haven't filled in completely yet? Remember, not more than 1 inch of mulch so that groundcovers can spread, but summer weeds are germinating quickly now and it won't take long for them to get out of hand.

- Leaf and stem blight can be a serious problem on pachysandra, especially if it's planted in too much sun. Stem blight will be visible as blackened, sunken areas on the stems and leaf blight is visible as sunken brown areas that often have a bulls-eye pattern. In areas where you continue to have problems, it may be wise to consider an alternative that is more sun tolerant.

JUNE

- Keep an eye out for moles in newly planted groundcover beds. Moles love to dig through soft, freshly prepared soil and may push plants out of the ground if they haven't fully rooted yet. Check with your local garden center for best control methods.

Pachysandra grows well in the shade.

- Apply water as needed to keep newly planted groundcovers from wilting. It will only take a few weeks to get them established now that the soil and weather is consistently warm.

- Instead of using shredded bark or hardwood mulch on your groundcover beds, consider using "soil conditioner" instead. Shredded mulch packs down tightly, making it difficult for groundcovers to spread. Soil conditioner will remain loose while still suppressing weeds.

- Keep an eye out for crown rot in beds of ajuga and remove any infected plants. Bare patches will fill in quickly on their own.

JULY

- If you're planning a vacation and don't have automatic irrigation, consider buying battery-powered timers for outdoor faucets and set up hoses and sprinklers to do your watering while you're away. Timers are relatively inexpensive, will last for several years if well taken care of, and are a great insurance policy against losing plants to drought without you there to water.

- Fast-growing summer weeds seem to appear overnight. Most are easy to pull when they are small, but can become real problems if allowed to become established. Keep beds as clean as possible until groundcovers have become dense enough to control most of the weeds on their own.

- Aphids, spider mites, and Japanese beetles are very active this month. Most ornamental grasses are relatively pest free, but some groundcovers can occasionally be attacked. Consult your local garden center for advice if you find yourself with an insect infestation.

AUGUST

- August is a stressful month for doing any new planting in the South. Waiting until September, or even October, will be easier on you and on the plants. If you have plants that you feel would be better off in the ground, soak them thoroughly in a bucket of water before planting and again once they are in the ground.

- Watering will be at the top of your to-do list this month. Remember that you want to water deeply and less frequently to encourage roots to reach far into the soil searching for water and nutrients. This will greatly reduce how much you have to water in the future.

- August is a perfect time to walk your garden in the early morning, journal in hand, and make notes of which plants are performing well and which ones are not. Are there problem areas where groundcovers may be a good solution?

SEPTEMBER

- Fall is prime planting season for groundcovers, but September can still be hot and very dry. Be sure that you can water new plantings if it turns out that we don't get a break in the weather after Labor Day.

- If you have established areas of groundcover that have a few bare spots, try transplanting a few sprigs from the areas that are thick and lush into the bare spaces. Dig 3- to 4-inch plugs, making sure they have good roots attached. Keep them watered until established.

- Avoid fertilizing this month, as it could spur your plants into growth, and they may not have time to harden off before cold weather sets in later in the fall.

- Clean up fallen leaves in groundcover beds. They block light to evergreen groundcovers that are still working to store energy before winter comes and may harbor insects and diseases too.

OCTOBER

- If you have a slope whose steepness makes mowing dangerous, consider planting groundcovers as a low-maintenance solution. Their deep roots will also help to stabilize the ground. In full sun, creeping juniper is an excellent option. For shade, try liriope.

- Spring-flowering bulbs like daffodils, grape hyacinths, crocus, and others can be planted among your groundcovers in October. Early flowering varieties are best for this so they will have already flowered and their foliage will be dying down by the time the groundcovers begin growing actively later in spring.

Chickweed will be easier to eliminate if you start pulling it when it is small.

- In colder parts of the South, leaf removal begins in earnest this month. While leaves can break down and feed the soil, they can also harbor insects, fungal spores, and, most importantly, they provide a perfect cover for marauding voles! Compost your leaves into valuable leaf mold before adding it back to improve your soil.

NOVEMBER

- In warmer areas, container-grown groundcovers can still be planted. Winter rainfall will help to ensure they become well established by spring, and you will get a great first season's growth from them.

- Watch for mole activity. They do not hibernate and can do a great deal of damage to newly planted groundcover beds as they burrow through in search of underground worms and grubs. Be sure to replant any plants they may push out of the ground as soon as possible.

- Fall can be a dry time of year in the South. Be sure to keep up with watering throughout the garden for first-year plantings that are just getting well established.

- Winter and early spring weeds like chickweed, henbit, and dandelions will be germinating now. It is easiest to eradicate them while they are small. Be careful when hoeing or cultivating around shallow-rooted groundcovers or landscape plants.

DECEMBER

- Don't forget to water beds of groundcovers that were installed this fall. They probably haven't rooted completely yet and will need some supplemental water, especially if late fall and early winter are dry.

- If you haven't removed leaves from groundcover beds yet, it is essential to get it done as soon as possible. Fallen leaves can harbor insects and diseases that will overwinter and cause problems come spring. They also provide excellent cover for voles that can wreak havoc as they chew and burrow their way through groundcover beds.

- Continue pulling winter weeds. They grow amazingly fast during the cool days and nights of late fall and early winter.

- If you had scale or spider mite problems on any groundcovers this season, now is the time to spray with horticultural oil sprays to help smother the insects and their eggs that are overwintering for next year.

LAWN GRASSES
for the South

When it comes to climate, soil, and geographic features, there are few other regions of the country that are as diverse or as unpredictable as the South. In Tennessee, where I have lived and gardened for more than twenty years, you can drive from one end of the state to the other and experience the flat river basin of the Mississippi and the sweltering summertime heat and humidity of Memphis, the rolling hills of Middle Tennessee around Nashville, cross the high and flat Cumberland Plateau, enter the foothills around Knoxville, and be in the Great Smoky Mountains, all in the space of a six or seven hours and fewer than 500 miles.

Along with this array of geographic regions and features come just as many weather conditions and even more soil types. Most of the other Southern states are no different, and when you combine geography with the latitudes encompassed by "the South" and the vast difference in temperatures those latitudes bring, the climatic diversity is greater than almost anywhere else in the country. As you move from north to south, you'll find cold temperate regions in the mountains and progress all the way to subtropical climates along the Gulf Coast. It becomes a daunting task, then, to recommend any "best way" to be successful growing a lawn—or any plant, for that matter— since climates and microclimates are nearly as numerous as the plants that will thrive in them. With a little bit of research and some regionally accurate information, you can choose the best grass for your lawn wherever you live.

THE SOILS OF THE SOUTH

Soils in the South vary as greatly as the climate, much of it containing a high percentage of clay that increases the challenges of growing lawns successfully. There are some pockets where good, loamy soil exists, and along the east and southern coasts, sandy soils prevail. Your soil type has a lot to do with which turf grasses you will be able to grow successfully. One way to help determine what type of lawn you can grow well is by doing a basic assessment of your soil's texture. By doing a simple test right at home, you can determine whether or not you need to add amendments and the amount of watering that might be required, and establish what other regular maintenance tasks may be needed to keep your lawn happy and healthy. You'll find the instructions for performing this soil texture test near the end of this chapter.

The acidity or alkalinity of your soil, the measurement called pH, will also play a key role in what types of turf grasses will thrive in your area. There are a variety of home test kits for measuring soil pH, but many of these are not especially accurate, and there are too many factors that can come into play that may cause mistaken readings. It is best to take soil samples from several places in your yard and have them accurately tested through your local County Extension Service. In addition to pH, a professional soil test will often tell you what amounts of nutrients are already present in your soil, which nutrients (nitrogen, phosphorous, or potassium) should be applied, and in what quantities.

CHOOSING A HARDY LAWN GRASS

In addition to choosing a type of grass that will adapt to your soil conditions, you also have to choose one that is hardy where you live. Your lawn will be just as affected by the range of temperature extremes throughout the year as any of the rest of your landscape and garden plants. In addition to being cold hardy in your zone, you need to choose a lawn grass that is tolerant of the heat and humidity that prevails through most of the South. Tolerance of summertime heat and humidity is just as important as choosing a grass that will survive the winter.

In the Upper South, cool-season grasses tend to prevail. Homeowners like the fact that they remain green throughout the year and are willing to give them a little extra water in summer to keep them healthy and growing. That said, if the fact that they go dormant and turn brown in winter doesn't bother you, warm-season grasses like Bermudagrass and zoysia are well suited to colder zones, as well. Once you get into the deeper South in Zones 8 and warmer, cool-season grasses will begin to suffer during the extended heat and humidity of summer and warm-season lawn grasses are better choices.

WATER AND YOUR LAWN

The availability of water is just as much a determining factor in what type of turf to choose for your lawn as your soil type and the hardiness zone where you live. Whether you rely on natural rainfall or have an irrigation system, how much you can or are willing to water is the final determining factor in which type of lawn grass will thrive in your yard. In the broadest view, cool-season lawns will require considerably more water than warm-season grasses in most parts of the South. In order to survive the long, hot, and humid summer, they must be irrigated. Warm-season grasses tend to require less irrigation, so this may be an important consideration as you decide what kind of lawn you want.

If you do not have irrigation for your lawn—and many of us do not—another important factor to consider when choosing what kind of grass to plant is *when* the majority of precipitation occurs where you live. The amount of precipitation that occurs annually and when most of that precipitation occurs can vary greatly from state to state and region to region. In some areas, the most rainfall occurs in spring and early summer, while in other parts of the South, autumn and winter rainfall may be more prevalent. If you live where summers are typically dry, choosing a warm-season grass that is more drought tolerant may be a wiser choice for your lawn, while in cooler, mountain climates or in areas where summer rainfall is prevalent, cool-season grasses may thrive.

A WORD ON IRRIGATION

One of the most critical and costly mistakes when it comes to lawn care is improper watering. This is especially true for lawns with automatic irrigation systems, but 99 percent of the time it's not the fault of the system. It's the fault of the owner. The typical line of thinking is that we have spent all of this money on automatic irrigation and now we want to see it run. The truth of the matter is this: If you run your irrigation for a brief period of time every day or, in some cases even *twice* a day (yes, people do that), you are only saturating the uppermost surface of the soil. Roots only go where they have to in order to get water, so if all of the water is in the upper 2 inches of soil, so are the roots. Then, when dry weather comes you find yourself watering constantly and paying exorbitant water bills trying to keep your lawn alive. Whether you water by hand or by automated system, the rule to follow is "deep and infrequent." The type of grass doesn't matter. The deeper you water and the deeper the roots have to go in search of that water, the better off your lawn will be in the long run.

MAINTAINING YOUR SOUTHERN LAWN

Regular maintenance is a fact of life if you desire a lush, green, carpetlike lawn. Most gardeners already know that lawns require watering, fertilizing, and weed control, and they probably suspect there are other things they need to do as well. The easiest way to ensure that your lawn is getting what it needs, when it needs it, is to establish a regular schedule of watering, fertilizing, and pest control. As we become more conscientious about pouring chemicals into our soil, look for natural and organic fertilizers, as well as earth-friendly fertilizers, weed controls, insecticides, and disease treatments.

The experts at your local garden centers and your County Extension agents are invaluable resources in helping to determine the best time of year and the best products for various lawn maintenance needs. Fertilizing, pest and disease treatments, and weed control schedules for lawns will vary from region to region and from one type of grass to another, so it's best to consult an expert who can give advice based specifically on where you live and the type of lawn you are trying to maintain.

BERMUDAGRASS
Cynodon dactylon

Why It's Special—If a tough, fast-growing, and hardy turf grass that quickly forms a lush, green carpet is what you're looking for in a lawn, Bermudagrass may be your answer. Bermudagrass is one of the most adaptable of turf grasses, tolerating heat, humidity, and cold better than almost any other grass.

How to Plant & Grow—Bermudagrass can be planted several ways. It can be seeded, sprigged, or plugged with excellent results. Most commonly, 2-inch plugs are cut from sheets of sod, planted on 6- to 12-inch centers, and allowed to fill in during the course of the first season.

Care & Problems—Like many plants that are tough and adaptable, Bermudagrass is not without problems. It can be aggressive to the point of being invasive and is almost impossible to eradicate from landscape beds. It also has no tolerance for shade, quickly becoming thin and bare in shady corners of the yard, allowing weeds to make a mess of it.

Hardiness—Zones 6a to 10, excellent heat tolerance

Type—Warm-season grass

Texture—Fine

Water Needs—Very drought tolerant, once established

Mowing Height—½ inch to 2 inches

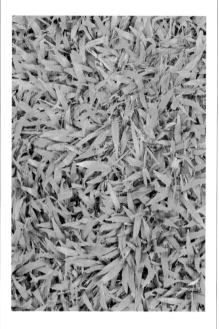

CARPETGRASS
Axonopus fissifolius

Why It's Special—Carpetgrass is one that many gardeners are unfamiliar with, but where conditions are difficult— in poor, wet, acidic soils—it may be worth considering as a replacement for other, much fussier turf grasses. It is especially adaptable to coastal climates.

How to Plant & Grow—Carpetgrass can be seeded, sprigged, or plugged. It is a warm-season grass that will establish quickly as the weather warms up in spring and early summer and active growth begins. It is also tolerant of lean, less fertile soils and overfeeding can contribute to disease problems and the abundant production of unsightly seedheads.

Care & Problems—While it is a lower maintenance turf grass than most, the biggest problem with carpetgrass is that its seedheads grow quite tall and very quickly, making frequent mowing necessary to keep it looking its best. This may be a worthwhile tradeoff for very difficult areas in wet, acidic soils where no other turf grasses will grow.

Hardiness—Zone 8b and warmer

Type—Warm-season grass

Texture—Coarse

Water Needs—Tolerant of both wet and dry conditions

Mowing Height—1 to 2 inches

CENTIPEDE GRASS
Eremochloa ophiuroides

Why It's Special—Centipede grass can be used as an alternative to Bermudagrass in areas of the South where it is hardy. Centipede grass is slower growing and has shorter stolons than Bermudagrass, making it less worrisome when it comes to invading landscaping and flower beds.

How to Plant & Grow—Centipede grass is usually started by seeding between April and June when the soil and air temperatures are warm and conducive to fast germination and establishment. It can also be sprigged or plugged as with many of the other warm-season grasses.

Care & Problems—Centipede grass is slow growing and may be better suited to relatively flat lawns where erosion will be less problematic while it gets established. Its lighter green color is less desirable in some peoples' eyes, but selections have been bred with deeper green color. Its tolerance to salt is lower than some other species, so centipede grass may not be the best choice for coastal areas where soil salinity can be a problem.

Hardiness—Zone 7a to 9b

Type—Warm-season grass

Texture—Medium

Water Needs—Medium, water during drought

Mowing Height—1 to 2 inches

KENTUCKY BLUEGRASS
Poa pratensis

Why It's Special—Kentucky bluegrass may be the ideal image of what a "perfect" lawn should be—thick, soft, and cushiony underfoot and green year-round. Unfortunately, it is a cool-season grass and is not especially well suited to most areas of the South, where it suffers in summer's heat and humidity.

How to Plant & Grow—Sow seed in autumn when the soil is warm, but air temperatures have begun to moderate. The use of a commercial seeder may be beneficial to ensure that the seed is in firm contact with the soil and, once sown, seed must be kept consistently and evenly moist while it germinates.

Care & Problems—Kentucky bluegrass must have deep, thorough watering in the summer months, and regular fertilizing will help keep it looking its best. Grub worms, brown patch, and rust can be problems in areas where high temperatures are coupled with high humidity.

Hardiness—Zones 5a to 7a

Type—Cool-season grass

Texture—Fine

Water Needs—Deep, thorough watering throughout summer

Mowing Height—2 to 2½ inches spring and fall; 3 to 3½ inches summer

ROUGH BLUEGRASS
Poa trivialis

Why It's Special—Rough bluegrass is little known outside of the Deep South, but is very useful in warm climates for overseeding warm-season lawns during the winter months. It is a cool-season grass, so is short-lived once summer's heat and humidity sets in, but makes a beautiful, lush, green carpet through the coldest months of winter while warm-season lawns are brown and dormant.

How to Plant & Grow—Sow seed in autumn when the soil is warm, but air temperatures have begun to moderate. Rough bluegrass can also be useful in shady locations under deciduous trees where warm-season grasses may get thin due to lack of sun. While it won't last the summer, it is helpful in keeping erosion down during the winter months.

Care & Problems—Because it grows during the winter months when most common lawn diseases are less prevalent, rough bluegrass is fairly maintenance free in that respect. It will require mowing to keep it looking neat and tidy.

Hardiness—Zones 7a to 9a

Type—Cool-season grass

Texture—Fine

Water Needs—Survives in normal rainfall

Mowing Height—2 to 2½ inches in winter

ST. AUGUSTINE GRASS
Stenotaphrum secondatum

Why It's Special—One of the greatest attributes of St. Augustine grass is its shade tolerance. Where canopies of oak and pine make it difficult to grow less shade-tolerant species like Bermudagrass and zoysia grass, it may be your go-to lawn grass. St. Augustine grass thrives in heat and humidity and is fairly tolerant of saline soils, making it a good choice for coastal regions of the South.

How to Plant & Grow—St. Augustine grass is most commonly sprigged or plugged in spring and early summer when soil and air temperatures are warm and the sprigs or plugs will root and establish quickly. Regular watering is required until the lawn is well established and occasional feeding will encourage it to grow and fill in quickly.

Care & Problems—Thick, dense thatch can build up at the soil surface, harboring insects and fungal diseases, and while it is rated hardy to Zone 7b, frequent or long drops in temperature below 20° can be damaging.

Hardiness—Zones 7b to 10

Type—Warm-season grass

Texture—Very coarse

Water Needs—Low, once established

Mowing Height—2 to 3 inches or taller

RYE GRASS
Lolium spp.

Why It's Special—Rye grass comes in two forms: annual rye and perennial rye. In the South, both types are grown as annuals since neither will tolerate the intense heat and high humidity. Both are used for overseeding warm-season grasses, like Bermudagrass and zoysia grass, to lend some green color to the lawn during the dormant season, when warm-season grasses are brown.

How to Plant & Grow—Rye grass is seeded into warm-season lawns in October and November, where it germinates quickly, and as the warm-season lawn goes dormant and brown, the rye is green and thriving. The following summer, the rye grass will die out as the warm-season lawn greens up.

Care & Problems—Green winter color also means winter mowing. Rye grass should be maintained at about 2½ inches through the winter. Take care not to use high-nitrogen fertilizers on rye grass or it can cause problems for the dormant warm-season grass beneath it.

Hardiness—Grown as an annual

Type—Cool-season grass

Texture—Fine

Water Needs—Moderate, winter precipitation is usually adequate

Mowing Height—2½ inches

TALL FESCUE
Festuca arundinacea

Why It's Special—Tall fescue is a fairly tough, cool-season grass that thrives in the Upper and Mid-South. It is also one of the most shade-tolerant of all turf grasses. It does require some irrigation during the summer months, which should always be deep and infrequent, encouraging roots to grow deep into the soil.

How to Plant & Grow—Seeding is done from late September through October when soil is still warm and seed will germinate and grow quickly. Thorough and regular watering is a must to ensure the seed bed stays moist during germination and while grass is young and tender.

Care & Problems—Tall fescue is not as drought tolerant as some species, and summer irrigation is required to keep it from going dormant. The name "tall" fescue is a good reminder to keep your mower set high in summer. Mowing too short stresses the grass, giving an open invitation to a variety of insect and disease problems.

Hardiness—Zones 5a to 7b

Type—Cool-season grass

Texture—Medium to coarse, depending on variety

Water Needs—Medium, but higher in summer

Mowing Height—3 to 3½ inches

ZOYSIA GRASS
Zoysia japonica

Why It's Special—Many Southern gardeners consider zoysia grass to be the ideal lawn grass for the South because of its fine leaf blades and thick, carpetlike growth. As warm-season grasses go, it is one of the more shade tolerant and its ability to tolerate winter cold—as well as high summer heat and humidity—makes it a highly desirable turf grass.

How to Plant & Grow—Zoysia grass is either sprigged or plugged between April and June when both soil and air temperatures are warm and conducive to fast root growth and establishment. Zoysia is somewhat drought tolerant, but is a heavy feeder and needs regular applications of fertilizer to look its best.

Care & Problems—Zoysia needs very regular mowing. It can be mowed very short to give that golf course-like appearance, but this requires even more diligence on your part. Thatch buildup can be a problem and good drainage is essential. It doesn't mind moisture, but will not tolerate heavy, wet clay.

Hardiness—Zones 6a to 10

Type—Warm-season grass

Texture—Fine

Water Needs—Drought tolerant, once established

Mowing Height—¾ inch to 1½ inches

HOW SOIL AFFECTS YOUR LAWN

Lawns cover more soil in most American landscapes than any other group of plants. As homeowners, we expect lawn grasses to grow almost everywhere in our yards where there isn't landscaping. Yet, as much amending of soil as we do for landscape beds, flower beds, perennial beds, vegetable gardens, and almost any other soil where we expect plants to grow, we rarely consider the condition of our soil when it comes to our lawns. Instead, we throw down some grass seed, lay sod, or plant plugs in whatever existing soil is onsite and expect a beautiful, lush carpet of lawn to grow—and get frustrated when it doesn't.

Soil preparation for lawns is just as important as soil preparation for any other part of your landscape. Fortunately, most lawn grasses just ask for a little good topsoil to sink their roots into, so we're not talking about adding massive (and expensive) quantities of organic soil amendments to areas where we want lawns to grow. However, if you really want a great lawn, the investment in a few truckloads of great topsoil will pay you back many times over.

Before you start, it might be helpful to know what your existing soil is made of, and there is an easy—and kind of fun—way to find out.

LEARNING WHAT YOUR SOIL IS MADE OF

One of the primary factors that helps determine how often you will have to feed and water your lawn is the texture of your soil. Sandy soils that are loose and open tend to dry out quickly and retain few nutrients, while heavy clay soils stay wet and grab tightly to nutrients, making them unavailable to plants, including lawn grasses. A simple test to determine your soil texture and the percentage of its three basic components—sand, silt, and clay—will help reveal how your soil might need to be amended, as well as how to water and fertilize for the best results with your lawn. The following test will help determine how much sand, silt, and clay your soil is made of. Here's how to do it:

1. Fill a quart jar two-thirds full of water and add one teaspoon of liquid dishwashing detergent as a wetting agent.

Keep grass plugs well watered until they are established.

2. Dig several small samples of soil from various locations around your yard and mix them thoroughly together in the bottom of a bucket. Remove any rocks or other debris. Slowly add this soil blend to the jar of water until the water line approaches the neck of the jar and cap the jar tightly.

3. Vigorously shake the jar for one-and-a-half to two minutes and set it on a level surface to settle. The sand, being heavy, will settle very quickly. After a minute or so and without picking the jar up, mark the sand level with a permanent or waterproof marker on the outside of the jar. The sand will have stopped moving but the clay and silt particles will still be in suspension in the water.

4. Wait another four hours without disturbing the jar, and most of the silt will be settled. Mark the silt level with the pen. The remainder that settles in the next twenty-four hours should be clay. Mark again to identify the clay level.

5. Observe the thickness of the three distinct sections. In general, if all three layers are about equal, your soil is loamy; if the top layer is the deepest, your soil is mostly clay; and if the bottom layer is the deepest, your soil is sandy.

When all of the soil has settled completely, you're ready to do some measuring. With a ruler, measure the total depth of all of the soil in the jar. Then measure the depth of each layer—sand, silt, and clay. Let's say that the total soil depth is 3 inches. Then, when you measure the depth of the bottom layer (sand), you come up with 0.5 inches. Simply divide 0.5 by 3 and you get 0.166666, or 16.6 percent. This means that 16.6 percent of your sample is sand. Perform the same calculations for the silt and clay layers in the jar, and you will know the rough percentages of the makeup of your soil.

Now that you have a rough estimation of the contents of your soil, consider the following:

- Sand is the least water-retentive of the three particles and dries out the fastest. Soils with a large percentage of sand tend to dry out quickly and have little nutrient-holding capacity.

- Silt retains some moisture and although nutrients will bind and stick to silt particles, they are also easily released and made available to a plant's roots. Silty soils are moisture retentive, but rarely waterlogged and will readily exchange nutrients with the plants growing in them.

- Clay is the smallest particle of soil and binds very tightly to both water and nutrients, not wanting to let go of either one. Clay soils tend to become sticky when wet and will not willingly give up the nutrients that are tightly bound to them.

Armed with this information, it is easy to understand that if you find your soil to be mostly sand, it will likely dry out quickly and retain few nutrients. You will have to water frequently and fertilize on a very regular basis to keep plants—including your lawn—thriving. At the opposite end of the spectrum, if your soil is mostly clay, you may want to adjust your watering schedule to keep lawns from being waterlogged and encouraging a variety of diseases. You can also deduce, if your soil is primarily clay, that nutrients may not be readily available because the clay soil binds them so tightly they cannot be absorbed by roots and used for plant growth.

So for soils that are either sandy or clay-based in their makeup, how do we correct the associated problems? Organic matter—garden compost, composted manures, soil conditioners, and so forth—is the problem solver. It is organic matter that helps increase the water- and nutrient-holding capacities of sandy soils and it is organic matter that helps to break the tight bonds between clay particles and loosen up those sticky clay soils, allowing water and nutrients to pass through them more freely. When preparing large areas of soil for new lawn, add a minimum of 2 to 3 inches of good organic matter and till it thoroughly into the existing soil. On established lawns, a topdressing of a ½-inch layer of compost or topsoil can be applied to be incorporated by earthworms and other soil organisms.

JANUARY

- In all but the very warmest parts of the South, lawns are largely dormant this time of year. There is little to be done in the way of maintenance, but if you are considering hiring a lawn-care company for the coming season, now is a great time to begin interviewing.

- If you seeded or sodded your lawn last fall, be sure to keep young lawns or new sod well-watered through the winter. When temperatures are warm and soil is not frozen, it is important to keep the top 4 to 6 inches of soil moist so that roots continue to grow down into the soil in search of water and nutrients.

- January is the perfect time to perform mower maintenance, cleaning air filters, changing spark plugs and oil, and sharpening mower blades for the upcoming season. Regular maintenance of your mower and other equipment will ensure that it works well for many years.

FEBRUARY

- Take the time to calibrate your fertilizer spreader to be sure you are not over- or under-applying fertilizer. Settings on spreaders and instructions on fertilizer bags are not universal, so never assume that a spreader setting and a "recommended" spreader setting on a fertilizer bag are the same. Calibration instructions can be found online.

- In warmer regions of the South, sod can be installed this month. New sod must be kept evenly moist for the first three to four weeks after it is installed. Roots will grow quickly as long as sod is kept moist, and by the end of the second week, if you gently tug on the sod in a few places, it should be firmly connected to the soil.

- If you have overseeded your warm-season lawn with rye, you may have to continue mowing right through the winter. Ryegrass overseeded into zoysia or Bermudagrass should be maintained at about 1½ inches tall. Be sure to maintain sharp mower blades to keep your lawn looking its best.

MARCH

- Mowing season will begin across much of the South this month, if it hasn't already. In warmer areas, you might have been mowing for a month or more. If you haven't done the regular annual maintenance on your lawnmower, do it soon. Oil and air filters should be changed and gas tanks and lines should be cleaned to keep your equipment in top shape.

- If you have a cool-season lawn—bluegrass or fescue in most of the South—spring fertilizing can happen this month, if necessary. Fall is the most important time to fertilize cool-season lawns, but a supplemental feeding can be done in early spring if you have especially poor soil or if a soil test indicates a need for fertilizer.

- In warmer regions of the South, warm-season lawns will be coming out of dormancy this month. Be sure to keep them well-watered, especially if conditions are dry. You'll want to get them off to the best possible start as they wake up for the spring and summer growing season.

- Fungal diseases, especially brown patch, can be a problem in warm-season grasses as they emerge from dormancy in spring—now in the warmer regions of the South and through April and early May in cooler regions. Avoid over-fertilizing warm-season grasses in spring to help control fungal diseases, and if outbreaks are especially bad, apply a fungicide specifically targeted at lawn diseases. Some are difficult to treat.

APRIL

- Bare patches in warm-season grasses can be repaired by digging small sprigs of plugs from healthy, lush sections of the lawn and planting them in the bare spots. As warm-season grasses emerge from dormancy, the small plugs you've removed will fill in fast and the patched areas will fill in over the next month or two.

- Newly seeded, plugged, or sodded lawns will need frequent, thorough watering to keep the soil moist until germination and rooting have begun. Once grass is established, slowly reduce the amount of water to encourage roots to grow deep into the soil.

- Lawn diseases will be rearing their ugly heads this month. Rust, dollar spot, brown patch, and spring dead spot can all be problems. Fungal diseases can spread with amazing speed and wipe out large sections of lawn very quickly, if not controlled. Local garden centers or your County Extension office are excellent resources for information about treatment.

MAY

- Encourage your lawn's roots to grow deep into the soil in search of water and nutrients by reducing the frequency of watering and by watering thoroughly and deeply each time. Lawns with deep roots require less maintenance, will be more tolerant of hot, dry weather and, in the long run, will use less water overall than lawns whose roots don't run deep.

- Fertilizing can be done now on warm-season grasses, like zoysia and Bermudagrass, as they enter their most active phase of growth. It is best to do this once they have greened up fully and have been mowed a few times.

- Southern chinch bugs can be problematic on all warm-season grasses, but are especially troublesome on St. Augustine grass. The nymphs (young insects) suck sap from the leaves and can cause severe yellowing or even death of leaves, causing the lawn to look pallid and sick. Check with a local garden center for the best method of control.

- Pre-emergent herbicides that were applied earlier in the spring for control of crabgrass have probably lost their effectiveness by now. Most are only effective for about six weeks. Crabgrass and other grassy weeds will continue to germinate right through the warm season of summer, so regular application of crabgrass preventer may be necessary.

JUNE

- The best way to determine fertilizer requirements for your lawn is to have your soil tested at least every three years through your local Cooperative Extension Service office. Have your soil tested this month to make plans for fall.

- In the upper regions of the South, you can still renovate warm-season lawns by sodding, plugging, or sprigging. Farther south, where the temperatures are hotter, it may be too late to do any patching unless you can really stay on top of the watering. Remember that overwatering your entire lawn just to keep a few small patches going may cause more harm than good.

- Water your lawn any time that it shows signs of stress. These signs could include having a bluish gray tint to the color, footprints remaining in the lawn when you walk on it, and wilted, curled, or folded leaves.

- If you have a fescue or bluegrass lawn, keep an eye out for brown patch this month and treat it immediately if there are any signs of it at all. Brown patch can wipe out entire sections of lawn, almost overnight. A preventive application of fungicide is recommended in areas where night temperatures and humidity remain high.

JULY

- Lawns that were newly seeded, sodded, or sprigged in spring will need attention to watering until their root systems are thoroughly established and have grown deeply into the soil. Even established lawns will need at least 1 inch of water per week through the hottest and driest summer months. On sandy soils, lawns may need even more water.

- Newly sodded lawns can be mowed once they have firmly rooted into place. Raise the mowing height by one or two notches to decrease "pull" on the new sod as you cut. It may be a good idea to push-mow new sod the first couple of times to avoid tearing tender roots with a heavy riding mower.

- Pythium wilt or blight is a fungal disease that thrives during the hot summer months. Like brown patch, it can wipe out large sections of lawn, seemingly overnight. Be on the lookout this month for leaves that appear water-soaked or greasy looking, as this is a sure sign. Consult experts at a local garden center or County Extension Office for recommended treatments.

AUGUST

- If your cool-season lawn has gone dormant, which can happen during the hottest and driest summer months, begin watering thoroughly and deeply every two weeks, knowing they will soon begin growing again. Overseeding may be necessary for bare spots once autumn arrives.

- Mow regularly and only remove one-third of the total leaf blade each time you mow. This reduces the stress on your lawn and keeps it healthy and looking its finest. It is not necessary to remove grass clippings as long as you are mowing regularly. They will return valuable organic matter and a small amount of nutrients back to the soil.

- White grubs are extremely active this month. Milky spore disease can be used for grub control and is especially effective against Japanese beetle grubs. Getting milky spore disease established in your lawn requires multiple applications, but once you've followed the steps, it will be effective for several years.

SEPTEMBER

- Aerating is one of the most important autumn activities for lawns. It is beneficial for all lawns, but is especially important for those growing on clay-based soil. An aerator pulls a small core of soil from the ground and increases air, water, and nutrient penetration.

- In cooler areas, overseeding cool-season fescue or bluegrass lawns can begin in mid to late September. Once seed is sown, it must remain moist until it germinates and for several weeks afterward. If seed begins to sprout and then dries out, it will die.

- Warm-season grasses should not be fertilized in the fall. The large amount of nitrogen in most lawn fertilizers can force soft, lush growth that will be more susceptible to winterkill when cold temperatures arrive.

- Cool-season grasses *should* be fertilized now to encourage lush, thick growth during the cool days of autumn and early winter. This is the season when cool-season lawns really thrive, and the better you treat them now to get them as healthy as possible, the better they'll survive the summer seasons that are less to their liking.

OCTOBER

- Leaves will need to be removed from your lawn as they fall. Consider putting leaves in their own pile, separate from the compost, to break down into leaf mold, a tremendous source of organic matter. Shredding, if you have access to a shredder, will help them break down faster.

- October is the prime month for new seeding or overseeding of cool-season fescue and bluegrass lawns. Seed will begin sprouting in seven to ten days in the warm soil and moderate daytime temperatures paired with cool nights will encourage it to grow and develop quickly.

- If you haven't applied an autumn application of fertilizer, waiting until late November and applying a winterizer-type fertilizer will keep your lawn looking its best through the winter and will give it a jumpstart, come spring.

- Mow cool-season grasses often and keep the mower height raised as high as recommended for the type of grass you're growing. Mowing cool-season grasses too short causes undue stress on the plants, while tall mowing encourages roots to grow deep into the soil.

- Henbit, chickweed, dandelions, and other broadleaf weeds begin germinating this month. For severe infestations, post-emergent herbicides may be necessary. Weeds are easiest to kill when they are small and before they get their roots firmly established in the soil.

NOVEMBER

- November is the perfect month to sod cool-season lawns. If you're considering a total lawn renovation or have a new home site where you've been waiting to get the lawn established, now is the time. Be sure you can keep new sod thoroughly watered until it is well established. New sod should root down within two weeks.

- If the fall is especially dry, warm-season grasses may need to be watered, even though they are going dormant. This is a bit of a balancing act, keeping them healthy, but not overwatering while they are beginning to shut down for the season.

- Wild garlic is an annoying weed in lawns across the South. It can be treated with a broadleaf herbicide when the air temperature is above 50 degrees or it can be hand-pulled or dug with a small trowel as long as you are sure to remove the entire plant, bulb and all.

DECEMBER

- Make plans to winterize the lawnmower before putting it away for the winter to keep interior parts from rusting and to ensure that the mower will start when you need it to in the spring. If possible, store your mowers indoors over winter to keep them dry. If you must store them outdoors, keep them under an awning or carport and cover with a tarp to help keep them dry.

- Cool-season lawns may need to be mowed through the month of December. Be sure to mow them at the proper height. Ryegrass overseeded into Bermudagrass or zoysia can be maintained at 1½ to 2 inches through the winter. Fescue and bluegrass, if they need mowing at all, should be mowed at 2½ to 3 inches.

- Spot treat any chickweed, henbit, or dandelions by hand-pulling or with a broadleaf weed killer as they continue to germinate and grow.

Power aerating your lawn creates openings for air and nutrients to get deep into the root system. It also creates hundreds of dirt cylinders that can be left to dry and then worked back in.

ORNAMENTAL
GRASSES
for the South

There was a time in the not-too-distant past when ornamental grasses were largely overlooked in Southern gardens. Many gardeners felt that grasses didn't "fit in" here. We were more into the neat and tidy, evergreen boxwood hedge or the romantic look of a garden strewn with roses and azaleas. Ornamental grasses were looked on as being too untidy and unkempt, and they offended the sense of structure and orderliness upon which so many Southern gardens are built. Thankfully, our views have softened a bit and ornamental grasses are now found growing in gardens throughout the South, softening beds with their graceful beauty or adding dramatic architectural focal points to the landscape.

USING ORNAMENTAL GRASSES IN THE LANDSCAPE

Ornamental grasses come in an enormous range of sizes, shapes, and colors, from low-growing, almost groundcoverlike forms to bamboo-like giants 15 feet tall. Some grow as rounded, almost formal-looking mounds, while others are loose, open, and willowy, bending and swaying in the slightest breeze. Still others may be staunchly upright, creating dramatic vertical accents in the landscape. Because of their wide range of forms and growth habits, ornamental grasses can be used in an equally wide range of landscape settings. Shorter varieties can form "feet" for taller-growing perennials and shrubs, medium varieties can be used as fillers in landscape beds and perennial borders, and the largest varieties can be dramatic focal points, commanding attention from afar.

In addition to their architectural value, some ornamental grasses provide dramatic color in the landscape with their richly colored or variegated leaves. 'Cabaret' miscanthus, with its boldly variegated leaves of green-and-creamy white, offers the perfect balance of color and texture when paired with the dark and dramatic leaves of a red-leafed canna. Blue fescue's powder blue leaves form the perfect foreground for brightly colored annuals like narrow-leaf zinnia or angelonia, and the pleated, ribbonlike leaves of variegated palm grass,

borne on remarkable maroon-red stems, provide striking contrast when planted with black-leaved elephant ears.

One of the most dramatic effects that ornamental grasses bring to the garden is movement with their long, ribbonlike leaves catching the slightest breeze or their late summer and autumn plumes bobbing and dancing on the wind. This is an ornamental quality that many gardeners fail to consider as they design their gardens, but one that can be used very effectively.

Ornamental grasses can also serve functional purposes in the landscape. They can divide the larger landscape into distinct spaces or be used as backdrops to borders and other plantings. Larger growing species can be used effectively as screens, hedges, and even windbreaks. Most have tough root systems that grow deep into the soil, helping control erosion by wind and water, while spreading varieties can be used very effectively as groundcovers and for stabilizing steep banks. Some even provide an attractive and unusual alternative to turf grasses, making beautiful and artistic lawns that never need mowing.

If space allows and the natural style of gardening appeals to you, ornamental grasses can be used to great effect, creating garden meadows and prairie-style plantings using large swaths of grasses combined with perennials, annuals, and wildflowers to create great sweeps of color and movement across your landscape. These can be created to mimic nature as closely as possible or they can be given an avant-garde, artistic flair using the landscape as a canvas for your living masterpiece.

Some varieties of ornamental grasses make perfect subjects for outdoor pots and containers. Larger growing varieties can be used as centerpieces and focal points for large containers, while smaller varieties make excellent fillers when paired with colorful annuals and tropicals. Their roots will reach deep into the pots to take advantage of moisture that the roots of other plants don't grow deep enough to reach, making them highly compatible in mixed container plantings. When choosing ornamental grasses for containers, use their mature size as the guide for required size of

Native grasses can be both functional and ornamental.

our heat and humidity and, for the most part, are well adapted to our less-than-perfect soils. Their foliage can range in color from deepest green to steely blue and the seedheads of some provide outstanding color and texture in the garden. With native species, there is little concern for them invading nearby lands, since more than likely they already reside there anyway. In addition to having tremendous ornamental value, native grasses are extremely functional in today's world where greener living and being more sensitive to our environment are not just a passing fad, but a way of life. For land restoration, erosion prevention, dune stabilization and even for the renovation of pasture lands, native grasses should be at the top of the list. Many of these species do double duty as beautiful garden ornamentals, as well as being workhorses for the environment.

A WORD ON BEHAVIOR

There is much talk today of invasive exotic plants and how much havoc they wreak in our native habitats and ecosystems. While this is not an issue to be taken lightly—and certainly there are some ornamental grasses that may fall into this "invasive exotic" category in some locales—it is generally confined to one or two problem species that are problematic in certain climates or regions. With some education and good stewardship, the problem can be largely solved and future problems avoided. One excellent example is the very popular and highly ornamental maiden grass, or *Miscanthus*.

Driving through some parts of the South you will see the straight species, *Miscanthus sinensis*, popping up along roadsides and spreading to natural meadows and river bottoms. However, the cultivars 'Cabaret', 'Morning Light', and several others make excellent garden subjects and rarely, if ever, produce a single seedling. In coastal regions of the South, Japanese blood grass, which is shy and well-behaved in colder climates, can be a belligerent thug in the delicately balanced dune ecosystems along our seashores. By being good stewards and making wise choices about what we grow, we can ensure that our natural ecosystems stay healthy and intact while still enjoying many well-behaved and beautiful plants from around the world.

the pot to plant them in. Many perennial grasses will reach their full height—even if they don't reach their full width—in the first season so choose accordingly. They look small in their nursery pots, but will grow quickly once their roots are in good potting soil with some room to spread.

Wildlife habitats and gardens made to attract an array of living creatures wouldn't be complete without ornamental grasses. Plumes full of seeds will be picked clean by smaller birds and the dense foliage of some grasses makes good cover for others. Many birds will weave nests from the leaves of ornamental grasses, and the fluffy seedheads will be stripped to make soft nest linings for delicate eggs and young hatchlings. Ornamental grasses provide cover for a variety of other animals as well, and help to create well-rounded and healthy garden ecosystems.

USING NATIVE GRASSES AS ORNAMENTALS

Many of our favorite ornamental grasses, including the muhly grasses, switch grasses, Indian grass, and many others, are native to the South. They thrive in

BLUE FESCUE
Festuca glauca

Why It's Special—Blue fescue is one of the smallest of the ornamental grasses, its densely tufted, silvery blue foliage reaching only a foot tall. When planted *en masse*, it makes a dramatic and beautiful alternative lawn. Attractive tan seed heads appear in late summer.

How to Plant & Grow—Blue fescue grows best in lean, dry, well-drained soils and frequently rots in winter if planted in clay. If a lawn-like effect is what you're after, plant on 18-inch centers so that plants will grow together and touch when they are mature. Once established, it is quite drought tolerant and will only need watering during extended periods of dry weather.

Care & Problems—Blue fescue, once established, requires almost no care in the landscape. In early spring, just before new growth starts, simply trim back old foliage to tidy up the clumps, and that's all there is to it! Clay soils that stay cold and wet in winter can lead to root and/or crown rot and the death of the plants.

Foliage Color—Silvery blue

Bloom Season—Early summer

Hardiness—Zones 4a to 8a

Texture—Very fine

Water Needs—Drought tolerant, once established

FEATHER REED GRASS
Calamagrostis × acutiflora 'Karl Foerster'

Why It's Special—Feather reed grass is a shoulder-high, strictly vertical grass suitable for gardens of any size because of its narrow, upright habit. Deep green foliage is attractive from early spring until late fall, and the feathery plumes, appearing in early summer, are pinkish when they're young, changing to a golden tan at maturity.

How to Plant & Grow—Feather reed grass is a cool-season grass that greens up very early in spring and can be planted either in spring or in fall in a sunny location with good air circulation. While it prefers well-drained, fertile soil with sufficient moisture, it will adapt to heavier clay soils and drier sites.

Care & Problems—Heavy rain or winds may temporarily bend the stems. They will usually right themselves soon after. In Zone 8, heat, humidity, and poor air circulation can cause fungal leaf spot. Korean feather reed grass, *Calamagrostis brachytricha*, can tolerate hot, humid summers.

Foliage Color—Green or variegated

Bloom Season—Early summer to fall

Hardiness—Zones 5a to 7b

Texture—Fine

Water Needs—Evenly moist to slightly dry

FOUNTAIN GRASS
Pennisetum alopecuroides

Why It's Special—Broad, arching fountains of foliage make it easy to see how "fountain grasses" got their name. Easy to grow and highly adaptable, they are particularly effective planted *en masse* or as focal points in large containers. From midsummer through autumn their plumes put on a showstopping display.

How to Plant & Grow—Fountain grass should be planted in spring or early summer when it will establish quickly and easily as the soil warms. Water regularly for the first month to get it rooted and then only as needed to keep the leaves from curling. Large varieties may need as much as 5 feet between plants while small varieties can be planted as close as 2 feet.

Care & Problems—Fountain grass is relatively pest free. In early spring, cut plants back to 8 to 12 inches to remove the last season's growth. The variety 'Moudry', although very popular and beautiful, can reseed and become weedy. Divide fountain grasses every three to five years to maintain their vigor.

Foliage Color—Green

Bloom Season—Midsummer through fall

Hardiness—Zones 5b to 8b

Texture—Fine

Water Needs—Moderately drought tolerant

FOUNTAIN GRASS, PURPLE
Pennisetum setaceum 'Purpureum'

Why It's Special—Purple fountain grass is an annual ornamental grass, growing extremely fast and putting on a spectacular show in only one season. It can be planted *en masse* or mixed in individually with colorful perennials and annuals. It also makes an excellent specimen for containers. Foxtail plumes will appear from midsummer through fall.

How to Plant & Grow—Plant in mid- to late spring when the soil is warm to the touch. Purple fountain grass loves the heat and will languish if planted in cold soil. Give it well-amended, rich garden soil and provide plenty of moisture. Fertilize at planting time and once per month throughout the summer to encourage lush growth and lots of plumes.

Care & Problems—Purple fountain grass is not hardy and is grown as an annual. Even in climates where it is hardy, it is often less attractive in subsequent seasons and is still commonly replaced each year. Other than having to be replaced, it is care-free and beautiful.

Foliage Color—Deep burgundy-purple

Peak Season—Early summer through fall

Hardiness—Grown as an annual

Texture—Medium

Water Needs—Regular watering is necessary

GIANT REED 'PEPPERMINT STICK'

Arundo donax 'Peppermint Stick'

Why It's Special—Giant reed is one of the largest-growing of all ornamental grasses and, under ideal conditions, it can reach as much as 25 feet tall! In the garden, though, 10 to 15 feet is more common. 'Peppermint Stick' is an exceptionally beautiful form with its green leaves broadly edged in white.

How to Plant & Grow—Plant giant reed in spring in rich soil with plenty of moisture. Once established, its roots will reach many feet into the soil to extract water, but it is native to swampy areas and thrives in those conditions. Plant it with its mature size in mind, understanding that the base of the clump may eventually reach 8 feet wide or more.

Care & Problems—The old canes of giant reed should be cut to the ground in late winter or very early spring so that new growth can emerge unimpeded. It will reach its full height in a single growing season.

Foliage Color—Green-and-white striped

Bloom Season—Very late autumn

Hardiness—Zones 6 to 10

Texture—Coarse

Water Needs—Average to wet

MISCANTHUS 'CABARET'

Miscanthus sinensis var. *condensatus* 'Cabaret'

Why It's Special—'Cabaret' miscanthus is a strikingly variegated and well-behaved cultivar that deserves a place in every garden. Its long, ribbonlike leaves are dramatically enhanced by a creamy white stripe down the center of each one, making it a perfect accent plant for the perennial garden or mixed border or a striking focal point in the larger landscape.

How to Plant & Grow—As with all warm-season grasses, miscanthus are best planted in spring to get them well-established during their first growing season. While they are tolerant of drier and leaner soils, they will be most robust and beautiful given rich, well-drained soil and ample summertime moisture.

Care & Problems—Old foliage can be allowed to stand through winter for architectural interest, cutting back just before new growth starts in early spring. In some climates, some miscanthus can re-seed and be invasive. 'Cabaret' sets almost no viable seed and not a problem.

Foliage Color—Green with a creamy white central stripe

Bloom Season—Late summer and autumn

Hardiness—Zones 5 to 9

Texture—Medium, very graceful

Water Needs—Average to moist

MISCANTHUS 'MORNING LIGHT'

Miscanthus sinensis 'Morning Light'

Why It's Special—'Morning Light' maiden grass forms large clumps of finely textured, silvery green foliage. In autumn, it is topped by fan-shaped plumes that start out pinkish tan turning to silvery white. 'Morning Light' is one of the best varieties of maiden grass, suitable for gardens of any size, and is noninvasive.

How to Plant & Grow—Maiden grass is best planted from early spring to early summer to get it established as warm temperatures arrive. It prefers full sun and will tolerate an enormous range of soil types, from wet areas to dry, rocky slopes. Avoid overfertilizing, which will cause stems to stretch and topple.

Care & Problems—Cut clumps back to 12 inches in early spring. Tie the clumps together with twine and then cut below the twine to keep the dried leaves from creating an enormous mess in the garden. It may require gas-powered hedge shears to cut through the clump in this way, but the ease of cleanup is worth it.

Foliage Color—Green or variegated

Bloom Season—Late summer through fall

Hardiness—Zones 5a to 8b

Texture—Fine to medium

Water Needs—Moderately drought tolerant

MUHLY GRASS, BAMBOO
Muhlenbergia dumosa

Why It's Special—Bamboo muhly has delicate, fern-like foliage on tall, slender stems that resemble a graceful, arching bamboo. Its airy texture provides an accent in the landscape or as a dramatic focal point in a pot. It also makes an excellent cut stem for arrangements and can be used fresh or dried.

How to Plant & Grow—Plant bamboo muhly in spring in very well-drained, fertile garden soil or as focal points in containers. Once established, it is extremely heat and drought tolerant, but will respond well to summertime watering and feeding. It is very tolerant of coastal conditions.

Care & Problems—Bamboo muhly is a tolerant and care-free grass. Occasionally, stems will turn brown and can simply be clipped off at ground level and a new one will take its place. There are usually so many that the removal of a few goes completely unnoticed. Bamboo muhly is not tolerant of cold, wet clay, especially in winter.

Foliage Color—Light green

Bloom Season—Summer, inconspicuous

Hardiness—Zones 8 to 10, annual in colder regions

Texture—Very fine

Water Needs—Very drought tolerant, once established

MUHLY GRASS, LINDHEIMER'S
Muhlenbergia lindheimeri

Why It's Special—Lindheimer's muhly grass is a lesser-known form of muhly that deserves to be much more widely grown. Its aqua-blue foliage softens the landscape through the summer months and the flowers, emerging purplish in September, mature to silvery gray in late autumn and early winter. Its tidy growth habit makes it an excellent choice for perennial borders.

How to Plant & Grow—Plant muhly grass in spring or early summer to establish it while its actively growing. It prefers moist, but very well-drained, fertile soil and full sun, although it is more tolerant of rocky soils and clay than one might guess.

Care & Problems—Muhly is a care-free grass, once established. It may be tender in colder parts of the South, and excellent winter drainage will help ensure that it comes through the winter north of Zone 7. It responds very well to summertime water, growing lush and sending up quantities of plumes in autumn.

Foliage Color—Aqua-blue

Bloom Season—Early autumn to early winter

Hardiness—Zones 7 (6b with protection) to 10

Texture—Fine

Water Needs—Average to moist, well-drained

MUHLY GRASS, PURPLE
Muhlenbergia capillaris

Why It's Special—If it is a truly show-stopping ornamental grass you are looking for, look no further than purple muhly grass. Its summertime foliage is average as ornamental grasses go, but come late summer and autumn, when it turns into a hazy mist of purplish red flowers, there is nothing average about purple muhly!

How to Plant & Grow—In warmer zones, purple muhly can be planted in autumn, but in Zones 6b (where it needs some protection) and Zone 7, spring planting is probably best. It prefers very well-drained soil, especially in the winter, when it will not tolerate being wet at the roots.

Care & Problems—Seedheads will stand until midwinter to extend the seasonal display. Purple muhly is one grass that does not like to be cut back hard. Trim it in early spring, just enough to tidy it up, but leave as much of the plant intact as possible. Cutting it back by more than half will probably cause it to sulk.

Foliage Color—Gray-green

Peak Season—Autumn

Hardiness—Zones 7a (6b with protection) to 9a

Texture—Fine

Water Needs—Very drought tolerant, once established

PALM GRASS
Setaria palmifolia 'Variegata'

Why It's Special—Palm grass is grown for its unique leaves that look as though they have been pressed flat and run through a pleating machine. The cultivar 'Variegata' is highly desirable with leaves that are edged in white, held on purplish red stems that make for a dramatic contrast. It is an annual grass in all but the warmest climates.

How to Plant & Grow—Plant small transplants from 4- or 6-inch pots in late spring when the soil is warm to the touch. This is a tropical grass and it *loves* the heat and humidity! It prefers rich, moist, well-drained soil and will respond especially well to regular summer watering and feeding.

Care & Problems—Where it is hardy, in Zones 9 and 10, and where the growing season is long enough, it may set seed and can be invasive in some areas. It is extremely frost tender and in most climates will not live late enough in the season to set any seed at all, so its invasive tendencies are of no consequence.

Foliage Color—Green or variegated

Bloom Season—Very late autumn, if at all

Hardiness—Zones 9 to 10

Texture—Coarse

Water Needs—Moderate to moist

PAMPAS GRASS
Cortaderia selloana

Why It's Special—Pampas grass is perhaps the most impressive of all of the ornamental grasses. Enormous, arching mounds of foliage from dramatic fountains of green in the landscape and in autumn, the spectacular plumes—each as much as 3 feet long—can rise as high as 12 feet on sturdy, upright canes. 'Pumila' is a smaller form.

How to Plant & Grow—Pampas grass is best planted in spring to get the roots established during the warm summer months. In the colder end of its hardiness range, it is very important that it be well established before cold weather comes along. Pampas grass will adapt to almost any soil type.

Care & Problems—Plants should be cut back hard in early spring, after the coldest weather has passed. You will need long sleeves and gloves to perform this task. Pampas grass leaves are razor sharp and can inflict nasty cuts. This is another good one to tie up tightly with twine before you begin cutting.

Foliage Color—Deep green or variegated

Bloom Season—Autumn

Hardiness—Zones 7a to 10a

Texture—Medium to coarse

Water Needs—Very drought tolerant

SWEET FLAG
Acorus gramineus

Why It's Special—Sweet flag is not a true grass, but is actually a distant cousin to the iris. However, its grassy texture means that it is more commonly used as a dwarf grass in the landscape. The varieties 'Ogon', with golden striped foliage and 'Minimus Aurea', a tiny gold form growing only 2 inches tall, are very popular. 'Variegatus', a green-and-white form, is quite striking.

How to Plant & Grow—While it is native to wet areas, sweet flag will adapt very well to moist, partially shaded areas of the garden. Many ornamental grasses are not well suited to wet sites, so sweet flag and its close relatives make excellent alternatives where a grassy texture is needed but the site may be too wet for traditional grasses.

Care & Problems—Divide garden plants in early spring, just as new growth appears. In boggy areas or pond edges it can be quite vigorous. It can suffer from fungal leaf spot or rust if it is stressed, but these are rarely serious.

Foliage Color—Green, gold, variegated

Peak Season—Spring to fall

Hardiness—Zones 5a to 9a

Texture—Fine

Water Needs—Needs moisture, even shallow standing water

SWITCH GRASS
Panicum virgatum

Why It's Special—Along with the native bluestems, switch grass was a major component of the tall-grass prairies of the great plains. Before the arrival of the settlers, it stretched in vast green oceans across the central United States. Now, many beautiful selections have been made for inclusion in today's gardens.

How to Plant & Grow—Full sun is required and switch grass will perform best when planted in spring to take advantage of early rains to get it established and the heat of the summer to encourage it to grow. Roots grow very deeply and it makes an excellent choice for erosion control. Do not overfertilize or growth will be weak and floppy.

Care & Problems—Give it some hard pruning back to 8 inches at the end of each winter and in two or three seasons, most switch grasses will spread from 1-gallon pots to 4- to 5-foot-wide clumps. For smaller gardens where spread is a problem, try the very vertical and strictly clumping *Panicum virgatum* 'Northwind'.

Foliage Color—Green to blue-green

Peak Season—Midsummer through late fall

Hardiness—Zones 3a to 8b

Texture—Medium-fine

Water Needs—Very drought tolerant, once established

TALL MOOR GRASS
Molinia arundinacea 'Skyracer'

Why It's Special—Tall moor grass is one of the best ornamental grasses for wet areas. In the wild, it is frequently found in bogs and wetlands. Its attractive, gray-green foliage arches upward to form a 2- to 3-foot-tall mound. In July, the purplish brown flower spikes rise to almost 6 feet, but are very light, open, and airy.

How to Plant & Grow—Plant tall moor grass in early spring in full sun and in soil that is rich, well-amended, and moist throughout the year. Moor grass is not one of the more drought-tolerant grasses, but where it's happy, it will be nothing short of spectacular.

Care & Problems—The only drawback to tall moor grass is that, compared to other ornamental grasses, it is very slow to establish. Often, it does not reach its full stride until the third or even the fourth year. Be patient with it. It is more than worth the wait.

Foliage Color—Green

Bloom Season—Late summer through autumn

Hardiness—Zones 5 to 9

Texture—Fine to medium

Water Needs—Damp to wet

GROWING ORNAMENTAL GRASSES IN YOUR GARDEN

Most ornamental grasses will grow in unimproved soil. However, they will establish more quickly and produce better-looking plants in amended soil. If you are among the fortunate few with clay loam soil, adding amendments will result in only marginal increases in performance. However, on red clay Piedmont soils, incorporating limestone and a 2-inch layer of organic soil conditioner or aged pine bark will improve drainage, water intake, and microbiological activity in the soil. On sandy soil near the coast and on the old sand dunes running southwest from Pinehurst to Columbia and Aiken, generous amounts of limestone and moistened peat moss or leaf compost worked into the soil will greatly improve its moisture retention. Aged pine bark generally works best on clay soils, peat moss, or sand. Initially and thereafter, yearly applications of organic mulch will help maintain a healthy organic content in your soil.

LONG-TERM CARE AND MAINTENANCE OF ORNAMENTAL GRASSES

Leaving large clumps of ornamental grasses to fend for themselves leads to their eventual failure. Even near the coast, clumps freeze back partway, and farther west some grasses may freeze essentially to ground level each winter. Emerging new blades are partially obscured by the old foliage and the visual effect is messy. Cutting old clumps to the ground each spring can be approached ritually or with trepidation, depending on your age and energy level. Even with electric or gas-powered hedge shears the job isn't easy, and you are left with large piles of hay. Fortunately, ornamental grasses make good raw material for composting.

If you find yourself needing to dig and divide large clumps of grasses, be prepared for a difficult job. Old clumps of miscanthus, pampas grass, and other large-growing types have tremendous root systems that spread both deep and wide. In some instances, it may even take a truck or other piece of equipment to pull or dig grasses out. Division may have to be done with an ax or even a chain saw. Grasses are tough! These are extreme cases, though, and if you will divide very fast-growing grasses every three years, and slower ones every five years, on a regular schedule, they should remain manageable. Regular division will also keep large clumps from dying out in the center as they are sometimes known to do.

THE FOOLPROOF WAY TO SHEAR LARGE GRASSES

One trick-of-the-trade that many professional landscapers use is to tie your ornamental grasses up in tight bundles *before* you cut them. Starting at the base of the plant, wrap a piece of sturdy jute twine around the plant about 18 inches above ground level and tie it as tightly as you can. Then wrap the twine around the plant three to four times, working your way toward the top. Tie off again at the top, as tightly as possible. Now use your gas-powered hedge shears or a large pruning saw to cut through the stems about 6 inches *below* the first round of twine near the base of the plant. Once you've cut all the way through, the top of the grass will be neatly bundled and can easily be removed.

FURTHER NOTES ON INVASIVE PLANTS

"Invasive exotic" is certainly a hot buzzword in horticultural circles these days and while this is a worthwhile concern, it's not always just the exotic species that can be troublesome in the garden. Potential problems with *Miscanthus* were mentioned at the beginning of the chapter. Near the coast, Japanese blood grass (*Imperata cylindrica*), which spreads by underground runners, can get out of control in moist, fertile soil.

But in a garden setting, even some of our native species can turn into aggressive thugs. Northern sea oats or river oats are a great example of a native grass that drops so many seeds that the phrase "like hair on a dog's back" accurately describes the crop of volunteer seedlings. Even though it is a native species, in a garden setting it can be very invasive and problematic. The same can be said for some of the switch grasses, which can spread to form large clumps very quickly and run right over the tops of smaller plants that may be in their way. This does not make them any less garden-worthy, it just means that you—the homeowner—need to educate yourself on the front end and know what to expect.

The more responsible garden centers and mail-order suppliers of ornamental grasses are sensitive both to environmental and garden issues and present the advantages and disadvantages of ornamental grasses in their descriptions.

GRASS LOOK-ALIKES

If you're interested in expanding your plant palette and learning even more about ornamental grasses and grasslike plants, be sure to take a look at the genus *Carex*, commonly known as the sedges. This is one of the most diverse groups of plants you can grow. There are forms with broad leaves an inch or more wide and forms with leaves so fine they look like mounds of hair. There are green forms, blue forms, golden forms, and beautiful variegated forms. There are also species that grow on dry, shady rock outcroppings in forests and others that grow in standing water in full sun at the edges of streams and ponds. In size, they can range anywhere from a diminutive 3 inches tall to over 3 feet tall when they are full grown. All of them have interesting and sometimes showy "flowers," and some have spectacular seedheads. No matter the site, soil, or amount of moisture, there is a sedge that will fit the bill.

Other grasslike plants include the sweet flags, one of which was described in the plant profiles, the mondo grasses of which there are many forms and varieties, and for the true plant collectors there is a "newer" group of grasslike plants from South Africa called "restios." The restios are actually not new at all, but are ancient grass relatives and are extremely fascinating and beautiful. Not all of them are tolerant of hot, humid climates, but part of the fun in gardening is experimenting with new, unusual plants to learn how they grow and perform where we live. Ornamental grass look-alikes are valuable garden subjects, adding color, texture, and sometimes dramatic architecture to parts of the garden where traditional ornamental grasses may not thrive.

Sedges, from the genus *Carex*, can find a spot in almost any garden.

JANUARY

- January is a great month to plan for the upcoming gardening season. Give special consideration to problem areas in your garden where other plants have struggled and see if you can find a grass or grasslike plant that will thrive there. Many of them are highly adaptable and tolerant of less-than-ideal conditions.

- In all but the warmest regions of the South, it is too cold to plant or transplant any of the ornamental grasses now. Most of our common ornamental grasses are warm-season grasses and need the warm air and soil temperatures of spring and early summer to get established. Planting in winter in cold, wet clay soil is risky at best.

- Some ornamental grasses may be starting to shatter now. Go ahead and cut back any that are really making a mess of the garden. Last year's foliage does help to protect the crowns, so if you are growing some grasses whose hardiness may be in question, it is better to leave the old foliage for a little while longer. Hardy perennial grasses will be largely unaffected by cutting back now if they've become too unsightly.

FEBRUARY

- For shady areas where most ornamental grasses won't grow and where you have a difficult time growing a lawn, consider grasslike plants as alternatives: dwarf sweet flag, liriope, and mondo grass are all possible alternatives for areas where you want a grasslike texture, but it's too shady to be successful with true grasses.

- In Zones 8 and warmer, you may be able to divide ornamental grasses this month. Watch for new growth to begin emerging around the base of the plant. As soon as you see any green at all, you can dig and divide. New growth indicates that the plant has "woken up" from its winter slumber and is heading into its active phase of growth.

- If you use organic fertilizers that take a few weeks to become active in the soil, you may want to fertilize your ornamental grasses this month in the warmer regions of the South. Look for new growth at the base of the plant to indicate that they are beginning to break dormancy and feed then. If you don't see new growth, wait a little longer to feed.

MARCH

- Garden centers will begin stocking their shelves this month. Warm-season plants, including ornamental grasses, will start appearing toward the end of the month in warmer regions, while it may be April before they are stocked in cooler regions. The best garden centers will stock plants at the appropriate time for planting in your area, so follow their lead.

- In cooler parts of the South, ornamental grasses will start waking up from their winter sleep this month. The time to do any necessary digging and dividing, as well as early spring feeding with a good, organic fertilizer, is when you begin to see new growth appearing at the base of the plant.

APRIL

- Give serious consideration to ornamental grasses as you think through your current season's planting scheme or as you design new garden beds or landscape areas. They can be strong unifiers in the landscape, helping to tie your home, outdoor entertaining areas, and garden together into one cohesive space.

- April is the prime month for planting ornamental grasses in most of the South. Soil and air temperatures have warmed, and grasses are actively growing and will establish quickly. Be sure to keep newly planted ornamental grasses watered well if you are not having regular rainfall in your area. They are especially susceptible to drying out when they are newly planted.

- If you haven't fertilized your ornamental grasses, a light feeding now will encourage robust summer growth. Don't overdo it, though, or the stems may become weak and plants may flop.

- Dividing ornamental grasses can be done while they are pushing their first flush of new growth. Large-growing grasses like some of the *Miscanthus* should be divided every third year. Dig the entire clump, divide it into three or four pieces, and replant the most vigorous sections from around the outer edge. These will quickly develop into robust new clumps.

MAY

- Rabbits can be troublesome for newly planted ornamental grasses, eating the tender, young new growth. They may also nibble on established plantings of smaller-growing grasses, like blue fescue or some of the dwarf fountain grasses, but the grasses will usually recover quickly and will eventually outpace the little nibblers.

- Be sure to keep mulch on areas where ornamental grasses haven't completely filled in yet. Summer weeds are germinating quickly now, and it won't take long for them to get out of hand if you don't stay on top of them. A 2-inch layer of mulch will dramatically reduce the amount of weeds in your beds and will reduce water loss from the soil by up to 50 percent.

- Ornamental grasses have very few pest or disease problems, but crown rot can occur in some species if the spring has been especially wet. Keep an eye out for plants whose leaves seem to be curling up or drying out even though the soil seems damp. They could be victims of crown rot and may need a fungicide treatment.

JUNE

- You can still plant container-grown ornamental grasses from nurseries and garden centers. Many of our most popular ornamental grasses are warm-season grasses and will establish very well during the warm days of early summer.

- Water as needed to keep newly planted ornamental grasses from wilting or curling. It will only take a few weeks to get them established now that the soil and weather is consistently warm, but drying out during this time is especially hard on them.

- Instead of using wood mulch on your ornamental grasses, consider using well-rotted horse manure if it is available in your area. It is relatively free from weed seeds and will quickly enrich your soil while suppressing weeds. It is low enough in nitrogen that it will not cause weakening of the stems and flopping of plants, but as with any manure, it must be well composted before you apply it.

- The stems and leaves of some ornamental grasses, *Miscanthus*, for instance, make great fillers for flower arrangements. Clip a few small stems to tuck into vases with purple coneflower, phlox, rudbeckia, and other flowers you have cut from your garden.

JULY

- Many small- and medium-sized ornamental grasses thrive in containers, the smaller varieties making excellent fillers and those that are a little larger, excellent focal points when combined with other plants. Grasses have large root systems and can quickly become potbound. By mid- to late summer, they made need almost daily watering to keep them from curling up and the tips of their leaves from turning brown.

- Fast-growing summer weeds seem to appear overnight. Be sure to keep them under control among your ornamental grasses until the grasses are thick and tall enough to shade out most weeds on their own.

- Grasshoppers are one of the few pests that may be a problem for ornamental grasses and July is one of their most active months as they feed on the leaves, leaving them ragged-looking. If they become a serious problem, grasshoppers can be treated with carbaryl.

AUGUST

- August is a stressful month for planting any new plants, including ornamental grasses. In fact, your ideal window of time for planting ornamental grasses—spring and early summer—has already closed. If you have plants that must get in the ground right away, be sure to keep them well watered during this hot, dry month.

- Watering will be at the top of your to-do list this month for all of your garden plants and not just ornamental grasses. Remember that you want to water deeply and less frequently to encourage roots to reach far into the soil searching for water and nutrients. This will greatly reduce how much you have to water in the future.

- August is a perfect time to walk your garden in the early morning, journal in hand, and make notes of which plans are performing well and which ones are not. You may want to add more of those that are proving themselves and replace those that aren't.

SEPTEMBER

- Ornamental grasses are at their peak in September and October. If you want to preserve any dried plumes for use in dried floral arrangements, fall decorations, or Christmas décor, now is the time to dry them in a warm, dry place. Once they have had a couple of weeks to dry, spray them with a light coat of shellac or hair spray to help keep them from shattering.

- Feeding now won't spur your ornamental grasses (most of them, anyway) into fall growth, but any fertilizer you applied now would likely not be used by the plants and would just go to waste. Better to put the fertilizer bag, at least for your ornamental grasses, back in the garden shed and make yourself a note to feed them early next spring, just as they begin to green up.

- Clean up fallen leaves in flower beds and around ornamental grasses. If allowed to remain on the ground for the winter, they can harbor insects and diseases that can cause problems for the next growing season, and, for ornamental grasses, they can harbor voles, which may burrow into the crowns of the plants and do serious damage to the crowns and roots.

OCTOBER

- If you have a slope whose steepness makes mowing dangerous, consider planting ornamental grasses as a low-maintenance solution. They require almost no maintenance, once established, and their deep roots will also help to stabilize the ground.

Interplanting grasses with annual flowers can make for a beautiful garden.

- Interplant spring-flowering bulbs, such as miniature daffodils, grape hyacinths, crocus, and others with your ornamental grasses for splashes of color next spring. The smaller, earlier-flowering bulbs are best for this, so that their foliage will be dying down by the time the grasses begin growing actively.

- Autumn is the perfect time to freshen up the garden's mulch. Wait until after all of the leaves have fallen and been cleaned up. A fresh layer of mulch will show off ornamental grasses' architectural form in the garden to great effect during the winter months.

NOVEMBER

- Avoid planting ornamental grasses now since winter is just around the corner. They may not have time to become well established before cold weather sets in, and crown rot can cause losses of up to 50 percent or more if plants sit in cold, wet soil through the winter.

- Autumn is often the driest season of the year in the South, so be sure to keep up with watering throughout the garden—especially for first-year plantings that are just getting well established. Ornamental grasses are going dormant now and will require little or no additional watering, but their neighbors could be suffering!

- Winter and early spring weeds, like chickweed, henbit, and dandelions, will be germinating now. It is easiest to eradicate them while they are small. Be careful when hoeing or cultivating around ornamental grasses, since they frequently have a lot of roots near the surface of the soil in addition to the ones that are going deep in search of water.

DECEMBER

- If you're into natural décor during the holiday season, consider using the feathery plumes of ornamental grasses as part of this year's Christmas scheme. They can be tucked into Christmas trees or added to dried arrangements for a soft and natural effect.

- Continue pulling winter weeds from around your ornamental grasses and in your flower beds. They grow amazingly fast during the cool days and nights of late fall and early winter. The larger and more deeply rooted they become, the harder they will be to remove, so stay on top of the weeding and get them while they're small.

- Keep an eye out for voles throughout the winter. They are nasty little creatures that look like mice, but with shorter tails and bigger teeth. They can make quick work of almost any garden plant, but they especially love ornamental grasses and hostas. Keeping your garden free from debris where they can hide and not mulching too deeply (they love to burrow just under the mulch) will help discourage them.

- Grasslike plants, such as liriope, mondo grass, and sweet flag, that remain evergreen through the winter can be divided while they are dormant. Unlike warm-season grasses, the roots of these grasslike plants will continue to grow through the winter and will be reestablished by the time spring arrives.

PERENNIALS
for the South

What is a perennial? In the broadest sense of the term, a perennial is any plant that lives three or more years. Trees, shrubs, and some vines are all perennials by definition, but gardeners use the term most often to refer to herbaceous perennial flowers. We ask, "Do you have a perennial garden?", or "Have you grown that new perennial phlox?" For most gardeners, perennials are plants that, in winter, will die to the ground while their root system and a crown or growth point of some type overwinters beneath the soil. In spring, new growth emerges from this crown and the process of growing and flowering begins again.

This ability to return year after year, multiplying and putting on a bigger show with each passing season, is one of the best traits of perennial garden flowers. The finest perennials will flower abundantly and multiply without too much fussing on your part. Some will tolerate considerable neglect, and a few, like artemisia, even prefer it. Perennial gardens enjoy enduring popularity among gardeners for their beauty that increases with each year and their ability to brighten our landscapes with bold and beautiful color.

Southern gardeners enjoy another advantage over gardeners farther north in that we benefit from mild winters in much of our region. Evergreen perennials like yucca show off their dramatic, spiky leaves in sunny locations while Christmas ferns keep their delicate green fronds right through the winter in shady corners. Some of the most special, though, are those perennials that have the ability to flower during the winter in spite of any cold or inclement weather we may endure. Lenten rose (*Helleborus* × *hybridus*) and its kin are some of the best examples. Depending on which variety you choose, you can have Lenten rose, Christmas rose, or the bear's foot hellebore (all featured in the following pages) in flower beginning in late autumn and early winter, continuing right on through early spring. Paired with winter-blooming bulbs and shrubs, your garden can be a showplace year-round.

Perennials are also some of the most adaptable garden plants and can perform a variety of functions. Showstopping displays of summertime blooms are the reason many perennials are so popular, but what about after they flower? Are there other ways perennials can be useful? Of course there are!

Many perennials have beautiful leaves and stems even when they aren't in bloom, adding to the green layers of the garden. Some have interesting structure or form that adds architectural interest to the garden, flowers or no flowers. Others have beautiful pods or seedheads that remain decorative long after the flowers themselves have faded. Some perennials grow from a slowly creeping or spreading root or stem that acts much like a groundcover, or they reseed themselves to form large patches or colonies in the garden and can be used in place of traditional groundcovers in many instances.

HOW HARDY ARE PERENNIALS?

In Southern gardens, there are two types of hardiness to consider when it comes to perennials. Winter hardiness is what first comes to mind, and you will recall that's simply a plant's ability to survive a winter in a given hardiness zone that is determined by the lowest average winter temperature that region experiences. If a perennial is listed as hardy to Zone 6, it should be hardy enough to survive winters in most of the South. If a perennial is hardy only to Zone 8, that means it would survive only in Zones 8 and warmer. Those in zones colder than Zone 8 would need to find an alternative.

Heat tolerance in perennials should also be considered. Peonies are the perfect example of a much-loved perennial that more Southern gardeners wish they could grow successfully. Peonies need a certain amount of cold weather every winter in order to thrive and Southern climates often don't get cold enough to suit them. They will thrive well up into the northern tier of states and Canada, but once you move them into zones that are warmer than Zone 7, their winter chilling requirements may not be met, the plants will suffer, flowering will be sparse, and they may eventually die out.

Many plants will thrive outside their zones, and microclimates play important roles in that success. In my garden on the border between Zones 6a and 7b, I have success with peonies in the open garden at the north end of the property where cold winter winds prevail, but in a shady, protected corner near the south end of the house, I grew a plant only hardy to Zone 8 for several years because of the protection offered it there. Knowing your garden and its microclimates will let you grow the broadest range of plants that are "hardy" in your area.

SUCCESS IN THE PERENNIAL GARDEN

One of the challenges with many perennials is that they bloom only a few weeks each season, causing waves of bloom in the garden. As one variety finishes, another may just be starting. When planning a garden, I carefully consider the foliage of perennials and what it looks like when the plants stop blooming, blending those with great foliage with those having beautiful blooms. Perennials grown more for their foliage like 'Powis Castle' artemisia, coral bells, and lamb's ear are as important in your garden's design as those with spectacular displays of blooms for a few weeks, but with little to offer the rest of the year.

Further success will come by selecting the best possible site for your perennial garden and the plants you want to grow. Proper soil preparation, with the addition of soil conditioner and plenty of organic matter, will enhance drainage and alleviate many problems from the outset. The one time of year that most perennials will not tolerate moisture at their feet is winter. Cold, wet conditions during the cold months of the year can easily lead to root and crown rot—a death sentence for many perennial plants.

MADE IN THE SHADE

When growing perennial flowers, you are not limited to sunny borders. Many perennials flourish in shade. Some of the best plants, such as lungwort, ferns, wild ginger, and hosta, can be used to magnificent effect in the shade of a large oak or as the understory planting in a beautiful woodland. Shaded sites can be problematic. Tree roots will quickly invade well-watered and well-fed beds. Many shade-loving perennials are used to root competition and will adapt well, but be prepared to do some supplemental watering and feeding as the need arises.

For native plant enthusiasts, shade gardens with spring wildflowers are the ultimate display of Mother Nature's beauty. Survival of many wildflowers has to do with their ability to grow and flower in early spring when light and moisture are plentiful, going dormant for the long, dry summer when conditions are less conducive to the survival of smaller plants. By storing up water and energy before the trees leaf out, these plants are able to thrive in difficult conditions.

GARDEN AGGRESSORS

There is some confusion in today's world about plants that are invasive versus plants that are aggressive. Many gardeners now associate the word "invasive" with plants from other parts of the world that may invade native habitats and displace the naturally occurring plant life there. While this is true, there can also be garden invaders or garden aggressors. Garden aggressors may be non-native, but they can just as easily be native plants that are perfectly behaved in their natural habitats, but when you move them to the garden, with good soil, plenty of water, and regular feeding, they become monsters. Plants like pink evening primrose come to mind, as do bee balm and other members of the mint family, goldenrod, and obedient plant. These plants and many others, while beautiful, will tear through the garden at breakneck pace, running over, under, around, and through anything that stands in their way.

PERENNIAL MAINTENANCE

Maintenance is an inescapable part of gardening and perennials are no exception. Weeding beds is simply a necessary evil, which, if you can learn to embrace it, may be quite cathartic. Proper spacing of plants will help control weeds by shading the soil, and a light layer of mulch will inhibit the stronger types. Some plants will require staking and others deadheading to encourage repeat flowering. Regular watering during the hot months of summer and a once or twice yearly application of fertilizer will be important to keep your perennials growing and looking their very best.

The gardener's goal—always—is to encourage the plants to grow larger and healthier with each passing season, providing more flowers or more colorful foliage to make the garden lush and full.

AROMATIC ASTER
Aster oblongifolius

Why It's Special—The foliage of aromatic aster provides a perfect, soft green backdrop for earlier-blooming perennials until late summer and autumn when the plant becomes hidden in a cloud of lavender-blue flowers. Aromatic aster is native and well adapted to our Southern climate.

How to Plant & Grow—Plant in full sun or light afternoon shade at any time through the early summer. Be careful about too much shade, though, or stems may become weak causing plants to splay open in the middle. Space aromatic asters on 3-foot centers. Within a season or two they will more than fill their space.

Care & Problems—In early spring, cut perennial asters back 4 to 6 inches in height. New growth will come from the base of the plant. Pinching the growing tips once or twice between May and July will make for bushier plants and more blooms later in the summer and fall.

Hardiness—Zones 3a to 8b

Bloom Color—Lavender-blue

Peak Season—Early summer to late fall

Mature Size (H x W)—2 to 2½ ft. × 2½ to 3 ft.

Water Needs—Moderately moist to slightly dry

ARTEMISIA 'POWIS CASTLE'
Artemisia × 'Powis Castle'

Why It's Special—Silver foliage helps to blend and unify colors in the perennial border, and for Southern climates, this plant is one of the best. In most areas, 'Powis Castle' will be nearly evergreen, looking good throughout the year. It is the only well-behaved artemisia that thrives in the heat and humidity of the South.

How to Plant & Grow—'Powis Castle' is best planted in spring when soil temperatures begin to warm in late April or early May. Site in a full-sun location and give it some elbow room, as it will grow 2 to 3 feet high and wide very quickly. Soil should be well drained, particularly in winter, when cold, wet conditions may lead to root rot.

Care & Problems—Pinching or light pruning to manage plant size can be performed anytime during the summer months. Hard pruning should be reserved for spring only, just as new growth begins.

Hardiness—Zones 6a to 9a

Bloom Color—Grown for silvery foliage

Peak Season—April to November

Mature Size (H x W)—2 to 3 ft. × 2 to 3 ft.

Water Needs—Moderately drought tolerant, once established

BAPTISIA
Baptisia spp. and hybrids

Why It's Special—One of our toughest native perennials, baptisia, or false indigo, is an indispensible garden perennial. New hybrids have been introduced ranging in color from soft lavender to midnight blue, creamy yellow, white, and even some new bronze bicolors and blends.

How to Plant & Grow—Plant in spring, handling carefully as new growth is very brittle. Baptisia are slow to establish, so if this is the plant to splurge on then buy the largest size you can afford. Baptisia will frequently live in the garden for twenty years or more with little to no care.

Care & Problems—Be sure to site baptisia where you want them the first time. They will quickly grow large, fleshy taproots and resent being moved. Foliage is attractive throughout the growing season and should not be trimmed back until late fall. Seedpods remain ornamental through winter if allowed to stand.

Hardiness—Zones 3a to 8b

Bloom Color—Shades of violet-blue, yellow, white, bronze

Peak Season—Spring to early summer

Mature Size (H x W)—1½ to 4 ft. × 1½ to 4 ft.

Water Needs—Very drought tolerant, once established

BEE BALM
Monarda fistulosa

Why It's Special—Red or common bee balm is the most widely found variety in garden centers, but some other native species, like *Monarda fistulosa*, are more disease resistant and less aggressive in the garden. All bee balms are extremely attractive to beneficial pollinators like hummingbirds and butterflies.

How to Plant & Grow—Bee balm can be planted anytime from spring to early summer. The more sun you give it, the stronger your plants will be and the more blooms you will have. Although many consider it to be tough and drought tolerant, the truth is that moist, well-drained soil suits bee balm best.

Care & Problems—Some bee balms can be aggressive in the garden, although this species is better behaved. It performs well with other large plants like ornamental grasses, asters, and perennial sunflowers. Although all bee balms spread to a certain degree, it is still a welcome addition to almost any sunny garden and is easy to pull where it isn't wanted.

Hardiness—Zones 4a to 9a

Bloom Color—Soft lavender-pink to white

Peak Season—Early to midsummer

Mature Size (H x W)—4 ft. × 3 ft.

Water Needs—Evenly moist soil is best

BLACK-EYED SUSAN
Rudbeckia fulgida var. *sullivantii* 'Goldsturm'

Why It's Special—Durable and easy to grow, the unmistakable, rich yellow flowers of 'Goldsturm' are a welcome sight when they appear in July. Its flowering time fills an important bloom gap in the perennial border when early summer perennials have finished flowering and fall bloomers have yet to begin.

How to Plant & Grow—Plant black-eyed Susans anytime the soil can be worked, although the preferred season is spring. Choose the most vigorous looking plants. It adapts to most conditions and soil types, but is ideal in well-drained, moisture-retentive soils.

Care & Problems—Black-eyed Susans are durable once established and are virtually maintenance free. After several years in the garden, clumps will have spread considerably and may begin to thin toward the center. Dig vigorous plants from the edges of the clump and transplant back to the middle, discarding any unwanted plants to control the size of the clump.

Hardiness—Zones 4a to 9a

Bloom Color—Brilliant, golden yellow

Peak Season—Mid- to late summer

Mature Size (H x W)—1½ to 2 ft. × 2 to 2½ ft.

Water Needs—Adaptable, but evenly moist is best

BUTTERFLY WEED
Asclepias tuberosa

Why It's Special—Butterfly weed is a tough, roadside native that thrives on neglect! Its brilliant orange flowers light up the midsummer garden, attracting bees, butterflies, and other desirable pollinators. It is the host plant for Monarch butterfly caterpillars, so if you see something munching on the leaves, don't despair and *don't spray!*

How to Plant & Grow—Plant butterfly weed in spring to early summer in full sun. It has a deep taproot that makes it difficult both to transplant and to divide. Choose where you want it to grow, plant it, and let it alone. It will tolerate both clay and sandy soils, but does not like wet feet.

Care & Problems—Hot temperatures and dry soils are all this tough, native wildflower needs to thrive. Deadheading after the first flush of bloom and a light application of organic fertilizer may encourage it to flower a second time later in the summer or autumn.

Hardiness—Zones 3a to 8b

Bloom Color—Deep orange, occasionally red or gold

Peak Season—Midsummer

Mature Size (H x W)—1½ to 2 ft. × 1½ to 2 ft.

Water Needs—Extremely drought tolerant

CARYOPTERIS 'SNOW FAIRY'
Caryopteris divaricata 'Snow Fairy'

Why It's Special—You may be familiar with caryopteris as a shrub (sometimes called "bluebeard" or "blue spirea"), but this species is a true perennial, dying to the ground each autumn and returning the following spring. Deep green leaves are brightly edged in white and form the perfect backdrop to the sky blue flowers that appear in mid- to late summer and early autumn.

How to Plant & Grow—Plant container-grown plants in spring to get the plant well established during the warm summer months. 'Snow Fairy' will die to its base during the winter, but will return in spring and grow vigorously as soon as the weather warms up.

Care & Problems—Good drainage is essential and drier conditions suit the plant better than wet, although this species has proven quite tolerant of heavy clay soils. Overfertilizing may cause plants to grow excessively and flower less.

Hardiness—Zones 5b to 8b

Bloom Color—Blue

Peak Season—Late summer to early fall

Mature Size (H x W)—3 ft. × 3 ft.

Water Needs—Moderate to slightly dry, well-drained

COLUMBINE
Aquilegia × hybrida

Why It's Special—The delicate and beautiful foliage of columbine resembles that of a maidenhair fern, and the spectacular blooms light up the spring garden. It reseeds itself where it's happy and will mix and mingle with other shade garden plants without becoming a problem.

How to Plant & Grow—The ideal location for columbine is in morning sun with afternoon shade or in high dappled shade throughout the day. Best growth and flowering are in rich, woodland soil. Once established, plants will be quite drought tolerant.

Care & Problems—Columbine is known as a short-lived perennial and typically has a life expectancy of three to four years, possibly shorter in the warmest climates. Buy new plants or transplant seedlings routinely to keep new, robust plants coming along continually. Leaf miners may burrow between the layers of the leaves. They are unsightly, but fortunately, not generally life threatening.

Hardiness—Zones 3a to 8a

Bloom Color—White, pink, yellow, red, purple, blue

Peak Season—Spring

Mature Size (H x W)—1 to 3 ft. × 1 to 1½ ft.

Water Needs—Average to moist soil

CORAL BELLS
Heuchera spp. and hybrids

Why It's Special—Thanks to a few enterprising plant breeders, today's generation of coral bells boast beautiful flowers, evergreen foliage in an array of colors, and tolerance of hot, humid weather. The inclusion of two Southern native species in many breeding programs has changed the game when it comes to growing coral bells in the South! It's one of the best perennial plants for dry shade.

How to Plant & Grow—Plant coral bells in spring or fall. Most prefer dappled light and are happiest in partial shade. They are extremely adaptable, tolerant of less-than-ideal soils and even some degree of drought, but they will be most beautiful and dramatic when well cared for.

Care & Problems—Water deeply twice a week until well established. Rabbits and slugs and snails can disfigure young, tender growth in spring. Diatomaceous earth or a non-toxic slug bait sprinkled on the ground around the plants will help to eliminate slugs and snails.

Hardiness—Zones 4a to 8a

Bloom Color—White, pink, red

Peak Season—Spring to fall, depending on species

Mature Size (H x W)—Foliage, 8 to 10 in. × 1½ to 2 ft.

Water Needs—Moderately drought tolerant

COREOPSIS 'FULL MOON'
Coreopsis × 'Full Moon'

Why It's Special— 'Full Moon' coreopsis is a hybrid coreopsis that has proven itself in the garden time and again. Buttery yellow flowers are borne profusely from early summer until frost, and plants show excellent resistance to powdery mildew.

How to Plant & Grow—Plant coreopsis anytime from spring through fall. Once established, the plants are quite drought tolerant, but blooms will last longer and continue to appear for many weeks if they receive some irrigation and an occasional application of liquid bloom booster-type fertilizer.

Care & Problems—As with many perennial garden flowers that bloom for very long periods of time, some coreopsis can be short-lived. Dividing clumps every two to three years helps maintain vigor and keeps plants producing new, healthy growth and lots of blooms. If plants begin looking worse for wear in late summer, cut them back 6 inches to encourage a new flush of growth and bloom.

Hardiness—Zones 5 to 8

Bloom Color—Butter yellow

Peak Season—Early summer to frost

Mature Size (H x W)—1½ ft. × 1½ ft.

Water Needs—Moderately drought tolerant, once established

DAYLILY

Hemerocallis spp. and hybrids

Why It's Special—One of the largest groups of plants on the market, there are more than 25,000 registered varieties of daylilies. Gone are the days when the old-fashioned orange "ditch lily" reigned supreme. Today's magnificent hybrids come in every size, shape, form, and color.

How to Plant & Grow—Plant in full sun in early spring or late fall. They will tolerate part sun conditions, but may bloom less. In heavy clay, amend with generous quantities of organic matter for best growth, but otherwise daylilies are nearly care-free.

Care & Problems—Deer can be a serious problem. Daylilies are near the top of their "preferred foods" list, and, in areas where deer are a problem, fencing is a must if you ever want to see a flower. Other than deer, daylilies are more or less pest free. For reblooming varieties, deadheading is important to keep new scapes and buds forming.

Hardiness—Zones 4 to 9

Bloom Color—All colors, bicolors, and blends

Peak Season—Mid-spring to early fall

Mature Size (H x W)—1 to 6 ft. × 1 to 3 ft.

Water Needs—Even moisture for lush growth and flowers

DIANTHUS 'BATH'S PINK'

Dianthus gratianapolitanus 'Bath's Pink'

Why It's Special—*Dianthus* 'Bath's Pink' has allowed those of us who garden in warmer climates, where many dianthus struggle, to share in the joy and fragrance that cottage pinks provide in the garden each spring. 'Bath's Pink' makes an outstanding groundcover in full sun.

How to Plant & Grow—Container-grown plants can be planted in the garden in spring or fall. Choose a location in full sun with excellent drainage. 'Bath's Pink' is especially beautiful planted at the edge of the wall where its blue-green foliage and pink flowers can cascade and soften the wall.

Care & Problems—Good drainage is essential with all dianthus. Stem and crown rot can be a problem in cold, wet soils in winter. Only a few varieties are well suited to growing in the South since heat and humidity take a quick and deadly toll on the plants. Deadhead by shearing old blooms all at once when flowering is finished.

Hardiness—Zones 3 to 8

Bloom Color—Pink

Peak Season—Spring

Mature Size (H x W)—6 in. × 3 ft.

Water Needs—Moderately drought tolerant, once established

FERN, CHRISTMAS

Polystichum acrostichoides

Why It's Special—Christmas ferns are easy to transplant and will brighten up dark corners where almost nothing else will grow. They are compact, clump-forming plants with delicate fronds whose evergreen qualities make them perfect year-round additions to any shade garden.

How to Plant & Grow—Christmas fern is truly a low-maintenance and resilient plant once established. Watering is essential during the first season but only in dry spells in the following years. An organic mulch of compost is the best fertilizer, releasing its nutrients slowly and improving the quality of the soil as it breaks down.

Care & Problems—Essentially pest free, Christmas fern requires little in the way of additional care. In late winter or early spring, last year's foliage should be trimmed off before new fronds begin to unfurl. On rare occasions, slugs may attack soft new growth in early spring. Diatomaceous earth or a non-toxic, iron-based slug bait will correct this problem.

Hardiness—Zones 3a to 9a

Bloom Color—Grown for its evergreen foliage

Peak Season—Year-round

Mature Size (H x W)—1½ to 2 ft. × 1½ to 2 ft.

Water Needs—Moderately drought tolerant, once established

FERN, CINNAMON

Osmunda cinnamomea

Why It's Special—Cinnamon fern has delicate, lacy fronds of light green that mix and mingle perfectly with the broader leaves of other shade lovers like hosta, Lenten rose, coral bells, and others. It is a clump-forming fern, which, once planted, stays put. Spore-bearing fronds will appear in the center of the plant covered in cinnamon-brown, dustlike spores.

How to Plant & Grow—Plant cinnamon fern from early spring to early summer. It is easiest to plant them when they are still dormant or just as new fronds are emerging to avoid breaking delicate fronds. Allow them a couple of years to settle into the garden and really begin performing to their fullest potential.

Care & Problems—One of the more care-free ferns, cinnamon fern only has a handful of drawbacks. In very dry summers, it may become ratty looking or even head into an early dormancy if it doesn't have water available. Fronds are brittle and easily broken.

Hardiness—Zones 3 to 8

Bloom Color—Green, grown for foliage

Peak Season—Early spring through late summer

Mature Size (H x W)—2½ ft. × 2½ ft.

Water Needs—Evenly moist

FERN, OSTRICH

Matteuccia struthiopteris

Why It's Special—In an open woodland with space for a stunning fern that will form great colonies over time, ostrich fern is one of the best. Light green, lacy fronds are especially beautiful in the early part of the season. Ostrich fern spreads by underground runners, sending up new plants as far as 3 feet away from the mother clump.

How to Plant & Grow—Plant ostrich fern in damp, shady woodlands where its spreading roots can crawl through the soil and establish large patches. Well-grown ostrich ferns may stand nearly 5 feet tall (3 feet is more common) and spread several feet in every direction.

Care & Problems—Deer may occasionally nip the tips off the fronds, but they rarely eat it to the point of doing real damage. Slugs and snails can be a problem in early spring as new, tender fronds emerge, but a plant usually outgrows them unless the infestation is particularly bad.

Hardiness—Zones 3 to 7

Bloom Color—Green, grown for foliage

Peak Season—Early to midsummer

Mature Size (H x W)—3 to 5 ft. tall, forming large colonies

Water Needs—Moderate to moist

FERN, SOUTHERN WOOD

Thelypteris kunthii

Why It's Special—This is one of our most forgiving and adaptable native ferns with delicate, lacy, light green fronds emerging in spring and looking great through summer's heat, right up to frost. Deer tend to leave it alone in preference of other shade garden plants.

How to Plant & Grow—Plant in spring for a good summer growing season to get established. Spreading by underground runners, southern wood fern will begin colonizing within a few weeks of planting though is never invasive. A 1-gallon pot planted in April could easily be an 18-inch-wide, full but tidy clump by autumn.

Care & Problems—Southern wood fern thrives in rich, moist, woodsy soil but will be tolerant of less-than-ideal conditions. With the ability to grow new fronds almost immediately, it can be cut back hard in midsummer, lightly fed, watered, and in a few weeks will have completely rejuvenated and look fresh until fall.

Hardiness—Zones 6 to 9

Bloom Color—Light green, grown for foliage

Peak Season—Spring to fall

Mature Size (H x W)—2 ft. × 4 ft.

Water Needs—Moderate to moist

HARDY HIBISCUS
Hibiscus moscheutos

Why It's Special—Hardy hibiscus grows in damp sites and roadside ditches throughout the South. With blooms up to 10 inches across, it's a showy addition to the summer perennial border that thrives, even in drier conditions, with minimal care.

How to Plant & Grow—Plant in spring as soil begins to warm. Plants are late to break dormancy, often not appearing until late April, but growing rapidly once they start. A sunny garden and moist, average soil will encourage rapid growth. Plants are shrublike in proportion, so allow plenty of room.

Care & Problems—Hardy hibiscus is a low-maintenance plant with few pests, although Japanese beetles can be a problem in early summer. Pick them off by hand and drop them in a jar of soapy water, or carbaryl is an effective method of control for severe infestations. When clumps grow too large, dig and divide in early spring before new growth starts.

Hardiness—Zones 5 to 9

Bloom Color—Shades of red, rose, pink, white

Peak Season—Midsummer

Mature Size (H x W)—2 to 5 ft. × 2 to 5 ft.

Water Needs—Average to moist soils

HELLEBORE, CHRISTMAS ROSE
Helleborus niger

Why It's Special—Christmas rose is one of those truly exceptional plants that defies all logic, blooming in midwinter. Pristine white flowers appear as early as Thanksgiving on some varieties and continue right on through the winter months without hesitation.

How to Plant & Grow—Plants may be available as they flower in late autumn or in spring as pots full of beautiful green leaves. Plant Christmas rose in dappled shade to shade where it will receive some summer moisture, but should be well drained in winter. Rich, woodland soil suits it better than cold, wet clay.

Care & Problems—Christmas rose and its close cousins (included in other profiles in this chapter) are some of the most care-free of shade garden perennials. Deer will not touch them and even voles generally leave them alone. The one thing that most will not tolerate is being planted in heavy clay soil that is cold and wet during the winter. They're best in Zone 7 and cooler.

Hardiness—Zones 4 to 7

Bloom Color—White

Peak Season—Winter

Mature Size (H x W)—1 ft. × 1 ft.

Water Needs—Moderate, well drained

HELLEBORE, LENTEN ROSE
Helleborus × hybridus

Why It's Special—With flowers that appear at a most surprising time of year, Lenten roses, also known as hellebores, reign supreme when much of the garden is drab and dormant. Lenten roses may begin flowering as early as February, putting on a spectacular show with early spring-flowering shrubs, bulbs, and wildflowers.

How to Plant & Grow—Fall is the best time to plant, as plants are making new roots at that time and establish easily. Hellebores perform best in rich, well-drained soil. A spring application of composted manure or organic fertilizer will encourage lush growth and abundant blooms the next year.

Care & Problems—Hellebores grow slowly at first, but once established will "fatten up" quickly and get bigger and more beautiful as the seasons progress. Mature clumps can have literally hundreds of blooms over a period of several months from winter through spring.

Hardiness—Zones 5b to 8b

Bloom Color—Shades of white, pink, green, deep purple

Peak Season—Winter through spring

Mature Size (H x W)—1 to 1 ½ ft. × 2 to 2½ ft.

Water Needs—Moderately drought tolerant, once established

HOLLYHOCK
Alcea rosea

Why It's Special—Hollyhock is an old-fashioned favorite, passed along from one Southern gardener to the next as far back as anyone knows. Tall and statuesque, they are a classic cottage garden plant, their spires of showy blooms opening over the course of many weeks from late spring through midsummer.

How to Plant & Grow—Hollyhocks are usually sold "in the green" (without blooms) in spring. Most will not flower their first season while they grow roots deep into the ground, forming a healthy clump of round, boldly textured leaves that are interesting even when the plant is not in bloom.

Care & Problems—Japanese beetles and lace bugs can both be problems on hollyhocks. The fungal disease rust can be safely treated with copper fungicide. Staking may be required if you live where wind is a problem. Cut the entire plant to the ground after flowering to encourage a flush of fresh new growth.

Hardiness—Zones 3 to 9

Bloom Color—White, pink, rose, yellow, red, maroon

Peak Season—Early summer

Mature Size (H x W)—3 to 6 ft. × 3 ft.

Water Needs—Moderate, drought tolerant once established

HOSTA
Hosta spp. and hybrids

Why It's Special—With more than 2,000 varieties readily available in the retail nursery trade and many more than that from specialty nurseries, hostas may be the ultimate shade perennial. With sizes ranging from 4-inch-tall miniatures to giants that spread more than 7 feet wide at maturity, there is a hosta for every garden.

How to Plant & Grow—Hostas can be planted anytime the ground is not frozen, but they establish particularly well if planted in early autumn. Root growth will continue through winter and plants will burst into growth the following spring. Hostas prefer rich, fertile, well-drained soil.

Care & Problems—Unfortunately, hostas are at the top of the list when it comes to deer favorites, and voles can also be a real problem, especially in winter and very early spring. Most garden centers will be able to offer suggestions for control methods that have been successful in your area.

Hardiness—Zones 3a to 8a

Bloom Color—White, lavender

Peak Season—April to October

Mature Size (H x W)—4 in. to 2½ ft. × 4 in. to 7 ft.

Water Needs—Average to moist soil

IRIS, JAPANESE

Iris ensata

Why It's Special—Japanese iris have some of the most spectacular flowers in the plant kingdom. Crepe paper-like blooms can be nearly 8 inches in diameter on some varieties, and while their bloom season is limited to a few weeks, it is spectacular when it occurs. Their swordlike leaves lend vertical drama to the garden.

How to Plant & Grow—Best planted in spring, Japanese iris benefit from spring and early summer rains to get established. They are well adapted to growing in average garden soil, but in the wild, they grow near ponds or stream banks, making them well suited to damp or wet areas in the garden.

Care & Problems—Japanese iris have few problems, but deer will occasionally browse the foliage and may nibble the blooms as they begin to open. Grasshoppers can chew leaves in mid to late summer, but are usually not a serious problem. Feeding in autumn will encourage flowering the following summer.

Hardiness—Zones 4 to 8

Bloom Color—White, pink, lavender, purple, blends

Peak Season—Early to midsummer

Mature Size (H x W)—3 to 4 ft. × 3 to 4 ft.

Water Needs—Moist to wet

JAPANESE ANEMONE

Anemone × hybrida

Why It's Special—Japanese anemones pick up the floral show where summer perennials leave off, flowering in part sun to part shade from mid-August until frost with long, wand-like flower stalks and large but delicate poppylike flowers that dance and sway in the wind.

How to Plant & Grow—Japanese anemones are best planted in spring in order to have the benefit of the summer growing season to become well established before winter. Soil should be well prepared and thoroughly amended. Morning sun is the ideal setting, although plants that are very well irrigated will take nearly full sun, with just a little shade during the hottest part of the day. They do like moisture and will not perform well in particularly dry sites.

Care & Problems—Some varieties have been known to spread aggressively where they are happy. This trait varies from variety to variety and, sometimes, from garden to garden. 'Honorine Jobert' is one of the less-aggressive varieties with perfectly formed flowers of pure white.

Hardiness—Zones 5b to 8b

Bloom Color—Shades of pink, white

Peak Season—Late summer through fall

Mature Size (H x W)—2½ ft. to 4 ft. × 2½ ft.

Water Needs—Evenly moist soil

LAMB'S EAR
Stachys byzantina

Why It's Special—The silvery white, felted leaves of this vigorous and drought-tolerant plant are as soft and velvety to the touch as the ears of a lamb. 'Helene von Stein', also known as 'Big Ears', is a more heat- and humidity-tolerant selection that is perfect for Southern gardens.

How to Plant & Grow—Lamb's ear can be planted anytime from spring through fall and will perform best in full sun, in average soil with excellent drainage. Lamb's ear likes "sweet" or alkaline soils, so if your soil tends to be on the acidic side, a handful of lime at planting time may be helpful.

Care & Problems—Overhead irrigation can be a problem during the heat of summer, causing plants to melt in the heat and humidity. Once established, plants are extremely drought tolerant and very little additional water is required. A light feeding in early spring will encourage lush growth.

Hardiness—Zones 4a to 8b

Bloom Color—Grown for silvery foliage

Peak Season—Year-round

Mature Size (H x W)—10 to 12 in. × 2 to 3 ft.

Water Needs—Drought tolerant, once established

LUNGWORT
Pulmonaria spp. and hybrids

Why It's Special—Lungwort is a durable early-spring bloomer that mixes extremely well with our native wildflowers in the shade garden. The small blooms in shades of pink or cobalt blue appear on short stalks that reach just above its spotted foliage.

How to Plant & Grow—Lungwort can be planted in spring or fall. Because they do most of their growing before the trees leaf out, they are more tolerant of deep shade than some perennials. They thrive in moist, rich soil with morning sun or high dappled shade throughout the day.

Care & Problems—By midsummer, the heat may have taken its toll on some varieties. These can be cut to the ground, lightly fertilized, and thoroughly watered for a few weeks and they will rebound beautifully by growing new foliage that will be attractive through autumn. Some varieties are extremely susceptible to powdery mildew. Many of the new hybrids are more mildew resistant.

Hardiness—Zones 4a to 8b

Bloom Color—Pink, cobalt blue

Peak Season—Early spring

Mature Size (H x W)—8 to 12 in. × 1 to 2 ft.

Water Needs—Evenly moist soil

NEW ENGLAND ASTER
Symphyotrichum novae-angliae

Why It's Special—New England aster is a flowering powerhouse in the late summer and fall garden, covered so densely with rich purple blooms that you can barely see the foliage. Most garden centers offer inferior dwarf cultivars that are grown to look like cupcakes and sold alongside equally cupcakelike mums in autumn. The larger growing species, perfectly suited to the wild autumn garden, is where it's at!

How to Plant & Grow—You may have to go to a wildflower nursery or mail-order catalog to find the straight species of New England aster, but it's worth the effort. Plant in early spring and allow plenty of room for it to expand and grow. Pinch as necessary from early May to July 1 to help with branching and bud set.

Care & Problems—New England aster is one of the easiest and most care-free of garden perennials. It can grow tall, if not pinched, and may require staking to keep it upright. It is insect, disease, and deer resistant.

Hardiness—Zones 4 to 9

Bloom Color—Purple

Peak Season—Autumn

Mature Size (H x W)—4 ft. × 4 ft.

Water Needs—Moderate

PHLOX, GARDEN
Phlox paniculata

Why It's Special—This old-fashioned, easy-to-grow perennial has been grown for generations. New breeding programs for garden phlox are firmly focused on creating and introducing disease-resistant varieties, new colors, and sturdier, more compact plants.

How to Plant & Grow—Plant phlox in early spring in full to part sun. Rich, evenly moist soil and good air circulation are essential to keep the plants growing vigorously and free from disease. Use phlox as a companion plant for other sun-loving perennials such as purple coneflower.

Care & Problems—Garden phlox should be divided every two to three years to keep it growing vigorously. In spring, thin the clumps to the strongest four to six stems in each clump by pinching out the others to increase air circulation. Highly refined horticultural oil mixed with 1 teaspoon of baking soda per gallon of water can be applied as an effective mildew preventer.

Hardiness—Zones 4a to 8b

Bloom Color—Shades of purple, magenta, orange, pink, white

Peak Season—Mid- to late summer

Mature Size (H x W)—1½ to 4 ft. × 1½ to 2½ ft.

Water Needs—Evenly moist soils

PHLOX, PRAIRIE
Phlox pilosa

Why It's Special—Prairie phlox deserves wider attention as a terrific addition to prairie and meadow plantings, as well as naturalistic perennial gardens. It bears fragrant clusters of pale pink to lavender flowers from late spring to early summer. Where it's happy, it will politely reseed itself but is never invasive.

How to Plant & Grow—You may only find prairie phlox at native plant nurseries or by mail order but it is worth the search to add it to the garden. It prefers full to part sun in slightly moist to average soil. Excellent drainage is a necessity, and it will frequently self-sow into gravel walkways.

Care & Problems—Prairie phlox may be browsed by deer, as will most phlox. It may be more temperamental than common garden phlox, but when its needs are met—good drainage being at the top of its list of requirements—it can be spectacular. Prairie phlox is nearly mildew proof.

Hardiness—Zones 4 to 8

Bloom Color—Pale pink to deep lavender

Peak Season—Early summer

Mature Size (H x W)—1 to 2 ft. × 1 to 2 ft.

Water Needs—Moderate to moist, well drained

PURPLE CONEFLOWER
Echinacea purpurea

Why It's Special—Purple coneflower is a tough, sun-loving native that produces long-lasting, fragrant flowers from early summer through late fall. They make good cut flowers that may last ten days or more in a vase. Hybridizers have created many colors and varieties of flower forms.

How to Plant & Grow—Purple coneflower can be planted from spring through fall and is tolerant of a wide range of soils, provided they are well-drained and do not remain waterlogged during the cold months of winter. Cutting back hard after the first flowers fade will encourage a second flush in late summer.

Care & Problems—Deer will browse purple coneflower. Aster yellows is a disease that causes the flowers to be deformed. Plants should be dug up and thrown away, soil and all, and not composted, as aster yellows can be transferred back to the garden through the soil.

Hardiness—Zones 3a to 8b

Bloom Color—Pink, purple, white, red, orange, yellow

Peak Season—Early summer through fall

Mature Size (H x W)—1 to 3 ft. × 1 to 1½ ft.

Water Needs—Average to moist, but well drained

PURPLE HEART
Tradescantia pallida

Why It's Special—Purple heart is a tough yet beautiful garden plant, flourishing in heat and humidity. It has extremely deep roots and is excellent for helping to stabilize difficult banks where little else will grow, but its royal purple foliage also makes an excellent addition to the perennial border or containers.

How to Plant & Grow—Plant after danger of frost is past, since tender new growth can be nipped by frost. Purple heart thrives in full sun and is drought tolerant, but will also perform well in part shade, as well as moist areas. It is truly one of the most versatile plants you can grow.

Care & Problems—If plants look ratty, cut them to the ground, feed and water them, and they will respond with lush new growth in a matter of weeks. Keep in mind that it may not resprout in spring until the soil is thoroughly warm— possibly as late as May.

Hardiness—Zones 7 to 10

Bloom Color—Grown for its deep purple foliage

Peak Season—Spring through fall

Mature Size (H x W)—10 in. × 2 to 3 ft.

Water Needs—Very drought tolerant, once established

ROSE CAMPION
Lychnis coronaria

Why It's Special—In Southern gardens, rose campion may act like a biennial or even a reseeding annual. Individual plants usually grow and flower for two to three years before dying off and leaving seedlings behind. The felted, silvery leaves set off the small but screaming magenta flowers borne on 1½- to 2-foot-tall, wandlike stems.

How to Plant & Grow—Plant rose campion in spring or fall in extremely well-drained soil. It may be beneficial to leave the top 1 inch or so of the rootball sticking out of the soil, mounding soil up to its edge, but not into or over the crown of the plant. Crown rot in winter is the number one reason for loss of plants.

Care & Problems—Rose campion is extremely low maintenance with few to no problems from insect pests or marauding deer. Its one enemy is winter moisture combined with clay soil. Excellent drainage is an absolute must.

Hardiness—Zones 3 to 9

Bloom Color—Magenta, pale pink, white

Peak Season—Late spring to midsummer

Mature Size (H x W)—1½ to 2 ft. × 1 ft.

Water Needs—Drought tolerant

RUSSIAN SAGE
Perovskia atriplicifolia

Why It's Special—One of the best "see through" plants for the perennial border, Russian sage provides color all season long, either from its airy stems clothed in small, silver-white leaves or from its long, slender, lavender-blue flower spikes.

How to Plant & Grow—Russian sage thrives in the heat of summer and its only real requirement is excellent drainage. It will grow in heavier clay soils, but may not survive the winter because of its intolerance of being cold and wet at the roots. Clay soils should be thoroughly amended at planting time.

Care & Problems—Outer stems of older plants become woody and may flop. Trim them off so others will take their place. Allow the semi-woody structure of the plant to stand through the winter, both for winter interest and because the plants usually experience some dieback, and pruning is best done in spring. Flowering stems can be cut for bouquets.

Hardiness—Zones 4b to 9a

Bloom Color—Lavender-blue

Peak Season—Midsummer to fall

Mature Size (H x W)—3 to 4 ft. × 3 to 4 ft.

Water Needs—Established plants are drought tolerant

SAGE, ANISE-SCENTED
Salvia guaranitica

Why It's Special—Anise-scented sage is one of those special perennials that deserves a spot in every garden. Why? It will flower from May through October and sometimes longer, giving you the long bloom season of an annual with the yearly return of a perennial. Its cobalt blue flowers are extremely attractive to hummingbirds, butterflies, and other beneficial pollinators.

How to Plant & Grow—Anise-scented sage prefers full sun to part sun in moist, well-drained soil. It grows very quickly once planted, and a 4-inch pot will easily grow into a 3-foot by 3-foot shrublike perennial by midsummer. A bloom booster-type fertilizer at planting time will ensure that this vigorous grower has plenty of nutrients to keep it flowering profusely.

Care & Problems—Regular deadheading is beneficial to keep the plant looking tidy and to keep new blooms appearing. Mid- and late summer feedings with your favorite liquid fertilizer will keep the plant growing and flowering until frost.

Hardiness—Zones 7 to 10

Bloom Color—Purple, dark blue, light blue

Peak Season—Early summer until frost

Mature Size (H x W)—3 ft. × 3 ft.

Water Needs—Moderate to evenly moist

SAGE, AUTUMN
Salvia greggii

Why It's Special—Autumn sage is a tough and resilient sun-loving perennial for Southern gardens and is perfectly suited to the hottest and sunniest locations in the garden. Blooms are a favorite of hummingbirds, appearing nonstop from early summer through autumn.

How to Plant & Grow—Plants are often rootbound in their pots by the time you buy them. Cut through the outer tangle of roots with a sharp knife or pruner blade to encourage new roots to grow deep into the soil. Overfertilizing leads to more leaves and new growth than flowers.

Care & Problems—Autumn sage is one of the most care-free plants in the garden. Almost no pest or disease bothers it. It can suffer from root rot diseases during cold, damp winters if it is planted in heavy clay soil. Excellent drainage is essential to it surviving the winter, making it an excellent choice for rock gardens or steep, sunny slopes.

Hardiness—Zones 6 to 10

Bloom Color—Red, pink, white, coral, yellow, purple

Peak Season—Early summer through frost

Mature Size (H x W)—1 to 2 ft. × 1 to 2 ft.

Water Needs—Very drought tolerant, once established

SAGE, LILAC
Salvia verticillata

Why It's Special—Lilac sage is a lesser known salvia that performs extremely well in Southern climates. Its heat and humidity tolerance make it an excellent choice for perennial beds, rock gardens, and cutting gardens. Lilac-purple flowers open from late spring through midsummer. The variety 'Purple Rain' bears deep, indigo-violet blooms.

How to Plant & Grow—Plant in spring as you are setting out other perennials in the garden. Sages quickly become rootbound in pots, so be sure to loosen the roots around the edges and at the bottom of the rootball so they will quickly grow out into the surrounding soil. Deadheading will promote a longer season of bloom.

Care & Problems—Lilac sage has very few problems. Snails and slugs may occasionally attack in early spring, but can be controlled with diatomaceous earth or an iron-based slug and snail bait. Flower stalks become ratty after flowering is finished and should be cut to the ground. A new flush of foliage will emerge.

Hardiness—Zones 4 to 9

Bloom Color—Lilac-purple to indigo

Peak Season—Late spring to early summer

Mature Size (H x W)—1 ft. × 2 ft.

Water Needs—Moderate

SAGE, MEXICAN
Salvia leucantha

Why It's Special—Mexican sage is a garden workhorse that flies under the radar for most of the summer. Its felty, gray-green leaves form the perfect backdrop for other summer-blooming perennials. In late summer and autumn, it becomes the star of the garden as the fuzzy, indigo-blue blooms emerge on long slender stalks, nearly hiding the plant.

How to Plant & Grow—Plant Mexican sage in spring and allow plenty of room for the plant to develop throughout the summer and into autumn. Even small plants will reach their full grown size in the first season. Pinching once or twice early in the season will keep the plants more compact, but don't pinch after July 1.

Care & Problems—Mexican sage is an easy, drought tolerant, tough plant that no Southern garden should be without. It can be tender in gardens that are colder than Zone 7, so be prepared to replace it occasionally when winter's chill really bites. It is worth the effort.

Hardiness—Zones 7 to 10, reliably

Bloom Color—Purple

Peak Season—Autumn

Mature Size (H x W)—3 ft. × 3 ft.

Water Needs—Moderate, drought tolerant once established

SHASTA DAISY
Leucanthemum × superbum

Why It's Special—The traditional white daisy of cottage gardens, the Shasta daisy is one of our most enduring perennials. Most varieties were poorly suited to Southern gardens, despising heat and humidity, until the 1990s when the variety 'Becky' was discovered thriving in Georgia.

How to Plant & Grow—Shasta daisies are best planted in spring in loose, well-drained soil. Planting holes should be dug at least twice the width of the rootball and soil thoroughly amended with compost and soil conditioner to allow for quick and easy rooting.

Care & Problems—Shasta daisies generally have few problems and no serious insect pests. If deer are a problem in your area, they may browse the flower buds. Don't overfertilize, as this may encourage weak growth and stems that flop. Crown rot can be a problem in winter. Do not bury plants too deeply when planting.

Hardiness—Zones 5a to 9a

Bloom Color—White

Peak Season—Early to late summer

Mature Size (H x W)—1 to 3 ft. × 1 to 3 ft.

Water Needs—Evenly moist

SPIDERWORT
Tradescantia virginiana

Why It's Special—Spiderwort is a tough, native perennial that is highly adaptable in the garden, thriving anywhere from heavy, wet clay to dry-ish woodlands. Given good garden soil, regular feeding, and water when the weather gets dry, it will astound you with its performance.

How to Plant & Grow—Fertilize once each spring, just as new growth appears to encourage a spectacular show during the first flush of bloom. When plants begin to look ratty in midsummer, cut them all the way to the ground, feed and water them, and they will flush out and rebloom until autumn.

Care & Problems—Some varieties reseed readily and can occasionally become a problem in smaller gardens. Roots run deep and babies are difficult to pull without the aid of a trowel or weeding tool. The variety 'Sweet Kate' has spectacular golden yellow foliage with cobalt blue flowers.

Hardiness—Zones 4b to 9b

Bloom Color—Shades of blue, purple, white

Peak Season—Late spring to late fall

Mature Size (H x W)—1 to 3 ft. × 1 to 2 ft.

Water Needs—Average to very moist, tolerant of wet areas

SOLOMON'S SEAL
Polygonatum spp. and hybrids

Why It's Special—Solomon's seals are some of the most beautiful of all shade garden plants. They are tough, resilient, and easy to grow, spreading slowly underground by creeping rhizomes. Variegated forms add color and interest to the garden throughout the growing season, and cut stems will last for weeks in a vase.

How to Plant & Grow—Solomon's seal can be planted anytime the soil can be worked. Take care not to break the tips of the rhizomes as you pull them from their pots. Even if the rhizomes have grown into the side of the pot and look deformed, don't try to cut or straighten them. They are very brittle and will likely snap.

Care & Problems—Solomon's seal is extremely care-free in the shade garden. Slugs and snails can be a problem on tender new growth in early spring or if infestations are particularly bad later in the season. Deer may browse the tips.

Hardiness—Zones 3 to 8

Bloom Color—White, but grown for foliage

Peak Season—Spring to fall

Mature Size (H x W)—1½ ft. × 3 ft.

Water Needs—Moderate, but drought resistant once established

STOKES ASTER
Stokesia laevis

Why It's Special—One of the bluest of the blues when it comes to flower color, this daisy relative is a welcome addition to any garden. Even the taller varieties are a very manageable size and will not overwhelm, even in smaller spaces. The varieties 'Omega Skyrocket' and 'Peachies Pick' are exceptional.

How to Plant & Grow—Plant in full sun and well-drained soil. Fertilize in spring and again in midsummer to encourage a late flush of bloom. You might wish to leave the old flower stalks, as the seedpods can be very ornamental, although this will discourage later flowering.

Care & Problems—Stokes aster is relatively pest free, with no major insect or disease problems. Division can be carried out in early spring, just as new growth begins, and plants will reestablish and bloom by midsummer. Rabbits can be a problem early in the season when new growth is soft and tender.

Hardiness—Zones 5 to 9

Bloom Color—Blue

Peak Season—Early to midsummer

Mature Size (H x W)—1 to 2½ ft. × 1 to 1½ ft.

Water Needs—Evenly moist, especially when in bloom

THREADLEAF BLUESTAR
Amsonia hubrichtii

Why It's Special—Multiple seasons of interest from early spring until late autumn make threadleaf bluestar an indispensable native wildflower for the perennial garden or border. Pale blue to nearly white flowers are borne in large clusters in spring, carrying on for several weeks before the plant turns into a soft and billowing mound of foliage for the summer. Its leaves turn brilliant gold in autumn.

How to Plant & Grow—Threadleaf bluestar (and all bluestars, for that matter) have long, fleshy, deep taproots. Plant them where you want them to grow and leave them alone. They will thrive in the same location for many years, decades even, but resent being moved.

Care & Problems—Extremely hardy, resilient, and care-free, plants just don't come much tougher than threadleaf bluestar. Left alone by browsing deer and marauding rabbits, few pests seem to bother it. It may show some yellowing and iron deficiency in highly alkaline soil.

Hardiness—Zones 6 to 9

Bloom Color—Pale blue, white

Peak Season—Spring to fall

Mature Size (H x W)—2½ ft. × 4 ft.

Water Needs—Moderate, drought tolerant once established

YUCCA
Yucca filamentosa

Why It's Special—Many gardeners have a love-hate relationship with yuccas, but the truth is that for dramatic architectural form throughout the year, few perennials can offer what the yucca does with its spiky, swordlike foliage. 'Colorguard' is a newer variety with beautiful green-and-yellow variegated leaves.

How to Plant & Grow—Plant in spring so that plants have the opportunity to become well established during the warm summer months. Yuccas will take two to three seasons to settle in and begin blooming, but their foliage value is worth it even before any flowers appear.

Care & Problems—Yuccas are extremely care-free and are one of the lowest-maintenance plants you can grow in the landscape. They also make excellent groundcovers for difficult sites, especially steep slopes, in full sun. Once a plant flowers, that portion of the plant will die, but the many pups that are produced will quickly fill and you will never know that one is gone.

Hardiness—Zones 5a to 10

Bloom Color—White

Peak Season—Year-round

Mature Size (H x W)—2½ ft. × 3 ft.

Water Needs—Very drought tolerant

JANUARY

- If you wish to grow perennials from seed, January is a good month to start. You don't have to have a greenhouse, but fluorescent lights can be very helpful. As seeds begin to germinate, keep lights 3 to 4 inches above the soil surface to prevent stretching.

- Some perennial seeds may require the cold treatment called "stratification" to break their dormancy before they will sprout. This can be done very easily by mixing them with 1 teaspoon to 1 tablespoon of damp sand, depending on the size and quantity of the seed you're sowing, sealing them in a small ziptop bag, and storing them in the refrigerator for the prescribed period of time, usually two to four weeks.

- The fungal disease *damping off* can cause the sudden dying of young seedlings. Seedlings should be kept damp, but not wet, the soil just moist to the touch. Good air circulation and a light hand with the watering can will help to prevent this problem.

- As you design your garden, consider creating island beds, which can be viewed from all sides and help to separate large expanses of lawn, giving seasonal color and interest, as well as texture and height variation, to what might be a less interesting part of the yard.

Select a variety of perennials with varying bloom times, flower colors, and plant heights.

FEBRUARY

- Some perennials will begin emerging by the end of this month. Be prepared to divide and replant summer- and fall-flowering perennials just as their new growth emerges. Most perennials won't need to be divided more often than every three years and sometimes longer.

- If there are any perennials, such as purple coneflower, black-eyed Susan, or others whose seedheads or seedpods have been left standing for winter interest, now is the time to cut them back. Birds will have picked the heads clean of seed by now and cutting them back will make way for new growth that will begin appearing in March and April.

- In warmer regions of the South, garden centers may begin stocking perennials in February. Lenten rose and other perennials that will be unfazed by cold weather can be planted as long as the soil is not frozen.

- Winter weeds, such as chickweed and henbit, are at their most active and robust right now. Control as necessary by pulling and then re-mulching perennial beds as necessary. Be sure not to pile mulch over the crowns of perennial plants, as this may encourage crown rot.

MARCH

- Perennial planting can begin across much of the South this month, as shipments of plants begin arriving at local garden centers. Be sure that you are buying the fresh, new stock and not plants that are leftovers from last year. The best garden centers will carry plants that are in season, hardened off, and ready to go in the ground. The selections will change weekly as the planting season progresses.

- Some perennials have a tendency to heave or push themselves out of the ground over a period of several years, and winter freezing and thawing only compounds the problem. This exposes tender buds that should be below the level of spring frosts. These plants can be dug and replanted slightly deeper in their holes before they begin growing to protect the crown from damage by spring frosts, marauding animals, or an errant foot while weeding.

- Most perennials benefit from a boost with fertilizer just as new growth begins to emerge in the spring. Slow-release and/or organic or all-natural fertilizers are generally best, as they last the longest in the soil and are less likely to burn tender new growth.

APRIL

- Some taller growing perennials may become top-heavy and need staking to keep them standing upright. Dahlias and lilies are perfect examples, but many other plants benefit as well. Staking should be done early in the season, with young stems tied loosely to firmly set and sturdy bamboo sticks. The stakes will be visible for a short time, but will be hidden as the plants grow. Trying to stake plants that have already flopped or fallen over is a thankless task.

- If you started seeds indoors, young plants must be hardened off before planting them in the garden. Do this by gradually exposing them to outdoor conditions. A screened porch or covered patio is a great first step, where plants are sheltered from wind and sun. Gradually expose them to more sun and the elements and after a week to ten days, they should be ready for the garden.

- Keep newly planted perennials well-watered during the first few weeks to help them get quickly established. Water deeply and thoroughly to encourage roots to grow deep into the soil in search of water.

- Watch for aphids and whiteflies on tender new growth. A strong spray of water or an application of insecticidal soap will help with control.

MAY

- If you're serious about being successful in your gardening endeavors, now is a great time to start a garden journal. It will document your observations, thoughts, and plans for the future and give you a reference to look back on and remember your successes and lessons from previous years. Keep notes on which perennials meet or exceed your expectations in the garden, as well as those that don't and may need to be replaced.

- Taller-growing perennials should be staked when they reach one-third of their mature height. Place the stakes close to the plant, but take care to avoid damaging the root system and secure the stems to the stakes with loosely tied twine so that it will not cut into the stems. Perennials are growing quickly now and staking should be done before they get too tall so the plants will hide the stakes as they grow and fill out.

- When watering, apply sufficient water to soak the soil deeply, wetting the entire root zone of the plant. Deep and thorough watering encourages roots to grow deep into the soil in search of water and nutrients and prepares them for summer days ahead when water may be scarce near the soil's surface.

- Avoid leaf spot diseases by watering your perennials from below and limiting water on the leaves. Proper spacing with plenty of air movement will also reduce fungal infections.

JUNE

- Slow and deep watering of recently planted perennials is important to get them established and to encourage roots to grow deep into the soil. As temperatures reach above 90 degrees, perennials that were planted this spring will still need supplemental watering to keep them healthy and growing vigorously.

- If you used a slow-release fertilizer early in the season, it may be time for another application. A three-month formula that was applied in early March will have reached the end of its usefulness by early June. An early summer feeding will nourish plants slowly and constantly through the long, hot days of summer.

- Many perennials will benefit from a light pinching of the growing tips at this time of year—especially late-blooming species like chrysanthemums, 'Autumn Joy' sedum, asters, Joe-pye weed, and perennial sunflowers. Pinching helps keep plants bushy and compact and encourages branching and, eventually, more blooms.

- Slug and snail baits containing iron phosphate are very effective against these destructive beasts while being safe to use in the garden where children and pets may be at play. They are some of the most effective, non-toxic snail and slug controls on the market and these are available at most garden centers.

JULY

- If you maintain a garden journal, July is a great month to do a close inspection of the garden. Which plants are thriving and which are struggling? Which have grown too large for their allotted space and may need transplanting or dividing come autumn? Which plants seem to have constant insect or disease problems and are they worth the trouble?

- Many nurseries and garden centers will be running deep discount sales this month in order to clear out spring stock. This can be a great way to expand your garden without breaking the bank, but remember they will need some extra care in order to thrive. Most will respond quickly to good garden soil, water, and fertilizer.

- The garden needs at least 1 inch of water per week during the hot days of summer for plants to continue growing and looking their best. Some plants may need more. If natural rainfall isn't providing enough water to the garden, it will be up to you.

- If you're leaving on vacation this month, be sure to have the irrigation system set to run while you're away. If you don't have an irrigation system, sprinklers and battery-powered timers attached to outdoor faucets will do the trick.

- If you have been pinching any late-blooming perennials—such as mums and asters—to keep them more compact, you should stop all pinching this month so that buds will set for fall.

AUGUST

- Spider mites are one of the most difficult garden pests to control, and they love the heat and humidity of late summer. Plants with spider mites will have lighter colored or white stippling or speckling on their leaves, and you may be able to see the "cobwebs" that the mites build when infestations are severe. Spray the upper- and under-sides of leaves with a gentle spray of water and use horticultural oil sprays to smother the mites.

- If you're planning a vacation this month, be sure to have someone keep an eye on flower beds and especially on containers while you're away. It doesn't take long for plants to dry out during hot weather.

- The early morning hours are the perfect time to get out and do essential garden tasks like deadheading and weeding. You'll be surprised at how much you can accomplish in just a few minutes of focused time and you can be back indoors before the heat of the day sets in.

- Avoid irrigating perennial beds with overhead sprinklers. Wet foliage can lead to powdery mildew and various other fungal diseases. If overhead watering is your only option, do it as early in the morning as possible to allow foliage to dry during the day.

SEPTEMBER

- The fall-blooming season really begins this month as asters, perennial sunflowers, and dahlias come into flower. In the shade garden, Japanese anemones, toad lilies, and late-blooming hostas are the stars.

- Early autumn is a great time to divide hostas throughout most of the South. Do not cut them back before you divide them, but divide them "in the green"—with their leaves attached—into clumps with at least three to five eyes. They will reestablish quickly and will return with great vigor the following year.

- Fall is the driest season throughout much of the South. Remember that perennial plants are storing energy for next year and keeping them well watered and actively growing will ensure that they get off to the best possible start next season.

- As leaves begin to fall, regular cleanup helps to ensure that insect eggs and disease spores do not overwinter in fallen debris.

OCTOBER

- Autumn is a great time for garden projects. The days are comfortably warm, but the humidity has begun to drop and the evenings are cool and pleasant. If the creation of new beds or garden areas is on your to-do list, there is no time like the present! Soil prep can be done now and beds will be ready to receive plants later in the fall or next spring, as your schedule and budget allow.

- When starting new beds, be sure to have your soil tested. The results of your soil test will tell you what the pH of your soil is, as well as its nutrient content. This will let you know whether or not you need to add lime to raise the pH and will tell you how you need to fertilize to achieve maximum performance from your plants.

- Autumn is the perfect time to dig, divide, and replant crowded perennials. If you noticed any perennials in the summer garden that looked weaker or less vigorous than normal, it may be time to divide. October is an ideal month to divide and replant hostas. They'll emerge next spring as lush and beautiful as ever.

- Many perennials benefit from a light application of organic fertilizer as they go dormant. They'll take the nutrients directly into their roots and store them to use next spring.

NOVEMBER

- The latest flowering perennials, like aster and sunflower, may just be finishing up their bloom. Leave seedheads in place for the birds to enjoy. Goldfinches are particularly attracted to the seeds of perennial sunflowers and other daisylike blooms.

- Planting perennials can continue across much of the South well into the late days of fall and early winter. Most plants need about four weeks to root in before regular freezing weather sets in. If you live in the deeper South and periods of cold weather are brief, you may be able to plant right through the winter.

- Be sure to cut back and clear away the foliage of peonies, bee balm, phlox, and other plants that are known to have problems with fungal diseases, like botrytis and powdery mildew. Spores can overwinter in old foliage and debris.

- Winter weeds will be appearing now. Henbit, chickweed, and others can be pulled and removed from perennial beds most easily while they are young and before their roots become entangled in dense clumps of perennial plants.

DECEMBER

- As winter weather sets in, now is a good time to catch up on reading those gardening magazines that you may not have gotten around to in the past couple of months. Make notes of good plant combinations or plants you haven't grown that you may want to try.

- If you planted new perennials or divided old ones this fall, be sure to mulch them well before cold winter weather arrives. Mulch will conserve moisture and help to keep plants from heaving during periods of freezing and thawing.

- Garden cleanup should be finished this month, except for perennials such as purple coneflowers, black-eyed Susans, and perennial sunflowers, whose seed heads offer food for the birds and winter interest through their form and texture. They're especially pretty when we get the occasional winter snow in some parts of the South.

SHRUBS
for the South

A shrub, by definition, is a multistemmed woody plant that matures at less than 15 to 20 feet in height. Many common shrubs are considerably smaller than that maximum height and are used as foundation plants, as groundcovers, to soften corners of buildings, or to provide masses of color in the landscape. They come in every imaginable size and form—weeping, columnar, round, pyramidal, open, or compact and may be grown for their foliage, flowers, or both. Some, like azaleas, burst into vivid color in springtime; others, like sasanqua camellias, bloom for weeks in autumn. Still others, like arborvitae and Japanese plum yew, perform important functions in the landscape by creating year-round interest with their evergreen foliage. The largest-growing shrubs, like Chinese snowball viburnum, can even be limbed up to form very attractive, multistemmed "trees" that serve as excellent focal points in the landscape.

TYPES OF SHRUBS

Evergreen shrubs have a long and enduring history in the South. Boxwoods have been a staple of the Southern landscape for more than 200 years; historic gardens and plantations take great pride in their old and majestic specimens. Evergreens come in a wide variety of forms, from the needle-bearing types like false cypress and juniper to the broadleaf evergreens like cleyera, evergreen azaleas, and camellias. Each serves a different function in the landscape and offers different textures, forms, and growth habits for adding year-round interest to the garden.

In the past two decades, conifers have soared in popularity in the landscape because of the wide range of colors, forms, and textures they offer throughout the year. The most restrictive factor when it comes to growing conifers in the South is that of heat tolerance, especially when nighttime temperatures remain above 80 degrees at night. The more serious gardeners among us are really pushing the limits of conifers to determine which ones will thrive in our climate and which ones simply are not meant to thrive here.

Deciduous shrubs, of course, lose their leaves in the winter and include many of our most common landscape shrubs. Forsythia, oakleaf hydrangea, and rose-of-Sharon are all examples of popular deciduous shrubs. Even though they lose their leaves, deciduous shrubs offer valuable architectural interest in the garden during the winter months, and many have attractive bark, colorful stems, and some may even flower in midwinter to early spring when their branches are bare.

THE NATIVE VS. NON-NATIVE DEBATE

There is great debate, these days, about planting and growing native species versus those that hail from other parts of the world. Certainly, some of the concern of "invasive exotic" species is warranted. Chinese privet, Japanese bush honeysuckle, tree of heaven, paulownia, and many more plants from abroad have invaded our natural landscapes and wreaked havoc on native plant habitats. This does not mean, however, that all plants from other parts

AMERICAN BEAUTYBERRY

AMERICAN WITCH HAZEL

of the world are bad. Some of our best landscape shrubs—including our "signature" boxwoods, hydrangeas, and gardenias of Southern landscapes and gardens—are not native plants. They are well-behaved, non-threatening varieties that have coexisted in our gardens without ever becoming problems for many (sometimes hundreds of) years.

On occasion, a problem plant will rear its ugly head. For instance, I have voluntarily removed the Japanese species of beautyberry (*Callicarpa dichotoma*) from my garden because of the copious quantities of seedlings it produced each year. They began germinating by the thousands each spring and not only was I tired of pulling them, I also didn't want them to invade the surrounding native landscape— and they were headed in that direction. I have since taken Japanese beautyberry off the list of plants I use in other peoples' gardens, as well, and replaced it with our native American beautyberry (*Callicarpa americana*). Part of being a good gardener is being a good steward, and while I do not support the carte blanche banning of plants from other parts of the world, I do believe in being responsible.

THE BEAUTY OF FLOWERING SHRUBS

Many shrubs are grown for their beautiful blooms, and we have a distinct advantage when it comes to

growing flowering shrubs in the South. When chosen wisely and well cared for, you can have shrubs in bloom in your garden nearly year-round.

In spring, azaleas, forsythia, quince, viburnums, and others light up the landscape with their dazzling displays of flowers. Some are also intoxicatingly fragrant and make great cut flowers for indoors too. Most of these spring-blooming shrubs are hardy, resilient plants, which, once established, will thrive in the landscape for many years with minimal care.

In summer, the brightly colored blooms of butterfly bush, mophead hydrangeas, St. John's wort, and oleander take center stage. If it's cooler shades of green and white that you love, summer offers the creamy blossoms of smooth hydrangea ('Annabelle' is the most famous of these) and oak leaf hydrangea partnered with the intoxicating and spicy fragrance of gardenia.

Autumn opens its doors with the flowering of sasanqua camellias, American witch hazel, and the fragrant, silvery gray berries of wax myrtle, or bayberry, perfume the air. In some parts of the South, reblooming azaleas may also put on a respectable show in September and October.

You may be wondering what winter-flowering shrubs you can add to your landscape and the good news is that in the South, we have options. In the

Deep South, Chinese snowball viburnum may open some of its flowers sporadically throughout the winter, especially during warm spells. Where they are hardy, camellias may start flowering as early as January, peaking in February and March. Alongside the camellias come the deciduous Chinese witch hazels and their hybrids, unfurling their brightly colored, fringelike blooms on bare stems from January to March.

HYDRANGEAS—CLEARING UP THE CONFUSION

Hydrangeas thrive in Southern gardens; not just one kind of hydrangea, but a variety of different types and forms, each of which requires different care, pruning, and growing conditions to be successful. Let's try to quickly clear up any confusion before addressing each of them in their own profile later in this chapter.

- FRENCH HYDRANGEA (*Hydrangea macrophylla*), also called mophead hydrangea because of its large, rounded heads of flowers, is the hydrangea that everyone wants to grow. Their vast popularity stems from the fact that when grown in acidic soils, the flowers of some varieties can be the most luscious shade of blue. These plants need rich, moist soil that is loose, open, well-drained, and very high in organic matter. They flower on their previous year's growth and should be pruned immediately *after* they flower. Spring pruning should be limited to the removal of dead wood and cutting individual stems back to the fattest and sturdiest pair of live buds.
- LACECAP HYDRANGEA (*Hydrangea serrata*) is very similar to and by some authorities considered the same plant as (or a variant of) the French hydrangea. It is different, by gardener's standards, in that it is hardier and less susceptible to late spring frosts. The leaves are smaller and narrower, and the blooms, instead of being full, rounded heads, are flat and broad with sterile florets around the edges surrounding the tiny fertile flowers in the center. Growing conditions and pruning are the same as for the French hydrangea described above.

- OAKLEAF HYDRANGEA (*Hydrangea quercifolia*) is a very fine and highly desirable species that is native to the South. Growing quite large and forming a perfect understory shrub, its creamy white blooms put on a dazzling display in very late spring and early summer. Oakleaf hydrangea flowers on the previous year's growth and should be pruned after it flowers. This can be confusing because it flowers later in the season. Pruning is best done just as the flowers pass their peak and begin turning from white to pink or tan. Oakleaf hydrangea is tolerant of a wide range of soils, including clay.
- PANICLE HYDRANGEA (*Hydrangea paniculata*) has become one of the most popular hydrangeas for Southern gardens. Preferring full sun across most of the South, it will thrive where other hydrangeas wilt and scorch. Its enormous heads of white flowers are borne from mid- to late summer, after most of the other hydrangeas have finished and the blooms on the best varieties will go through a dramatic color change—from white to pink to red—as they age, extending the show well into late summer or early autumn. Panicle hydrangea flowers on new wood and can be pruned hard in spring to encourage lush new growth and abundant blooms.
- SMOOTH HYDRANGEA (*Hydrangea arborescens*) is another native species that is tougher than it looks. Where it grows naturally it is often found hanging off the sides of cliffs in damp seeps, barely clinging to the rocks with almost no soil around its roots. In good garden soil it will grow into a robust and impressive shrub. 'Annabelle' flowers profusely on its new growth and can be pruned hard in spring. The "wild" forms—with lacecap-type blooms—flower better on their older wood, and pruning should be limited to removing dead wood and light shaping.

With the amazing array of species and cultivars of hydrangea available to gardeners today, gardeners can find one suited to almost any spot in the garden. I hope this additional bit of information helps to clear up any questions when it comes to growing them successfully.

ARBORVITAE
Thuja occidentalis

Why It's Special—Arborvitae comes in a wide array of forms, shapes, and colors. 'Emerald', the slender green form that everyone knows, is an attractive and useful plant that is well adapted to our Southern climate. Other selections are those with golden or variegated foliage, as well as forms that range from tight, round globes to broad-bottomed pyramids.

How to Plant & Grow—Arborvitae can be planted in fall, winter, or early spring, establishing easily during the dormant season when the tops of the plants are not growing, but roots continue to work their way into the ground. Arborvitae will adapt to almost any soil that is not waterlogged.

Care & Problems—Keep an eye out for bagworms and spider mites. Both can slip by unnoticed until the infestation is so great that they have done irreversible damage and are impossible to eradicate.

Hardiness—Zones 4b to 8b, depending on variety

Bloom Color—No blooms

Mature Size (H × W)—5 to 40 ft. × 5 to 20 ft.

Water Needs—Evenly moist to slightly dry

Special Features—Evergreen, year-round color and form

AZALEA
Rhododendron hybrids

Why It's Special—Few flowering shrubs epitomize the Southern landscape the way azaleas do. From front yard displays in suburban subdivisions to the massive spectacles in public parks and gardens across the South, bright and bold azaleas shout spring's arrival from the rooftops.

How to Plant & Grow—Plant azaleas anytime from spring to fall, as long as they are irrigated. They will tolerate full sun to full shade, but are best in morning sun or bright dappled shade throughout the day. Some sun is required to ensure a good floral display. Well-drained soil, heavily amended with compost and soil conditioner, is a must.

Care & Problems—Prune azaleas after they bloom in late spring to early summer. June 15 is the deadline to ensure bloom the next year. Fertilize at the same time and in early autumn. Lace bugs are a problem. Systemic insecticides are the most effective treatments for lace bug.

Hardiness—Zones 6b to 9b

Bloom Color—White, red, pink, fuchsia, bicolors

Mature Size (H × W)—4 to 6 ft. × 4 to 6 ft.

Water Needs—Evenly moist

Special Features—One of the most spectacular floral displays of spring

AZALEA, DECIDUOUS
Rhododendron spp. and hybrids

Why It's Special—Deciduous azaleas are primarily woodland species that flower in early spring before the leaves appear. A few species flower later in the summer after they leaf out. Almost all are spectacular when well grown and deserving of wider use in woodland gardens. Several species are intoxicatingly fragrant when in bloom.

How to Plant & Grow—Plant deciduous azaleas anytime from spring through fall in morning sun or filtered shade. Soil is extremely important—rich, well-drained, and very loose, "woodsy" soil suits them best. Some moisture at their roots is needed during summer, but drainage is equally important during the winter months.

Care & Problems—Deciduous azaleas should be fertilized immediately after they finish flowering and six to eight weeks later. If needed, prune after flowering, trimming out individual branches and lightly tipping back errant shoots to maintain a natural appearance. Water is essential during the hottest and driest months of summer.

Hardiness—Zones 4a to 9b

Bloom Color—White to deep pink, yellow, orange

Mature Size (H × W)—5 to 12 ft. × 5 to 10 ft.

Water Needs—Evenly moist

Special Features—Beautiful fragrant flowers

BOTTLEBRUSH BUCKEYE
Aesculus parviflora

Why It's Special—When it comes to spectacular floral displays, few shrubs can compete with the foot-long spires of white blooms that appear on the bottlebrush buckeye in late spring and early summer. The butterflies agree, and it is not uncommon to see fifty or more butterflies at a time on a mature bottlebrush buckeye in the garden.

How to Plant & Grow—Plant bottlebrush buckeye from fall to very early spring while they are dormant. Try to find container-grown specimens, as they will transplant better than balled-and-burlapped plants whose taproots have been cut. Some sun is required to ensure a good floral display.

Care & Problems—Once established, bottlebrush buckeye is tough, resilient, and care-free. In dry summers, they may drop their leaves early as a defense mechanism against the drought. The following spring they will leaf out and flower normally without skipping a beat.

Hardiness—Zones 5 to 9

Bloom Color—White

Mature Size (H × W)—10 ft. × 15 ft.

Water Needs—Average, drought tolerant once established

Special Features—Exceptional butterfly attractant

BOXWOOD
Buxus sempervirens

Why It's Special—"American" boxwood, the name it frequently goes by, really isn't American at all. It is actually native to southern and western Europe, but its rich history here since Colonial times means that we have laid special claim to it. Historically, it is one of the most important shrubs of the Southern landscape.

How to Plant & Grow—Boxwoods can be planted year-round, but it is best to avoid the hottest and driest months of the summer. They will grow in full sun, but the most beautiful specimens are usually found in part sun to part shade. Avoid wet areas and heavy clay soil.

Care & Problems—Prune or shear boxwoods in February, just before new growth starts in spring. Leaf miners can be a significant problem and cause the leaves to look blistered and off-color. Their treatment is best done by professionals. The one condition that boxwoods will not tolerate is wet feet. Good drainage is essential.

Hardiness—Zones 6a to 8b

Bloom Color—None

Mature Size (H × W)—2 to 15 ft. x 2 to 15 ft.

Water Needs—Average to slightly dry

Special Features—Evergreen shrub with aristocratic character

BUTTERFLY BUSH
Buddleia davidii

Why It's Special—Butterfly bush is one of the staples of the summertime perennial garden or mixed border, with arching sprays of fragrant flowers attracting swarms of butterflies and beneficial pollinators. Old forms are weedy in some climates, but new, sterile hybrids are seedless and pose no threat to the native flora and fauna.

How to Plant & Grow—Plant butterfly bush in full sun anytime from early spring to late summer. Plants are often potbound when you buy them, so lightly score the roots around the outer edge of the rootball to encourage them to grow out into the surrounding soil.

Care & Problems—Prune hard in late winter, cutting plants back to 12 to 18 inches tall to encourage vigorous new growth and a spectacular display of blooms in early summer. Water and feed regularly during summer and keep old blooms removed to encourage continual flowering from spring to frost.

Hardiness—Zones 5a to 8b

Bloom Color—Pink, purple, white, lavender

Mature Size (H × W)—5 to 10 ft. × 5 to 10 ft.

Water Needs—Evenly moist to slightly dry

Special Features—Attracts butterflies, bees, and hummingbirds

CAMELLIA
Camellia Japonica

Why It's Special—Camellias, with their large rose or peonylike blooms opening from late winter to early spring, are another of those "signature" Southern plants. Some collectors have entire gardens dedicated to camellias. New hybrids have increased the camellia's hardiness well into Zone 6, dramatically expanding their growing range.

How to Plant & Grow—Plant camellias from early spring through early autumn while the soil is warm and they'll root in quickly. Well-drained soil that has been amended with organic matter is critical to camellias' success. Camellias thrive in morning sun or high, dappled shade.

Care & Problems—Camellias require a certain amount of attention and care to reach their fullest potential. Pruning is especially important and should be done carefully and thoughtfully to enhance the shape and beauty of the shrub and the presentation of the bloom. It is best to prune immediately after they finish flowering.

Hardiness—Zones 6b to 9b

Bloom Color—Shades of pink, white, red, variegated

Mature Size (H × W)—6 to 15 ft. × 5 to 10 ft.

Water Needs—Moist but well-drained

Special Features—Newer varieties are hardy to Zone 6

CAMELLIA, SASANQUA
Camellia sasanqua

Why It's Special—These fall- and early winter-flowering camellias usually go by the common name of "sasanqua." They are vigorous and free-flowering, and, because they flower in autumn, there are no worries of flower buds freezing during cold winter weather and losing that year's show.

How to Plant & Grow—Plant sasanquas from March through October to establish roots during warm weather. This species is more sun tolerant than the Japonica types, but still perform best in partly sunny to partly shady conditions. Sasanquas need loose, well-drained soil that is high in organic matter.

Care & Problems—Leaf scorch can occur during winter months on plants that are planted in too much sun or on windswept sites. Prune in very early spring before new growth begins. Blight can be a problem, and any shoots that die back quickly should be pruned out immediately. Some can grow very large over time. Site appropriately.

Hardiness—Zones 6b to 9b

Bloom Color—White, red, shades of pink

Mature Size (H × W)—10 ft. × 5 to 10 ft.

Water Needs—Moderately drought tolerant, once established

Special Features—Very showy late autumn and early winter blooms

DWARF CRAPE MYRTLE
Lagerstroemia hybrids

Why It's Special—Most gardeners think of multitrunked trees when it comes to crape myrtles, but there are just as many on the market today that provide small to mid-sized shrubs. They provide the same bright, cheerful blooms as the trees. They fit perfectly into perennial beds, mixed borders, courtyards, and smaller landscapes.

How To Plant & Grow—Crape myrtles love the heat and should be planted in spring or early summer to grow quickly and become well established before having to go through the winter. Their only real requirement is full sun. They will adapt to almost any soil, but will respond with fast growth and profuse flowering when given good soil and plenty of summer moisture.

Care & Problems—Japanese beetles can be a serious problem in early summer, nearly stripping the plants bare just as they are producing flower buds and getting ready to bloom. This is more true for shrub forms than the larger, treelike varieties. Late spring freezes may nip early new growth, but plants usually recover quickly.

Hardiness—Zones 6 to 9

Bloom Color—White, pink, red, lavender

Mature Size (H × W)—2 to 10 ft. × 2 to 10 ft.

Water Needs—Moderate, but fairly drought tolerant, once established

Special Features—Showy blooms from summer to autumn

FALSE CYPRESS
Chamaecyparis spp. and cultivars

Why It's Special—False cypress are truly a diverse group of plants. The smallest may be tiny, round buns of foliage only a foot tall, while the largest and most elegant of the group can reach treelike proportions. Foliage comes in a wide range of colors from steely blue to golden yellow, offering year-round color in the landscape.

How to Plant & Grow—Plant in spring or fall in moist, but well-drained soil. They are not as tolerant of clay soil as our native cedars and other junipers, so amend soil well. Some varieties are fairly shade tolerant, but their growth habit will be looser and more open than when grown in full sun.

Care & Problems—False cypress can be slow to establish and suffer in dry soils. Keep them well watered for at least the first year. Pruning should be done in late winter or early spring, selectively pruning to enhance the plant's natural shape.

Hardiness—Zones 5b to 8b

Bloom Color—No flowers

Mature Size (H × W)—6 to 10 ft. × 3 to 6 ft.

Water Needs—Evenly moist soil

Special Features—Colorful foliage, many interesting forms

FORSYTHIA
Forsythia × intermedia

Why It's Special—Few shrubs signal spring's arrival like forsythia. Its golden yellow blooms burst forth from leafless twigs as the gray days of winter finally lose their grip. Bloom time can range from early February to mid-March depending on where in the South you live and how quickly the weather warms in late winter.

How to Plant & Grow—Plant forsythia anytime the soil can be worked. It will grow almost anywhere and in any soil; it's truly a tough plant, once established. Forsythia will flower most profusely in full sun, but can be found blooming in considerable shade on old farmsteads around the South.

Care & Problems—Prune forsythia immediately after flowering by removing one-third of the oldest growth each year to encourage new growth from the base of the plant. A second, light pruning can be done in early summer to shape, but next year's buds are set by July, so no late pruning.

Hardiness—Zones 4b to 8a

Bloom Color—Golden yellow

Mature Size (H × W)—6 to 10 ft. × 6 to 10 ft.

Water Needs—Drought tolerant, once established

Special Features—Early spring blooms, red fall color.

FOTHERGILLA
Fothergilla gardenii

Why It's Special—Fothergilla is a native shrub that is well adapted to Southern gardens. Its honey-scented, white, bottlebrush blooms open before or just as leaves appear in spring. It is an excellent addition to the woodland wildflower garden. Fall color can range from brilliant yellow to orange and scarlet and is one of the plant's best features.

How to Plant & Grow—Fothergilla can be planted in spring or fall. It will flower and show its best fall color in full to part sun, but is shade tolerant. It is not especially drought tolerant, and, in the wild, may be found growing on creek banks or at pond edges where moisture is readily available.

Care & Problems—Keep fothergilla well watered during its first growing season and anytime the garden is experiencing prolonged heat or drought. If pruning is needed, do so immediately after flowering, selectively, to maintain an open and natural form.

Hardiness—Zones 5a to 8b

Bloom Color—White

Mature Size (H × W)—4 ft. × 5 ft.

Water Needs—Evenly moist soil

Special Features—White spring blooms; yellow, orange, red fall color

FRINGE FLOWER
Loropetalum chinense

Why It's Special—Fringe flower is a showy, semi-evergreen shrub with wide-spreading branches laden with fringelike pink or white flowers in spring. Newer varieties range in size from very compact, ground-hugging forms to broad, open specimens that can be limbed up into small, multistemmed "trees." Leaf color may be olive green to deep purple.

How to Plant & Grow—Fringe flower is best planted in spring and summer, while soil is warm and active root and top growth can begin right away. Foliage color develops best in full sun, becoming bronzy or brownish purple in too much shade. Fringe flower is tolerant of clay soils. Provide protection from cold winter wind.

Care & Problems—Fringe flower can be sensitive to sudden cold winter weather, sometimes freezing back to the ground in colder zones. Usually, it will resprout and grow quickly from the base of the plant. Prune immediately after flowering to shape plants and remove erratic growth.

Hardiness—Zones 7a to 9b

Bloom Color—Pink, burgundy, white

Mature Size (H × W)—3 to 8 ft. × 3 to 8 ft.

Water Needs—Evenly moist soil

Special Features—Semi-evergreen leaves provide winter color

GARDENIA
Gardenia jasminoides

Why It's Special—Where they are hardy, gardenias are another of those signature plants that no Southern garden should be without. Intensely fragrant, waxy white blooms are borne from May to July. Gardeners in Zones 6 and 7 may try 'Kleim's Hardy', with single white blooms and reportedly hardier than most of its kin.

How to Plant & Grow—Gardenias thrive in the heat and humidity and should be planted in spring or early summer so they are well established before winter weather arrives. Soil is very important! Rich, organic soils high in organic matter or even sandy soils will suit them. They will struggle, though, in heavy clay.

Care & Problems—Gardenias must have moisture, and irrigation of some kind is recommended. Fertilize twice each year with a bloom booster-type fertilizer or with a formula made especially for acid-loving plants like gardenias, camellias, and azaleas. Scale insects and mealybugs can be a problem when plants are stressed.

Hardiness—Zones 7b to 9b

Bloom Color—White

Mature Size (H × W)—3 to 6 ft. × 3 to 5 ft.

Water Needs—Evenly moist soil

Special Features—Long season of fragrant white blossoms

GLOSSY ABELIA
Abelia × grandiflora

Why It's Special—Glossy abelia is one of the workhorses of the Southern garden. A handsome shrub, its glossy green leaves turn burgundy in winter. It flowers freely from early summer to fall, attracting honeybees and butterflies to the garden. Variegated and colored foliage make beautiful accent plants in the landscape.

How to Plant & Grow—Abelia loves the heat and will establish quickly from spring or early summer planting. It is not finicky about soil types and is quite drought tolerant, once established. In full sun, it will grow dense and full, flowering profusely. In shade, growth will be more open and loose and flowers will be sparse.

Care & Problems—Abelia is truly a low-maintenance shrub, once it is well established. If plants become overgrown and full of dead twigs and limbs, they can be cut back hard to rejuvenate them. More compact forms are available that require virtually no maintenance whatsoever.

Hardiness—Zones 6a to 9b

Bloom Color—White to pale pink

Mature Size (H × W)—4 to 8 ft. × 4 to 8 ft.

Water Needs—Drought tolerant, once established

Special Features—Glossy, evergreen foliage and fragrant blooms

HYDRANGEA, FRENCH
Hydrangea macrophylla

Why It's Special—One of the most recognizable plants of the Southern garden, the French or mophead hydrangea boasts large, showy blooms in shades of white, pink, and blue. Recent selections flower more reliably on new growth and are less prone to losing their flowers to late spring freezes.

How to Plant & Grow—Hydrangeas require good garden soil that has been well amended with large quantities of compost, manure, leaf mold, or other organic matter. A steady supply of moisture is essential, especially in summer. Feed in spring, just as new growth emerges and again in early to midsummer when flower buds are being set for next year's bloom.

Care & Problems—French hydrangeas can be susceptible to extreme winter cold, killing stems to the ground, as well as to early spring frosts that may kill opening flower buds. Site them in protected areas for best results.

Hardiness—Zones 6 to 9

Bloom Color—Shades of white, pink, blue

Mature Size (H × W)—3 to 6 ft. × 3 to 6 ft.

Water Needs—Consistently and evenly moist

Special Features—Floral display can be showstopping when it's well grown

HYDRANGEA, LACECAP
Hydrangea serrata

Why It's Special—*Hydrangea serrata* is a lesser-known, but highly desirable hydrangea for Southern gardens. It is hardier and less susceptible to spring frosts than its mopheaded close cousin. The delicate, lacecap blooms appear in late spring and early summer, and, while not as large as some hydrangeas, are borne in great quantity.

How to Plant & Grow—Plant lacecap hydrangeas in spring and keep them well watered through their first summer to get the plants established before winter. Amend soil well with compost, composted manure, or other organic matter. At least a half-day of sun will encourage prolific flowering each year.

Care & Problems—Freeze damage may occur in very cold winters, but less so than with other hydrangeas. Flowering occurs on old wood, so prune with care. Wait until leaves begin emerging in spring and then trim out any dead wood and cut stems back to where the strongest growth is emerging.

Hardiness—Zones 5 to 9

Bloom Color—White, pink, blue

Mature Size (H × W)—2 to 4 ft. × 2 to 5 ft.

Water Needs—Moderate to moist

Special Features—Beautiful lacecap blooms in spring, early summer

HYDRANGEA, OAKLEAF
Hydrangea quercifolia

Why It's Special—Oakleaf hydrangea is one of the finest native shrubs, with large, deeply notched leaves that resemble those of red oak. Large panicles of showy white flowers fade to rosy pink as they age. For a truly outstanding display, look for the 'Snowflake', a double-flowered form whose enormous blooms cascade in a white, frothy waterfall for nearly two months!

How to Plant & Grow—Oakleaf hydrangea can be planted year-round, but summer-planted specimens will require close attention to watering in order to thrive. In cooler climates, oakleaf hydrangea will tolerate full sun, but morning sun or very bright, dappled shade suits it best.

Care & Problems—Pruning can be tricky with oakleaf hydrangea. It flowers on old wood, so should only be pruned after it flowers, but timing can be tricky. Wait until the flowers have turned from their white "full bloom" stage back to beige, then prune as needed.

Hardiness—Zones 5a to 8b

Bloom Color—White

Mature Size (H × W)—4 to 10 ft. × 4 to 10 ft.

Water Needs—Evenly moist soil

Special Features—Showy, long-lasting blooms in early summer

HYDRANGEA, PANICLE
Hydrangea paniculata

Why It's Special—Panicle hydrangea (often called "Tardiva" hydrangea, although 'Tardiva' is one specific cultivar) is one of the best choices for our hot and humid Southern climate. Large trusses of showy pale green to white blooms appear in mid- to late summer after most other hydrangeas have finished flowering.

How to Plant & Grow—Plant in spring or fall in rich, well-amended, and well-drained garden soil. Unlike most hydrangeas, panicle hydrangeas need full sun to perform to their fullest potential. Part sun is suitable, but without at least a few hours of direct sun each day, growth will be lax and blooms sparse.

Care & Problems—Some varieties grow very large. Do your research before buying and purchase a variety that grows to the appropriate size for your space. There are many to choose from. Panicle hydrangea, unlike most hydrangeas, flowers on its new growth. Pruning can be done in spring to encourage summertime bloom.

Hardiness—Zones 3 to 8

Bloom Color—Pale green, white

Mature Size (H × W)—5 to 15 ft. × 5 to 15 ft.

Water Needs—Moderate to moist

Special Features—Spectacular blooms

HYDRANGEA, SMOOTH
Hydrangea arborescens

Why It's Special— 'Annabelle' is the best known of the smooth hydrangeas, with enormous heads of creamy white flowers in early summer. It is easy to grow and very forgiving, since it is native to the South. The wild form bears a lacecap-type flower instead of the full head of the sterile forms.

How to Plant & Grow—Plant in spring to get it well established in its first growing season. It will grow very quickly—almost like a perennial—often flowering its first year. Tolerant of a wide range of soils and conditions, it is best in good garden soil with regular water.

Care & Problems—Deer will browse the new growth and emerging flower buds, so spraying with deer repellent may be necessary early in the season. Voles can be a problem in winter, when they burrow around the base of plants, chewing on roots. Plants flower on new growth and can be pruned hard in early spring.

Hardiness—Zones 4 to 9

Bloom Color—Creamy white

Mature Size (H × W)—4 ft. × 4 ft.

Water Needs—Moderate to moist

Special Features—Pink-flowered varieties are being introduced

JAPANESE AUCUBA
Aucuba japonica

Why It's Special—For shady locations where little else will grow, aucuba is your answer. Few shrubs—and really only a handful of plants—thrive in the shade the way aucuba will. If its speckled leaves are not to your liking, choose a solid green form. For deep shade, there is no better shrub!

How to Plant & Grow—Aucuba loves warm weather and is easiest to establish during the summer months, anytime from April to October. Aucuba only asks for well-drained soil and plenty of shade. Its leaves will actually burn and turn black, even in winter, if it receives too much sun.

Care & Problems—Root rot can be a problem in heavy clay soil that retains water in winter. Cold, wet feet are not to its liking. Just make sure it has plenty of shade and aucuba will be one of the most care-free plants in your landscape.

Hardiness—Zones 6b to 9b

Bloom Color—Inconspicuous flowers; red berries on female plants

Mature Size (H × W)—4 to 8 ft. × 4 to 8 ft.

Water Needs—Evenly moist, well-drained soil

Special Features—Bold texture and brightly colored foliage

JAPANESE PLUM YEW
Cephalotaxus harringtonia

Why It's Special—The soft texture, dark green foliage, and excellent heat tolerance make Japanese plum yew incredibly versatile in the landscape. Where common yew frequently suffers in the heat and humidity of the South, Japanese plum yew thrives. Forms ranging from low, spreading groundcovers to vertical columns can fill any niche in the garden.

How to Plant & Grow—Time has proven that full to part sun produces fuller, denser, faster-growing plants, although in the hottest climates, part sun to part shade may be more preferable. Excellent drainage is critical. It *will not* thrive in heavy clay soil.

Care & Problems—Japanese plum yew can be planted in spring or fall. Young plants are brittle and easily broken, so plant carefully. Soil should be very well amended, and heavy clay soils should be avoided altogether. Root rot and stem dieback will be prevalent in soil that does not drain.

Hardiness—Zones 6a to 9a

Bloom Color—Green, insignificant

Mature Size (H × W)—2 to 6 ft. × 5 to 10 ft.

Water Needs—Evenly moist to slightly dry

Special Features—Soft, feathery foliage provides year-round interest

JAPANESE TERNSTROEMIA
Ternstroemia gymnanthera

Why It's Special—While you may not guess it at first glance, this useful, evergreen shrub is a relative of the camellia, although without the camellia's showy blooms. In the trade, it is most commonly sold as "Japanese cleyera," which, while related, is an entirely different and less ornamental plant. Ternstroemia is grown for its bronze- or red-colored new growth and makes excellent evergreen screens or hedges.

How to Plant & Grow—Plant anytime the soil can be worked during fall, winter, or early spring. Amend soil thoroughly with compost, manure, and soil conditioner, especially in clay or sandy soils. Apply an all-purpose fertilizer in early spring for thick, lush, new growth each season.

Care & Problems—Once established, ternstroemia is relatively pest and disease free, as well as drought tolerant. Poor drainage can cause root rot, and lean, sandy soils may lead to chlorosis and weak growth. Prune lightly to shape, as needed.

Hardiness—Zones 7a to 10b

Bloom Color—White, insignificant

Mature Size (H × W)—10 ft. × 6 ft.

Water Needs—Drought tolerant, once established

Special Features—Look for varieties with bronzy red new growth

OLEANDER
Nerium oleander

Why It's Special—Oleanders are only suited to the warmer regions of the South, but where they are hardy, they make tough, durable, and beautiful evergreen shrubs with a bloom season that stretches from late spring to autumn. It's very tolerant of lean, sandy soils, and salt spray in coastal areas.

How to Plant & Grow—Plant oleanders in spring and early summer to get them well established before colder winter weather. They will grow in a wide range of soils and flower best in full to part sun. Feed and water regularly during the season to encourage abundant blooms.

Care & Problems—Young plants will need some winter protection in the colder parts of their hardiness range. Once established, most varieties will be hardy to Zone 8. **Warning:** Oleander is poisonous. Do not burn clippings, as even the smoke can be dangerous and keep away from areas where children are regular visitors.

Hardiness—Zones 8a to 10b

Bloom Color—White, pink, red, salmon, light yellow

Mature Size (H × W)—4 to 12 ft. × 6 to 12 ft.

Water Needs—Very drought tolerant

Special Features—Superb for difficult seaside locations

PITTOSPORUM
Pittosporum tobira

Why It's Special—In warmer regions of the South, pittosporum has become a staple broadleaf evergreen in the landscape. Excellent for planting informal hedges, its broad, evergreen leaves and fragrant, white, springtime blooms give it multiple seasons of interest. Where it's hardy, it also makes an excellent subject for large pots or tubs.

How to Plant & Grow—Plant in late winter and early spring to ensure the plants are well established before winter. Standard varieties will grow in full sun, with irrigation, while dwarf and variegated forms are best suited to part sun or part shade. Keep well-watered through their first growing season. It's adaptable to sandy soil and salt spray along coasts.

Care & Problems—Pittosporum should be allowed to grow into its natural, rounded shape. Prune immediately after flowering to enhance its natural growth habit. Scale and mealybugs can be problems. Severe infestations may require systemic chemical treatments to get them under control.

Hardiness—Zones 8a to 10b

Bloom Color—Creamy white

Mature Size (H × W)—5 to 15 ft. × 5 to 12 ft.

Water Needs—Drought tolerant

Special Features—Rhododendronlike, evergreen foliage, fragrant white flowers

ROSE OF SHARON
Hibiscus syriacus

Why It's Special—When most other garden shrubs are green and doing well just to survive a hot, humid, Southern summer, rose of Sharon is at its peak. Beginning in late July to early August and continuing through September, its hibiscuslike flowers appear when the garden needs them most.

How to Plant & Grow—Rose of Sharon can be planted anytime soil can be worked. Full sun will ensure the most flowers, but it is quite tolerant of part sun and even part shade conditions. Some gardeners use it as a deciduous, flowering hedge, which can be achieved by planting them on 3-foot centers and allowing them to grow together.

Care & Problems—Pruning should be done in early spring, if necessary. Water is important during dry summers, especially when the plants are flowering. Japanese beetles may be a problem on foliage in June and July and should be treated.

Hardiness—Zones 5a to 8b

Bloom Color—White, lavender, pink, red

Mature Size (H × W)—8 to 12 ft. × 6 to 12 ft.

Water Needs—Drought tolerant, once established

Special Features—Showy blooms in late summer and early fall

ST. JOHN'S WORT
Hypericum frondosum

Why It's Special—A tough and resilient native shrub, St. John's wort produces bright, golden yellow flowers in midsummer against attractive, blue-green foliage. It is very tolerant of less-than-ideal growing conditions and is particularly tolerant of clayey and rocky soils. The best cultivar is 'Sunburst'.

How to Plant & Grow—Plant St. John's wort in spring or fall. Once established, it is extremely drought tolerant and will thrive in lean, clayey soils where other plants might suffer. Full sun suits it best and produces the most blooms, but it will grow well even in part sun, although blooms may be sparser.

Care & Problems—It's tough, resilient, and care-free, once established. Some species are intolerant of overwatering and may wilt or melt almost overnight from a variety of blight and/or root rot diseases. Getting them well established and then leaving them alone is key to their survival. Light pruning, just enough to shape it, can be carried out in early spring.

Hardiness—Zones 5 to 8

Bloom Color—Yellow

Mature Size (H × W)—3 ft. × 4 ft.

Water Needs—Drought tolerant, once established

Special Features—Tough resilient native

VIBURNUM, CHINESE SNOWBALL
Viburnum macrocephalum 'Sterile'

Why It's Special—One of the most impressive floral displays of spring comes from the Chinese snowball viburnum as its impressive, near-football-sized blooms expand and change from apple green to white over a period of several weeks. Many people mistake the shrub for a gigantic white hydrangea when it's in bloom.

How to Plant & Grow—Plant potted or balled-and-burlapped specimens in spring or fall. Once established, they'll grow into impressive and very large shrubs. Snowball viburnum is a tough plant, once established, but responds to good soil and irrigation.

Care & Problems—The only real problem with Chinese snowball viburnum is that gardeners underestimate its potential size. In the South, it has the potential to reach 15 ft. × 15 ft. or more, if left unpruned. The best way to manage it is to remove one-third of the oldest wood each spring, immediately after flowering.

Hardiness—Zones 6 to 9

Bloom Color—Apple green to white

Mature Size (H × W)—15 ft. × 15 ft.

Water Needs—Moderate, but somewhat drought tolerant, once established

Special Features—Grown for its magnificent spring floral display

VIBURNUM, DOUBLEFILE
Viburnum plicatum f. *tomentosum*

Why It's Special—Few plants can rival the spectacular floral display of the doublefile viburnum when it is well grown and happy. Flowers are borne on top and along the length of the horizontal branches. It is deciduous, but grows large and dense enough to make an effective screen, and, in autumn, leaves turn reddish purple before dropping.

How to Plant & Grow—Plant potted or balled-and-burlapped doublefile viburnum in spring or fall. Its best growth and flowering will be in rich, moist, well-drained soil. It is not especially drought tolerant nor will it thrive in very heavy clay. Drainage is important.

Care & Problems—Old, overgrown specimens can be rejuvenated by cutting them back to 12 inches and allowing them to regrow from the base. Scorched leaf margins may appear if the plants suffer drought, but these are usually cosmetic and not detrimental to the plant.

Hardiness—Zones 5 to 8

Bloom Color—White

Mature Size (H × W)—10 ft. × 12 ft.

Water Needs—Moist

Special Features—Spectacular spring floral display, red fall color

VIBURNUM, KOREANSPICE

Viburnum carlesii

Why It's Special—If you love fragrance, there is no more fragrant, spring-blooming shrub than the Koreanspice viburnum. In early spring, clusters of rosy pink buds open to 3-inch white clusters that perfume the air with their warm, spicy fragrance.

How to Plant & Grow—Koreanspice viburnum can be planted in spring or fall. Potted plants often appear sparse, but plants will grow and fill in quickly once they are planted in the ground. Avoid heavy clay soils and amend planting holes thoroughly with a combination of compost and soil conditioner.

Care & Problems—Koreanspice viburnum grows with little care and attention. In wet summer weather, leaf spot can occur, but is mostly cosmetic and not a problem. Pruning to remove the occasional errant branch may be necessary, but otherwise, the plant can largely be left alone. Root rot can be a problem in heavy clay soils.

Hardiness—Zones 5a to 8a

Bloom Color—Pink buds, white blooms

Mature Size (H × W)—6 to 10 ft. × 6 to 10 ft.

Water Needs—Evenly moist soil

Special Features—3-inch clusters of fragrant white blooms, semi-evergreen

VIRGINIA SWEETSPIRE

Itea virginica

Why It's Special—Virginia sweetspire is a highly desirable native shrub with drooping spikes of sweetly fragrant flowers. They appear in midsummer when few shrubs are showy. Crimson fall color adds to the show later in autumn. It is especially adaptable to difficult wet areas where other plants fail due to poor drainage. 'Henry's Garnet' grows vigorously and turns rich, ruby red in autumn.

How to Plant & Grow—Plant Virginia sweetspire in spring or fall in full sun to part shade. It grows best in fairly rich, moist soil, but is very adaptable and will tolerate drier conditions with few adverse effects.

Care & Problems—Once established, sweetspire is a low-maintenance plant that spreads slowly by underground stolons and will become a dense, thick "groundcover" with time. Slugs and snails can chew holes in the leaves and while it is unsightly, it is not life-threatening.

Hardiness—Zones 5a to 9b

Bloom Color—White

Mature Size (H × W)—2 to 5 ft. × 4 to 5 ft.

Water Needs—Moist to wet

Special Features—A tough, resilient native that thrives in wet locations

WAXMYRTLE

Myrica cerifera

Why It's Special—This tough, resilient, native evergreen will grow where most other shrubs would fail, including the dry, sandy soils of the coast. Both foliage and berries are extremely fragrant and are the source of the "bayberry" fragrance so popular for candles and potpourri. Berries are very popular with birds in the garden.

How to Plant & Grow—Plant waxmyrtle in spring, summer, or fall in full sun to part shade. Waxmyrtle prefers moisture during its active summer growth phase, but needs good drainage in winter. While it is very adaptable to clay, it should not stand in water.

Care & Problems—Pruning should be done with care. While it will tolerate fairly heavy pruning and will re-sprout and fill out even from bare wood, it will not tolerate shearing. This may seem odd but is, nonetheless, true. It responds very well to feeding and will grow quickly into a large and beautiful specimen.

Hardiness—Zones 7a to 10a

Bloom Color—Insignificant

Mature Size (H × W)—5 to 20 ft. × 5 to 20 ft.

Water Needs—Evenly moist

Special Features—Fragrant, evergreen foliage and fragrant gray berries

WITCH HAZEL
Hamamelis spp. and hybrids

Why It's Special—With flowers that open from late autumn through winter and into early spring, witch hazel is the perfect shrub for adding winter interest to the garden. 'Arnold Promise', a hybrid with yellow blooms, is one of the best spring bloomers and 'Pallida', a pale yellow form, often flowers in midwinter.

How to Plant & Grow—Plant witch hazel from late winter through spring or in early fall. They prefer evenly moist soil, rich in organic matter in morning sun or bright dappled shade. Amend soil with copious quantities of compost and soil conditioner to ensure robust growth and large quantities of flowers.

Care & Problems—Prune these shrubs after they bloom in late winter to open up the centers of the plants and to control size. Plants are best left to grow in their natural, upright to vase-shaped form. Borers can be a problem in plants that are stressed.

Hardiness—Zones 4a to 8a

Bloom Color—Yellow, orange, red

Mature Size (H × W)—8 to 12 ft. × 8 to 12 ft.

Water Needs—Average to evenly moist

Special Features—Unique, ribbonlike blooms in autumn and winter

YAUPON HOLLY
Ilex vomitoria

Why It's Special—Yaupon holly is one of the most versatile shrubs or small trees in the Southern landscape. With dwarf forms growing only 2 feet tall and as wide, to weeping tree forms 15 feet tall, there is an appropriate cultivar for almost any site. In late fall and winter, the clear gray stems are adorned with bright red berries.

How to Plant & Grow—May be more cold hardy than once thought, but plants should be installed in spring to allow them to become well-established before winter temperatures arrive. This plant thrives in the heat and humidity!

Care & Problems—Yaupon holly, while tough, is not the most cold-hardy of hollies and may not survive in the coldest parts of the South. Even where it is hardy, it can suffer considerable dieback if cold temperatures arrive suddenly in autumn before it has had a chance to harden off.

Hardiness—Zones 7a to 10a

Bloom Color—Insignificant

Mature Size (H × W)—3 to 16 ft. × 3 to 16 ft.

Water Needs—Dry to wet, very adaptable

Special Features—Bright red berries can be spectacular on good cultivars

GETTING THE MOST FROM YOUR SHRUBS

Shrubs, like trees, are permanent features of your landscape—or at least they should be. Choosing the right plant for the right place and making wise decisions will be important so that your shrubs thrive in the right light, the right soil, and with the proper care. Shrubs can be prominent features of your landscape as foundation plantings, or they can blend into the understory, creating those all-important "layers" that we are all trying to achieve. Well-grown shrubs will be both beautiful and functional. They can serve as windbreaks, screens, and privacy hedges or they can simply be ornamental and valued for their colorful foliage, picturesque form, or striking blooms.

PLANTING

Planting shrubs properly is not difficult. Most are readily available in sizes that are easy for the gardener to handle. Some, like certain camellias, viburnums, or arborvitae, may be found in larger sizes as field-grown balled-and-burlapped specimens. These may require some assistance, since they will be too large and too heavy for one person to safely move or plant. Whether you are doing the planting yourself or you have hired a landscape company to assist you, be sure that the planting is done properly. Hopefully, you will only be planting shrubs one time, so treat them well from the beginning to ensure they do their job as they grow and mature.

While there are certain shrubs that are tough and adaptable to less-than-ideal growing conditions, most are going to grow and flower best (if they are flowering types) in good, well-amended garden soil with at least moderate moisture at their roots. If you garden where the soil is heavy clay or very sandy, adding plenty of organic matter in the form of compost, well-composted manure, soil conditioner, leaf mold, or a combination of any of those will be important. Organic matter helps to loosen and break up clay soil, allowing air, water, and nutrients to move through it. In sandy soils, it helps retain water and nutrients that otherwise evaporate or leach rapidly from the soil. Ideally, it is best to work organic matter into larger areas or beds instead of individual planting holes. If that is not possible, then at least some amending of the holes will get plants off to a good start.

When you are ready to plant:

1. Dig your planting hole the same depth as the rootball of the shrub, but at least twice as wide. This gives the roots of the plant some soft soil to grow quickly into.
2. If you were unable to amend and till a larger planting area, mix amendments into the soil that you dig out of the individual planting holes at a ratio of about one-third amendments to two-thirds native soil. This will give some boost to your soil without it being so good that the roots will stay confined to the planting hole.
3. Backfill around the roots with the amended soil and lightly tamp the soil with your hands or the handle end of your shovel. Do not pound or stomp the plants into the ground. This only serves to compact the soil and drive out air, eliminating spaces for water and nutrients to move through the soil.
4. Water thoroughly to settle the soil and add a little more soil, if necessary, based on how much settling there is. When finished, the top of the rootball should just be covered so that water is not wicked away through evaporation, but the base of the plant should not be buried.
5. Keep newly planted shrubs watered well until they are established.

FERTILIZING

Some gardeners like to use root stimulators or starter fertilizers when they are planting trees and shrubs. This is a personal choice. Certainly, it does not hurt to give the plant a few additional nutrients as it starts life in the garden, but any heavy fertilizing should wait until the plants are well established. Usually, I use a root stimulator solution at planting time and again about three weeks later and then save any other fertilizing until the spring of the following year, when I am certain that the plant is well established.

Fertilize anytime from early spring, just before the plants leaf out, until early fall, just before the shrubs go dormant. During this time, roots are actively taking up water and nutrients and utilizing them fully for both root and top growth. Be sure to water fertilizer into the soil and to keep the soil moist after feeding. Fertilizer works by being dissolved in and carried by water, so if conditions are dry, the fertilizer will not move into the root zone and cannot be used by the plants.

There are literally hundreds of kinds of fertilizer on the market. There are chemical and organic types and within those two larger groups there are fertilizers for specific plants or groups of plants. There are fertilizers for blooming shrubs, fertilizers for acid-loving shrubs, and fertilizers for evergreens. There are dry, granular fertilizers that are spread directly on the soil and liquids or concentrates that are mixed with water and poured directly on the roots or sprayed onto the leaves. You may end up trying several types and brands over the years before you settle on which one works the best for you. The professionals at your local garden center can also be a tremendous help when it comes to choosing products that work well in your area.

WATERING

Watering correctly will ensure success with the shrubs you've chosen. For newly planted shrubs, you may find yourself watering frequently for the first several weeks to keep them from getting dry and wilting. Proper watering will also encourage roots to grow deep into the soil, giving plants greater access to water held in deeper layers of the

Dig a planting hole twice as wide as the rootball, but no deeper. The plant should sit at the same place it was growing in the container or maybe an inch or so above the surrounding soil to allow for settling.

soil during the hot and dry days of summer. By watering deeply and thoroughly each time you do water, you will actually reduce the amount of watering you will have to do as your shrubs grow and mature.

PRUNING

Pruning is a basic maintenance requirement for shrubs; it improves their health and appearance and keeps them in bounds. Pruning is an entirely different activity than shearing. Pruning is done by hand with a good pair of pruning shears, loppers for slightly larger branches, and a small pruning saw to remove the thickest branches when rejuvenating shrubs like forsythia or Chinese snowball viburnum.

TWO BASIC RULES OF PRUNING

1. Spring-flowering shrubs like forsythia, azalea, and camellia should be pruned immediately after they finish flowering, if possible, and no later than mid-June. These shrubs will begin setting new flower buds for next spring's bloom by midsummer and pruning after mid-June may result in you cutting off the following year's flowers. Some early summer-flowering shrubs, like oakleaf hydrangea, sweet azalea, and mophead hydrangea, also flower on the previous season's growth. These too should be pruned immediately *after* they flower in summer, giving them time to set next year's flower buds in late summer and autumn.

2. Summer-flowering shrubs, like butterfly bush, glossy abelia, panicle hydrangea, and crape myrtle, flower on the new growth of the season. This group should be pruned in late winter or early spring, just a few weeks before they begin to leaf out. This will encourage strong new growth and abundant flowering when warm weather arrives.

The removal of dead, damaged, or diseased wood can be done anytime. In summer, watch for branches that wilt and won't recover, that die off suddenly or that develop black or sunken spots along the stems. These may be symptoms of stem diseases that should be pruned out immediately and discarded. Never put diseased plants in the compost pile.

Many large, old, overgrown shrubs—especially flowering shrubs—can be rejuvenated and brought "back to life" by cutting them back hard. This can be done in stages, by removing about one-third of the oldest wood at ground level each year for three years, rejuvenating the plant entirely over a period of time, or by taking drastic measures and cutting the entire shrub back to 12 to 18 inches from the ground and allowing it to regrow. The former is obviously less traumatic, but takes time. The latter is a dramatic and quick method, but some follow-up pruning will be required as the plant regrows to keep it from getting rangy and overgrown again.

PEST CONTROL

Pest control on shrubs simply requires a watchful eye and a bit of diligence on your part. Keeping your shrubs well watered, fertilized, and pruned will encourage healthy and very active growth that is less susceptible to outbreaks of disease and attacks by insect pests, but in the event they should occur, treatment may be necessary. Prevention and early detection are the keys to managing both without having to haul out the toxic chemicals. When outbreaks do occur, consult the professionals at your local garden centers for treatment options. I always try to go with the safest option first and if that doesn't work, I may resort to more powerful treatments if it's a plant that is very rare or really critical in my landscape. If it is a plant that, over a period of years, requires constant treatment to keep it healthy, you may consider removing it entirely.

JANUARY

- In warmer regions of the South where the soil is not frozen, hardy shrubs and trees can be planted right through the winter months. Winter and early spring moisture will help get plants established before the heat of the summer sets in. Avoid planting heat-loving shrubs like crape myrtle and gardenia. They'll transplant better in spring and summer when the weather is more to their liking.

- Broadleaf evergreens like boxwood, gardenia, aucuba, and others continue to lose water through their leaves, even when the weather is cold. In dry winters, it is important to water broadleaf evergreens occasionally when the temperatures are above freezing and to keep their leaves from drying out from winter cold and wind. Anti-dessicants may also be helpful to keep broadleaf evergreens from suffering winter burn.

- If scale, mealybugs, or spider mites were problems on any shrubs last summer, dormant oil sprays can be applied in winter to smother any overwintering eggs or hibernating insects. Dormant oils should only be applied when shrubs are completely dormant in winter. If applied during the growing season, they can cause severe scorching of foliage.

FEBRUARY

- Branches from early spring-flowering shrubs like quince and forsythia can easily be forced into bloom indoors. Forcing cut stems to bloom indoors is as easy as cutting them, placing them in a vase full of water and placing them in a warm, well-lit room indoors. In about seven to ten days you will see the buds swelling and showing color and a few days after that, they'll be in full bloom.

- In warmer parts of the South, shrubs may need to be fertilized this month. Time your fertilizing with the swelling of leaf buds so that fertilizer is available as the shrubs leaf out and come into their most active phase of growth. Organic fertilizers take a little longer to become active in the soil, so they can be put down a little earlier to be sure they're working their way into the root zone when the plants need them.

- As buds begin to swell on the branches of your shrubs, it's time to think about pruning shrubs that flower on their new growth. Butterfly bush, dwarf crape myrtle, and panicle hydrangea are among those that bloom on the new growth of the season. Azalea, French or mophead hydrangea, oakleaf hydrangea, and others flower on last year's growth. *Do not* prune those now or you will be pruning off the flower buds that will be opening soon.

MARCH

- Across most of the South, air and soil temperatures are beginning to warm this month. Now is a great time to plant most shrubs, taking advantage of spring rains to get them established before the heat of summer sets in.

- As the blooms fall from your spring-flowering camellias, or "Japonicas" as they're sometimes called, be sure to keep the fallen blooms cleaned up under the shrubs. Decaying blooms can harbor fungal diseases, some of which are serious enough to cause damage to the plants.

- Most shrubs can be fertilized in March. Spring-flowering shrubs that have just finished flowering will be entering a stage of active growth, and summer-blooming shrubs that have just been pruned will use the nutrients to grow quickly and flower profusely later in the season. In cooler parts of the South, you may need to push your schedule back by a couple of weeks to time fertilizing correctly.

APRIL

- Keep an eye on shrubs that look like they may have suffered cold or wind damage during the winter. In most parts of the South, shrubs should be entering a very active phase of growth by now, and any damaged or dead growth may need to be pruned out to encourage healthy new growth from undamaged parts of the plant.

- Garden centers are fully stocked this month and the selection will be better than at almost any other time of year. Catalog pictures are beautiful, but there is no substitute for seeing in person a plant that you are thinking of adding to your garden. Visit your garden centers often to get the highest quality plants they have to offer.

- Unfortunately, warm spring weather also means the beginning of bug season. Aphids, whiteflies, and spider mites will be hatching this month as temperatures rise. Aphids are especially fond of tender, succulent new growth on shrubs and roses. Insecticidal soap is a safe method of controlling these springtime pests.

- If you haven't yet pruned summer-blooming shrubs like butterfly bush and dwarf crape myrtle, your window of time is closing fast. They should be leafing out well now and you can cut stems back to the very strongest new growth that is emerging.

MAY

- Watering becomes very important this month as summerlike temperatures begin arriving across much of the South. Be sure that hoses, sprinklers, automatic timers, and soaker hoses are all in good working order. Soaker hoses need to be replaced about every three years. Over time, their tiny pores in the hoses clog up with soil and other debris and they distribute water unevenly, causing some plants to dry out faster than others.

- Shrubs can still be planted in May as long as you pay careful attention to watering. Heat-loving varieties like gardenia and oleander prefer to be planted now when the soil has warmed up and their roots can grow quickly into the surrounding soil. Remember that roots are confined to a relatively small rootball, and plants will need regular watering until their roots have grown into the surrounding soil.

- Azaleas are one of the most popular flowering shrubs in the South and timing is everything when it comes to pruning. Evergreen varieties that flowered in March and April can be pruned between the time they finish blooming and June 15. Pruning after that time may ruin next year's floral display, since they will begin setting next year's flower buds by midsummer.

JUNE

- The kids and grandkids are out of school now and it's the perfect time to plan outdoor activities with the youngsters. Plan a picnic to a local park or botanical garden. Make a fun activity out of identifying shrubs that are especially attractive to butterflies and beneficial insects and make a list to add to your own garden.

- Summer heat and dry weather may be setting in across much of the South this month. Recently planted shrubs will almost certainly need additional water until they are well established. Try not to allow them to wilt repeatedly, as this is hard on the plants and it can affect their overall growth and flowering.

- Japanese beetles seem to appear out of nowhere this month and especially bad infestations can number in the thousands. Japanese beetles can be hand-picked and dropped in a jar of soapy water or for severe infestations, spray with carbaryl.

- If you choose to use Japanese beetle traps as a control method, be sure to place the traps in the farthest corners of the yard from your garden. Traps use pheromones to attract Japanese beetles to them, and you want to lure them out of the garden, not into it!

JULY

- Vacationing gardeners need to have plans in place for keeping the garden watered while they're away. If you don't have an automatic irrigation system, soaker hoses or sprinklers can be set up with battery-powered timers to keep plants watered while you're away.

- Water needs will vary from plant to plant. Be sure to keep a close eye on newly planted shrubs. They can dry out very quickly, and it doesn't take much time for permanent damage to occur when temperatures are high.

- Spider mites thrive in the heat and humidity of midsummer across the South. Their population can explode almost overnight and damage can be severe almost before you realize you have a problem. Sunspray or highly refined horticultural oils will help with severe spider mite outbreaks. Bagworms can also be active, especially on conifers like arborvitae and juniper.

- Even though it is hot and dry, overwatering can be a problem in heavy clay soils that stay wet. Hot, humid conditions and wet soil are the perfect formula for a variety of root rot

diseases. Often, these are not detected until plants begin to wilt or collapse, and by then, it may be too late to save the plant.

AUGUST

- August is the month to take advantage of early sunrises and cooler morning temperatures. Do your best to get out in the garden early to get any deadheading, weeding, or watering done before the heat of the day sets in. This is easier on the garden and on the gardener. If you do have to work later into the day, be sure to drink plenty of water and take frequent breaks.

- Shrubs that were planted in spring should be getting well established in the garden by now, but August can be a brutal month. Remember, when you're watering, to soak rootballs deeply and thoroughly to encourage roots to grow deep into the soil in search of water. This will make them all the more drought tolerant later in life.

- Redheaded azalea caterpillars are active this month and can completely defoliate branches if not detected early. Azalea caterpillars are a bigger problem in the deeper South than farther north. You can identify this caterpillar by its red head and yellow stripes. Control with the natural insecticide Bt (Bacillus thuringiensis).

- A variety of root rot diseases can be problems in the heat of the summer. They are most common in wet soils, but can attack stressed plants in drier locations too. They can also be passed from plant to plant in the soil and can be especially troublesome in mass plantings as they move from plant to plant.

SEPTEMBER

- Across much of the South, we will begin seeing occasional breaks in the heat during September, but we can also see a distinct lack of rainfall. Keep the garden well-watered to reduce stress on plants and allow them to store as much energy as possible for the coming winter.

- Fall is prime shrub-planting season in the South. Begin making plans for shrubs you want to add to your landscape during the months of October and November. Nurseries will have fresh plants in stock by the end of the month and if you're willing to do a little coddling, plants left over from spring and summer are often deeply discounted. They'll need a little TLC, but most will settle into the garden just fine.

- If shrubs have suffered any kind of dieback during the heat and drought of summer, prune out dead branches. Any other pruning should be reserved for the proper time of year, usually late winter to early spring. Avoid any pruning other than dead branch removal on shrubs like azaleas, oakleaf hydrangeas, or viburnums. Flower buds have already formed for next year and pruning now will cut off next spring's blooms.

OCTOBER

- Fall is the best time for planting shrubs and trees in the South. Warm soil temperatures encourage fast root growth and establishment, but cooler air temperatures keep plants from being stressed. Avoid planting heat-loving shrubs like butterfly bush and dwarf crape myrtle at this time of year. Their root growth slows to a minimum and plants may have difficulty getting established.

- October is often the driest month of the year across much of the South, so don't rely on natural rainfall to water newly planted shrubs or to take the stress off of established plantings. Water thoroughly and deeply to draw roots deep into the soil in search of water and nutrients.

- It is too late to do any shearing or pruning now, especially on evergreen shrubs like boxwood and holly. Shearing will leave you with brown-edged leaves all winter long and may encourage new growth to sprout from pruning cuts that will then freeze and die when cold weather arrives.

- Cool-season weeds like henbit, chickweed, and dandelions will be germinating this month. Pre-emergent herbicides will aid in their control. The key to success with pre-emergents is that they *must* be applied before the seeds germinate and once applied and watered in, the soil must be left undisturbed so that the seed-preventing barrier stays intact.

NOVEMBER

- November is prime planting time throughout the South. Both evergreen and deciduous shrubs can still be planted, and we should be settling back into a regular moisture pattern to keep plants watered as they get established.

- Many trees and shrubs will be dropping leaves this month and some may be dropping fruits or berries. Keep leaves blown out of beds and larger fruits and berries raked up. Both can harbor insect pests and diseases that can overwinter and re-infect the garden next spring.

- Broadleaved and tender evergreens can be susceptible to drying out and leaf desiccation by cold winds as winter weather arrives later in the month. Keep the plants well-watered if natural rainfall is scarce so the roots have plenty of water available to them to draw up into the leaves and keep them hydrated.

- Spruce mites are cool weather mites that are active this month on arborvitae, juniper, spruce, and other conifers. They attack in the cooler seasons of spring and fall across much of the South, but can be active throughout the summer in mountainous regions. They are best treated with miticides, but often go undiscovered until they have already caused serious damage to the plant.

Azaleas are a popular flowering shrub in the South.

DECEMBER

- Gardeners who would like to try their own hand at making new plants from cuttings may want to try taking hardwood cuttings of boxwood, camellia, holly, and juniper. Hardwood cuttings can be taken in December to be rooted in a cold frame or in pots of damp sand in an unheated but well lit garage or garden shed.

- In cold, dry, exposed sites, broadleaf evergreens must be watered through the winter months when the soil is not frozen. They don't want to be waterlogged, as this may cause root rot to set in, but keeping the soil damp will help keep moisture in the leaves and plants from desiccating due to winter winds.

- Evergreen hollies, boxwoods, aucuba, wax myrtle, and more can be used in holiday wreaths and other decorations this month. Prune thoughtfully and carefully to maintain the natural shape and overall health of the shrub as you're collecting for your holiday display. Deciduous hollies produce wonderful stems of berries this time of year as well.

TREES
for the South

What would we do without trees? Well, for one thing, none of us would be here. Trees, whether in the deciduous forests of the northern hemisphere or the tropical rain forests of the equatorial belt, produce a large majority of the oxygen we breathe and so without them, there would be no us. That is important to keep in mind in this day and age when it seems our modus operandi is to consume, consume, consume, instead of conserve, conserve, conserve! But before we get too deep and esoteric, let's consider trees' value in our daily lives. They shade our homes and reduce the amount of energy we consume. They add beauty to our surroundings. They provide shelter for a variety of flora and fauna that all—whether we like some of them or not—contribute to a healthy ecosystem. They provide lumber for building, pulp for paper, and wood for burning to heat our homes. What *would* we do without trees?

For those of us who love to garden, we understand all of the practical applications of trees, but we love them most for their beauty. Trees announce the arrival of spring with the flowering of the dogwoods and redbuds. In summer, the uniquely shaped leaves of the tulip poplar and the colorful foliage of 'Forest Pansy' redbud add texture and color to our landscapes. In autumn, the woods blaze with glorious color as red and sugar maples light up hills and valleys across the South. And in winter, trees like American beech, river birch, and others offer up their beautiful bark and their striking silhouettes to give us beauty even when their leaves have fallen.

SELECTING A TREE

A tree should be selected not only for its form in the landscape, but also for its function. Certainly, form is important. If we're going to plant trees, we do want them to be beautiful. But we need to give careful consideration of what that tree's intended function is, too. Do we need a tree to provide shade for the back yard? Do we need a tree to protect the front of our south-facing house from the brutal summer sun? Are we looking for an understory tree that will coexist with other trees we already have, helping to add another layer of interest and beauty to our landscape?

Do the trees we want to add to our landscape need to be evergreen or deciduous? Does it matter? Deciduous trees are often selected because they offer summer shade and allow the winter sun to warm our houses. The largest specimens, like the oaks, are known for their long lives and majestic form, while others provide outstanding fall color and ornamental appeal. Still others, like the ginkgo, have an ancient history, as well as a unique beauty all their own.

When it comes to evergreens, our selections are more limited, but no less beautiful. Southern magnolia, one of the signature plants in the landscape of the South, spreads its branches low across the ground bearing its pristine white, fragrant blooms from early to midsummer. American holly stretches its stately pyramidal form skyward and clothes itself in bright red berries in autumn and winter. And live oak, where it is hardy, is as much a part of

SOUTHERN MAGNOLIA

LIVE OAK TREE

the Southern psyche as pecan pie. Evergreens are not without their challenges. They shade the ground twelve months of the year and allow little else to grow under them. The few plants that aren't shaded out are likely strangled by the trees' large and impressive root systems. Evergreen trees like these serve a very specific purpose in the native habitats—shelter. Under the canopies of these evergreens is where the animals take refuge, so it isn't meant for a large number of plants to be growing there. There is a purpose, you see, to everything.

LETTING TREES WORK FOR YOU

Shade trees can frame a house the way a beautiful frame enhances a lasting work of art. Evergreens block objectionable views and divert strong winds. As a group, evergreens can add color to an otherwise bleak winter landscape. Although they never lose all their leaves, pines shed some of their needles each year in spring or fall, gifting you with coveted pine straw mulch.

During the dreary winter months, many ornamental trees provide colorful berries for our enjoyment and sustenance for birds. The seedpods and berries that follow the handsome flowers are a special treat in the garden. The Japanese flowering apricot, *Prunus mume*, is a winter-flowering gem whose blossoms will emerge as early as January in the deeper South and February where it's a little colder. If you're lucky enough to avoid a late hard freeze, you'll even find small apricots on the trees later in the season that are very attractive to birds and wildlife.

One often overlooked characteristic of deciduous trees is exfoliating bark, such as the bark of the river birch that flakes and peels in long, cream-, beige- and salmon-colored strips. The cinnamon-colored, mottled bark of crape myrtle is most appreciated in the winter garden, but is a characteristic that is often overlooked when initial choices are being made. Research the subtle seasonal characteristics of landscape trees before you plant, and site them where their traits can be most appreciated.

PLANNING AHEAD

Trees, as important as they are, can also be one of the biggest financial investments you make in your landscape. From a purely monetary standpoint, trees are big ticket items. They're not only more expensive to buy, but eventually they are going to need occasional maintenance to keep them strong and healthy. With trees, you're not just planning for this season or even five or ten seasons from now. You are truly planning for the future and wise planning is essential. Ask yourself why you need a tree for a particular location. Is shade your primary goal? What about privacy? Are there height restrictions in the space? If a tree produces fruit or drops twigs, would it create a hazard or maintenance concern? Do you desire pretty flowers, or is a conifer acceptable? Many trees attract wildlife; are you prepared for the litter that accompanies critters?

You can consult with an arborist, a horticulture professional at a local garden center, or your County Cooperative Extension agent for lists of trees for special situations. They can guide your tree selection by considering your particular soil types and environment, as well as any limitations your lot may create. Remember, too, that for many people living in modern-day subdivisions there are ordinances and rules that one must abide by. These ordinances may specify which tree species can be planted near streets or power lines and may also stipulate restrictions for protecting valuable, mature trees onsite.

UNUSUAL TREES FOR SOUTHERN GARDENS

In the following pages, you will find profiles for a wide range of trees that will thrive in our Southern climate—everything from the tallest shade trees to smaller and more ornamental understory species. Most of those chosen for the book were trees that are readily available, reasonably easy to grow, and varieties that you will meet with a certain degree of success. Hopefully, that will encourage you to branch out (pun intended) and explore more trees for your landscape. Following is a list of very unique, desirable, and highly useful trees that we didn't have room for in the book, but that you will find fascinating enough to research on your own. Enjoy!

COMMON NAME	LATIN NAME
Autumn Moon Maple	*Acer shirasawanum* 'Autumn Moon'
Pawpaw	*Asimina triloba*
Pecan	*Carya illinoinensis*
Blue Atlas Cedar	*Cedrus atlantica* 'Glauca'
Deodar Cedar	*Cedrus deodara*
Chinese Redbud	*Cercis chinensis*
Chinafir	*Cunninghamia lanceolata*
Snow Gum	*Eucalyptus gunnii*
Chinese Parasol Tree	*Firmiana simplex*
Fantasy Crape Myrtle	*Lagerstroemia fauriei* 'Fantasy'
Bigleaf Magnolia	*Magnolia macrophylla*
Dawn Redwood	*Metasequoia glyptostroboides*
Blackgum	*Nyssa sylvatica*
Sassafras	*Sassafras albidum*
Umbrella Pine	*Sciadopitys verticillata*
Fragrant Snowbell	*Styrax obassia*
Japanese Tree Lilac	*Syringa reticulata*

AMERICAN BEECH

Fagus grandifolia

Why It's Special—American beech is one of our most overlooked native trees for the Southern landscape. Popular in the past, with enormous specimens gracing estates and plantations across the South, at some point they fell out of favor. Few trees are as majestic with their smooth, silvery gray bark, broad crowns, and stately form lending a great sense of age to the landscape.

How to Plant & Grow—Balled-and-burlapped specimens should be planted while they are dormant. Potted trees may be planted while dormant or actively growing. Expect the trees to take one to two seasons to settle in before putting on any noticeable growth.

Care & Problems—Once established, American beech is a relatively pest- and disease-free tree. They will not win any races in the growth department, and it should be understood that even the young among us are planting for the next generation's enjoyment. American beech will not thrive in compacted soil.

Hardiness—Zones 4 to 9

Flowers/Beeries—Insignificant

Fall Color—Golden bronze

Mature Size (H × W)—50 to 70 ft. × 50 to 70 ft.

Water Needs—Moderate to moist, never wet

AMERICAN HOLLY

Ilex opaca

Why It's Special—American holly has been largely replaced by the much faster growing 'Nellie R. Stevens' and other hybrids, but this overlooked native evergreen is one of the most widely adaptable for Southern gardens. Young specimens are often awkward, but the ugly duckling will turn into the most beautiful of swans.

How to Plant & Grow—Plant balled-and-burlapped specimens in late winter or early spring before plants break dormancy and begin to grow. Potted plants can be planted spring or fall. Hollies have a broad-spreading, fibrous root system and benefit from a large planting hole and well-amended soil.

Care & Problems—Hollies prefer a well-drained, moist soil, but will tolerate drier sites as long as they are kept well watered while they are getting established. It may take two to three seasons after transplanting for berry production to start, and you must have both male and female plants nearby.

Hardiness—Zones 5b to 9a

Flowers/Berries—Small white flowers, showy red berries

Fall Color—None; leaves are evergreen

Mature Size (H × W)—30 to 45 ft. × 15 to 25 ft.

Water Needs—Evenly moist to slightly dry

AMERICAN YELLOWWOOD

Cladrastis kentukea

Why It's Special—American yellowwood is an excellent landscape tree that is native to the South. It is valued for its silvery gray bark and its wisterialike white flowers in spring, but its common name comes from the bright yellow color of its heartwood. It matures into a graceful, medium-sized tree suitable for any yard, large or small.

How to Plant & Grow—Plant yellowwood during its dormant season, late November to early March, in full sun to light shade. It prefers rich, evenly moist soil that is extremely high in organic matter and it may suffer in heavy clay.

Care & Problems—Prune in summer while the tree is young to encourage a strong, well-branched structure. Sap will flow freely when the tree is pruned, but will stop of its own accord. Yellowwood has no serious disease or insect pests. Flowering may be cyclical; impressive one year and less so the next.

Hardiness—Zones 4b to 8a

Flowers/Berries—White flowers in pendulous clusters in spring

Fall Color—Clear, beautiful yellow

Mature Size (H × W)—30 to 40 ft. × 20 to 30 ft.

Water Needs—Evenly moist to slightly dry

BALDCYPRESS
Taxodium distichum

Why It's Special—One of the few deciduous conifers, this native tree makes an imposing specimen in large landscapes. It is known for producing fascinating knees in swampy situations, but adapts perfectly well to the drier landscape and there, knees are not present.

How to Plant & Grow—Fall or winter, after the needles have dropped, is the best time to plant baldcypress. If you have an area of the yard that stays wet and is difficult to get other trees to grow, baldcypress may be the perfect answer. However, it will also tolerate drier sites and does not require standing water in order to thrive.

Care & Problems—Use care when planting baldcypress and be sure not to break the leader. If that happens, it may have a difficult time generating a new one. The beauty of a cypress is its near-perfect symmetry and improper pruning can quickly ruin it. Lower branches can be carefully limbed up as the tree ages.

Hardiness—Zones 5a to 10a

Flowers/Berries—Flowers inconspicuous, occasional small cones

Fall Color—Cinnamon/bronze before dropping

Mature Size (H × W)—50 to 75 ft. × 40 to 60 ft.

Water Needs—Average to wet soils

CHINESE FRINGETREE
Chionanthus retusus

Why It's Special—A Chinese fringetree is the Asian cousin to our much-loved American fringetree, also called 'Grancy Gray-beard' or 'Old-man's-beard'. This Chinese counterpart is larger in all respects, growing into a small, multistemmed tree to 25 feet tall with a similar spread. In spring, the plant literally turns itself into a cloud of white fringe-like blooms, almost hiding the leaves. Impressive!

How to Plant & Grow—Plant Chinese fringetree in spring, giving it the warm months of the summer to become established. It prefers deep, moist, fertile soils but is highly adaptable to less-than-ideal conditions. It prefers full sun to reach its fullest potential, but will adapt to part sun.

Care & Problems—Not extremely drought tolerant, fringetree will need supplemental watering during dry periods in summer. It is, however, very tolerant of and actually thrives in our heat and humidity. It is less hardy than our native fringetree, but not tender enough to be a problem in the South.

Hardiness—Zones 6 to 8

Flowers/Berries—White flowers, spring

Fall Color—Soft yellow, not reliable

Mature Size (H × W)—25 ft. × 25 ft.

Water Needs—Evenly moist soil, ideally

CRAPE MYRTLE
Lagerstroemia indica

Why It's Special—Crape myrtles thrive throughout the South, with few other flowering trees matching their colorful display or the length of their bloom period from midsummer to autumn. Many varieties also have beautiful flaking and peeling bark in shades of silver to cinnamon.

How to Plant & Grow—Crape myrtles thrive in the heat and humidity of the South and are best planted in early spring to take advantage of warming soil and air temperatures to get them established. They *must* have full sun. Even a few hours of shade each day will significantly reduce the number of flowers and will invite problems with powdery mildew.

Care & Problems—Crape myrtles must be well watered during their first season in the ground. **Important:** The mutilation-style pruning of crape myrtles that has become commonplace in the landscape is not only unnecessary, but is actually detrimental to the trees, so don't do it!

Hardiness—Zones 6a to 9b

Flowers/Berries—Blooms in white, lavender, red, pink

Fall Color—Yellow to red, depending on variety

Mature Size (H × W)—10 to 30 ft. × 10 to 25 ft.

Water Needs—Evenly moist soil

DOGWOOD, CHINESE

Cornus kousa

Why It's Special—A close cousin to our native flowering dogwood, the Chinese dogwood bears similar white flowers a month after ours has finished blooming, extending the dogwood flowering season well into late spring. On many varieties, flowers are followed by large and very showy bright red fruits.

How to Plant & Grow—Chinese dogwood prefers full sun to part sun to grow and flower its best. It will thrive in an open, sunny yard where our native dogwood may suffer sunburn or leaf scorch in midsummer. Deep, rich, moist soil will suit it best.

Care & Problems—Avoid pruning during borer season in June and July, as this can invite borers into open pruning cuts. Chinese dogwood is nearly immune to the anthracnose diseases that plague our native dogwood and is a great landscape choice for that reason alone.

Hardiness—Zones 5b to 9a

Flowers/Berries—Showy white blooms, red fruits

Fall Color—Red, in late autumn

Mature Size (H × W)—20 to 30 ft. × 20 to 30 ft.

Water Needs—Evenly moist to slightly dry

DOGWOOD, FLOWERING

Cornus florida

Why It's Special—Perhaps no other tree evokes more distinct images of spring in the South than the flowering dogwood. Flowering dogwood also contribute intense red fall color to our Southern forests, peaking over a period of several weeks in October and November.

How to Plant & Grow—Unlike most deciduous trees, dogwoods are best planted in spring rather than fall. This is particularly true of balled-and-burlapped plants. Dogwoods prefer well-drained, slightly acidic soil with plenty of organic matter. In heavier clay soils, amend deeply and thoroughly when planting.

Care & Problems—Avoid pruning during borer season in June and July, as this invites borers into open pruning cuts and makes an already serious problem worse. Leaf spot anthracnose is common and is worse in years when wet, rainy springs prevail. This is unsightly, but not life-threatening like the *Discula* dogwood blight that can weaken and kill trees outright.

Hardiness—Zones 5b to 9a

Flowers/Berries—White blooms, red fruits

Fall Color—Deep red, October/November

Mature Size (H × W)—20 to 30 ft. × 20 to 30 ft.

Water Needs—Evenly moist to slightly dry

GINKGO

Ginkgo biloba

Why It's Special—Ginkgo is an ancient conifer relative native to China. It is an excellent landscape tree with brilliant yellow fall color. Its distinctive fan-shaped leaves are 2 to 4 inches wide and flutter beautifully in the summer breeze.

How to Plant & Grow—Ginkgo should be planted in late winter or early spring while trees are dormant. Full sun and rich, fertile soil will get them off to a good start and encourage relatively fast growth while they are young. Investing a little extra time in their care after planting will pay off. Water thoroughly and deeply once a week, more if weather is hot and dry.

Care & Problems—The best feature of the ginkgo is that it is virtually pest, disease, and maintenance free! When buying a ginkgo, consult with your local garden center and purchase a cultivar that is known to be a male variety. With age, a female tree produces copious quantities of messy, bad-smelling fruit.

Hardiness—Zones 4a to 9a

Flowers/Berries—Undesirable fruits on female trees

Fall Color—Brilliant golden yellow

Mature Size (H × W)—60 ft. × 45 ft.

Water Needs—Average to slightly moist

JAPANESE CEDAR
Cryptomeria japonica

Why It's Special—Japanese cedar, or cryptomeria, is a cousin to the giant sequoia of the West Coast. Soft sprays of foliage appear in spirals along drooping branches. Mature specimens have attractive, reddish brown bark that peels off in long shreds. Many unusual variants are available, including dwarf and globe-shaped forms.

How to Plant & Grow—Cryptomeria is best planted in early spring and must be kept well watered through the first summer. They thrive in sunny locations with deep, rich, moist soil. Once established, they grow quickly, and it is not unusual to see 2 to 4 feet of growth per year from larger-growing varieties.

Care & Problems—Keep trees dense and full by shearing very lightly in early spring, just before new growth begins. Cutting the central leader is not recommended. It will ruin the shape of the tree. Japanese cedars will not tolerate long periods of drought and must be kept mulched and well watered, especially when young.

Hardiness—Zone 6a to 9a

Flowers/Berries—None significant

Fall Color—Evergreen

Mature Size (H × W)—5 to 50 ft. × 5 to 25 ft.

Water Needs—Evenly moist soil required

JAPANESE FLOWERING CHERRY
Prunus spp.

Why It's Special—Flowering cherry is known for its spectacular spring show of soft pink to white flowers that cloak the bare branches in early spring. 'Yoshino', with its pale pink, single flowers, and 'Kwanzan', with its deeper pink double pompons, are the two most popular.

How to Plant & Grow—Plant flowering cherries during the dormant season so that their roots have time to begin establishing before the heat of summer sets in. Cherries need excellent drainage and will suffer if planted in wet soil. Soil should be thoroughly amended with organic matter.

Care & Problems—Regular watering during the first year or two after planting is critical. Fertilize with an all-purpose nursery fertilizer each spring when the trees have finished flowering. Prune while dormant in winter or in August when dead wood can be distinguished from growth.

Hardiness—Zones 5a to 7b

Flowers/Berries—Pink or white blooms, early spring; no fruit

Fall Color— 'Kwanzan' is best in glowing gold to orange

Mature Size (H × W)—15 to 35 ft. × 20 to 25 ft.

Water Needs—Evenly moist, not wet

JAPANESE SNOWBELL
Styrax japonicus

Why It's Special—The pendent, bell-shaped, fragrant white flowers of Japanese styrax appear in May, just after attractive, emerald green leaves unfold. The variety 'Emerald Pagoda' is especially well adapted to our Southern climate and a weeping form, 'Carillon', is a beauty to behold.

How to Plant & Grow—The farther south you go and the warmer the climate gets, the more shade Japanese snowbell needs to keep from scorching in the summer sun. This can be alleviated by giving it the rich, deep, highly organic soil it needs to thrive. Amend the planting hole with a large quantity of compost, composted manure, and soil conditioner, and keep new plants well watered for the first growing season.

Care & Problems—Once established, snowbell is nearly care-free. Problems with borers have occasionally been reported and ambrosia beetle is the culprit. The telltale sign is small cores of frass (sawdust) sticking straight out of the trunk. Treat infected trees immediately!

Hardiness—Zones 5b to 8a

Flowers/Berries—White flowers in mid-spring

Fall Color—Yellow, flushed red

Mature Size (H × W)—20 to 30 ft. × 20 to 30 ft.

Water Needs—Evenly moist soil

MAGNOLIA, SOUTHERN

Magnolia grandiflora

Why It's Special—Southern magnolia, along with live oak, is a signature tree of the South. All over the region, magnolias are valued for their large, shiny green leaves and 10-inch, creamy white flowers. The sweet fragrance of magnolia blossoms perfumes the air on early summer nights.

How to Plant & Grow—Southern magnolias' fleshy roots make it sensitive to cold or dry conditions. Avoid balled-and-burlapped specimens, as these are difficult to transplant and frequently struggle to get established. Southern magnolia grows naturally in rich, moist soils along river swamps or in damp woods, but will tolerate drier sites as long as the soil is rich and high in organic matter.

Care & Problems—The biggest problem most gardeners face is the endless number of leaves that fall at the worst possible time of year—early summer. By letting your magnolias branch low and sweep the ground, you can disguise the problem and the leaves become natural mulch.

Hardiness—Zones 6b to 9b

Flowers/Berries—White blooms, summer

Fall Color—Evergreen

Mature Size (H × W)—30 to 70 ft. × 20 to 50 ft.

Water Needs—Evenly moist soil

MAGNOLIA, SWEETBAY

Magnolia virginiana

Why It's Special—Sweetbay magnolia is a lovely and graceful small specimen tree. Its handsome, semi-glossy green leaves are backed in silvery white, showing to great effect on breezy days. The flowers are small and not nearly as showy as its larger cousin, the Southern magnolia, but they are intoxicatingly fragrant and that alone makes it worth growing.

How to Plant & Grow—Native to swampy habitats around the South, sweetbay magnolia requires a deep, rich and constantly moist soil to look its very best. It will grow in less-than-ideal conditions, but always looks a little wan when its needs are not being met.

Care & Problems—Sweetbay magnolia has no serious pests or disease, but its roots form a completely impenetrable mass beneath the tree in a few short years. Nothing will grow successfully under them, and it is a waste of time to try.

Hardiness—Zones 5 to 9

Flowers/Berries—White, very fragrant

Fall Color—None, semi-evergreen

Mature Size (H × W)—15 to 20 ft. × 15 to 20 ft.

Water Needs—Evenly moist to boggy

MAPLE, JAPANESE

Acer palmatum

Why It's Special—Japanese maples offer more forms, colors, and growth habits than almost any other tree in our Southern landscapes. The gnarled and twisted trunks of an old Japanese maple are not to be rivaled when it comes to architectural form and interest. Many have spectacular fall color.

How to Plant & Grow—Plant Japanese maples from November through April while they are dormant and can make significant root growth before spring growth and hot summer weather. Maples will perform best in rich, well-drained, woodsy, humus-rich soil, but are adaptable as long as they are not wet.

Care & Problems—Water deeply during the summer months, especially during its first two seasons, to encourage roots to grow deep into the soil in search of water. This will help to keep foliage from burning and trees from suffering heat stress. Late freezes can damage tender new growth, but the trees will grow out of it.

Hardiness—Zones 5b to 8b

Flowers/Berries—None

Fall Color—Red, orange, gold

Mature Size (H × W)—4 to 30 ft. × 6 to 20 ft., depending on the variety

Water Needs—Average to moist soils

MAPLE, RED
Acer rubrum

Why It's Special—Red maple is the star of Southern maples. Its fast rate of growth and strong, upright growth habit make it the near-perfect shade tree for the modern urban landscape. The variety 'October Glory' is one of the finest on the market, holding its brilliant red color late into the season.

How to Plant & Grow—Red maples are available as potted or balled-and-burlapped specimens. Plant red maple in late fall or winter so that roots can begin to grow before hot summer weather arrives. Regular water is essential during the first two years. Then, trees will thrive on their own in all but the most extreme heat and drought.

Care & Problems—Try to develop a strong framework with a single trunk and branches growing perpendicular to the trunk. As the tree matures, remove weak branches and limbs with narrow crotches at the trunk, as these will become weak as the tree grows.

Hardiness—Zones 4b to 9a

Flowers/Berries—Red flowers in early spring

Fall Color—Scarlet red, in autumn

Mature Size (H × W)—40 to 60 ft. × 30 to 50 ft.

Water Needs—Drought tolerant, once established

MAPLE, SUGAR
Acer saccharum

Why It's Special—Across the South, few trees produce the truly stunning fall color of the sugar maple, lighting up the autumn landscape in shades of brilliant gold, orange, and vermillion. Strong-growing and resilient, sugar maple is an excellent shade tree for the more temperate regions of the South.

How to Plant & Grow—Container-grown trees can be planted anytime the soil is workable, while balled-and-burlapped specimens should be planted from late fall to late winter, while they are dormant. This gives the roots a chance to settle in and begin to grow before the tree leafs out. Sugar maple will require regular, weekly watering for the first two seasons.

Care & Problems—The greatest problem with sugar maple is its shallow root system, which will eventually make its way to the soil surface and render it nearly impossible to grow grass—or anything else, for that matter—within the root zone of the tree.

Hardiness—Zones 3a to 8b

Flowers/Berries—Insignificant

Fall Color—Truly stunning orange, gold

Mature Size (H × W)—60 to 70 ft. × 40 to 50 ft.

Water Needs—Evenly moist to slightly dry

OAK, LIVE
Quercus virginiana

Why It's Special—Live oak shares top billing with Southern magnolia when it comes to trees that make our Southern landscapes what they are. Their one-of-a-kind form, with enormous limbs sweeping low to the ground, evoke images of long driveways leading to the finest Southern homes.

How to Plant & Grow—Oaks, because of their strong taproot, may be finicky when it comes to transplanting. It is best to find container-grown trees that have all of their roots intact rather than balled-and-burlapped specimens whose taproots have been compromised. Container-grown plants should be checked for any girdling roots.

Care & Problems—Oak wilt can affect live oaks and chestnut blight can be an occasional problem in coastal areas of the South. Call a certified arborist at the first sign of decline so that the problem can be treated properly. These diseases can spread through contaminated saws and pruning tools, so use reputable care providers.

Hardiness—Zones 7b to 9b

Flowers/Berries—Acorns on older trees

Fall Color—Evergreen

Mature Size (H × W)—60 to 80 ft. × 70 to 100 ft.

Water Needs—Average to dry soils

OAK, SOUTHERN RED

Quercus falcata

Why It's Special—Southern red oak is one of our faster growing oaks and makes an outstanding street tree, as well as an excellent shade tree for larger landscapes. Its deep solid root system makes it a sturdy tree with few worries of it being uprooted during severe wind and thunderstorms.

How to Plant & Grow—Plant Southern red oaks anytime from November through March while they are dormant. Water thoroughly at planting time and then as needed to maintain soil moisture until the tree is well established. Be prepared to soak the soil at least once and possibly twice each week during hot summer weather for the first two growing seasons.

Care & Problems—Prune to encourage an open branch structure with strong side branches at perpendicular angles to the trunk. Oak wilt can be an occasional problem and a professional arborist or County Extension agent should be consulted at the first sign of possible trouble.

Hardiness—Zones 6a to 9a

Flowers/Berries—Small acorns when mature

Fall Color—Reddish to rusty bronze

Mature Size (H × W)—50 to 80 ft. × 40 to 60 ft.

Water Needs—Average to slightly dry

PALMETTO

Sabal palmetto

Why It's Special—Easily recognized by its single, straight trunk and compact, rounded crown, our native palmetto is one of the hardiest palm species known. Once established, it can regularly withstand temperatures of 10° and will tolerate colder temperatures for brief periods.

How to Plant & Grow—Container-grown plants can be planted anytime in late spring or summer. They transplant easily from May to July, thriving in the summer heat and humidity. Palmetto will grow in almost any well-drained soil, as long as they are not waterlogged in winter.

Care & Problems—Newly planted palmettos should be thoroughly soaked once or twice a week for the first two summers. After that, they should thrive on their own in all but the driest summers. Old leaves do deteriorate and should be pruned away, as needed. Extremely cold temperatures may cause leaf burn, but plants generally recover quickly during the next growing season.

Hardiness—Zones 7b to 9b

Flowers/Berries—Large fruit clusters on mature plants

Fall Color—Evergreen

Mature Size (H × W)—20 to 50 ft. × 6 to 10 ft.

Water Needs—Evenly moist, well-drained soil

RED BUCKEYE

Aesculus pavia

Why It's Special—The rosy red flowers of red buckeye appear in mid-spring and nearly always signal the arrival of hummingbirds to the garden. In fact, the ruby-throated hummingbird follows the bloom season of the red buckeye from south to north as spring makes its debut.

How to Plant & Grow—Red buckeye is best transplanted in late fall or winter, while it is dormant. Even container-grown plants will occasionally die if transplanted after they leaf out in spring. It is ideally planted as a specimen tree and while it will tolerate full sun, it is best suited to areas with moist soil and light afternoon shade.

Care & Problems—Red buckeye is pest free and extremely adaptable. Buckeyes are quite drought tolerant once established, but expect some leaf scorch in dry conditions. Leaves may drop as early as August. This is natural and harmless.

Hardiness—Zones 5a to 8a

Flowers/Berries—Red flowers in spring

Fall Color—None; leaves fall early

Mature Size (H × W)—15 to 20 ft. × 15 to 20 ft.

Water Needs—Evenly moist to slightly dry

REDBUD, EASTERN
Cercis canadensis

Why It's Special—Redbuds in full bloom are among the most striking sights of spring, and, in a good year, redbud and dogwood bloom will overlap. What a sight! A small, vase-shaped tree, redbud forms a rounded canopy of heart-shaped leaves by early summer, casting light, comfortable shade.

How to Plant & Grow—Container-grown redbuds can be planted either in spring or fall. Redbuds have a deep taproot that makes balled-and-burlapped transplanting a little trickier, but it can be done. Late fall or winter is ideal so that new root growth can begin while the tree is dormant.

Care & Problems—The only thing that redbuds will not tolerate is waterlogged soil, so be sure that drainage is adequate. Other than that, this is one of our toughest, and most rewarding native trees. Soak newly planted trees twice weekly for the first two to three months. Eventually, redbuds will require very little extra water or care.

Hardiness—Zones 4b to 8b

Flowers/Berries—Magenta flowers in early spring

Fall Color—Usually not showy, occasionally yellow

Mature Size (H × W)—20 to 25 ft. × 20 to 30 ft.

Water Needs—Average to dry

REDBUD, TEXAS
Cercis canadensis var. *texensis*

Why It's Special—Texas redbud is a very closely related subspecies of our native Eastern redbud that thrives in full to part sun, heat, and humidity. Its richly colored, reddish purple blooms are borne in early spring at the same time as other redbuds; the unusual weeping variety 'Traveler' is especially beautiful.

How to Plant & Grow—Texas redbud is best planted in spring to give it the growing season to become well established. Redbuds have a deep taproot that makes balled-and-burlapped transplanting a little trickier, but it can be done. Late fall or winter is ideal so that new root growth can begin while the tree is dormant.

Care & Problems—Texas redbud is even tougher than Eastern redbud and once established will require very little extra care or maintenance. Soak newly planted trees twice weekly for the first two to three months.

Hardiness—Zones 5 to 8b

Flowers/Berries—Magenta flowers in early spring

Fall Color—Not showy

Mature Size (H × W)—20 to 25 ft. × 20 to 30 ft.

Water Needs—Average to dry

SWEETGUM
Liquidambar styraciflua

Why It's Special—Many homeowners dislike sweetgum trees for their spiny round seedpods that drop from the trees in autumn. 'Rotundiloba' is a selection with round-lobed leaves instead of the typical pointed stars and very few fruit. Some sources say that it is fruitless, but it will produce a very small number of fruit in some years.

How to Plant & Grow—Plant in late winter or early spring to take advantage of spring rains for establishment. Sweetgums prefer a rich, moist, well-drained site, but will tolerate nearly anything you can dish out, except for waterlogged conditions. The best fall color will develop in full sun.

Care & Problems—Some sources list 'Rotundiloba' as being a smaller form of the tree and while it is more compact, it is by no means a small tree. After the tree has been planted for one season, begin pruning to encourage a single, strong leader in the center of the tree.

Hardiness—Zones 5a to 8b

Flowers/Berries—Inconspicuous flowers, few fruits

Fall Color—Spectacular burgundy, orange, gold

Mature Size (H × W)—50 ft. × 25 ft.

Water Needs—Average to evenly moist

TULIP POPLAR

Liriodendron tulipifera

Why It's Special—Tulip poplar is one of our largest and most magnificent native forest trees. When grown and developed, few trees are as impressive and almost none, at least in the South, are as large. Greenish orange, tulip-shaped flowers appear in late spring to early summer on trees that are at least six to ten years old.

How to Plant & Grow—Transplant potted trees anytime the soil can be worked as long as water can be provided during the summer months. Balled-and-burlapped specimens are best planted from late fall through winter. Tulip poplar will grow amazingly fast when planted in deep, rich, moist soil, but will adapt to even the worst growing conditions.

Care & Problems—Not the tidiest of trees, tulip poplars are probably best grown as lawn trees away from the house, but few trees are truly as impressive as a well-grown tulip poplar. Trees can be limbed up as they grow to show off their beautiful, straight trunks.

Hardiness—Zones 4 to 9

Flowers/Berries—Flowers greenish orange in late spring, early summer

Fall Color—Occasionally a clear yellow

Mature Size (H × W)—70 to 90 ft. × 40 to 50 ft.

Water Needs—Moist, ideally, but drought tolerant

TWO-WINGED SILVERBELL

Halesia diptera var. magniflora

Why It's Special—This small, native tree grows in moist, rich soil along streams and in bottomlands across the South. The name "silverbell" comes from the clusters of white bell-shaped flowers that appear just as the tree leafs out in spring. Two-winged silverbell is more heat tolerant and a better choice than Carolina silverbell for most of the South.

How to Plant & Grow—If possible, start with a potted specimen, as these will establish faster in the landscape than balled-and-burlapped trees. A natural understory tree, part sun to part shade suits it best. It prefers rich, deep, moist soil and will suffer in heavy clay.

Care & Problems—The key element to maintenance is moisture. Silverbell is simply not drought tolerant. Newly planted trees should be watered twice weekly for the first month and once weekly for the remainder of its first year in the ground. Borers should be treated at the first signs of invasion.

Hardiness—Zones 5b to 8a

Flowers/Berries—Flowers white in early sprin; winged fruit

Fall Color—Yellow, not always showy

Mature Size (H × W)—25 to 35 ft. × 25 to 30 ft.

Water Needs—Evenly moist soil

ZELKOVA

Zelkova serrata

Why It's Special—Originally touted as a replacement for the quickly declining American elm, zelkova is a neat, tidy, and attractive shade tree. It performs well in the heat and humidity of the South, and, while it will never have the magnificent presence of the American elm, it deserves greater popularity.

How to Plant & Grow—Container-grown and balled-and-burlapped specimens are best planted during the dormant season from December through early March. For maximum growth, plant where the soil is moist and deep in part to full sun. One reason that zelkova has become popular is that it transplants easily.

Care & Problems—Watering during the first two growing seasons is a must if the summers are dry. A soaker hose that can be turned on and allowed to drip slowly for one to two hours at a time is a wise investment. Good drainage is essential, and decline of plantings can often be attributed to heavy, wet, clay soils that are poorly drained.

Hardiness—Zones 4a to 8b

Flowers/Berries—None

Fall Color—Gold to bronze, sometimes

Mature Size (H × W)—70 ft. × 50 to 60 ft.

Water Needs—Evenly moist

TREES IN YOUR GARDEN

HOW TO PLANT A TREE

Trees are generally available for purchase in one of two ways: Growing in pots ranging in size from 5-gallon to 15-gallon in most garden centers (smaller and larger sizes are available from some nurseries) or as field-grown, balled-and-burlapped specimens. The former are easiest to handle by the average gardener. The latter are often slightly larger and more impressive, providing a little more instant gratification in the landscape, but are frequently heavy and difficult to handle without some assistance.

1. Before you head to the nursery looking for trees, study the location where you want your new tree to go. Look at the light levels, soil type, available moisture, and proximity to your house or other structures. Also be aware of drainage, salt spray (if you live near the coast), and other factors that may affect a tree's growth.

2. Dig a wide, shallow hole two to three times larger than the diameter of the rootball, but no deeper than the height of the ball. By making the hole as wide as possible, the roots will grow quickly into the loosened soil, speeding up the plant's establishment in its new home.

3. Slip the plant out of the pot and examine the rootball. Trees (or shrubs) growing in containers may have roots circling around the outside of the rootball. If so, take a knife, pruning shears, or the end of a sharp spade and score the rootball in three or four places. Make shallow cuts from the top to the bottom and gently tease the roots apart. Now, new roots will grow out into the soil, anchoring the plant quickly and taking up water and nutrients.

4. Remove any wire or twine entirely from balled-and-burlapped plants and cut away as much wrapping material as possible *after* placing the plant in the hole. Remove synthetic burlap entirely; it won't break down and will ultimately strangle the roots.

5. Plant even with or slightly above the surrounding soil. Look for the root flare on the tree—the point where the roots begin spreading out at the very base of the trunk. Is it buried in soil in the pot or in the rootball of the plant? If so, gently remove some of the soil from the top of the rootball to expose the flare. Burying this root flare too deep can cause roots to suffocate. In slowly draining soils, set the rootball an inch or two higher than the surrounding soil and cover it with mulch.

6. Start backfilling. Tamp the soil lightly as you go, but don't compact it. Never *stomp* the soil back into the hole with your foot. When half of the rootball is covered, add some water to settle out any air pockets and remoisten the rootball. Finish backfilling and water again. Let the soil settle for a day or two and then check to see if you need to add a little more soil around the roots.

7. Mulch your newly planted tree. Apply 2 to 3 inches of organic mulch, such as compost, leaf litter, shredded wood, or pine straw around its base. Extend the mulch to the drip line (the outermost reaches of the branches), leaving a space of 3 inches or more around the trunk to keep the bark dry. Mulch should *never* be built up around the trunk of the tree and high-sided tree wells (also known as mulch volcanoes) are not only unnecessary, they are harmful.

8. Water your newly planted trees regularly for the first several months after planting if you are not getting regular rainfall. During the first month, you may need to water as much as twice each week. After that, once per week will probably suffice unless you hit a dry spell. Then you may have to add a day back in until you get some rain. If you plant in spring, you will likely need to soak new trees thoroughly *at least* once a week and maybe more, throughout the summer.

WATERING YOUR TREES

Once established and growing well on their own, most trees will not need any irrigation from you in a normal year. Drought-tolerant trees can withstand long periods without rain or irrigation. When watering is required, it should be done thoroughly and deeply to encourage roots to grow far into the soil searching for moisture. Drip irrigation or soaker hoses are very effective because they put water right on the ground where it is needed, and they can be allowed to drip very slowly for several hours, thoroughly saturating the soil.

If you are watering with a sprinkler attached to a garden hose, follow a slightly different routine. Water for thirty minutes one day and then turn the sprinkler back on for an additional thirty to sixty minutes the following day. The first day, you are moistening the soil so that it will readily accept more moisture on the second day. This ensures getting water deep into the root zone where it is needed.

PRUNING YOUR TREES

Many gardeners and homeowners are afraid to prune their trees, but pruning is essential to the overall health and longevity of your trees. Trees are a long-term and sometimes expensive investment

The best time to prune is when trees are dormant. You can see their silhouette better, and the chances of disease and insect problems are reduced.

in your landscape, so be sure you take the best possible care of them. The main purpose of pruning young trees is to create a strong structure of well-spaced limbs that will increase in strength as the tree matures. Remember, those small branches on a newly planted tree will someday be the support system for an enormous and very heavy structure. Pruning helps make them sturdy and strong.

When you're pruning, especially if you are removing larger limbs, determine the limb you think needs to be cut. Then step back several paces from the tree and look closely at that limb. Follow it all the way from where it attaches to the tree's trunk out to its very tip and see how and where it crosses and interacts with other limbs and branches. Once you've checked it from several angles, then you can proceed. By doing this, you avoid opening up big holes and creating bare spots in the tree that cannot be fixed.

PEST CONTROL

The most proactive choice you can make when it comes to pest control is choosing the right plant for the right place from the very beginning. Trees that are properly sited and growing in the right conditions will be healthy, vigorous and able to defend themselves against most pest and disease outbreaks. If you have a severe infestation of insects or if a disease strikes and you are concerned about the tree's ability to survive, contact an arborist or get a recommendation from an expert at a local garden center. Your County Extension Service is also an excellent source for diagnosing insect and disease problems and for making recommendations for treatment.

FERTILIZING

Newly planted trees can be fertilized after they become established, which may take months or longer, depending on their size. Once established, fertilizing can stimulate growth and help them fill into their allotted space in the landscape. Established trees won't need to be fertilized more than once each year.

JANUARY

- Winter is an excellent time to prune many ornamental and shade trees. The branches are bare and it is easy to see what you are doing. Pruning could include removing dead or dying branches, thinning the canopy, removing branches that are rubbing or crossing over one another, or improving the tree's overall shape. Avoid pruning trees like crape myrtles right now. It is better to prune them as spring arrives, just before they leaf out.

- Do not coat pruning wounds with tar, paints, or other substances. There is no scientific evidence that this practice is actually helpful, and there are some who believe that covering the wound actually traps moisture and invites trouble.

- If you have newly planted trees that were staked last season, check to make sure that the bindings are not cutting into the trunks. Trees should be tied at the lowest point on the trunk to allow them to move just slightly. A little bit of movement in the wind encourages the trunk to develop strong and thick. Most trees should not be staked for more than one year after planting. By then they should be rooted in and able to stand on their own.

FEBRUARY

- Consider planting some fruit trees in your landscape. They have beautiful and often fragrant blooms, they attract beneficial pollinators to the garden when they're in bloom, and in a few years you can begin enjoying harvests of fresh fruit. Order them early in the season so they can be shipped at the proper planting time for your location.

- Large balled-and-burlapped trees can be planted this month anytime the soil is not frozen and a hole can be dug. By planting larger trees while they are still dormant, they settle in quickly and easily, barely knowing they have been moved.

- Newly planted trees must be kept moist. It is easy to forget to water during the winter, but it can be a very important task. This is especially true for conifers, like pines and junipers, that continue to lose water through their needles and for broadleaf evergreens, like Southern magnolia and rhododendron, that continue to lose water through their leaves, even in winter.

- Begin pruning when the coldest part of winter has passed and before new growth begins. When pruning large limbs, be sure to undercut the limb first by making a cut on the underside of the limb you're removing to help prevent it from cracking and stripping the bark down the trunk of the tree, thereby creating a large wound that then must heal.

MARCH

- If you have evergreens that need to be pruned, March is the perfect time. Do not cut needled evergreens like pine, cedar, spruce, and false cypress back past the point where they have active green growth. If you cut back into bare wood, they may not regrow and you'll be left with a bare stub. Broadleaf evergreens, like Southern magnolia and pittosporum, do have the ability to sprout from bare wood, but it is better not to prune them that hard if you can avoid it.

- If you regularly have scale, mealybug, or spider mite problems in your landscape, you can spray dormant oil this month—before trees start to leaf out—to help control them. Dormant oil smothers overwintering eggs and nymphs of destructive insect pests, but must be used while the plants are still completely dormant so that tender leaves aren't burned.

- If you are doing some pruning this month and the trees you are working on include things like flowering cherry, crabapple, or other early spring bloomers, take some of the branches indoors and put them in a vase full of water. In just a few days the buds will swell and the blooms will pop open for you to enjoy indoors.

APRIL

- You can still plant trees across much of the South, but you'll need to pay close attention to watering as the heat begins to increase and summer sets in.

- Mowing the lawn is top priority this month as the grass grows very quickly. Be careful not to bump into the trunks of your trees while you're mowing. This goes for mature trees, but is even more important for young, newly planted trees. Young bark is thin, tender, and easily damaged. Once damaged, it opens the tree up to infestation by insects or disease.

- If you grow hardy palms or palmettos where you live, it's time to feed with a slow-release palm fertilizer, such as 18-6-12 or 15-5-10, applied according to the label directions. Palms benefit from fertilizers that contain additional micronutrients, especially in coastal areas where soils are sandy and nutrients leach out quickly. Fertilizers made especially for palms will contain these necessary nutrients.

- Mites begin to get active this season and controlling them will be important, but remember, *plants are no longer dormant!* Put the dormant oil away. It's time to switch to highly refined horticultural oils or what some people refer to as sun spray oils. These oils are less likely to cause burning of tender young foliage when properly used.

MAY

- If you're the type of gardener who enjoys keeping a journal, it is very important to start your record keeping for the season now. Gardens change almost daily this time of year and trying to remember what happened and when is nearly impossible. Your notes will help to jog your memory about plants that performed well and plants that didn't.

- If you would like to add palms or palmettos to your landscape, they transplant best in late spring and summer when air and soil temperatures have warmed and the palms are in full, active growth. In areas where palms are hardy, now is the time to get them in the ground.

- If you're not receiving regular rainfall, be prepared to water newly planted trees regularly until rain resumes. Remember to water thoroughly and deeply. It may seem that you're standing there with the hose for a long time, but you have to water all the way to the bottom of the rootball to ensure that each plant is getting all of the water it needs.

- Aphids are out in force this month, especially on new tender leaves and stems. A medium-strong spray of water will generally dislodge them and alleviate the problem. For severe infestations, insecticidal soaps are a safe and easy way to treat them.

JUNE

- Are you planning a vacation this year? If so, look up some botanical gardens or other public gardens wherever you're going. They are great places to find inspiration for your own garden and even if you can't do something on the same scale that many public gardens do, you can still be inspired and adapt the ideas to your own space and needs.

- Newly planted trees are especially susceptible to heat and drought stress as summer sets in. Water thoroughly and deeply to encourage deep rooting. Mulch with a 2- to 3-inch layer of compost to conserve moisture, suppress weeds, and moderate soil temperatures.

- Be on the lookout for aphids, scale insects, spider mites, and dogwood borers on your trees. For severe infestations, treating early will be important for the overall health of your trees. Japanese beetles will be hatching this month as well. They are particularly fond of crape myrtles and anything in the rose-of-Sharon or hibiscus families.

- Keep bagworms at bay by applying the bacterial insecticide Bt (*Bacillus thuringiensis*). It is safe and non-toxic and does a good job of controlling these pernicious and persistent pests.

JULY

- If you are planning a summer vacation, be sure to arrange for someone to water your newly installed trees. Trees are a big investment and losing one (or more) while on vacation would make the return home disappointing.

- Trees should not be fertilized during the heat of the summer. To encourage soft new growth now means a higher need for water and the possibility of tender new growth scorching in the hot sun. It also opens that soft new growth up to attack by pests and diseases while the plant is under stress.

- Powdery mildew and leaf spot diseases are very active this month. Fungal diseases love the heat and humidity. Proper pruning to increase airflow within the tree can help alleviate these problems. Avoid wetting the foliage with overhead watering; this will help!.

AUGUST

- Many of our Southern states have coastlines where gardeners face challenges that are much different from those of us inland. Along the coast or on barrier islands, you may have a difficult time finding plants that will thrive in the salt breezes and poor sandy soils in your area. Look to native plants for tough and resilient options that will thrive under difficult conditions.

- August is usually our hottest and one of our driest months of the year in the South. Be sure to keep your plants (and yourself, as you're outdoors working) well hydrated. Trees that were planted in spring may be showing signs of heat or drought stress.

- Spider mites are very active during hot, dry weather, especially on junipers, arborvitae, hollies, and many other ornamentals. They can be controlled with insecticidal soap applied early in the morning while it is cooler outdoors. Several applications will probably be necessary for complete control.

- Powdery mildew and leaf spot diseases are still prominent this month. Select resistant cultivars when choosing trees for your landscape and avoid sprinklers that spray high overhead and wet the foliage on trees, such as dogwood and crape myrtle, which are particularly susceptible to powdery mildew.

SEPTEMBER

- As leaves begin to fall from the trees, consider composting them. It's a much easier way to "dispose" of them than bagging them and hauling them away and you get an enormous benefit from them in just a year or two when they go back into the soil. For a fine-textured mulch, shred the leaves with a lawn mower or leaf shredder.

- Avoid doing any major pruning at this time of year. Pruning now can stimulate new growth that will not have time to harden off before cold weather arrives and can then freeze and be killed.

- Fall can be deceptively dry. If a period of several days goes by with no rain, be sure to check and see what is wilting. Inevitably, something will be.

- Prepare now to protect your trees from deer and rodents. As the weather cools down and winter heads our way, hungry animals (and male deer in rut) can do irreversible damage to the garden. Protect trees from deer with fencing and repellents. Deter rabbits by installing wire or plastic guards around the trunks of young shade trees with tender, delicious bark.

OCTOBER

- Deciduous trees can light up the autumn sky with an assortment of fiery reds, oranges, and yellows. Look around you as trees begin to color up for fall and decide where you might want to add more colorful trees to your landscape. Some suggestions for excellent fall color include sugar maple, red maple, and crape myrtle, and there are many others.

- October is the start of prime tree-planting season across the Upper and Mid-South. The soil is warm, but air temperatures are beginning to cool down. Roots will establish quickly in the warm soil, while cooler air temperatures mean less stress on the plants and slower drying out of the soil.

- In fall and early winter, don't forget to water newly planted trees to help them become established. A few weeks after planting, start reducing water to every few days or longer, especially with cloudy, rainy, cool weather.

- Remove and destroy bagworm bags on evergreens and other trees. Eggs overwinter in the bags produced by females and will hatch next spring.

NOVEMBER

- When planning to include trees in your landscape, take advantage of their winter beauty. Peeling bark, twisting branches, and architectural forms all give deciduous trees great character and make our gardens more interesting.

- Fall is the best time of year to plant or transplant many trees, both deciduous and evergreen. To ensure success, wait until they have gone completely dormant in late November before you begin. Then, if you're transplanting, dig as big a rootball as you can reasonably manage and keep the tree as intact as possible. It will settle back in without skipping a beat.

- Fall rains may be adequate for newly planted trees, but keep a close watch on your soil and if it appears to be drying out too much, be prepared to water.

- As leaves fall from deciduous trees, be sure to remove them from the lawn. It doesn't take long for a thick layer of leaves to shade and/or rot out the grass beneath them, leaving you with large bare patches in the lawn.

DECEMBER

- You still have plenty of time to plant new trees in the yard if you're still thinking about adding some shade to a certain spot or could use some beautiful spring or fall color somewhere. As long as the ground is not frozen, you can plant trees in the South!

- Try to purchase your Christmas tree several days ahead of when you want to bring it indoors and decorate it. Make a fresh cut at the base—even if they cut it at the tree lot—and stand it up in a 5-gallon bucket of water in the garage for at least twenty-four hours (forty-eight is better) before bringing it indoors. Really saturating your tree this way will help it last longer indoors!

- It's Christmas time! Be sure to check the water in your Christmas tree stand every day to be sure that it does not dry out.

- When Christmas is over, check to see if Christmas tree recycling occurs in your area. Many cities and townships have one or more drop-off points where you can take your tree or trees, and the city will haul them away for free, often grinding them up and using them to mulch pathways in city parks or on woodland hiking trails.

To protect young trees from rabbits and rodents, place a cylinder of ¼-inch mesh hardware cloth around the trunk. The cylinder should extend 18 to 24 inches above the soil and 2 to 3 inches below ground.

TROPICALS
for the South

What makes a plant tropical? If we're going by definition alone, a tropical plant is one that originates in the tropics—the area that forms a belt around the middle of our planet, bound on the north and south ends by the Tropics of Cancer and Capricorn with the equator in the middle. The tropics are unique in that they experience almost no fluctuation in the length of days or in seasonal temperatures, since seasons, for the most part, don't exist—at least not as gardeners traditionally think of them. There is no spring, summer, fall, or winter as we know them. Instead, plant growth in the tropics is dictated by rainfall and the seasons are only two—wet and dry. The rainy season is the season of active growth and the dry season is the season of reduced growth or dormancy. Many tropical plants have special adaptations for surviving these periods of drought that, in some regions, may last many months. These adaptations are part of what allows those of us outside of the tropics to grow and, if we choose, to overwinter them successfully in what may seem like less-than-ideal conditions for most tropical plants.

For the purpose of gardening, we tend to broaden the definition of the "tropical plant" considerably and may include plants that originate in subtropical regions or occasionally even warm temperate climates, but that have that "tropical look" about them, or give the garden a tropical "feel" with their dramatic form, bold texture, or brightly colored blooms or leaves. Growing tropical and subtropical plants, usually just shortened to "tropicals" by gardeners, is more about the ambiance they bring to the garden—the feeling or impression of being transported to a land more exotic than where we actually reside—than it is about definitions.

THE TROPICAL LOOK

Gardening with tropicals, for the majority of gardeners, does not mean trying to recreate the tropical rain forest or an equatorial jungle in our back yard. Tropicals offer us a break from the ordinary and give us an opportunity to expand our palette of plants into a glorious realm that includes some of the showiest, most dramatic, and in some cases, most bizarre plants in the world. The challenge lies in pairing these plants with the more common ones of our temperate gardens in an effective and dramatic way, letting plants from all parts of the world mix and mingle; combining the striking architecture of a banana plant with the softening effect of *Miscanthus* or pairing the bold, elegant leaves of elephant ears with purple coneflowers, daylilies, and garden phlox. Tropicals elevate our temperate beds and borders to another level and help transport us to a realm beyond where we actually live and garden.

Because summer across much of our country—and especially the South—brings plenty of sun, heat, and humidity, tropical plants thrive here. Once the soil is warm and summer's heat settles in, tropicals kick into high gear, growing at an impressive rate and even plants that started small in spring will attain their full size by midsummer. Tropicals grow almost continuously from spring through fall, so they will only grow larger, fuller, and become more impressive as the season advances. By autumn, if

Japanese Fiber Banana is bold and dramatic.

you've planted a lot of tropicals, your garden just might feel like the rain forest has landed in your backyard.

The challenge in growing tropicals in regions outside of the tropics is finding plants that can thrive in spite of the fluctuations in temperature, moisture, and humidity that are commonplace in temperate climates. Remember that in the tropics, most of these factors stay nearly the same year-round. It is not 95 degrees one day and 66 degrees three nights later. It doesn't rain in fits and spurts with long stretches of excessive heat and no rainfall in between. In many places, the humidity is near 100 percent and remains there consistently without dramatic rises and falls. These are issues that all come into play when it comes to growing tropicals successfully. Some simply won't thrive outside of their native habitat. Fortunately, those plants are left mostly for the true collectors and botanists; the tropicals that are readily available to gardeners are plants that will thrive here.

THE VALUE OF TROPICAL PLANTS IN THE GARDEN

Their beauty is the most obvious reason to value tropical plants in the garden. It's what we see. Their bold leaves, dramatic displays of flowers, architectural form, or brilliant colors add dimensions to our gardens that many of our beloved temperate plants simply can't rival. But for Southern gardeners, it is just as much about *when* they provide that beauty as it is the beauty itself. Tropicals play an important role in filling the "summer bloom gap" in the South, the period from late summer when the main season perennials—coneflowers, black-eyed Susans, phlox, daylilies, and others—have passed their prime, but autumn's rich display of ornamental grasses, late-blooming perennials, and shrubs filled with berries has yet to begin. In some parts of the South, this gap can be weeks or even a couple of months long. Tropicals are the perfect plants to fill that gap, thriving in the heat and humidity of July, August, and early September, growing enthusiastically and wowing us with their tremendous show.

DESIGNING WITH TROPICALS

While tropical plants are often associated with bright and daring colors—and many of them *are* unabashedly brilliant and bold—it is the dramatic architectural form and texture of so many of them that should be given first consideration. The tropical look is achieved far better through extraordinary combinations of leaf texture and shape than through flowering, which, with many tropicals, is seasonal. "Foliage first" is a good mantra when designing with *any* plant and not just tropicals. If you have great foliage combinations, your garden will always look good even when it's not at its peak bloom, but with tropicals, vibrant displays of leaf form and texture should be given top billing. Flowers, when they occur, are an added bonus.

The leaves of tropical plants come in a tantalizing array of textures, fascinating shapes, and outlandish colors. Use this to your advantage. Many tropical leaves are big. Have you noticed that? Have you wondered why? Many of our favorite garden tropicals are actually understory or edge-of-the-forest plants where they grow in the wild and the canopy of the jungle or rain forest is overhead. Having big, broad leaves means they can soak up more sunlight, and gardeners can use that to great advantage to create remarkable combinations of plants.

Plan for high-contrast combinations when using tropical plants in the garden, but consider the contrast of broad leaves against finer textured ones paired together, making the bold appear bolder and the fine, finer. Use elephant ears with grasses and bananas with dahlias. Once you have a few good combinations under your belt, more will spring to mind almost like magic and you'll be creating stunning combinations and giving your own garden that tropical touch.

ANGEL'S TRUMPET

Brugmansia spp. and cultivars

Why It's Special—Angel's trumpet can take on almost treelike proportions and bear hundreds of foot-long, fragrant blooms in shades of white, soft pink, and yellow. It may flower periodically throughout the summer, but the greatest show comes in late summer and autumn.

How to Plant & Grow—Plant angel's trumpet in rich, moist, well-drained soil in full sun to part shade. The most blooms will be produced with at least some sun, but effective displays can still be had in a fair amount of shade. In Zone 7 (with protection) and warmer, angel's trumpet can be perennial, dying to the ground and returning from the roots each year.

Care & Problems—Like many tropicals, angel's trumpet is a hungry and thirsty plant. Water is critical to its success. Whiteflies can be a problem and if plants are drought stressed, spider mites may attack.

Bloom or Foliage Color—Enormous blooms of white, soft pink, yellow

Peak Season—Late summer to autumn

Mature Size (H x W)—5 to 10 ft. × 5 to 10 ft.

Water Needs—Frequent watering required

Good In Containers?—Yes. Excellent, as long as water is provided.

BANANA

Musa spp. and cultivars

Why It's Special—Bananas give the garden the ultimate tropical appearance with their tall, fleshy trunks, enormous leaves, and exotic blooms. If your summers are long enough and the trunks don't die clear to the ground in winter, they will frequently produce clusters of fruit.

How to Plant & Grow—Bananas are tolerant of a wide range of soils, but grow best where the soil has been amended with compost or leaf mold. They are some of the hungriest and thirstiest of all tropical plants, although old, established clumps can be quite drought tolerant. Plant in spring or summer to get them established during the hot and humid weather they thrive in.

Care & Problems—Bananas are reasonably care-free. Occasional removal of tattered and torn leaves will keep them looking fresh. Japanese beetles, where they exist, love the broad leaves of bananas, so spraying may be necessary to keep them from skeletonizing the leaves.

Bloom or Foliage Color—Grown primarily for enormous green leaves

Peak Season—Summer and fall

Mature Size (H x W)—3 ft. to 20 ft. × 3 ft. to 10 ft.

Water Needs—Even moisture is best

Good In Containers?—Yes, but only smaller varieties thrive in containers.

CASTOR BEAN
Ricinus communis

Why It's Special—Grown for its giant, tropical-looking leaves, castor bean is an old-fashioned plant that has stood the test of time in Southern gardens. Some say that castor beans are useful for controlling moles. **Note:** Castor bean seeds are *extremely poisonous*. Use caution when planting them where children or pets may be intrigued by them.

How to Plant & Grow—Castor beans grow quickly when the weather gets hot and humid. Seed can be sowed directly in the ground or they may be started in pots, indoors. They do have a large taproot and sometimes suffer from being potbound. Feed and water copiously to produce the most impressive plants.

Care & Problems—Castor beans are essentially pest free. Very large plants may need to be staked to prevent them from falling over. Castor beans respond well to heavy feeding. As noted, the seeds are extremely poisonous—use care!

Bloom or Foliage Color—Leaves in shades of green to red

Peak Season—Summer to frost

Mature Size (H x W)—6 to 15 ft. × 6 to 15 ft.

Water Needs—Moderate to moist

Good In Containers?—No. Too large for containers.

CENTURY PLANT
Agave spp. and cultivars

Why It's Special—Typically thought of as desert plants from the American Southwest and California, many varieties of century plant will thrive in Southern gardens. Their dramatic architectural form and beautiful colors add interest in the garden or in containers throughout the year.

How to Plant & Grow—There is one key to success with century plants: *drainage*. Most species will not tolerate wet feet, especially in winter. Plant in low berms in soil heavily amended with very coarse sand or small gravel. Plant so that the crown of the plant is above the soil level and mulch up to the base of the plant with gravel to ensure perfect drainage.

Care & Problems—Some varieties are not cold hardy. Do your research and find plants rated hardy for your zone before adding them to your garden. The importance of winter drainage cannot be overemphasized.

Bloom or Foliage Color—Spikey leaves in green, blue, steely gray

Peak Season—Year-round

Mature Size (H x W)—1 to 6 ft. × 1 to 6 ft., depending on the species

Water Needs—Moderate during summer, very well drained in winter

Good In Containers?—Yes. Striking in containers.

CHINESE RICE PAPER PLANT
Tetrapanax papyrifera

Why It's Special—Chinese rice paper plant is a bold-leaved, tropical-looking plant that has become popular in gardens across the South. Leaves may reach an impressive 3 feet across on some varieties, and plants can grow 10 to 15 feet tall in a single season. It is perennial from Zone 7 and warmer.

How to Plant & Grow—Plant in late spring or early summer to take advantage of summer heat and humidity that Chinese rice paper plant thrives in. Highly adaptable to a wide range of soils, it will grow almost anywhere. Avoid root disturbance to help prevent the plant from spreading.

Care & Problems—Chinese rice paper plant has one potentially serious problem, which is the rate at which it can spread. In warmer climates, where cold winters do not keep it in check, it can be invasive. It will require regular maintenance to keep it in-bounds.

Bloom or Foliage Color—Enormous green leaves up to 3 feet across

Peak Season—Summer to frost

Mature Size (H x W)—6 to 15 ft. × 6 to 15 ft.

Water Needs—Moderate to moist

Good In Containers?—No. Too large for containers.

COPPERLEAF
Acalypha cultivars

Why It's Special—Copperleaf is grown for its dramatically colored leaves in shades of copper, red, orange, pink, yellow, and green, often with a blend of several colors on the plant at once. A multitude of leaf forms also exist, from broad, wavy forms to skinny, almost pencillike leaves. Copperleaf makes a stunning display *en masse* in the garden, but holds its own as a focal point in a pot, too.

How to Plant & Grow—Plant in rich, well-amended garden soil in late spring after all danger of frost has passed and the soil is warm to the touch. Most varieties branch well on their own, but occasional pinching will keep plants bushy and compact.

Care & Problems—Copperleaf is one of the toughest tropicals in the garden and few pests or diseases bother it. Whiteflies can be an occasional problem if plants are stressed; treat with insecticidal soap.

Bloom or Foliage Color—Brilliantly colored foliage

Peak Season—Late spring to frost

Mature Size (H x W)—2 to 4 ft. × 2 to 3 ft.

Water Needs—Moderate

Good In Containers?—Yes. An excellent focal point in containers.

ELEPHANT EAR
Colocasia spp. and cultivars

Why It's Special—The old-fashioned green elephant ear has been grown throughout the South for more than a century. Newer and improved varieties include those with leaves in shades of near-black, bronze, and chartreuse, as well as forms that are variegated or have highly contrasting, colored leaf veins.

How to Plant & Grow—Plant elephant ears in late spring or early summer. They thrive in heat and humidity and once rooted will grow with astonishing speed. Elephant ears thrive on regular feeding and watering, producing an abundance of dramatic leaves in bold shapes and colors. In Zone 7 and warmer, many will be reliable perennials.

Care & Problems—Japanese beetles can be an occasional problem and will quickly skeletonize the leaves. They can be controlled by picking them off and dropping them in a jar of soapy water; severe infestations may require spraying.

Bloom or Foliage Color—Large leaves in black, bronze, chartreuse, variegated

Peak Season—Early summer to frost

Mature Size (H x W)—3 to 8 ft. × 3 to 8 ft.

Water Needs—Moist to wet

Good In Containers?—Yes. Use the most compact varieties.

EUCALYPTUS
Eucalyptus spp.

Why It's Special—Eucalyptus is typically seen as a fragrant "herb" whose silvery blue color and interesting leaf form add interest to the summer garden. In many parts of the South, though, it is semi-hardy and may live for several years, eventually taking on the form of a large, multistemmed shrub or small tree.

How to Plant & Grow—Eucalyptus can either be grown as a summer annual to be removed at the end of the season or, in warmer areas, it may live for several years to become a semi-permanent addition to the garden. Eucalyptus needs full sun and very well-drained soil to thrive.

Care & Problems—Virtually pest free, but root rot can be a problem in areas where winters are cold and wet. While it may be hardy for several years throughout much of the South, sudden temperature plunges in winter can split the tender bark. It's best not to count on it being a permanent garden resident.

Bloom or Foliage Color—Blue-green leaves

Peak Season—Spring to frost

Mature Size (H x W)—Variable, from shrublike to tree form

Water Needs—Drought tolerant

Good In Containers?—Yes. Excellent filler for containers.

GOLDEN DEWDROPS
Duranta erecta

Why It's Special—An unusual tropical shrub that produces sprays of sapphire blue, light blue, or white flowers from late spring to late summer, which eventually turn into clusters of greenish gold berries in autumn. New forms flower more than older varieties, and some have variegated or chartreuse leaves to add to their colorful display. Some growers train them into small standards, which is very effective.

How to Plant & Grow—Plant golden dewdrops in rich, well-amended soil in full sun to part shade. Feed regularly during the summer with a bloom booster-type fertilizer. Feeding too much nitrogen will cause abundant growth with few flowers.

Care & Problems—Golden dewdrops are relatively pest free. Rabbits can be a problem on young plants and aphids may occasionally attack tender new growth. Some old-fashioned varieties flower in cycles instead of providing season-long color. Trim wild shoots as necessary.

Bloom or Foliage Color—Blue to white

Peak Season—Early to late summer

Mature Size (H x W)—2 to 3 ft. × 2 to 3 ft.

Water Needs—Moderate to moist

Good In Containers?—Yes. Excellent container plants.

GOLDEN SERPENT FERN
Phlebodium aureum

Why It's Special—A grand and bold tropical fern with large, blue-green fronds that are held well above the soil on long, wiry stems. It grows from a creeping rhizome and will form a substantial plant in a relatively short time. One of the best ferns for a bold, tropical effect in shadier corners of the garden.

How to Plant & Grow—Plant golden serpent fern in late spring or early summer in rich, well-amended soil that stays evenly moist or in containers, where it will fill a large pot in a single season. As with most ferns, it prefers part shade to shade. It can also be effective in hanging baskets.

Care & Problems—Slugs and snails can be a problem, chewing holes in the leaves and sometimes chewing into the plant's creeping rhizomes. Golden serpent fern is not difficult to overwinter and can be moved indoors to a well-lit room for the winter if you desire to keep it.

Bloom or Foliage Color—Bold, blue-green leaves

Peak Season—Summer to frost

Mature Size (H x W)—2 ft. × 3 ft.

Water Needs—Evenly moist

Good In Containers?—Yes. Outstanding in containers.

MEXICAN SHRUB SPURGE
Euphorbia cotinifolia

Why It's Special—Mexican shrub spurge is a unique and unusual tropical plant that bears an eerie resemblance to the very popular smoke tree (*Cotinus*) that has long been popular in Southern gardens. Its round leaves, in a deep shade of burgundy, look very similar to smoke tree but it does not bear the plumes of "smoke."

How to Plant & Grow—Usually available as small plants in 4- or 6-inch pots in spring, shrub spurge will grow quickly once it's planted in warm, amended soil. Being a spurge, it is somewhat drought tolerant once established, but does respond well to summertime feeding and watering. Softwood cuttings taken in late summer can be rooted and overwintered.

Care & Problems—Mexican shrub spurge has few problems. Its milky sap keeps most animals and insects from chewing on it. That same sap may cause mild skin irritation in people with sensitive skin, but is not troublesome to most people.

Bloom or Foliage Color—Burgundy foliage

Peak Season—Early summer to frost

Mature Size (H x W)—3 ft. × 3 ft.

Water Needs—Moderate

Good In Containers?—Yes. Excellent in containers.

MIOGA GINGER
Zingiber mioga

Why It's Special—A stylish member of the tropical ginger clan, Mioga ginger is most often found in several very striking variegated forms. 'Nakafu' or 'Dancing Crane' is exceptional. Hardier than one might expect, it is reliably perennial well into Zone 7 and even the warmer parts of Zone 6, with protection.

How to Plant & Grow—While it grows from an underground, creeping rhizome, it is usually found already growing in 4-inch or quart pots, ready to go into the garden. It needs rich, moist garden soil to reach its full potential. Fertilize in spring just as new growth emerges and again in early to midsummer.

Care & Problems—Snails and slugs can be a problem on tender new shoots as they emerge from the soil in spring. A non-toxic, iron-based snail and slug bait will make quick work of them. Voles can be a problem, burrowing around the base of the plant to eat the rhizomes.

Bloom or Foliage Color—Elegant variegated leaves

Peak Season—Early summer to frost

Mature Size (H x W)—3 ft. × 3 ft.

Water Needs—Moderate to moist

Good In Containers?— Yes, but best in the garden.

PALMS
Various genera and species

Why It's Special—Palms and palmettos are typical of the coastal regions of the South, but many are perfectly hardy much farther north than some gardeners might guess. In fact, there are entire societies of people dedicated to growing hardy palms. Several palms are hardy to Zone 7 and a few into Zone 6, with protection.

How to Plant & Grow—Palms must be planted in spring or early summer to take advantage of the warm weather and the long growing season to get them established. Winter drainage is critical to their success; they will languish and die in cold, wet, clay soils. Trunks may need wrapping for extra winter protection in colder zones.

Care & Problems—Scale can be a serious problem in some climates and spider mites may attack during periods of hot, dry weather. Both are difficult to control once they've gained a strong foothold, so keep a watchful eye.

Bloom or Foliage Color—Bold green to bluish leaves

Peak Season—Year-round, where hardy

Mature Size (H x W)—5 to 25 ft. × 5 to 10 ft.

Water Needs—Moderate, but well drained

Good In Containers?—Yes, when plants are young.

PAPYRUS
Cyperus papyrus

Why It's Special—Growing papyrus goes all the way back to biblical times, when it was used to make parchment. Today, we grow it for its elegant and luxuriant beauty with its round heads of "fluffy" leaves held high aloft on slender green stems. Excellent for mixing into beds and borders for dramatic effect.

How to Plant & Grow—Plant papyrus in full to part sun in beds that have been well amended with organic matter like compost or decaying leaves. It needs plenty of moisture at its roots to grow big and put on the best show. Feed it regularly throughout the summer months to encourage fast and luxurious growth.

Care & Problems—The biggest enemy of papyrus is wind. The stems, while thick, are spongy on the inside and where large gusts of wind are common they are commonly bent over or broken off, which ruins the look of the plant.

Bloom or Foliage Color—Green stems and leaves

Peak Season—Early summer to frost

Mature Size (H x W)—6 ft. × 3 ft.

Water Needs—Moderate to very wet

Good In Containers?—Yes. Very dramatic in large containers.

213

PRINCESS FLOWER
Tibouchina urvilleana

Why It's Special—Most flowering tropicals need full sun to produce the most blooms and really put on a show, but princess flower thrives and blooms in part sun to part shade. It will grow readily in the ground, but really excels as a container specimen where its vibrant purple flowers can be enjoyed up close.

How to Plant & Grow—Plant princess flowers in spring after the danger of frost has passed and soil feels warm to the touch. Pinch the branch tips once or twice to encourage plants to branch and fill out. Feed with a bloom booster-type fertilizer to encourage the development of flower buds. Heaviest flowering occurs in late summer and autumn.

Care & Problems—Keep well watered throughout the growing season. Mealybugs can be an occasional problem, but they usually attack plants that are already stressed for other reasons. Happy, well-grown plants rarely have any problems.

Bloom or Foliage Color—Velvety green leaves, rich purple flowers

Peak Season—Late summer to autumn

Mature Size (H x W)—3 ft. × 2 ft.

Water Needs—Moderate to moist

Good In Containers?—Yes. Excellent container plant.

RED ABYSSINIAN BANANA
Ensete ventricosum 'Maurelii'

Why It's Special—One of the most dramatic of tropical plants, the leaves of red Abyssinian banana are emerald green, dramatically and intensely suffused with ruby red. On exceptionally well-grown specimens, individual leaves may be 8 feet long and 3 feet wide!

How to Plant & Grow—Plant in late spring to early summer. It thrives in the heat and humidity of our Southern summers and will not begin to grow well until the temperatures are into the 80s during the day and above 60 at night. The more you water and feed, the bigger and more impressive this plant will grow.

Care & Problems—Wind is the biggest enemy of this and other bananas and their relatives. A good windstorm can completely shred the plant, destroying its dramatic look. It is less cold hardy than many of its cousins and north of Zone 8b should probably be considered an annual.

Bloom or Foliage Color—Dramatic ruby red leaves

Peak Season—Summer to frost

Mature Size (H x W)—8 ft. × 8 ft. or larger

Water Needs—Moderate to moist

Good In Containers?—Yes, but only young specimens.

STICKS-ON-FIRE
Euphorbia tirucalli

Why It's Special—Sticks-on-fire is a unique and brightly colored relative of your grandmother's old-fashioned "pencil cactus." Thornless, leafless stems grow in a dense mass and, on this species, are brightly colored in shades of green, golden yellow, and red, looking almost as though the plant is on fire. It makes an outstanding focal point in a container.

How to Plant & Grow—Sticks-on-fire is a succulent and therefore needs very well-drained soil and is extremely tolerant of dry to even drought-like conditions. The plant will develop its most intense color in full sun.

Care & Problems—In soils that are too moist or if plants are overfed, stems may become weak and lax, and the plant may grow so fast that it collapses under its own weight. Even for well-grown plants in drier and leaner soil, staking may be needed if you like your plants staunchly upright.

Bloom or Foliage Color—Brilliantly colored stems of red, yellow, green

Peak Season—Summer to frost

Mature Size (H x W)—4 ft. × 3 ft.

Water Needs—Very drought tolerant

Good In Containers?—Yes. Very dramatic in containers.

TAPIOCA
Manihot esculenta 'Variegata'

Why It's Special—The large, palmate (hand-shaped) leaves of tapioca make a dramatic statement in the garden. To add to the drama, the form 'Variegata' has leaves that are even more dramatically marked in creamy yellow, making it a showstopper in the garden. Exquisite when paired with other brightly colored plants like anise-scented sage, whose cobalt blue blooms are perfection against tapioca's variegated leaves.

How to Plant & Grow—This plant thrives in the heat. In fact, the hotter and more humid it gets, the faster tapioca grows. Plant in rich, but very well-drained soil, feeding and watering regularly throughout the summer. Avoid pinching or breaking the growing tips. The plants will branch on their own as they grow.

Care & Problems—If you plant it too early in the season, before the soil warms sufficiently, it will languish and may even rot. Mealybugs can be a problem if you try to overwinter plants indoors for the next year.

Bloom or Foliage Color—Dramatic variegated leaves

Peak Season—Early summer to frost

Mature Size (H x W)—4 ft. × 3 ft.

Water Needs—Moderate

Good In Containers?—Yes. Good in larger containers.

THALIA
Thalia dealbata

Why It's Special—Thalia is usually grown as a water plant, taking up residence in large pots in water gardens and lily ponds. Its broad, cannalike leaves are held on long stems in an almost flat plane, giving the plant a unique appearance. Blue-purple flowers dangle in small clusters from tall, wandlike stems in summer.

How to Plant & Grow—Often found growing at the water's edge or even slightly submerged, thalia will adapt well to life in mixed beds or borders as long as the soil does not dry out severely. It prefers deep, rich soil so its roots can grow deeply in search of moisture and nutrients.

Care & Problems—Thalia is primarily pest free. Grasshoppers may occasionally chew on the leaves, but it is rarely a serious problem. The more you feed and the more you water, the better this plant will respond and the more dramatic it will be.

Bloom or Foliage Color—Blue-purple blooms in summer

Peak Season—Summer to frost

Mature Size (H x W)—6 ft. × 3 ft.

Water Needs—Average to wet

Good In Containers?—No. Too large for most containers.

UPRIGHT ELEPHANT EAR
Alocasia spp. and cultivars

Why It's Special—This is an enormous family of plants that range from diminutive species only a few inches tall to true giants that may be 12 feet tall and wide. Some of the most popular forms are the easy-to-grow species like *Alocasia macrorhizos*, whose leaves may approach 6 feet long and 4 feet wide on very well-grown plants.

How to Plant & Grow—Plant in rich, very well-amended garden soil. For the most part, these are forest- (or occasionally grassland-) dwelling species and are accustomed to drier conditions than their water-loving counterpart, *Colocasia*. Upright elephant ear responds well to summertime feedings.

Care & Problems—The largest species have few problems. They simply outgrow and outsize anything that might chew on or otherwise harm them. Smaller-growing species can be attacked by slugs and snails on occasion, which can be safely and effectively controlled with an iron-based slug and snail bait.

Bloom or Foliage Color—Dramatic heart-shaped leaves

Peak Season—Summer to frost

Mature Size (H x W)—Highly variable, depending on species

Water Needs—Moderate to slightly dry

Good In Containers?—Yes, some species. Depends on size.

VARIEGATED SHELL GINGER
Alpinia zerumbet 'Variegata'

Why It's Special—Vividly variegated leaves are striped in shades of yellow and green. Where plants are happy, they'll quickly grow into large clumps, and the effect in shadier parts of the garden can be extraordinary when plants are paired with more common denizens of the shade garden like hostas, ferns, and hellebores.

How to Plant & Grow—Variegated shell ginger can often be found in the foliage plant section of the garden center, rather than with the outdoor garden plants, even though it makes a very effective outdoor plant. Plant in deep, rich, moist soil in part sun to part shade. Large plants can often be picked up very inexpensively, giving some instant gratification in the summer garden.

Care & Problems—Frost tender in colder regions, shell ginger can be perennial in Zone 8 and will be almost evergreen farther south. It makes an excellent potted specimen and is not difficult to overwinter indoors.

Bloom or Foliage Color—Dramatically variegated leaves

Peak Season—Late spring to frost

Mature Size (H x W)—3 ft. × 3 ft.

Water Needs—Average to moist

Good In Containers?—Yes. Good in larger containers.

YOUR TROPICAL GARDEN

OVERWINTERING TROPICAL PLANTS IN COLD CLIMATES

In their native habitats, most tropical plants are perennials, growing year-round in the sunny, warm, and mild climate found in the equatorial belt. When brought out of that environment and into less hospitable surroundings, especially those where cold winters prevail, they quickly transform from perennials to annuals based on the weather alone. Most will not survive prolonged freezing temperatures.

The other factor that affects tropical plants in temperate climates is day length. Most of the regions of the world where tropical plants are native experience days that are of equal length throughout the year. When you move those plants out of the equatorial belt and into regions that experience dramatic changes in the number of daylight hours from one season to the next, the plants are affected. They thrive during the long and bright days of summer, but as the days grow shorter and cooler in autumn, tropicals often begin going dormant, and gardeners can use this to their advantage to overwinter tropicals from one season to the next.

The goal in overwintering tropical plants is to allow them to experience a natural period of dormancy without letting them freeze. Some plants that are truly tropical, growing year-round without any rest period, may need to be overwintered indoors as houseplants or in a greenhouse where they can be kept actively growing through the winter. Others have certain adaptations that allow them to survive occasional dry periods—fleshy or woody water-storing trunks, underground rhizomes or corms, or the ability to drop all or most of their leaves to reduce water loss and quickly regrow them when rains come again. These are all advantages when it comes to overwintering tropicals in temperate climates because it allows them to be stored without benefit of a greenhouse or having to fill the guest room so full of plants that winter visitors are not allowed!

METHODS OF OVERWINTERING TROPICALS

Tropicals can be overwintered in a variety of ways and many of them actually benefit from a period of dormancy during the cold months of winter, so use that to your advantage. Some, like banana trees, can be dug after the first hard frost, their trunks cut back to 3 feet or so high, and then the entire plant wrapped in burlap or landscape fabric and stored in a crawl space or basement where it is cool, or even cold, but doesn't freeze. They will remain there, in suspended animation, through the winter and can be replanted the following spring. Some palms can be overwintered in the same way in climates where they have no chance of surviving the winter.

Most plants in the ginger family—variegated shell ginger, mioga ginger, and others—grow from thick underground rhizomes. These can be dug after frost cuts the plants to the ground and stored in dry peat moss or vermiculite in an unheated garage or garden shed, where it is cool, but doesn't freeze, until time to plant them back out the next spring. Some gingers are quite hardy, so this is only necessary in Zone 7 and colder and will vary among species. Other tropicals also grow from tubers, corms, or rhizomes and can be overwintered in the same way.

In my garden, I have the advantage of having a garden shed that, while not heated, rarely freezes. If the weather turns extremely cold, I can set up a small space heater to keep the chill off until the weather moderates. I dig many of my tropicals in autumn, pot them, pack the pots tightly into the garden shed, and overwinter many of them very successfully this way. It is especially effective with elephant ears, agaves, angel's trumpets, and succulents that need to be kept drier in winter. There are two windows that offer some light, but no direct sun, and this is enough to keep plants alive through the winter until they are able to be planted back in the garden the following spring. The chill in the air in the garden shed also keeps insect pests at bay during the winter.

TROPICALS AS WINTER HOUSEPLANTS

Some tropical plants do make satisfactory houseplants during the winter months. Banana trees and elephant ears may be a little difficult to accommodate indoors, but tropical ferns, smaller palms, and agaves, along with many others, can help bring beauty to the indoors when the weather outside turns cold. You will have the most success moving plants indoors that are already growing in pots. Perhaps they were outdoors on a screened porch or covered patio, or resided on a small terrace in the shade garden for the summer.

The best candidates for moving indoors for the winter are plants that were growing in shady locations outdoors. Plants that were growing in full sun will have a hard time adapting to indoor light conditions, even if your house seems bright. Usually, they drop an enormous number of leaves and make a terrible mess. These may be better candidates for the garden shed, where their appearance during the winter is less important. Likewise, plants that were growing in the ground in the garden generally don't make good candidates for houseplants. They simply don't adapt well, so using the dormant storage method in a crawl space, garden shed, or garage may be a better option.

Fungal diseases can be controlled by using appropriate fungicide sprays.

If you decide to move some of your smaller tropicals indoors for the winter, there are a few important steps to take before you do. Before frost arrives, do a little trimming or pruning on plants that have leaves that they will shed (not as necessary for plants like agaves and other succulents). They are going to shed many of their leaves anyway, so you may as well help them along so they're not shedding all over your floor, and cutting them back to make them smaller means they take up less room indoors.

The second thing you'll want to do is spray your plants for insects several times over a period of several weeks before you bring them inside. You can use insecticidal soaps, horticultural oils, and other less or non-toxic products, but if you don't spray at all, you will inevitably carry a variety of problematic insect pests indoors. Trying to control them indoors during the winter months is almost always an effort in futility; far better to get any insect pests under control *before* moving plants inside.

At the end of winter, when it's time for tropicals to go back to the garden, you'll need to reintroduce them slowly—just like hardening off seedlings you've started indoors in late winter and early spring. Suddenly moving them back out into bright, outdoor light will likely give your plants a sunburn, since they have gotten used to lower light conditions indoors over winter. Start them out in shady locations and gradually expose them to brighter conditions. Even if they are succulents that typically grow in full sun, they'll need to be reacclimated.

Plants that have been overwintered in a garden shed, garage, or crawl space will probably lose all of their leaves over the winter. They may even die down to their crowns. As long as stems or crowns are green and show some signs of life, they will come back and grow fast once temperatures are warm. Tropicals that are completely dormant (or close) *can* go directly back into the garden in spring. When they sprout or leaf out, they will automatically be acclimated to whatever conditions they're growing in.

JANUARY

- Check tropicals that are overwintering in garages or garden sheds for insect infestations. Insects are surprisingly tough and may be multiplying and causing problems without you knowing it. Mealybugs and scale are not uncommon pests to find thriving, even in winter.

- Insects can also be problematic on tropicals that are living as houseplants indoors. Warm temperatures and dry air can cause population explosions in spider mites that are especially hard to control once they get a foothold.

- Mealybugs and scale can also be problems on tropicals overwintering indoors as houseplants. If leaves feel sticky or if you find sticky "sap" on floors or furniture, your plants may have scale. Both can be controlled with rubbing alcohol. For severe infestations, take plants outdoors on a warm winter day and spray with a systemic insecticide.

- If plants seem to be badly stretched or pale in color, they may need more light. When you move them indoors, even if the interior of your house seems bright, light levels can be cut in half or more and plants may have a difficult time adapting. If possible, move them to a location with brighter light.

FEBRUARY

- Bromeliads make excellent tropical houseplants. They are frequently found at greenhouses and garden centers in winter and will add a bright splash of color to the indoors with their jewel-tone blooms. In summer, they can be moved outdoors or incorporated into mixed containers.

- Water tropicals should be overwintered indoors as needed. When the weather is cloudy outside and temperatures are cool, plants in sunrooms or enclosed porches may dry out more slowly and need less water than they will when the sun is shining through the glass and warming the room. Tropicals that are in the house may dry out more quickly if they are placed near heat registers, so water accordingly.

- Keep a watchful eye out for spider mites on indoor plants. They are hard to detect at first, and by the time an infestation is visible to the naked eye, the plants may be past the point of rescue. Spider mites can be detected by visible speckling or stippling of the leaves or by holding a sheet of white paper under the leaves and tapping the plant. Watch for tiny red specks running around on the paper. If found, treat with a miticide.

MARCH

- In the warmest regions of the South, temperatures may be warming up enough by the end of the month to put the tropicals back in the garden and move those that have overwintered indoors as houseplants back to their places on outdoor terraces and patios.

- Insect pests can be a problem every month that plants are indoors, and some are difficult to control without spraying. They get down into the tiniest nooks and crannies between stems and leaves and "hide" from any kind of natural insecticides you might be using to try to control them. When spraying for insect pests, be sure to saturate both upper and lower leaf surfaces and any joints where leaves and stems meet.

- Spider mites hate humidity. If you notice a spider mite problem on some of your plants, put them in the shower and run warm water over them for several minutes once or twice a week to help reduce the population. Severe infestations may require treatment with a miticide.

- If it's warm enough to move potted tropicals back outdoors where you live, take the time to repot them into fresh soil. Plants are probably rootbound, and old soil can harbor insects and fungus spores. Dumping the old potting soil will reduce transfering pests from old soil to new. Repotting will stimulate the plants to grow and will also remove insect eggs and fungus that could be problems later.

APRIL

- In all but the uppermost regions of the South, it is warm enough to begin moving tropical plants that were overwintered inside back outdoors and to get others out of their winter storage and back into the garden. Those that have overwintered in the garden shed, crawl space, or garage can go directly back into the garden where they will acclimate as they leaf out.

- Toward the end of the month, the soil and air temperatures in most areas will be warm enough to plant tropical bulbs, corms, rhizomes, and so forth, back in the ground. They'll grow quickly once the soil is warm, but may languish or even rot if they are planted when it is too cold, especially if it is cold *and* wet. For most tropicals, soil should *feel* warm to the touch (65 to 68 degrees or warmer) before planting. It is often better to wait an extra week or two than to plant them too soon.

- Keep a close eye out for insect pests on all of the tropicals you have moved back outdoors. Their new growth is soft now and perfect for attack by aphids and other sucking insects.

MAY

- All across the South, even in the colder parts of our region, tropicals can go in the garden by mid-May. The soil will have warmed enough to support their growth and those that have been indoors since late last fall will practically be begging to get back in the garden!

- As you're planting or replanting tropicals in your garden, change them around each year. Part of the beauty of using tropicals and annuals is that they give you the opportunity to change the look of the garden seasonally and to create new and exciting plant combinations each year.

- Mix a generous handful of a slow-release, organic fertilizer right into the planting hole as you are getting your tropicals in the ground. Tropicals are hungry plants and the sooner you start feeding them, the more and faster they will begin to grow. Continue feeding them regularly throughout the summer.

- In warmer parts of the South, where tropicals may have been in the ground for a month or more now, keep them well fed and well watered as the temperature and humidity begins to rise. You want them to be well-established by the time real summer weather arrives.

JUNE

- Japanese beetles will hatch by the thousands in some areas this month. The most effective control against them is carbaryl. For those of you who don't like to spray, they can be picked off by hand and dropped into a jar of soapy water. Japanese beetles *love* bananas, elephant ears, and any other plants with broad, flat leaves.

- If you choose to use Japanese beetle traps, understand how they work. The scent of the traps draws Japanese beetles *to* them from long distances. If you place the traps in your garden, you'll draw every Japanese beetle in a two-block radius right to it. Place traps at points in the yard that are *farthest* from your garden to draw them away.

- Angel's trumpets may just be emerging from the ground this month in some climates. Don't worry if the first of June arrives and you don't see them yet. They can be very slow to emerge if spring was cool and damp. Once they start to grow, you'll be amazed at just how quickly they reach full size.

JULY

- This is the month that tropicals really begin to shine in the garden. Early summer perennials are beginning to wind down, and it will be September or even October before autumn perennials are at their peak. Tropicals fill that all-important summer bloom gap with their bold leaves, elegant forms, and bright colors.

- Be on the lookout for spider mites this month. They love the heat and will be especially prevalent if we have a dry period, which is not unusual across much of the South. Spider mite populations can explode almost overnight and once out of control are difficult to rein back in.

- If you grow bananas in your garden, you may want to limb them up (or "leafing" them up, as the case may be). By occasionally trimming the lowest leaves off at the trunk, you will expose the trunks, making the plants appear taller and opening up room for plants under them to fill in nicely.

AUGUST

- Keep tropicals well fed and watered through the month of August. They thrive in the heat and humidity this time of year and will be at their most robust when other plants are hoping for a break in the weather.

- Continue your diligent patrols of the garden for any insect pests or diseases that may be popping up and treat them before they become a problem.

- August is a good month to take a little bit of time out of the garden and catch up on your garden journal indoors in the air conditioning. Making notes now will keep you from having to remember it all later, and you can make accurate assessments of which tropicals you want to keep and which might find themselves staying in the garden when cold weather arrives this year.

- Never be afraid to edit. The best gardeners don't just keep planting more plants. They also edit the ones who aren't performing up to snuff. Don't coddle and baby struggling plants just because they still have a few green leaves. If a plant is a consistently poor performer or always looks unhappy, it brings the whole garden down. Remove it.

SEPTEMBER

- Make a visit to a local public garden or take a short road trip with a friend and visit a few gardens along the way. Check out their displays and see how they use tropicals in their displays. It's an easy way to glean ideas for your own garden.

- Angel's trumpets will really come into their own in autumn. Keep them well watered and fed during this time and as the nighttime temperatures begin to drop, they will set huge numbers of buds. On large, well-established plants, you may find as many as fifty to 100 blooms open all at one time!

- In warmer regions of the South, summer may not loosen its grip until sometime in October. Be sure to keep your tropicals well watered, especially if rain isn't falling regularly. As the nights begin to cool, those with colorful leaves will become even more intensely colored.

OCTOBER

- In the Mid- and Upper South, frosts may be likely by the end of the month. Be prepared and ready to move potted tropicals inside, if necessary. Tropicals that will be stored in garden sheds or garages in a dormant state can be left in the ground until a good frost blackens their leaves later in autumn.

- October is one of the driest months of the year across much of the South. Keep the garden well watered to get the most life out of all of your tropicals and other garden plants.

- Begin spraying plants that will be overwintered indoors. You don't have to use toxic chemicals, but spraying regularly with insecticidal soaps or sun spray oils will help kill any insects that might otherwise hitch a ride indoors when cold weather arrives. Controlling an insect population outdoors is much easier than controlling it indoors.

Tropicals like this jade plant can be moved indoors for the winter if they are planted in containers.

- If any of your tropicals can be rooted easily from stem cuttings, October is the perfect time to do it. Softwood cuttings can be rooted, several to a pot, in 4- or 6-inch pots and can then be overwintered indoors in these community pots to be planted next year instead of having to overwinter big plants inside.

NOVEMBER

- Will you be visiting any warm climates during the upcoming winter? If so, take pictures of the plants you see and how they are used in the landscape or, if you're really lucky, how they grow in their native habitats. You just might get some great ideas for your own garden!

- Any outdoor pots that have been emptied out for the winter and will not be used for winter annuals will last longer if they are stored somewhere out of the winter weather. Moisture is their biggest enemy.

- As you empty pots for winter, use the soil in your compost pile. It will be full of good microbes that will give your compost pile a boost.

- Tropicals make great additions to the compost pile too. Their leaves are often full of water, and they'll break down quickly and give the good bacteria and other organisms in your compost pile plenty of "food."

DECEMBER

- Tropical plant season has ended across most of the South now. Clean the garden up thoroughly so that insects and diseases have a harder time overwintering. Leaf litter and other debris just give them a place to hide from the cold and they'll be back in even greater force next spring.

- If you have tropicals stored in the garden shed or garage, keep an eye on them in case there are any insect or disease outbreaks. By now, the plants are mostly dormant, but even so insects can hang on.

- For tropicals that have been brought indoors to be used as houseplants for the winter, keep an even closer eye out for insect pests. Hopefully, you sprayed them several times before you brought them inside, but even so, some insects may have hitched a ride. Once they're in where it's warm and dry, they can multiply with amazing speed.

- Be careful not to overwater tropicals that are wintering indoors. Their growth will be much slower indoors during the winter and their need for water much less. Overwatering can cause root rot diseases, which are nearly impossible to control once they start.

VINES
for the South

Too often, gardeners are hesitant when it comes to planting vines. I'm convinced that this is due in part to the fact that throughout the South our trees are draped in kudzu, an insidious invader, and somehow we're afraid that any vine we plant is going to turn into the same destructive monster. This simply is not true. Vines can fill a variety of roles in the garden and, when thoughtfully selected and planted with a purpose in mind, can add beauty and drama that is difficult to achieve with any other group of plants.

Vines lend a sense of age to the garden. They creep, climb, and crawl up walls, over trellises, and through neighboring plants. They drape themselves through the limbs of nearby trees, over railings, or on top of a stump or wall, softening hard lines and giving the garden a romantic ambiance and an air of mystery. Consider the appearance of a blank stone wall with its austere façade and harsh lines versus one that is draped and swathed along its length with a well-placed vine softening its edges and lending it a sense of purpose and belonging.

MAKING WISE VINE CHOICES

When planting vines, do your research and choose the one that will suit your needs and grow within whatever limitations the space may provide. Do you need a small, delicate vine to grow up the mailbox post, or are you trying to cover a large expanse of bare wall? In the garden, are you looking for a sturdy vine to cover an arbor or pergola, or are you looking for a dainty vine to grow over or through a nearby shrub? The vines you need to fulfill these vastly different purposes will be entirely different from one another. To cover a large expanse quickly, you may choose five-leaf akebia, but that same choice would overwhelm a mailbox or handrail—probably in just a few weeks' time! To gracefully climb a corner post on the carport, you may choose Carolina jessamine or trumpet honeysuckle, but if you're trying to screen the view of the neighbor's house, these may not grow large enough to do the trick.

Gardeners commonly make the mistake of selecting vines that will eventually grow much larger than the space available to them. While a vine's ultimate size can be controlled to a certain extent with regular trimming and pruning, this can turn into a nightmare scenario—not to mention a tremendous amount of never-ending work—if you choose a vine which, in the end, is the wrong plant for the wrong place.

Remember that while you may be planting a specific vine for a specific purpose, *some* vines may still be problematic if left to their own devices. They can outgrow their space, overgrow nearby plants, and even escape into nearby woodlands and natural areas and become pests. Vines are wonderful plants and not something that gardeners should fear, but they are not maintenance free; there is a certain amount of dedication that goes along with planting vines in order to keep them from becoming a nuisance.

PLANTING AND CARING FOR VINES

Planting perennial vines is no different than planting a potted tree or shrub in the garden. Planting can be done either in spring or fall, avoiding the hottest and driest months of summer. You will also find vines available in a range of sizes, from small plants in 1-gallon pots to large specimens in 5-gallon or even larger containers. Large vines can be a little unwieldy to get in the ground, so choose a size that is easy for you to handle. Vines are usually some of the fastest-growing plants in the garden, so starting small is rarely a disadvantage. Many vines have very large root systems, which is one of the reasons they are so vigorous. Often, they will be potbound when you buy them, so be sure to loosen the roots—or even cut through large, woody roots with a pair of pruners—before placing them in the planting hole.

Vines, because of their large and vigorous root systems, need a large and generous planting hole. Dig the hole slightly deeper and at least twice as wide as the rootball it needs to accommodate. Mix the soil you have removed from the hole with a generous quantity of soil conditioner and add some compost from your compost pile or some well-composted manure to the mix. Put enough of this mixture back into the hole to place the top of the rootball evenly with the top of the surrounding soil once you have filled in around it. Backfill the hole with this blend of garden soil, soil conditioner, and compost, and water thoroughly. Mulching around the base of the plant will help keep weeds at bay. If you plant your vines in the spring, be sure to keep them very well watered through their first summer to encourage their roots to grow deep into the soil.

Annual vines, such as morning glory, hyacinth bean, and moon vine, grow best if direct-seeded where the plants are to remain. They resent transplanting and root disturbance, so there really is little advantage to starting them early indoors or even at the garden center. Amend your seed bed thoroughly before you sow the seeds, just as you would if you were preparing a hole for a growing vine. Sow the seeds at the proper depth, according to package directions, and keep the soil evenly moist until the seedlings emerge, usually in about seven to ten days for most vines.

SUPPORTS FOR VINES

Vines can be grown on or over a number of supports. Most gardeners grow their vines on trellises or fences. They can also be grown on walls, up trees, over arches, arbors, or pergolas. Some vines can be grown as groundcovers, while smaller vines may be grown successfully in pots as accents or colorful, flowering focal points.

When deciding which vines to grow, give careful consideration to your end goals. Is the objective to cover all or part of an existing structure? If so, what is that structure made of and how much weight will it support? Is the vine strictly decorative, growing on a small garden trellis or tuteur? Is the purpose of the vine to grow up the flat face of a wall and if so, will it have supports or will it need to stick itself to the surface? Some vines are self-clinging and have the ability to attach themselves to the surface they are growing on while others use twining stems or curling tendrils to work their way skyward. Those with twining stems or clinging tendrils will need at least some support to grab onto and grow. Self-clinging vines have small aerial roots (or sometimes small tendrils with suction cups on them) that stick to whatever surface they're going to climb. These can stick to nearly any surface, including wood siding, window frames and sills, door frames, and soffits, as well as stucco, brick, stone, concrete, and more. These will either leave "tracks" behind when they are removed or—in some cases—may pull the paint right off!

Not only should you consider the physical growth habits of vines, but also think about how they present their blooms. An open pergola or arbor allows the pendulous flowers of wisteria to hang down through it, while a stone mailbox or a fence may be the perfect backdrop for morning glory flowers. A flat trellis may be the best choice for large-flowered hybrid clematis whose flowers are flat and outward facing. Perhaps the roof of a garden shed or the top of a gazebo is the ideal place to grow the vigorous sweet autumn clematis where its stunning floral display can be seen from across the garden and its exquisite fragrance can be carried on the breeze.

EXOTIC VINES?

If commonplace ornamental vines do not excite you, consider a more exotic alternative. Tropical vines grow quickly and can add marvelous color while inviting bees and butterflies to the garden. Passionflowers (*Passiflora* spp. and hybrids) are some of the most exotic-looking vines you can grow. Their spectacular and complex flowers never fail to elicit comment and the leaves play host to several desirable species of butterfly. Many passionflowers are rampant growers and several are quite hardy. Give careful consideration to where you plant them so they don't become problematic. If a vine that is both beautiful and edible appeals to you, try Malabar spinach (*Basella rubra*) whose rhubarb-red stems bear fleshy, green edible leaves that look and taste like spinach, but thrive in the heat of summer long after spring's spinach has bolted and gone to seed. Coral vine (*Antigonon leptopus*) and Spanish flag vine (*Mina lobata*) are also exotic-looking vines whose blooms will stop garden visitors in their tracks! Whether you choose some of these exotic beauties or stay with more traditional choices, vines are important additions to the garden for their versatility and beauty throughout the seasons.

CAROLINA JESSAMINE
Gelsemium sempervirens

Why It's Special—Carolina jessamine is a native vine of moderate size whose showy blooms appear in late winter and early spring in small clusters and put on a great show. 'Pride of Augusta', a double-flowered form with small, roselike blooms, is worth searching out.

How to Plant & Grow—Plant in spring or summer to allow plants to become well established before cold winter weather arrives. Carolina jessamine responds well to being planted in rich, moist garden soil, growing into a frothy green mass bearing hundreds, or maybe even thousands, of showy yellow blooms each spring. Fertilize once a year, just after flowering.

Care & Problems—Carolina jessamine may need some help getting started on its ascent by tying the older growth to whatever you wish it to cover until vigorous new growth begins. The new growth will wind itself around whatever support it is to grow on. Carolina jessamine has no serious pest problems.

Color—Yellow

Bloom Period—Late winter to early spring

Type/Hardiness—Evergreen, Zones 6 to 10

Height—15 to 20 ft., but can be kept smaller

Water Needs—Drought tolerant, but responds well to moisture

AMERICAN WISTERIA
Wisteria frutescens

Why It's Special—American wisteria is a well-behaved vine native to the southeastern United States with none of the invasive qualities of its Chinese and Japanese cousins. Look for the variety 'Amethyst Falls', which has purple blooms in spring and repeats up to two times during the summer. 'Clara Mack' has white flowers.

How to Plant & Grow—American wisteria is best planted in spring to grow rapidly and become well established in its first growing season. Wisteria is tolerant of clay soil and often flowers better when grown in poorer soils and not fed excessively.

Care & Problems—Prune in mid- to late spring, after the first flush of bloom, to shape and train the vine. Second and third flushes of bloom will occur in summer on the new growth that appears after the initial spring flowering and trimming. Because the vines are much less rampant than the Asian wisterias, less additional pruning is required.

Color—Lavender, white

Bloom Period—Spring, with summer repeat

Type/Hardiness—Deciduous, Zones 5b to 9a

Height—15 to 20 ft.

Water Needs—Average moisture, summer water encourages re-bloom

CLEMATIS
Clematis hybrids

Why It's Special—Large-flowered clematis hybrids such as 'Jackmanii' have been popular for more than 100 years, and few vines can rival their beauty when well grown. Modern hybrids continue to expand the color range and flower form.

How to Plant & Grow—Clematis should be planted in rich, deep, moist garden soil. The plants themselves should be set deeply in the planting hole with the crown of the plant 1 to 2 inches below soil level. This encourages deep root growth and the formation of a crown below the soil surface, an important precaution against clematis wilt disease.

Care & Problems—Clematis like their tops in the sun and their roots in the shade, making them perfect for planting in between other garden subjects. Clematis wilt, though aggravating, is usually not lethal and as long as plants were planted deeply, new growth will sprout quickly from the underground crown.

Color—Shades of purple, lavender, pink, red, white

Bloom Period—Spring to fall

Type/Hardiness—Mostly deciduous, Zones 5a to 8b

Height—5 ft. to 15 ft.

Water Needs—Moderate, irrigate during extended drought

CLEMATIS, ARMAND
Clematis armandii

Why It's Special—Armand clematis is perfectly suited to covering larger garden structures or walls. Showy clusters of fragrant white flowers appear in early spring and the long, leathery evergreen foliage provides interest in the garden year-round. A variety of songbirds like to nest among its dense, evergreen leaves.

How to Plant & Grow—Plant in spring or fall in rich, well-drained, and thoroughly amended garden soil. Prune and fertilize in spring immediately after flowering. Armand clematis is a vigorous grower and in most gardens will need occasional trimming to keep it in check. Winter water may be necessary during dry periods since it is evergreen.

Care & Problems—Pruning and trimming can be an issue. This particular clematis is a vigorous grower and needs some elbow room. It flowers very early in the spring and can be nipped by early frosts. Hardiness may be a problem in the coldest parts of its range. Protection from winter wind is beneficial.

Color—White

Bloom Period—Late winter to early spring

Type/Hardiness—Evergreen, Zones 7 to 9b

Height—25 ft.

Water Needs—Moderate, water during dry periods

CLEMATIS, SCARLET
Clematis texensis

Why It's Special—This tough and resilient vine is native to Texas and, while lesser-known, is a perfect addition to Southern gardens. Its scarlet red blooms may be bell-shaped or a more open, four-petaled cross-shaped bloom. Several cultivars of the species have been selected and are in the trade and a number of hybrids are also available.

How to Plant & Grow—Scarlet clematis is native to the open plains and grasslands of Texas, where it grows alongside native prairie grasses and wildflowers. Full sun will give you the most flowers, but it will grow well in part sun also. Scarlet clematis is adaptable to a wide range of soil types, but may need added lime if your soil leans to the acidic side.

Care & Problems—Scarlet clematis can be pruned hard in early spring to rejuvenate vines and remove tangles of old, dead wood. Training should begin as soon as the vine sprouts in spring to keep the vine from overtaking nearby plants and structures.

Color—Scarlet red to deep pink

Bloom Period—Early to midsummer

Type/Hardiness—Deciduous, Zones 5a to 9b

Height—10 to 15 ft.

Water Needs—Drought tolerant once established

CLEMATIS, SWEET AUTUMN

Clematis terniflora (Clematis paniculata)

Why It's Special—In autumn, this vigorous vine becomes a cloud of fragrant, white, 1-inch flowers that perfume the air with their vanillalike scent. Its rambling habit makes it perfect for covering an arbor or pergola, as well as for winding its way up through the branches of a sturdy shade tree.

How to Plant & Grow—Sweet autumn clematis is not picky about soil type; you frequently see it growing along the side of the road in areas where the soil is thin, lean, and clayey. Full sun will give you the most flowers, but it is also quite shade tolerant and will still put on a good show in part shade.

Care & Problems—Extremely vigorous sweet autumn clematis can be pruned hard in early spring to rejuvenate vines and remove tangles of old, dead wood. Training should begin as soon as the vine sprouts in spring to keep the vine from overtaking nearby plants and structures.

Color—White

Bloom Period—August and September

Type/Hardiness—Deciduous, Zones 5a to 9b

Height—20 ft. or more

Water Needs—Drought tolerant once established

CLIMBING ASTER

Ampelaster carolinianus

Why It's Special—Climbing aster is a unique and unusual member of the aster clan that is native to the southeastern United States. Its scrambling habit will send it clamoring up and over a fence, arbor, pergola, or porch rail. In late autumn, it covers itself in small, lavender-purple blooms.

How to Plant & Grow—Plant climbing aster in spring, when it is available from nurseries specializing in native plants or from a variety of mail order sources. It is tolerant of a wide range of soil conditions and thrives in leaner, less fertile soils. In the wild, it is found growing among the shrubs in full to part sun at a woods' edge.

Care & Problems—Eventually, climbing aster will become a jumbled mass of unsightly twigs and stems. At this point, your only choice is to cut the entire plant to the ground in early spring and let it rejuvenate from the base. Don't over-fertilize or you may get all leaves and few blooms.

Color—Lavender-purple

Bloom Period—Mid to late autumn

Type/Hardiness—Semievergreen, Zones 6 to 9

Height—6 to 8 ft.

Water Needs—Moderate, somewhat drought tolerant

CONFEDERATE JASMINE

Trachelospermum jasminoides

Why It's Special—Confederate jasmine is an excellent evergreen vine for Zones 8 and warmer, where its highly perfumed white flowers send their fragrance through the garden for six to eight weeks each spring. It can be sheared and kept growing tight or allowed to grow into a large, voluptuous vine and is a good choice for covering chain link fences or screening views.

How To Plant & Grow—Plant Confederate jasmine in spring in colder zones to get it well established during the growing season or anytime in warmer zones where its hardiness is not in question. It is very tolerant of the sandy soils found in some areas of the South and grows well in lean, infertile soils.

Care & Problems—Confederate jasmine is not reliably hardy in cold climates. It may grow into Zone 7, with protection, but it may not survive long term. Spray with horticultural oil sprays during winter while the plants are dormant to help control infestations.

Color—White

Bloom Period—Spring

Type/Hardiness—Evergreen, Zones 7b (with protection) to 9b

Height—15 ft. to 20 ft.

Water Needs—Moist until established, then moderate

CORAL HONEYSUCKLE
Lonicera sempervirens

Why It's Special—If you want to attract hummingbirds to your garden, perhaps no other vine will do a better job than our native trumpet or coral honeysuckle. The very word "honeysuckle" strikes fear into the hearts of many gardeners, but coral honeysuckle is a well-behaved native vine. In good soil, coral honeysuckle will grow into a lush and robust vine laden with blooms from spring to autumn.

How to Plant & Grow—Trumpet honeysuckle can be planted in spring or fall when regular rainfall will help to get the plants established. If your soil is well drained, there is no need to amend. If you have heavy clay, adding soil conditioner and compost will be beneficial.

Care & Problems—Pruning should be done after the first big flush of bloom in early to midsummer. Powdery mildew may be a problem and is unsightly, but not life threatening. Prune hard to rejuvenate every three to four years.

Color—Coral red, soft yellow

Bloom Period—Early summer with repeat

Type/Hardiness—Semi-evergreen, Zones 5b to 9a

Height—15 ft. to 20 ft.

Water Needs—Moderate, once established

CORAL VINE
Antigonon leptopus

Why It's Special—Coral vine is a fast-growing tropical vine that bears masses of bright pink to white, chainlike blooms in late summer and autumn. It may survive the winter and come back from the roots in Zone 8. In colder climates, it makes an excellent, late-blooming annual vine.

How to Plant & Grow—Coral vine should be planted in spring in very well-amended garden soil. Feed and water regularly in the summer months while the vine is actively growing to encourage the best possible floral display late in the year. Fertilize with a low-nitrogen or bloom booster-type fertilizer to encourage flowering.

Care & Problems—In the Deep South, where it is hardy and has the ability to set seed, coral vine may be invasive in some regions. In most of the South, where the vine is not hardy and frost kills it before it is able to set seed, it is a *non-invasive* and beautiful annual vine.

Color—Pink, white

Bloom Period—Late summer and autumn

Type/Hardiness—Evergreen Zones 9-10, annual elsewhere

Height—10 to 15 ft. as an annual

Water Needs—Average to moist

CREEPING FIG
Ficus pumila

Why It's Special—Creeping fig is popular for covering stone, brick, or concrete walls in warmer regions of the South. Its tiny leaves and delicate stems form a solid mat and turn whatever structure they are growing on into a living green wall.

How to Plant & Grow—Plant creeping fig in spring to get it well established through the warmest part of the growing season. Creeping fig will grow well in average garden soil to very sandy soil, but it may struggle in heavy clay. If you need it to cover a large surface, starting with several small plants will get you faster coverage than one or two larger ones.

Care & Problems—Where it's hardy, creeping fig is relatively pest free, although scale and mealybugs may occasionally attack, especially if the vine is under stress. From Zone 8 south, creeping fig makes an excellent perennial vine. In colder regions it can be grown as an annual.

Color—Grown for foliage

Bloom Period—Flowers are insignificant

Type/Hardiness—Evergreen in Zones 8 to 10

Height—25 ft. or more, where hardy

Water Needs—Average to moist soil

CROSS VINE
Bignonia capreolata

Why It's Special—Cross vine is a popular flowering vine native to the southeastern United States. Its beautiful, orange-red, trumpet-shaped blooms are borne in spring against evergreen or semi-evergreen leaves that turn purplish maroon in winter. Its fast growth rate makes it an excellent choice for covering trellises and arbors or for growing up the trunks of large shade trees.

How to Plant & Grow—Cross vine is tolerant of a wide range of soil conditions, from dry clay to sand, but thrives in rich, well-drained garden soil in full to part sun. Good soil will encourage lush growth and spectacular bloom. The cultivar 'Tangerine Beauty' flowers repeatedly during summer.

Care & Problems—Cross vine attaches itself with tiny "suction cups" that glue themselves very tightly to their support and is best suited to growing on stone or brick walls or posts, avoiding wooden structures. It should be pruned immediately after flowering and then as needed to keep it in-bounds.

Color—Orange-red

Bloom Period—Spring

Type/Hardiness—Evergreen or semievergreen, Zones 6a to 9b

Height—Up to 30 ft. or more

Water Needs—Drought tolerant, once established

FIVE-LEAF AKEBIA
Akebia quinata

Why It's Special—Akebia is a tough, semi-evergreen vine that will cover walls, provide shade over arbors, or rapidly cover a trellis. The attractive foliage remains evergreen in warmer climates and will hold on well into winter, even into the Mid- and Upper South. Clusters of small, but fragrant, dark purple or white flowers appear in early spring.

How to Plant & Grow—Akebia is tolerant of a wide range of growing conditions and is one of the best vines for problem areas and heavy clay soil. Plant in early spring and keep it well watered during the first summer. Once established, akebia is nearly indestructible and will survive with minimal care.

Care & Problems—Pruning should be done immediately after the flowers drop in spring and then as needed through the summer to control errant or rampant growth. Akebia is a large-growing vine and should be planted on a sturdy structure that will support its bulk and weight.

Color—Dark purple, white

Bloom Period—Spring

Type/Hardiness—Evergreen to semievergreen, Zones 5b to 9a

Height—20 ft. to 40 ft.

Water Needs—Drought tolerant, once established

HYACINTH BEAN
Lablab purpureus

Why It's Special—This fast-growing annual vine bears beautiful purple flowers and large quantities of showy purple "beans." Hyacinth bean will quickly cover a garden arbor or trellis. Hummingbirds also find it attractive and it is an excellent choice for children to grow since the seeds are large, easy to handle, and grow quickly.

How to Plant & Grow—Sow seeds outdoors where you want them to grow when the soil feels warm to the touch in mid- to late spring. They will germinate within seven to ten days and grow rapidly up whatever support you have provided for them. They will flower from midsummer through frost.

Care & Problems—Japanese beetles can be a problem. Pick them off and drop them in a jar of soapy water or spray with carbaryl for severe infestations. The showy purple pods are not edible, but are highly ornamental in late summer and fall. Harvest seeds when pods dry in autumn to replant next spring.

Color—Purple flowers and pods

Bloom Period—Midsummer until frost

Type/Hardiness—Grown as an annual

Height—Up to 10 ft.

Water Needs—Moist until established, then moderate

MALABAR SPINACH

Basella rubra

Why It's Special—Malabar spinach is a lesser known, but highly ornamental annual vine that does double duty in the garden. Its attractive, rhubarb-red stems and semi-glossy green leaves grow rapidly in summer's heat and humidity to cover nearly any structure in full sun. That they are edible and a superb replacement for cool-weather-loving spinach is an added bonus!

How to Plant & Grow—Malabar spinach can be grown from seed sown directly in the garden once the soil is warm to the touch or from transplants started indoors or purchased from your local garden center. It prefers rich, well-amended, evenly moist soil and, given good growing conditions, will quickly cover a trellis, arbor, or decorative support.

Care & Problems—Rabbits and slugs can be a problem when plants are small and deer will browse if it's within their reach. Insects are rarely a problem. Any repellents or insecticides should be used with caution if you plan to eat the spinach.

Color—Grown for foliage and stems

Bloom Period—Blooms are insignificant

Type/Hardiness—Annual

Height—10 to 12 ft.

Water Needs—Moderate to moist

MOON VINE

Ipomoea alba

Why It's Special—Moon vine's captivating, saucer-sized, pure white blooms unfurl each night as the sun sets and remain open until the following morning. Their rich fragrance attracts a variety of nighttime moths and other pollinators, and on moonlit nights, the blooms glow from afar.

How to Plant & Grow—Moon vine seed should be sown directly in the garden where you want it to grow when the soil feels warm to the touch in late spring. They resent being transplanted so direct sowing is best. Plant in rich, deep, thoroughly amended garden soil and stand back! Keep the plants well watered throughout the growing season.

Care & Problems—These rapidly growing vines are fairly pest and disease free. They do grow large, so give them room to climb and spread on a fence, arbor, or large trellis. They can easily reach 20 feet by the end of the season and are difficult to prune, since the flowers appear continually as the vine grows.

Color—Pure white

Bloom Period—Midsummer to frost

Type/Hardiness—Annual, not hardy

Height—20 ft., at least

Water Needs—Evenly moist for best growth

MORNING GLORY

Ipomoea purpurea

Why It's Special—The old-fashioned morning glory has been a garden staple for as far back as anyone has written about gardening. For many of us, it brings back memories of grandmother's garden with morning glories growing up the clothesline pole, on the fence, or over an old stump in the back yard. Blue-flowered forms are especially popular.

How to Plant & Grow—Plant morning glory seed directly in the garden where you want them to grow once soil is warm to the touch. Some suggest that soaking the seed overnight is helpful to crack the tough seed coat and speed germination. Given full sun, good garden soil, and adequate moisture, morning glories will delight you daily from midsummer to frost.

Care & Problems—Nibbling rabbits may be a problem on young plants, but morning glories grow exceptionally fast and once they are out of reach will race up whatever support they are growing on or over.

Color—Blue, lavender, purple, pink, white, red, bicolors

Bloom Period—Midsummer to frost

Type/Hardiness—Annual

Height—8 to 15 ft.

Water Needs—Moderate to moist

PASSIONFLOWER
Passiflora spp. and hybrids

Why It's Special—Passionflowers offer some of the most unusual and beautiful flowers in the plant kingdom, their flat and often brightly colored petals topped with a crown of distinctively banded filaments. Few flowers are as obviously identifiable as the passionflower.

How to Plant & Grow—Plant passionflowers in spring when they are actively growing. There are both hardy and non-hardy species, depending on which part of the South you live in. *Passiflora incarnata*, our native "Maypop," grows throughout the southeastern United States. Subtropical and tropical species can be grown as annuals in colder areas, but may be perennials in warmer regions.

Care & Problems—Where they are hardy, some species can spread aggressively by underground runners and once you have them, they can be difficult to eradicate. Some gardeners find them welcome additions, while others find them a nuisance. Tropical varieties will freeze out in colder climates.

Color—Lavender, pink, blue, white, red

Bloom Period—Early summer to frost

Type/Hardiness—Zones 6 to 10, depending on species

Height—6 to 30 ft., depending on the species

Water Needs—Moderate to moist soil, some tolerate wet feet

PIPEVINE
Aristolochia durior

Why It's Special—Pipevine is a beautiful and large-growing vine native to the southeastern United States. Its large, velvety, heart-shaped leaves offer outstanding texture in the garden and its unusual blooms, while usually hidden by the leaves, are great fun to show off to children and grandchildren. Pipevine is the primary host for pipevine swallowtail butterfly larvae.

How to Plant & Grow—Plant pipevine in early spring. It is readily available through native plant nurseries, as well as better garden centers that cater to gardeners wanting unique and unusual plants. Pipevine is very tolerant of less-than-ideal conditions, but will really reward you when given good garden soil and ample water.

Care & Problems—Pipevine is a tough and durable plant with few problems. It can be a shock to walk through the garden one day and see it being devoured down to the stems by caterpillars, but these are the highly desirable pipevine swallowtail and should be left alone. The plant will recover quickly.

Color—Pale yellow

Bloom Period—Summer

Type/Hardiness—Deciduous, Zones 6 to 9

Height—10 to 15 ft.

Water Needs—Ideally average to moist, but somewhat drought tolerant

SPANISH FLAG
Mina lobata

Why It's Special—Spanish flag is an annual vine, easily grown from seed in spring and with the heat of summer will quickly grow 6 to 8 feet or more. Beginning in late summer and continuing until frost, deep red flower buds fade to yellow and eventually creamy white as the flowers open in succession up the stem. With fifty to 100 clusters of blooms open at once on large, well-grown vines, they are nothing short of traffic-stopping.

How to Plant & Grow—Sow seed in peat pots in early spring to get a jumpstart on the season or sow the seed directly in the garden when the soil feels warm to the touch. Seedlings will grow quickly and begin climbing within a couple of weeks of sprouting. Flowers will appear beginning late summer through autumn.

Care & Problems—Spanish flag is relatively pest free, although slugs and snails may be a problem on young plants. Keep the soil moist and feed plants regularly, and they will quickly cover a good-sized trellis or arbor. Use bloom booster-type fertilizers that are low in nitrogen.

Color—Multicolored in red, yellow, cream

Bloom Period—Late summer through autumn

Type/Hardiness—Annual vine

Height—6 to 10 ft.

Water Needs—Regular water throughout the season

TRUMPET VINE
Campis radicans

Why It's Special—Another of our tough—some may say indestructible—native flowering vines that provides a spectacular display of tubular, deep orange flowers from late June to September. A magnet for hummingbirds, it thrives in the hot, humid summers of the South and in difficult, rocky, clay-based soils. Again, this plant is *tough*.

How to Plant & Grow—Trumpet vine can be planted in spring, summer, or fall as long as you can keep it watered long enough to get it established. Once it's off and growing, just stand back and let it go! Flowering will be best in full sun, but it will grow and flower well even in light shade.

Care & Problems—With vines, extremely tough can also mean extremely aggressive, and trumpet vine is no exception. Even though it is native, it can still swallow an arbor, pergola, gazebo, or the side of a house in short order. Give careful consideration to where you want it to grow. Also be aware that it sticks itself to its support with woody roots that sprout from the stem and are nearly impossible to remove once they're stuck.

Color—Orange to red, rarely yellow

Bloom Period—June to September

Type/Hardiness—Deciduous, Zones 4a to 9b

Height—20 ft. to 30 ft.

Water Needs—Drought tolerant, once established

THE INS AND OUTS OF VINES

HOW VINES CLIMB

Vines have a variety of methods for clinging to whatever support it is they are climbing on. Some will cling to a structure and have very little effect on that structure's long-term well-being, while other vines are so tenacious and strong they can actually damage a structure that wasn't meant to take their weight or the strength of their twining stems and trunks. It is also recommended to keep very dense growing vines off of wooden structures or walls where they can trap moisture and cause decay. Smaller vines and those that climb by tendrils (explained below) are best suited to wooden structures.

Twining vines twist their stems around supports. With a little coaxing, American wisteria (*Wisteria frutescens*) and confederate jasmine (*Gelsemium sempervirens*) happily wrap themselves around mailbox posts, lampposts, railings, or the posts of an arbor or pergola as they wind their way skyward. Twining vines, especially those that are perennial and grow large each year, need a sturdy structure to grow on or over.

Clematis (*Clematis* spp. and hybrids), cross vine (*Bignonia capreolata*), and others have specialized structures called tendrils that quickly and tightly wrap themselves around their supports to pull the stems and leaves of the vine upright and into position. While not always the case, many vines that use tendrils as a means of support are slightly smaller or lighter weight vines that are perhaps better suited to smaller structures or trellises that can't accommodate the size or weight of a larger vine.

Finally, some vines use specialized roots to give them a foothold. Creeping fig (*Ficus pumila*) and trumpet creeper (*Campsis radicans*) produce rootlets along their stems that have adhesive, suction-cup-like disks at their tips for attaching to surfaces. These can be especially difficult to remove, often requiring a wire brush or even sandblasting (in really severe cases) to remove them from a stone or brick surface where they were attached. They will also pull the paint off of any painted surface they are removed from.

HOW TO PLANT A VINE

1. Dig a hole that is at least two to three times the diameter of the rootball and the same depth as the height of the rootball. Thoroughly amend the soil you dig out of the hole with compost, composted manure, or soil conditioner (or a combination of those) so that the vine's roots can grow quickly into the loosened soil and speed up the plant's establishment in its new home. In heavy clay soils, additional amendments will help to ensure good drainage so that the plant doesn't sit in wet soil and rot.

2. Slip the plant out of the pot and examine the rootball. Vines (or groundcovers) growing in plastic or other hard-sided containers may have roots circling around the outside of the rootball. Lightly score the rootball with a sharp knife and cut through any roots that are larger than your little finger with a pair of pruners. This may seem harsh, but will encourage roots to break out of the rootball and grow into the surrounding soil in search of water and nutrients.

3. Place the rootball of the vine into the hole and measure the height of the rootball against the surrounding soil. With large plants, lay your shovel handle across the top of the hole to see if the rootball is even with or slightly above the handle. If the hole is too deep, add some soil to the bottom of the hole and reposition the vine in the hole. In especially heavy clay, it's wise to plant the rootball just slightly high, building up to the base of the plant to cover the rootball instead of sinking it into a hole that may hold water and drown the plant.

4. Backfill the hole with the amended soil that you dug out of the hole in Step 1. Tamp the soil into the hole with your hands, but not so heavily that you compact the soil. *Never* "stomp" a plant into a hole with your feet. This compacts the soil around the roots and drives water and air from the soil, both of which are essential to root growth. Water when you have filled half of the hole back in with soil to settle out any air pockets and to remoisten the soil in the

rootball. Finish backfilling and water again. Apply 2 to 3 inches of mulch around the base of the vine, keeping it clear of the stems so you don't invite insect or disease problems.

5. For the first month, soak your newly planted vines thoroughly at least twice each week. If the weather turns especially hot, you may need to water more. Try to keep the soil evenly moist, but never wet, while your newly planted vines are getting established. After the first month, you should be able to reduce the frequency of your watering, but always thoroughly soak the rootball each time you do water. The goal is to encourage the roots to grow deep into the soil to support the vine.

PRUNING YOUR VINES

Methods and timing of pruning will vary from vine to vine, much of it based on their bloom time. Some vines, like sweet autumn clematis, flower on their new growth and can be pruned hard in early spring to encourage lush, vigorous growth that will bear flowers in the fall. Wisteria and Carolina jessamine flower in spring on growth that was made the year before. These vines should be pruned in spring, immediately *after* they finish flowering and then only as needed to keep them shaped and in-bounds for the rest of the year.

TIPS AND TRICKS FOR PRUNING CLEMATIS

Clematis can be tricky when it comes to pruning, but don't despair. Here are some basic guidelines for knowing when to prune your clematis. They are divided into three groups:

Group I contains the early spring-flowering evergreen clematis and early and mid-spring-flowering species. Armand clematis (*Clematis armandii*) falls into this group. These clematis flower on the previous year's wood and should be pruned after the flowers fade but no later than July. The only pruning really needed is to remove weak or dead stems and to confine the plant to its allotted space.

Group II consists of clematis that also flower on the previous year's growth but will produce a second flush of bloom on new growth. Many of the large-flowered hybrids, such as 'H.F. Young', 'Nelly Moser', 'Will Goodwin', and many, many others are in this category. Remove all dead and weak stems in late winter or early spring, and cut the remaining stems back to a pair of strong buds that will produce the first blooms. Occasional pinching after flowering will stimulate branching. If these vines get leggy, they can all be cut to the ground in early spring, before growth starts, and will produce luxurious new growth and flower slightly later in the season.

Group III consists of late-flowering cultivars and species that flower almost exclusively on the current year's new growth, like the classic 'Jackmanii', as well as the scarlet clematis (*C. texensis*), and the herbaceous species. These can also be pruned in late winter or early spring. For the first two or three years they may be cut back to a foot from the ground. Later, cut them back to 2 feet. If not cut regularly, this group can become very leggy and overgrown.

The boundaries between these three groups are not absolute. Group I's requirements are fairly strict, but the pruning methods between Groups II and III are nearly interchangeable, especially for the hybrids. The groups simply serve as a rough guide to keeping your clematis vines growing and flowering profusely.

JANUARY

- With the arrival of spring gardening catalogs, be on the lookout for new and unusual vines that will add extra interest to the layout and design of your garden. Vines, like groundcovers, are often overlooked when it comes to creating layers, depth, and visual interest in the garden.

- Evergreen vines will continue to lose water through their leaves, even in winter, and may need additional water during the winter months when the soil is not frozen. If they become severely dry at the roots and we have an especially severe round of cold weather accompanied by wind, evergreen vines can be almost "freeze dried" because they can't take any additional water into their leaves if the soil is frozen.

- Scale insects can be a problem on some evergreen vines. To help kill these difficult-to-control pests, use a dormant oil spray during the winter when the vines are completely dormant. This will help to smother any overwintering insects that may be lurking in tiny nooks and crannies. Be sure to spray thoroughly, covering as many surfaces as possible, including the undersides of the leaves where pests can hide.

FEBRUARY

- In Zones 8 and 9, planting season is upon us. Keep newly planted vines well watered to help them establish quickly. Water twice weekly for the first month and then at least once each week, soaking them thoroughly, until the vines are well established. In sandy soils or if the weather gets unexpectedly hot, you may need to water more.

- An early spring application of organic, slow-release fertilizer can be applied to vines now to get them off to a good start as they begin to grow in spring. Use low nitrogen types of fertilizers like bloom boosters (even if you're feeding a vine that doesn't flower) to give it the nutrients it needs without forcing an inordinate and difficult-to-control amount of growth that requires constant maintenance to keep in check.

- Vines that have outgrown their space can be cut back now, when it is easy to see what you're doing, but avoid pruning vines such as wisteria and Confederate jasmine that will be blooming in just a few weeks on the growth they made last year. Prune those vines immediately after they finish flowering and just as they enter their most vigorous phase of growth.

- Once the coldest winter weather has passed, prune summer- and fall-flowering vines, such as sweet autumn clematis, climbing aster, and trumpet creeper. They will flower on their new spring and summer growth.

MARCH

- In the Lower South and some of the Mid-South, the main planting season arrives this month. This is the perfect time for planting hardy, perennial vines to get them established before the heat of the summer sets in.

- Wait to plant annual and tropical vines that are frost tender and need warmer soil temperatures until all danger of frost has passed and the soil feels warm to the touch. Dig a shovelful of soil and if it still feels very cold a few inches under the surface, it's still too early to plant heat-loving vines like moon vine, Spanish flag, and hyacinth bean. Wait until at least April.

- Spring is rarely dry, so newly planted vines may not need frequent watering, but be sure to check the soil to a depth of 4 to 6 inches at least once a week to be sure that the roots remain moist during the first six to eight weeks they are in the ground.

- Early spring-flowering vines, like Carolina jessamine, Armand clematis, and cross vine, should be pruned as necessary after flowering. Remove any dead or damaged shoots and cut back others to keep the vine in-bounds. Pruning also encourages side shoots and branching, making the plants fuller and more robust.

- Summer- and fall-flowering vines, like trumpet creeper and sweet autumn clematis, can be pruned now to flower on their new growth later in the season.

APRIL

- Seeds of moon vine and morning glory can be planted in the warmer areas of the South this month if the top 2 to 3 inches of soil is warm to the touch. Both have very hard seed coats, and it is helpful to knick them with a file or rub them between two pieces of coarse sandpaper and then soak them in water overnight to allow the seeds to absorb water before sowing.

- Tropical vines, like mandevilla, that you may have overwintered indoors can be planted back in the garden now to bloom throughout the summer until frost threatens next fall. A good spraying to kill any scale, mealybugs, or spider mites that have hung on over the winter may be in order.

- If you haven't pruned early-flowering vines, like wisteria, Carolina jessamine, and Armand clematis, do it now before new growth becomes so rampant it becomes difficult. Regular pruning may be necessary to keep particularly vigorous species, like wisteria, in-bounds.

MAY

- Continue planting seeds of summer-flowering annual vines, such as moon vine, hyacinth bean, and morning glory. They will germinate and grow quickly as the soil warms in the late spring sunshine.

- As the days begin to go from warm to hot, a good layer of mulch around the base of your vines will help keep them well hydrated and their roots cool. This is especially important for clematis, which love to have their tops in the warm sunshine, but want their feet in the cool shade.

- Give annual vines a helping hand getting started onto their trellises or whatever structures you want them to cover. Tie a string to a small stake in the ground near the plant and to the trellis at the other end to give the vines something to twine on as they begin their ascent skyward. Once they reach the trellis or other support they'll go right up on their own.

- Watch for signs of clematis wilt. Although it is rarely fatal, it can be devastating to vines that are just getting ready to flower. Carefully trim out any stems that wilt and die suddenly. Sterilize your pruner blades with rubbing alcohol to prevent passing the disease from plant to plant.

JUNE

- Take notes on your vines over the next few months and record your observations in your journal. Notes on bloom time, ornamental features, growth rates, and pest problems will be helpful in making plans to relocate or replace any poorly performing plants.

- Train rapidly growing vines to the trellis, arbor, or other structure they are meant to grow on. You may have to attach some temporary strings or wires to the structure to get the vines started. You can recycle twist ties from the kitchen to loosely tie vines to their supports until they attach themselves.

- Japanese beetles are at their most active this month. They *love* wisteria and a number of other vines. Pick them off by hand and drop them in a jar of soapy water or spray with carbaryl for severe infestations.

- Stay on top of weeds around your vines and throughout the garden. They rob your good plants of nutrients and water. When the days begin to get too hot, early morning is a great time to weed. Even thirty minutes of deadheading and weeding each morning as you walk through the garden will go a long way toward keeping it neat, tidy, and weed free.

JULY

- If you're planning a vacation this month, don't forget to find someone to check on the garden and water as necessary while you're gone.

- Feed 'Amethyst Falls' wisteria this month with a bloom booster fertilizer to encourage a nice flush of late summer or autumn blooms. American wisteria is a much less rampant grower than its Japanese and Chinese cousins, and pruning should only be done to shape the plant and keep it in-bounds. Hard pruning is not necessary.

- Japanese beetles can still be active this month. Hand pick them and drop them in a jar of soapy water or spray with carbaryl for severe infestations. Spider mites love the hot summer months and are often recognized by the white speckling they cause on leaves. They can be controlled with regular applications of insecticidal soap, but be sure to spray the undersides of the leaves, as well, as this is where they love to hide!

AUGUST

- Collect seeds from annual vines, such as morning glory, moon vine, and hyacinth bean, and store them in paper envelopes or small paper bags for planting next year. Paper is better than a plastic zip-top bag because paper breathes and doesn't trap moisture, which can be detrimental to dormant seeds.

- As you begin collecting seeds from the garden, consider getting a shallow plastic bin to store seeds in. Even a plastic food storage container will work. If you're really organized, you can create small dividers with recycled cardboard and keep your small paper storage envelopes organized by type of plant—annuals, perennials, vines, and so on.

- Be diligent about watering vines this month, especially if natural rainfall is scarce. Vines that will flower early next spring, such as wisteria and Carolina jessamine, are forming their flower buds now, and drought stress during this time could affect next spring's floral display.

- Continue inspecting your vines for spider mite and aphid infestations. Spray only if necessary, but don't let your plants succumb to pests that can be controlled with just a little bit of help on your part. Early morning, before the heat of the day and while the wind is calm, is the best time to spray.

SEPTEMBER

- For a different approach and to create more visual layers in the garden, grow well-behaved vines on or through trees and shrubs. Draping vines over other plants allows you to create eye-catching combinations with contrasting foliage textures, as well as flower and foliage pairings.

- It is too late to do any major pruning now, especially for spring-flowering vines, such as wisteria, Carolina jessamine, and others. Their flower buds are already set for next spring's bloom and pruning now means cutting off those buds and ruining, or at least compromising, the display.

- Vines should not be fertilized this time of year. Fertilizing can force tender new growth that may not have time to harden off before cold weather arrives.

- Winter weeds, such as henbit and chickweed, as well as dandelions, begin germinating this month. Remove them now while they're young and easy to pull. Pre-emergent herbicides can be effective, but only when applied *before* weed seeds germinate.

OCTOBER

- October is prime fall planting season across much of the South, with warm days and cooler nights encouraging quick establishment. However, October can also be one of the driest months of the year so be certain that anything you plant is watered thoroughly and regularly.

- If you grow the colorful-leaved ornamental sweet potato vines in your pots or flower beds you can dig the tubers now and store them in a cool, dry location for replanting next spring after the danger of frost has passed. Some gardeners choose simply to replace them each year.

- In cooler parts of the South, annual vines may be killed by the first frosts toward the end of this month. At that point, it is time to cut them from their supports, pull up their roots, and add them to the compost pile.

- Many insects will still be active even after the weather cools off. Once perennial vines have gone completely dormant in late fall or early winter, spraying with dormant horticultural oil will help smother spider mite and other insect eggs to help reduce next year's population.

NOVEMBER

- If you're a do-it-yourselfer, make plans to build a new arbor, pergola, or trellis that can eventually support a vine. Winter is a great time to do the kinds of projects that many of us are too busy to do during the hectic summer season.

You can make your own trellis with some wood and copper pipe.

- Fall is often dry across the South, so don't rely on Mother Nature to water newly planted vines. Keep at least one hose handy, even if you have begun winterizing and storing some things away, to water any newly planted vines (or shrubs or trees) as necessary.

- Remember that evergreen vines, such as Armand clematis and Carolina jessamine, continue to lose water through their leaves, even though they are technically dormant. On warm days when the soil is not frozen (if it freezes where you live), it is especially important to water evergreen vines during periods of winter dryness.

- Rake up fallen leaves from the ground under your vines and compost them. Fallen leaves can harbor insects and disease that can then reinfect the plants next spring as they begin to grow.

DECEMBER

- If you have been taking notes throughout the growing season but have not had time to sit down and organize them into complete thoughts in your garden journal, now is the perfect time to do it while the growing season is still fresh in your mind.

- Now is also an excellent time to create a wish list for next year, since new plant catalogs may begin arriving as early as December and will definitely start arriving immediately after the first of the year. Were there any vines that you were particularly fond of that you would like to find other varieties of in different colors or different forms?

- Remember to keep vines off wooden walls. They can trap moisture, slow the drying of the wood, and encourage decay. This is especially true in winter when we tend to have damp weather in the South anyway.

- Dormant oil can be applied to vines this month to help control spider mites, scale insects, and mealybugs. Be sure to read the label for directions for proper mixing and for cautions regarding the limits of high and low temperatures at the time of application.

GLOSSARY

Acidic soil: On a soil pH scale of 0 to 14, acidic soil has a pH lower than 7.0.

Alkaline soil: On a soil pH scale of 0 to 14, alkaline soil has a pH higher than 7.0.

Annual: A plant that germinates (sprouts), flowers, and dies within one year or season (spring, summer, winter, or fall) is an annual.

***Bacillus thuringiensis* (Bt):** Bt is an organic pest control based on naturally occurring soil bacteria, often used to control harmful caterpillars such as cutworms, leaf rollers, and webworms.

Balled and burlapped (B&B): This phrase describes plants that have been grown in field nursery rows, dug up with their soil intact, wrapped with burlap, and tied with twine. Balled-and-burlapped plants may include both trees and shrubs, as well as deciduous and evergreen forms of both.

Beneficial insects: These insects perform valuable services such as pollination and pest control. Ladybugs, soldier beetles, and some bees are examples.

Biennial: A plant that blooms during its second year and then dies is a biennial.

Bolting: This is a process when a plant switches from leaf growth to producing flowers and seeds. Bolting often occurs quite suddenly and is usually undesirable, because the plant usually dies shortly after bolting.

Brown materials: A part of a well-balanced compost pile, brown materials include high-carbon materials such as brown leaves and grass, woody plant stems, dryer lint, and sawdust.

Bud: The bud is an undeveloped shoot nestled between the leaf and the stem that will eventually produce a flower or plant branch.

Bulb: A bulb is a plant with an underground storage organ, often round in shape, formed by the plant stem and leaves. Examples are tulips, daffodils, hyacinths, and onions.

Bush: *See* Shrub.

Central leader: The term used to describe the center trunk of an ornamental or fruit tree.

Chilling hours: Hours when the air temperature is below 45 degrees; chilling hours are most commonly referred to in fruit production, but are also important to hardy bulbs like tulips and daffodils and some perennials, such as peonies.

Common name: A name that is generally used to identify a plant in a particular region, as opposed to its botanical name, which is standard throughout the world; for example, the common name for *Echinacea purpurea* is "purple coneflower."

Contact herbicide: This type of herbicide kills only the part of the plant that it touches, such as the leaves or the stems.

Container: Any pot or vessel that is used for planting; containers can be ceramic, clay, steel, or plastic—or a teacup, bucket, or barrel.

Container grown: This describes a plant that is grown, sold, and shipped while in a pot.

Cool-season annual: This is a flowering plant, such as snapdragon or pansy that thrives during cooler months.

Cool-season vegetable: This is a vegetable, such as spinach, broccoli, and peas, that thrives during cooler months.

Dappled shade: This is bright shade created by high tree branches or tree foliage, where patches of sunlight and shade intermingle.

Deadhead: To remove dead flowers in order to encourage further bloom and prevent the plant from going to seed is to deadhead.

Deciduous plant: A plant that loses its leaves seasonally, typically in fall or early winter, is deciduous.

Diatomaceous earth: A natural control for snails, slugs, flea beetles, and other garden pests, diatomaceous earth consists of ground-up fossilized remains of sea creatures.

Divide: A technique consisting of digging up clumping perennials, separating the roots, and replanting. Dividing plants encourages vigorous growth and is typically performed in the spring or fall.

Dormancy: The period when plants stop growing in order to conserve energy; this happens naturally and seasonally, usually in winter.

Drip line: The ground area under the outer circumference of tree branches, this is where most of the tree's roots that absorb water and nutrients are found.

Evergreen: A plant that keeps its leaves year-round, instead of dropping them seasonally, is evergreen.

Flower stalk: The stem that supports the flower and elevates it so that insects can reach the flower and pollinate it is the flower stalk.

Four-inch pot: The 4-inch by 4-inch pots that many annuals and small perennials are sold in. Four-inch pots can also be sold in flats of 18 or 20.

Frost: Ice crystals that form when the temperature falls below freezing (32 degrees) create frost.

Full sun: Areas of the garden that receive direct sunlight for six to eight hours a day or more, with no shade, are in full sun.

Fungicide: A product used to control fungal diseases such as powdery mildew, blackspot, crown rot and many others.

Gallon container: A standard nursery-sized container for plants, a gallon container is roughly equivalent to a gallon container of milk.

Garden lime: This soil amendment lowers soil acidity and raises the pH.

Garden soil: The existing soil in a garden bed; it is generally evaluated by its nutrient content and texture. Garden soil is also sold as a bagged item at garden centers and home-improvement stores.

Germination: This is the process by which a plant emerges from a seed or a spore.

Grafted tree: This is a tree composed of two parts: the top, or scion, which bears fruit, and the bottom, or rootstock, which supports the plant's growth.

Graft union: This is the place on a fruit tree trunk where the rootstock and the scion have been joined.

Granular fertilizer: This type of fertilizer comes in a dry, pellet-like form rather than a liquid or powder.

Grass clippings: The parts of grass that are removed when mowing, clippings are a valuable source of nitrogen for the lawn or the compost pile.

Green materials: An essential element in composting that includes grass clippings, kitchen scraps, and manure and provides valuable nitrogen in the pile; green materials are high in nitrogen.

Hand pruners: An important hand tool that consists of two sharp blades that perform a scissoring motion; these are used for light pruning, clipping, and cutting.

Hardening off: This is the process of slowly acclimating seedlings and young plants grown in an indoor environment to the outdoors.

Hardiness zone map: This map lists average annual minimum temperature ranges of a particular area. This information is helpful in determining appropriate plants for the garden. North America is divided into eleven separate hardiness zones.

Heirloom: An open-pollinated plant that was more commonly grown pre-World War II.

Host plant: A plant grown to feed caterpillars that will eventually morph into butterflies is called a host plant.

Hybrid: Plants produced by crossing two genetically different plants, hybrids often have desirable characteristics such as disease resistance.

Insecticide: This substance is used for destroying or controlling insects that are harmful to plants. Insecticides are available in organic and synthetic forms.

Irrigation: A system of watering the landscape, irrigation can be an in-ground automatic system, soaker or drip hoses, or hand-held hoses with nozzles.

Larva: The immature stage of an insect that goes through complete metamorphosis; caterpillars are butterfly or moth larvae.

Larvae: This is the plural of larva.

Liquid fertilizer: Plant fertilizer in a liquid form, some types need to be mixed with water, and some types are ready to use from the bottle.

Morning sun: Areas of the garden that have an eastern exposure and receive direct sun in the morning hours are in morning sun.

Mulch: Any type of material that is spread over the soil surface around the base of plants to suppress weeds and retain soil moisture is mulch.

Nematode: Microscopic, wormlike organisms that live in the soil, some nematodes are beneficial, while others are harmful.

Naturalized: Plants that are introduced into an area, as opposed to being native to it, are said to be naturalized.

Nectar plant: Flowers that produce nectar that attract and feed butterflies, encouraging a succession of blooms throughout the season.

New wood (new growth): The new growth on plants, it is characterized by a greener, more tender form than older, woodier growth.

Old wood: Old wood is growth that is more than one year old. Some fruit plants produce on old wood. If you prune these plants in spring before they flower and fruit, you will cut off the wood that will produce fruit.

Organic: This term describes products derived from naturally occurring materials instead of materials synthesized in a lab.

Part shade: Areas of the garden that receive three to six hours of sun a day are in part shade. Plants requiring part shade will often require protection from the more intense afternoon sun, either from tree leaves or from a building.

Part sun: Areas of the garden that receive three to six hours of sun a day are in part sun. Although the term is often used interchangeably with "part shade," a "part sun" designation places greater emphasis on the minimal sun requirements.

Perennial: A plant that lives for more than two years is a perennial. Examples include trees, shrubs, and some flowering plants.

Pesticide: A substance used for destroying or controlling insects that are harmful to plants. Pesticides are available in organic and synthetic forms.

pH: A figure designating the acidity or the alkalinity of garden soil, pH is measured on a scale of 1 to 14, with 7.0 being neutral.

Pinch: This is a method to remove unwanted plant growth with your fingers, promoting bushier growth and increased blooming.

Plant label: This label or sticker on a plant container provides a description of the plant and information on its care and growth habits.

Pollination: The transfer of pollen for fertilization from the male pollen-bearing structure (stamen) to the female structure (pistil), usually by wind, bees, butterflies, moths, or hummingbirds; this process is required for fruit production.

Potting soil: A soil mixture used to grow flowers, herbs, and vegetables in containers, potting soil provides proper drainage and extra nutrients for healthy growth. *See also* Soilless potting mix.

Powdery mildew: A fungal disease characterized by white powdery spots on plant leaves and stems, this disease is worse during times of drought or when plants have poor air circulation.

Pruning: This is a garden task in which a variety of hand tools are used to remove dead limbs or stems from trees and shrubs, increase airflow within the plant, improve flowering and fruiting, and improve a plant's overall health.

Remontant: A word used to describe a plant that blooms again, sometimes repeatedly, outside of its normal blooming season. For example, remontant bearded iris flower heavily in spring, but have the ability to re-bloom in autumn.

Rhizome: An underground horizontal stem that grows side shoots, a rhizome is similar to a bulb.

Rootball: The network of roots and soil clinging to a plant when it is lifted out of the ground is the rootball.

Runner: A stem sprouting from the center of a strawberry plant, a runner produces fruit in its second year.

Scientific name: This two-word identification system consists of the genus and species of a plant, such as *Ilex opaca*.

Shade: Garden shade is the absence of any direct sunlight in a given area, usually due to tree foliage or building shadows.

Shop broom: A long-handled broom with a wide base used for efficiently sweeping a walkway or other hardscape.

Shredded hardwood mulch: A mulch consisting of shredded wood that interlocks, resisting washout and suppressing weeds, hardwood mulch can change soil pH.

Shrub: This woody plant is distinguished from a tree by its multiple trunks and branches and its shorter height of less than 15 feet tall.

Slow-release fertilizer: This form of fertilizer releases nutrients at a slower rate throughout the season, requiring less-frequent applications.

Slug bait: A pesticide used for controlling slugs in the garden. Iron-based slug baits are non-toxic to humans and pets, but are extremely effective against slugs and snails.

Soil conditioner: Finely ground pine bark that is commonly used as an amendment to improve soil quality, but may also be used as mulch. It is especially useful in perennial beds, where it suppresses weeds while still allowing perennials to emerge easily.

Soil test: An analysis of a soil sample, this determines the level of nutrients (to identify deficiencies) and detects pH.

Soilless potting mix: Soilless potting mixes are peat-based mixes that contain a variety of other ingredients to create a lightweight, well-balanced mix. They are popular for use in containers where good drainage is needed and where the light weight of the mix is useful to prevent pots from becoming immovable when filled full.

Succulent: A type of plant that stores water in its leaves, stems, and roots and is acclimated for arid climates and soil conditions.

Summer annual: Annuals that thrive during the warmer months of the growing season.

Systemic herbicide: This type of weedkiller is applied to and absorbed by the plant's leaves and transferred to its roots, killing the entire plant, roots and all.

Taproot: This is an enlarged, tapered plant root that grows vertically downward.

Thinning: This is the practice of removing excess seedlings to leave more room for the remaining seedlings to grow. The term may be used in reference to vegetables, especially rootcrops, where thinning allows the crop to develop fully; it is also a useful technique when direct sowing annual flowers, like zinnias, from seed to give seedlings room to develop.

Topdress: To spread fertilizer on top of the soil (usually around fruit trees or vegetables) is to topdress.

Transplants: Plants that are grown in one location and then moved to and replanted in another, seeds started indoors and nursery plants are two examples.

Tree: This woody perennial plant typically consists of a single trunk with multiple lateral branches.

Tree canopy: This is the upper layer of growth, consisting of the tree's branches and leaves.

Tropical plant: This is a plant that is native to a tropical region of the world, and thus acclimated to a warm, humid climate and not hardy to frost.

Turf: Grass and the surface layer of soil that is held together by its roots.

Variegated: The appearance of differently colored areas on plant leaves, often white or yellow, but variegation can be a variety of colors including various shades of green, pink, red, and others.

Vegetable: A plant or part of a plant that is used for food.

Warm-season vegetable: This is a vegetable that thrives during the warmer months. Examples are tomatoes, okra, and peppers. These vegetables do not tolerate frost.

Weeping: A growth habit in plants that features drooping or downward curving branches.

BIBLIOGRAPHY

Carolinas Gardener's Handbook, Toby Bost and Bob Polomski, Cool Springs Press/Quayside Publishing, Minneapolis, MN, 2012.

The Encyclopedia of Ornamental Grasses, John Greenlee, Michael Friedman Publishing Group, Inc., New York, NY, 1992.

The Green Gardener's Guide, Joe Lamp'l, Cool Springs Press, Franklin, TN, 2007.

Manual of Woody Landscape Plants, Fifth Edition, Michael A. Dirr, Stipes Publishing LLC, Champaign, IL, 1998.

Perennials for American Gardens, Ruth Rogers Clausen and Nicolas H. Ekstrom, Random House, NY, 1989.

The Southern Living Garden Book, John Alex Floyd, Jr., Oxmoore House, Inc., Birmingham, AL, 1999.

RESOURCES

Following are a few of my favorite gardening resources, both in print and online. While I encourage you to support local businesses and shop your local nurseries and garden centers first, I have also included some much-loved mail order nurseries for the more adventurous gardeners who are looking for plants beyond the typical offerings of most garden centers and nurseries.

RECOMMENDED READING

Christopher Lloyd's Garden Flowers, Christopher Lloyd
Daffodils for American Gardens, Brent and Becky Heath
The Encyclopedia of Ornamental Grasses, John Greenlee
Exotic Planting for Adventurous Gardeners,
    Christopher Lloyd
Fall Scaping, Stephanie Cohen and Nan Ondra
Garden Bulbs for the South, Scott Ogden
Garden Masterclass, John Brookes
Gardener's Guide Series (State-focused gardening
    books by Cool Springs Press)
The Green Gardener's Guide, Joe Lamp'l
Herbaceous Perennial Plants, Allan Armitage
Manual of Woody Lanscape Plants, 6th Edition,
    Michael A. Dirr
Perennial Gardener's Design Primer, Stephanie Cohen and
    Nan Ondra
Perennials for American Gardens, Ruth Rogers Clausen
    and Nicolas H. Ekstrom
The Well-Designed Mixed Garden, Tracy DiSabato-Aust
The Well-Tended Perennial Garden, Tracy DiSabato-Aust

MAGAZINES

Birds & Blooms (www.birdsandblooms.com)
The English Garden (www.theenglishgarden.co.uk)
Fine Gardening (www.finegardening.com)
Gardens Illustrated (www.gardensillustrated.com)
Horticulture (www.hortmag.com)
Organic Gardening (www.organicgardening.com)
State-by-State Gardening Magazines
    (www.statebystategardening.com)

MAIL ORDER NURSERIES

Annie's Annuals & Perennials (www.anniesannuals.com)
Antique Rose Emporium
    (www.antiqueroseemporium.com)
Arrowhead Alpines (www.arrowheadalpines.com)
Baker Creek Heirloom Seeds (www.rareseeds.com)
Blue Ridge Daylilies (www.blueridgedaylilies.com)
Brent & Becky's Bulbs (www.brentandbeckysbulbs.com)
Broken Arrow Nursery
    (www.brokenarrownursery.com)
Brushwood Nursery (www.gardenvines.com)
Cistus Nursery (www.cistus.com)
Cold Hardy Cactus (www.coldhardycactus.com)
Collector's Nursery (www.collectorsnursery.com)
Completely Clematis (www.clematisnursery.com)
Daylily World (www.daylilyworld.com)
Digging Dog Nursery (www.diggingdog.com)
Forestfarm (www.forestfarm.com)
High Country Gardens (www.highcountrygardens.com)
Johnny's Selected Seeds (www.johnnyseeds.com)
Klehm's Song Sparrow Farm (www.songsparrow.com)
Lazy S's Farm & Nursery (www.lazyssfarm.com)
Logee's Greenhouse (www.logees.com)
Old House Gardens (www.oldhousegardens.com)
Plant Delights Nursery (www.plantdelights.com)
Prairie Nursery (www.prairienursery.com)
Rare Find Nursery (www.rarefindnursery.com)
Swan Island Dahlias (www.dahlias.com)

OTHER ONLINE RESOURCES

American Community Garden Association
    (www.communitygarden.org)
Cornell University (www.gardening.cornell.edu)
Dave's Garden (www.davesgarden.com)
Farmer's Almanac (www.farmersalmanac.com)
Garden Web (www.gardenweb.com)
Kids' Gardening (www.kidsgardening.com)
National Gardening Association (www.garden.org)
National Garden Bureau (www.ngb.org)

COMMON NAME INDEX

SCIENTIFIC NAME INDEX

PHOTO CREDITS

Bill Adams: pp. 121 (right), 123 (right), 124 (right)

David Cavagnaro: pp. 92 (center), 93 (right), 101 (left)

Creative Commons/cc-by-2.0: pp. 231 (right)

Tom Eltzroth: pp. 98 (right), 109 (left), 111 (center), 121 (left), 122 (both), 123 (left), 124 (left), 178 (left)

Katie Elzer-Peters: pp. 177 (left)

Lorenzo Gunn: pp. 55 (right)

iStock: pp. 218

Troy B. Marden: pp. 16, 18, 20, 22, 25, 26, 28, 31, 33, 35, 36, 37, 38, 50, 52, 53, 54 (both), 55 (left and center), 56 (both), 57 (all), 58 (both), 59 (all), 60 (both), 61 (all), 62 (all), 63 (both), 64, 68, 71 (both), 72 (all), 73 (all), 74 (all), 75 (all), 76 (both), 77 (both), 78 (all), 79 (all), 80 (all), 81 (all), 82 (all), 83, 94 (left), 95 (left and right), 96 (left and center), 97 (right), 98 (left), 99 (center), 100 (left and right), 120 (left), 106, 109 (right), 110 (both), 111 (right), 112 (all), 113 (all), 114 (both), 130, 132, 133 (both), 134 (both), 135 (all), 136 (all), 137 (both), 138 (all), 144, 147 (all), 148 (both), 149 (both), 150 (all), 151 (all), 152 (all), 153 (all), 154 (both), 155 (right), 156 (all), 157 (all), 158 (left and center), 159 (all), 160 (both), 161 (both), 162 (all), 166, 167, 168, 170 (all), 171 (right), 172 (all), 173 (all), 174 (all), 175 (all), 176 (all), 177 (center and right), 178 (center and right), 179 (all), 180 (all), 181 (both), 192 (center and right), 193 (all), 194 (all), 195 (all), 196 (all), 197 (all), 198 (all), 199, 200 (all), 206, 207, 209 (both), 210 (all), 211 (all), 212 (all), 213 (all), 214 (all), 215 (both), 216 (both), 221, 225 (both), 226 (left and center), 227 (all), 228 (all), 229 (all), 230 (all), 232 (both)

Jerry Pavia: pp. 222

Shutterstock: pp. 19, 42, 44, 47, 48, 49, 84, 88, 89, 90, 92 (left and right), 93 (left and center), 94 (center and right), 95 (center), 96 (right), 97 (left and center), 98 (center), 99 (left and right), 100 (center), 101 (center and right), 102 (center and right), 104, 108, 111 (left), 116, 117, 121 (center), 140, 143, 155 (left), 158 (right), 171 (left), 187, 189, 1190, 192 (left), 226 (right)

Special thanks to the following people for helping to fill the gaps in my photo library:

Terri Barnes
Growild Nursery, Inc.
Fairview, TN
www.growild.com

J. Paul Moore
J. Paul Moore Photography
www.jpaulmoorephoto.com

Jason S. Reeves
Research Associate
University of Tennessee
West Tennessee Research & Education Center
www.ag.tennessee.edu

Jeff McMillian
Almost Eden
Merryville, LA
www.almostedenplants.com

NOTES

NOTES

NOTES

NOTES

MEET TROY MARDEN

Troy B. Marden is a plantsman, garden designer, and author with a passion for plants. His more than twenty-five years of professional experience include time spent in nearly every facet of the horticulture industry.

Not only a superb plantsman, Troy is a garden communicator who has been a cohost of Nashville Public Television's hit gardening show "Volunteer Gardener" for more than ten years. Marden writes regularly for some of the country's top gardening magazines, and Troy's blog, Gardener Cook, has become popular with plant lovers and food lovers alike. His latest venture, launched in late 2012, is a garden tour division of his business that will take other passionate gardeners on trips to some of the finest horticultural destinations in the United States and around the world. You can find more information at www.troybmarden.com.

Troy lives on a large property in Middle Tennessee near the tiny hamlet of Primm Springs, where he cultivates a large ornamental garden and fights off coyotes, bobcats, snakes, and hawks. Not to mention rabbits.

If you'd like to touch base with Troy, you can email him at troy@troybmarden.com, or you can find him on Facebook, his website, and on his blogspot Gardener Cook (http://troybmarden. blogspot.com/). In addition to this book, Troy is the author of *Plant This Instead!* also from Cool Springs Press.